STUDIES IN IRISH HISTORY, SECOND SERIES

edited by

T. W. MOODY
Professor of Modern History
University of Dublin

J. C. BECKETT
Professor of Irish History
Queen's University, Belfast

T. D. WILLIAMS
Professor of Modern History
National University of Ireland

VOLUME I

THE FALL OF PARNELL, 1890-91

THE FALL

OF

PARNELL

1890-91

by

F. S. L. LYONS

Fellow of Trinity College, Dublin

Routledge & Kegan Paul Ltd

LONDON

First published 1960
by Routledge & Kegan Paul Ltd
Broadway House, Carter Lane, E.C.4

Printed in Great Britain
by Hazell Watson & Viney Ltd
Aylesbury and Slough

To Jennifer

PREFACE

IT IS still not easy for Irishmen to take an objective view of Parnell, and much of the literature which has grown up around him has been partisan or controversial to an extreme degree. It is, indeed, only within the last twenty years that his career has been studied with any real detachment, and even then mainly in isolated articles by scholars writing for highly specialised readers. To this generalisation there are only two significant exceptions—J. L. Hammond's *Gladstone and the Irish nation*, published in 1938, and Dr Cruise O'Brien's *Parnell and his party, 1880–90*, which appeared two years ago.

I owe much to both these books, but since Hammond was by no means exclusively concerned with the Parnellite period, my principal debt is to Dr Cruise O'Brien's admirable and in many ways pioneering work, and I take particular pleasure in recording how much I have profited from it. I have leaned heavily on it in my earlier chapters, and especially the first; but perhaps I should make clear that while we have occasionally found ourselves on the same ground, our intentions have been very different. Dr Cruise O'Brien's main concern was with Parnell's relations with his party over the whole decade of his ascendancy, and the unity of his narrative is contained within the two fixed points of Parnell's election as chairman in 1880 and his deposition in 1890. My more limited purpose has been to analyse in detail the final crisis of Parnell's life and to explore it, not only as the crisis of an individual, or even of a party, but as a crisis in liberal-nationalist and, ultimately, Anglo-Irish relations. My unity, therefore, is not the same as Dr Cruise O'Brien's, for it comprises simply the eleven months between the hearing of the

vii

O'Shea divorce case in November 1890 and the death of Parnell the following October. Apart from the first two, largely introductory, chapters, the whole book is devoted to the events of these eleven months, and I have tried to pay particular attention to the development of the struggle in Ireland and elsewhere after, as well as before, the famous debate in Committee Room Fifteen. So far as I am aware, the later phases of the conflict between Parnell and his opponents have not hitherto been fully investigated.

To work upon a period so recent as this is both exciting and exasperating. Exciting, because new material is always coming to light, and exasperating, because one can be quite sure that more will continue to come to light after one's book has gone to press. We are still a long way from knowing all there is to know about Parnell—probably we shall never know it all—but at least it can be said that nowadays the archives are opening much more easily and rapidly than they used to do. I have been fortunate in obtaining access to various collections of private papers and I wish to thank the following for permission to consult them, and, where necessary, to publish, either in part or in their entirety, letters and other documents used in this book: Professor Thomas Bodkin, Professor Myles Dillon, Miss Gill, Mr C. A. Gladstone, Earl Granville, Viscount Harcourt, Colonel N. Harrington, Most Rev. Dr J. C. McQuaid (Archbishop of Dublin), Mrs G. Morley, Miss Eva Murphy, Madame S. O'Brien, Earl Spencer, Mrs M. Sullivan, the Director and Trustees of the National Library, Dublin, the Public Record Office, London, and the Trustees of the British Museum. I am especially grateful to Professor Myles Dillon, to Viscount Harcourt and to Earl Spencer for the personal interest they have taken in my work and for the facilities they gave me for my researches.

In addition to the collections listed in the bibliography I have also consulted the papers of the then Marquess of Hartington (later eighth duke of Devonshire) but found they had no direct bearing on my main theme. I regret that I have been unable to see the Balfour, Chamberlain and Manning papers, all of which are at present being arranged and catalogued.

I wish also to express my thanks to the Directors, Librarians and staffs of the Manuscript Department of the British Museum, the National Registry of Archives, the Public Record Office, *The Times* Library, the Royal Irish Academy, the Royal Dublin Society, the Library of Trinity College, Dublin, and the National Library, Dublin. Like every other student of Irish history my debt is particularly heavy to the Director of the National Library, Dr R. J. Hayes, and to his staff, amongst whom I must mention specially Mr John Ainsworth, Mr P. Henchy, Mr D. MacLochlainn and Mr T. P. O'Neill.

I have in addition benefited from conversation or correspondence with the following: Professor R. Dudley Edwards, the late Dr Henry Harrison, Mr C. H. D. Howard, Mr E. J. Kenny, Dr R. B. McDowell, Mr E. MacWhite, Captain A. D. Mateer, the late Dr M. F. O'Hea, the late Mrs W. A. Redmond and Mr. J. W. Robertson Scott.

I gladly record my deep indebtedness to the friendship, guidance and inspiration of Professor T. W. Moody of Trinity College, Dublin, whose help at every stage of my work has been beyond reckoning.

It gives me great pleasure to acknowledge a generous grant in aid of publication from the Board of Trinity College, Dublin.

Finally, I must thank my wife for her help in many different ways, but above all for her patience while this book was being written during the last five years.

F. S. L. Lyons

Dublin
October 1958

CONTENTS

ABBREVIATIONS

B.M., Add. MS	British Museum, Additional MS.
D.N.B.	*Dictionary of National Biography.*
F.J.	*Freeman's Journal.*
I.H.S.	*Irish Historical Studies.*
N.L.I.	National Library of Ireland.
P.R.O.	Public Record Office.

I

THE YEARS OF POWER

~~~~~~

(I)

IN THE HISTORY of modern Ireland the downfall of Charles
Stewart Parnell stands out as an event of immense significance.
His tragedy—romantic, total, irrevocable—overshadowed his
own generation and ever since has kept its hold upon the Irish
imagination. Yet, although the personal drama has an endless
fascination, there is scarcely less interest in the broad issues of
national policy which the crisis brought into the open. Any
study of the Parnell split must necessarily deal not only with
the clash of personalities, but also with such fundamental problems as the rôle of the church in politics, the rival claims of
constitutional agitation and physical force, the organisation and
conduct of a democratic Irish parliamentary party and its
relations with governments, parties and public opinion in
England. These problems, of course, were not problems of the
split alone. Their roots lay deep in Irish history and Parnell
himself was occupied with them from the very start of his career.
In his efforts to solve them he won many triumphs, contriving
with extraordinary skill to keep in equilibrium forces which
previously had seemed hopelessly incompatible. So great,
indeed, was his success that the crash, when it came at
last, took many of his contemporaries by surprise. Even in
1890, on the very edge of catastrophe, his power appeared
—superficially at least—to be as great as ever and there were

few who sensed how narrow was the basis on which it rested.

Every man is in some degree the prisoner of his own past decisions, and a political man more than most, since his decisions often have public repercussions which he cannot disregard, even if he would. In order to understand the disaster that overtook Parnell, it is essential to realise that what happened in the last year of his life was directly influenced by decisions he himself had taken earlier—sometimes much earlier—in his career. Within the last thirty years a great deal of new material has become available to historians, and much light has been thrown upon both the public and the more intimate aspects of that career. We are, therefore, in a much better position than the men of his own day to recognise the complexity and variety of the forces that brought about his overthrow. We can observe, especially, and this is perhaps the most striking fact to emerge from all this new information, how he, who seemed so much his own master, became progressively less so as the years passed. This was true not merely of his private life—as we shall see in the next chapter—but also of his leadership in Ireland and of his parliamentary manoeuvres at Westminster.

When Parnell first entered parliament in 1875 the Irish political scene was dominated by Isaac Butt's Home Rule League, a moderate and inoffensive body aiming at a moderate and inoffensive measure of self-government for Ireland. Butt was a distinguished lawyer and his approach to politics was essentially that of the advocate rather than that of the agitator. He was a scrupulous respecter of the forms and dignity of the house of commons and his appeals to English opinion were tactful and restrained—too much so, indeed, to have any very marked effect. However, although many Irish members followed his example, there was a discordant element represented mainly by the Belfast provision merchant, Joseph Gillis Biggar. Biggar, with his uncouth appearance and manner and his harsh northern accent, was in his way a portent as novel and significant in the house of commons as Keir Hardie with his cloth cap was to be in later years. He was in a tradition familiar enough to Ireland, but strange to Westminster. He was a fenian and at one time held a seat on the supreme council of the Irish Republican Brotherhood. For him and a few others like him, apart from the gratitude fenians in general felt to Butt for his defence of fenian prisoners between 1865 and 1869, the Home Rule League offered the only means available for active participation in politics. After the failure of the risings of 1867 the prospects of achieving independence by armed revolution had vanished and were likely to be remote for many years to come. Thereafter the alternatives seemed to lie between secret and fruitless conspiracy or joining the 'open'—or public—movement.

To this public movement, however, Biggar was bent on giving his own interpretation. For him the ancient traditions and conventions of the house had absolutely no appeal. On the contrary, the antiquated rules of procedure, designed as they were for the protection of a minority, gave him full scope for his policy of thwarting the majority by obstructing the progress of business in every way he could. The object of this obstruction was quite simply to demonstrate that if English members would do nothing in the interests of Ireland, Irish members would make it difficult for them to do anything in the interests of England. It could also of course be represented in Ireland as the translation into parliamentary terms of the never-ending struggle against English rule. But there was a difficulty. Although the fenian rebellion had failed, fenianism itself was far from dead. It still retained a widespread secret organisation and its ideas continued to have a powerful influence, especially upon the Irish emigrants in Britain and the United States. Between these irreconcilables who preferred to remain uncommitted to any open movement, and those who took the view that something might be done for Ireland by parliamentary action, there was a sharp divergence. This divergence was a major factor—perhaps the major factor—of which Parnell had to take account when he entered public life.

There seems little doubt that even before he became a member of parliament Parnell's attention had been caught by fenianism—or so at least he testified in later years.[1] But family influences and environment also played a part in his political education. Although a protestant landowner, he came of stock

---

[1] *Special commission act, 1888; reprint of the shorthand notes of the speeches, proceedings, and evidence taken before the commissioners appointed under the above-named act* (hereafter cited as *Spec. comm. proc.*), vii. 1; J. McCarthy, *Reminiscences*, ii. 109–10.

which was very far from conforming to the conventional opinions of its class. Through his father he traced his ancestry back to the Sir John Parnell who had vigorously opposed the act of union, and other members of the family, in the more recent past, had supported catholic emancipation. On the maternal side Parnell was descended from the American admiral, Charles Stewart, who had fought against England in the war of 1812. The admiral's daughter, Delia, was Parnell's mother and she was distinguished for her outspoken criticisms of English rule in Ireland. Some have deduced from this that her son's hatred of England was directly derived from her.[1] But since she dined on occasion at the Vice-regal Lodge, entertained English officers at Avondale (the family home), sent her son Charles to Cambridge and her daughters to be presented at Queen Victoria's court, perhaps not too much stress should be laid upon her political opinions. It is true, however, that she did have a genuine sympathy with the fenian movement and it is said that she gave temporary shelter to individual fenians on the run.[2] Parnell himself must obviously have been aware of his mother's tendencies, but there is no evidence that he felt any inclination to join a secret organisation of this kind. The pro-fenian atmosphere of the family circle no doubt had its effect upon him, but in the shaping of his ideas the countryside in which he grew up may also have had a share. County Wicklow, where his forbears had long been established, still nursed memories which went much further back than fenianism. When Parnell was a boy there were still men living in the neighbourhood who remembered the rising of 1798 and whose tales, as he afterwards recalled, had impressed themselves vividly upon his imagination.[3]

However, up to the time he entered parliament his views on politics appear to have been largely unformed. Vague memories of 1798, some sympathy with fenianism, a notion that the ballot act of 1872 establishing the secrecy of the vote might be

[1] For example, Thomas Sherlock, *Charles Stewart Parnell* (1945 ed.), p. 30; R. Johnston, *Parnell and the Parnells*, pp. 18–19; R. B. O'Brien, *Life of Charles Stewart Parnell*, i. 29; St. J. Ervine, *Parnell*, pp. 36–47; J. L. Hammond, *Gladstone and the Irish nation*, p. 149.

[2] Sherlock, op. cit., pp. 30–1; Johnston, op. cit., pp. 18–19; R. B. O'Brien, *Parnell*, i. 47.

[3] R. B. O'Brien, *Parnell*, i. 53–4.

turned to advantage in Ireland,[1] this is about all that can be attributed to him when in 1874 he first stood for parliament. During his election campaign he showed himself almost wholly inarticulate and had little to commend him save his famous name and his readiness to pay his own expenses.[2] Nor was he much more promising when the next year he was actually elected for Meath and took his seat at Westminster. He was so ignorant of the rudiments of procedure that he had no idea even how to set about asking a parliamentary question.[3] His first session was spent in total obscurity, though it was not wasted since he was able to watch Biggar mounting his first major effort at obstruction. Parnell found this line of tactics infinitely preferable to those of Butt and soon became expert in the art of enraging and frustrating the house of commons. But this was not all. In 1876 he startled the house by declaring that in his view the fenians who, at Manchester in 1867, had killed a policeman while attempting to rescue two of their comrades, had committed no murder.[4] This, together with his association with Biggar, brought him to the notice of the leading fenians in England and in 1877, with their support, he displaced Isaac Butt from the presidency of the Home Rule Confederation of Great Britain, a body which had a number of influential fenians among its members.

By 1877, then, although Parnell was still only in his thirty-first year, he had gained a wide reputation as a parliamentary obstructionist, he had won the respect of the fenians, and the Irish in Great Britain had accepted him as head of their organisation. But this sudden rise to eminence, dazzling though it was, brought with it the penalty of responsibility. With only two years' experience of public life to guide him Parnell was soon to be called on to make a grave decision, and one destined to have incalculable consequences for the whole nationalist movement. In the simplest terms it was the decision as to whether he would lead an extra-parliamentary agitation which might end by becoming revolutionary, or whether he would continue to rely on the constitutional approach as the best

[1] *Spec. comm. proc.*, vii. 1–2.
[2] O'Brien, *Parnell*, i. 72–5.
[3] Ibid., i. 85.
[4] *Hansard*, 3, ccxxx. 808.

means of reaching his goal. This was the problem which confronted him between 1877 and 1882 and in solving which he
first revealed the full extent of his political genius. It was not,
however, a simple choice between fenianism and parliamentary
action—if it had been his task would probably have been much
easier. True, what might be called 'official' fenianism, speaking
through the mouth of the supreme council of the Irish Republican Brotherhood, remained steadfastly opposed to constitutionalism and in August 1877 the two chief exponents of such
a policy—Biggar and J. O'Connor Power—were actually
expelled from that body.[1] However, this opposition from the
extreme left was only to be expected; it was not 'official' fenianism that set Parnell his problem, but rather that deviation from
it which came to be known as the 'new departure'.

This 'new departure' owed much to the energy and imagination of Michael Davitt. Davitt was born in Mayo in 1846 (the
same year as Parnell), but after his father had been evicted
from his holding the whole family emigrated to Lancashire,
where the boy lost an arm working in a factory when only
eleven years of age. He was a fenian before he was twenty and
when acting as an arms-agent was arrested in 1870 and sen-
tenced to fifteen years' penal servitude. After seven years—
mainly spent in Dartmoor in barbarous conditions—he was
released on ticket-of-leave. He at once rejoined the fenian
movement but, while not abandoning the idea of an eventual
appeal to force, soon began to advocate that the I.R.B. should
support the 'open movement' being carried on by the obstruc-
tionists, though he was also anxious—as apparently he told
Parnell—that 'there must be more immediate issues put before
the people, such as a war against landlordism for a root settlement of the land question.'[2] Visiting America in 1878, he found
that John Devoy, a leading spirit in Irish-American fenianism,
was thinking along parallel lines and was even in advance of
him on the land question.

From Parnell's point of view, this interest of prominent

[1] T. W. Moody, 'The new departure in Irish politics, 1878–9', in H. A.
Cronne, T. W. Moody and D. B. Quinn (ed.), *Essays in British and Irish
history in honour of James Eadie Todd*, p. 310. Two other able fenians, John
Barry and Patrick Egan, at the same time resigned from the supreme council.
[2] M. Davitt, *The fall of feudalism in Ireland*, pp. 111–3.

fenians in public action was an impressive tribute to the success
of his obstructionist tactics. But he had no intention of striking
up a hard and fast alliance with them, and although Devoy—
who met him at Boulogne and Dublin in March and June 1879
—later claimed that such an alliance—even if verbal—had
actually been concluded, the balance of the evidence suggests
that this was not so.[1] Parnell was prepared to utilise this new
factor in Irish politics, but not to be dominated by it. His task,
however, was certain to be difficult, since these allies still
looked to separation from England as their ultimate objective,
and had by no means abandoned the use of force as a possible
method of achieving it. But before he had had much chance to
develop his policy in this new situation, the situation itself was
radically changed by the onset of a grave economic crisis in
Ireland.

By 1879 the position of the Irish tenants and farm-labourers,
especially in the west and south, had become desperate. This
was due partly to bad harvests in 1877 and 1878 and to the
failure of the potato crop in the following year, but partly to
deeper and more permanent causes. One was the system of land-
holding which still left the bulk of the tenants liable to eviction
when they could not pay their rents—and rents which had
appeared reasonable in good times very easily came to seem
exorbitant in bad times. A second cause of the distress was the
impact of foreign competition—especially from America—
which drastically lowered Irish agricultural prices. And, since
the depression hit British farmers also, the prospects of seasonal
employment for Irish labourers in England dwindled alarm-
ingly, a factor particularly affecting the poorer districts of the
west of Ireland where the wages of migrant labour were often
an important element in the family budget. The situation was
further complicated by the virtual collapse of credit. Exaggerated hopes had been built on the land act of 1870, and banks
and gombeen men had lent freely to tenants who now found
themselves unable to pay their rents *and* repay their loans, and
often enough were incapable of doing either.[2]

---

[1] Moody, 'The new departure in Irish politics, 1878–9', in H. A. Cronne,
T. W. Moody and D. B. Quinn (ed.), *Essays in British and Irish history in
honour of James Eadie Todd*, pp. 328–30.

[2] R. B. O'Brien, *Parnell*, i. 175–6; M. Davitt, *Fall of feudalism*, p. 144; J. L.

Against this sombre background Davitt in the spring of 1879 launched the Land League, which was intended to provide the tenant-farmers with an organisation that would help them to resist rack-renting and would also work for the larger policy of making the occupiers the eventual owners of the soil. Beginning in Mayo the movement had an immediate success and it soon became clear that the agrarian situation in Ireland had in it all the elements of social revolution. The establishment of the Land League confronted Parnell with an extremely difficult problem. On the one hand, Davitt was urging him to lead the agitation—and for this there was much to be said. He and his supporters were still a very small minority of the Irish members at Westminster and his power to achieve anything constructive there was almost nil. If he headed the land agitation, not only would he have an opportunity of capturing the Irish imagination much more vividly than he could ever hope to do by even the most intransigent obstruction in the house of commons, but he would also be more formidable in parliament itself. On the other hand, the very gravity of the land crisis was enough to give him pause. Davitt and other responsible leaders might counsel peaceful measures, but who could tell how far a destitute and desperate peasantry might go? Might not the land agitation become in grim earnest what it was soon to be called—a land war? And if so, what place was there for a parliamentary leader in a convulsion of this kind? Might he not either lose control of the land movement or else be swept into illegal paths which would cut him off once and for all from constitutional methods?

On balance, the risk of letting the movement pass into other hands was probably greater than the dangers involved in putting himself at its head. At any rate, in October 1879 Parnell became president of the Land League and in doing so vastly increased his own power and prestige. Henceforward he was not merely the leader of a small and vociferous group in the house of commons, but also of a great and growing popular movement in Ireland. Almost immediately the general election of 1880 registered dramatically the extent of his success. For Parnell that election campaign was a personal triumph. He

Hammond, *Gladstone and the Irish nation*, pp. 104–5; N. D. Palmer, *The land league crisis*, pp. 64–5; E. Strauss, *Irish nationalism and British democracy*, p. 159.

himself was returned for three seats, the number of his followers was considerably increased and that very year he became chairman of the Irish parliamentary party. But his attempt to combine the popular and the parliamentary movements left him vulnerable on either flank. His preoccupation with the house of commons made him obnoxious to orthodox fenianism, while his connection with the Land League led the church, the *Freeman's Journal* (the leading nationalist newspaper) and many moderates to regard him with suspicion. So long as he pinned his hopes to a public or 'open' movement Parnell would have to resign himself to fenian hostility, but the opposition of the church and of moderate opinion was another matter, since no constitutional movement could hope to succeed if these forces were not behind it. In essence, therefore, Parnell's dilemma in 1880 and 1881 was how to win over moderate nationalism at a time when the situation in Ireland was offering every encouragement to extremism.

(2)

We can see now that the Irish problem of those years was two-fold. On the one hand, it was vital to restore order in a country on the verge of revolution. And on the other hand, it was no less necessary to remove the cause of the trouble by a fundamental reform of the land law. It is not surprising, however, that contemporaries, with the evidence of violence daily before their eyes, saw the situation primarily in terms of restoring order. Thus, although Gladstone's return to power in 1880 might have been expected to bring an improvement in Anglo-Irish relations, the immediate outcome was very different. True, the liberal government took up a measure originally introduced by an Irish member to give certain classes of tenants compensation for disturbance, but when the house of lords rejected it in August of that year, the cabinet appeared to have no constructive ideas about what to do next. In Ireland the action of the house of lords provoked a new crescendo of violence. Of the 2,590 agrarian crimes and outrages committed during 1880, more than half took place in the last three months of the year.[1]

---

[1] *Return of the number of agrarian offences in Ireland . . in* 1880, pp. 1–15, H.C. 1881, lxxvii. 619–33.

Inevitably, the Land League throve on the discontent and its influence increased by leaps and bounds.[1] Parnell, if he was not to lose control of the agitation, had no option but to make himself the spokesman for the seething unrest of the country. How faithfully he carried out this task is clear from the speeches he made that autumn, and especially from the meeting at Ennis where he warned his hearers that the land bill of the next session would be the measure of their determination not to pay unjust rents and not to take farms from which others had been evicted.[2] But the growth of Irish violence could only lead to English counter-measures and there followed in rapid succession the abortive state-trials of Parnell and other leaders in the agitation, the re-arrest of Michael Davitt and the passing of a coercion act so bitterly resisted by the Irish members that the government was obliged to introduce a notable change in parliamentary procedure—the closure of debate—in order to pass the measure through the house of commons.

Had this been all the liberals had to offer it is hard to see how an explosion could have been avoided. Fortunately, however, while the struggle to restore order was still raging, Gladstone was slowly working his way towards what was to become one of the great monuments of his Irish policy—the land act of 1881. Seen in retrospect it may not appear revolutionary, but to contemporaries it was precisely that, for it introduced a concept clean counter to English ideas. This was the idea of dual ownership, of partnership between the owner and the occupier of the soil. The most important concessions made by the act were of course the 'three Fs'—the provision for fair rents, fixity of tenure and the right of the tenant to free sale of his interest in his holding.[3] That the act resulted in endless litigation, that it left out of account those tenants who were in arrears with their rent, and that the judicial rents which *were* fixed were soon to be vitiated by a further decline in agricultural prices, all this should not be allowed to obscure the fact that this fresh attempt to solve the land question was by far the most serious threat the Land League had yet had to meet. If the machinery envisaged

[1] Hammond, *Gladstone and the Irish nation*, p. 192.

[2] *Freeman's Journal* (hereafter cited as *F.J.*), 20 Sept. 1880; R. B. O'Brien, *Parnell*, i. 236–7.

[3] *Statutes, United Kingdom*, 44 and 45 Vict., c. 49.

in the act were set up and worked efficiently, it would be difficult to prevent the tenants from crowding into the courts to have their rents fixed judicially, and once that began to happen it would be the death-knell of the League.

This new development placed Parnell in an awkward situation. The act of 1881 was too obviously valuable to be rejected out of hand, but to accept it over-enthusiastically would be to invite the hostility of the left wing, which was bound to regard it as being—what indeed it was intended to be—the English answer to the League. Parnell's tactics in this dilemma were subtle and dangerous, but in the long run brilliantly successful. In the house of commons he and some of his party abstained from voting on the second and third readings. But in Ireland he set himself to make the best of both worlds. On the one hand, he persuaded the League to experiment with the act by taking certain test cases into the land courts. On the other hand, he sought to strengthen his hold over the extreme section of the movement partly by a series of speeches hostile to the measure, and partly by launching the newspaper *United Ireland*, which immediately became a powerful propaganda weapon in the struggle against coercion. To Gladstone, the Irish leader's attitude seemed to indicate a deliberate intention of sabotaging the land act and in October the cabinet decided to arrest him. He was accordingly seized in Dublin and sent to join other Land Leaguers in Kilmainham jail.[1]

On the eve of his arrest Parnell is said to have observed that if he were imprisoned 'Captain Moonlight' would take his place.[2] The story of the winter of 1881-2 is largely a commentary upon this remark, for the dreary round of agrarian outrage and murder gained rather than lost momentum after he went to Kilmainham.[3] The immediate sequel was the issue of the 'No Rent' manifesto. This document, which called on the tenants to pay no rents to their landlords 'until the government relinquishes the existing system of terrorism and restores the constitutional rights of the people',[4] was signed by the heads of the

---

[1] R. B. O'Brien, *Parnell*, i. 305–14; Davitt, *The fall of feudalism*, pp. 331–2; Hammond, *Gladstone and the Irish nation*, pp. 248–9; C. Cruise O'Brien, *Parnell and his party, 1880–90*, pp. 65–72.   [2] R. B. O'Brien, *Parnell*, i. 312.
[3] Hammond, *Gladstone and the Irish nation*, pp. 266–7.
[4] *United Ireland*, 17 Oct. 1881; Davitt, *The fall of feudalism*, pp. 335–6.

League, almost all of whom were in Kilmainham jail.[1] Parnell himself, it is said, signed only with some reluctance,[2] and indeed it needed little insight to realise that whatever hope a general strike against rent might have had early in 1881, in October— with the coercion act in full force and the land act beginning to function—it stood no chance of success. And in fact its main consequence was to provoke the government into suppressing the Land League, thereby clearing the way for other and more extreme organisations.

Although Parnell's arrest caused an immense sensation at the time it is clear that from his own point of view it was exceedingly convenient. If he had remained at liberty he would either have had to continue at the head of an agitation which was becoming steadily more violent and thus risk a head-on clash with the authorities, or else break with the land movement and at one stroke lose much of the prestige he had gained in the past two years. His imprisonment allowed him to escape both horns of this dilemma, since at one and the same time it won him the halo of martyrdom for the cause and kept him out of the way while the League was in its death-throes.[3] Against this, however, had to be set the fact that the mounting violence in Ireland was potentially as great a threat to his movement as it was actually to the government of the country. A short spell in prison would set the ultimate seal of respectability on his record as a nationalist, a long one might amount to virtual abdication. It was not surprising, therefore, that after six months in Kilmainham Parnell began to feel his way back into politics. The moment was opportune, for a winter of terrorism in Ireland had shown all too clearly that the government, by shutting up the most responsible leaders in Kilmainham, had in effect removed from the scene one of the few stable elements in the country. Gladstone himself had only imprisoned Parnell as an enemy of the land act. At the first sign that he had abjured that rôle the case for keeping him in prison would disappear.

[1] The exceptions were Patrick Egan in Paris and Michael Davitt in Portland prison. It seems that Davitt's name was attached to the manifesto by Thomas Brennan (R. B. O'Brien, *Parnell*, i. 319, *n.* 1).

[2] R. B. O'Brien, *Parnell*, i. 320. There is, however, some uncertainty on this point; see C. Cruise O'Brien, *Parnell and his party*, pp. 73–4.

[3] For the personal factor which further complicated his position at this time see ch. II below.

With Parnell anxious to re-enter public life and Gladstone anxious to re-admit him the scene was set for the complicated negotiations of April 1882 which resulted in the so-called 'Kilmainham treaty'. The understanding—there was no 'treaty'—was, briefly, that the government would deal satisfactorily with the arrears question and would amend the land act of 1881 in certain particulars, especially by extending the benefit of its fair-rent clauses to leaseholders. In return Parnell would use his influence against outrage and intimidation in Ireland, while if the land act were adequately amended it would, he said, 'be regarded by the country as a practical settlement of the land question and would enable us to co-operate cordially for the future with the liberal party in forwarding liberal principles and measures of general reform . . .'.[1]

The Kilmainham agreement, so Davitt later wrote, 'was a vital turning-point in Mr Parnell's career and unfortunately he turned in the wrong direction'.[2] A vital turning-point it certainly was, but whether the direction be considered right or wrong depends upon the point of view. To those who had hoped for revolution, or at the very least for sweeping social change, Parnell's new orientation was bound to seem disastrous. And for them, indeed, it *was* disastrous, since the left wing of the movement was so shattered by the events of 1881-2 that for many years the parliamentary party had no rival in Ireland. But Davitt's criticism ignores the central fact of Parnell's whole career—the fact that it was firmly based upon his position as a parliamentary leader. At no time had he ever given any convincing evidence that he would abandon this position. For a time, it is true, he had managed to combine it with the land agitation, but even he could not walk that tight-rope for ever

[1] Hammond, *Gladstone and the Irish nation*, pp. 276-7. The 'treaty' was a complicated affair in which, besides Parnell, Captain W. H. O'Shea, Justin McCarthy (vice-chairman of the Irish parliamentary party) and Joseph Chamberlain were all involved. The basis of the understanding which led to Parnell's release is contained in a letter Parnell wrote to O'Shea from Kilmainham at the end of April; a copy of this letter was passed to Gladstone by the chief secretary, W. E. Forster. Forster resigned immediately afterwards. The best modern account is in Hammond, op. cit., ch. xv, but the whole episode needs further investigation.

[2] Davitt, *The fall of feudalism*, p. 349. A modern writer has similarly condemned the 'treaty' as 'a crass blunder' (E. Strauss, *Irish nationalism and British democracy*, p. 166).

and the Kilmainham 'treaty' left no doubt that, faced with the choice between a parliamentary and an extra-parliamentary movement, he had come down in favour of the former.[1]

The choice naturally involved the risk that he would be fiercely assailed from the left and especially by his late comrades of the Land League. Three things prevented this attack from becoming serious. One was the fact that the suppression of the League itself, combined with the operation of the land act, had slowed down the agitation. Another was the loyalty with which the agrarian leaders such as Davitt and Dillon accepted his decision. And the third was the extraordinary coincidence that, within a few days of Parnell's release, the chief secretary, Lord Frederick Cavendish, and one of his senior officials were murdered in the Phoenix Park. The crime was the work of a terrorist organisation with which Parnell had no connection, and he himself was so shaken by it that he offered to resign his seat, an offer which Gladstone did not accept, though he regarded it as an honourable and unselfish gesture.[2] However, English feeling was so roused by the atrocity that the government had no alternative but to impose fresh coercion upon Ireland. Parnell, for his part, had no alternative but to resist such a policy. In doing so he appeared to be resuming the rôle he had played so successfully in 1881, and whatever doubts the Kilmainham treaty might have raised amongst his followers seemed after all without foundation.

(3)

In reality the Phoenix Park murders, tragic as they were, turned out to be almost irrelevant to the central situation. Once the immediate excitement was over, the trend towards constitutionalism went steadily on and that very year provided the first indication of what this would mean in practice. By the end of 1882 a new organisation had sprung up in Ireland—the Irish National League—which from the outset was effectively

[1] It is significant that even in February 1881, when the temptation to secede from parliament was probably greatest, Parnell declined a suggestion from the Land League executive that he should go to America, and wrote them an open letter justifying his persistence in parliamentary action (C. Cruise O'Brien, *Parnell and his party*, pp. 61-2).

[2] Morley, *Gladstone*, iii. 70.

controlled by Parnell and the inner circle of the parliamentary party, and which was thus very different from the old Land League. There followed two years of comparative calm while Parnell consolidated his position as a constitutional leader, until in 1884 the new-found respectability of the movement received its most impressive recognition when the Irish hierarchy enlisted its aid to present in the house of commons the Roman Catholic viewpoint on educational matters. In that year also the extension of the franchise made it virtually certain that at the next general election the strength of the party would be considerably increased. And in fact, when the election came in 1885, the Irish constituencies returned 85 nationalists.[1] It was at this election that the machinery of county conventions, which in one form or another was to serve the party for most of its subsequent history, first played an important part. These conventions were organised by the Irish National League and consisted primarily of delegates from various branches of the League in the county where the convention was being held. The presence of the clergy at the conventions was not originally provided for in the constitution of the League, but it is a sign of the growing community of interest between the church and the party that they did nonetheless appear at these gatherings. The object of the conventions—which were normally presided over by a member of the parliamentary party—was to select a candidate for each constituency the nationalists hoped to contest. And the fact that the candidate selected had to sign a pledge binding him to sit, act and vote with the parliamentary party and to resign if a majority of the party should vote that he had not fulfilled this obligation, meant that the members eventually returned to the house of commons formed a closely-knit, highly-disciplined body, a world away from the old, miscellaneous collection of home-rulers of various shades of opinion who had sat on the Irish benches ten, or even five, years previously.

As might have been expected both from the increased num-

---

[1] The total strength of Parnell's party in the house of commons was 86, T. P. O'Connor having been returned for a Liverpool seat. The effect of the franchise extension should not, however, be overstated since two experts, Chamberlain and Parnell himself, reckoned that it would make a difference of only about ten seats. See C. Cruise O'Brien, *Parnell and his party*, p. 150, *n.* 3.

bers and from the rôle assigned to the county conventions, the
personnel of the new party showed many changes from that of
the old.[1] The chief differences were that there were fewer indi-
vidualists among the men of 1885, that more of them were
middle-class, that about half of them needed some degree of
financial aid from party funds,[2] and that they were more
genuinely representative of local interests, since many of them
lived in Ireland.[3] From the purely political viewpoint it is
probably also true to say that this greatly swollen party stood
further to the right than the group which had followed Parnell
in his earlier years. There were, indeed, still men of fenian
sympathies or experience in its ranks, and there were others
who were not afraid to go to jail when a fresh wave of agrarian
agitation demanded it. The fact remained, however, that from
1882 onwards the left wing was on the defensive. No man had
done more to achieve this than Parnell himself. By allowing the
movement to assume a middle-class, provincial, 'respectable'
character, and by allying it with the church, he had beyond
question made it more broad-based, more solid and more
powerful than ever before. But in doing so he had insensibly
limited his own freedom of action, for when in the last year of
his life he sought to invoke a more militant spirit, he found in
the party he had himself created a vested interest in constitutionalism which it was beyond his power to control.

The *raison d'être* of such a party was of course to win a satisfactory measure of home rule for Ireland. With its success at the
general election of 1885 the home rule issue became for the next
twelve months the dominant factor in British politics, since
Parnell controlled the balance of power at Westminster. The
story of that remarkable year is well known and need not be

---

[1] The fact that members of parliament habitually presided at county conventions no doubt gave the party—or at least Parnell and the inner circle of
the party—some control over the choice of candidates. This may well have
been the case in later years, but in 1885 the simple fact that there were so
many vacancies to be filled probably allowed the conventions to exert a real
influence upon the process of selection.

[2] C. Cruise O'Brien, *Parnell and his party*, p. 269 shows that between 1886
and 1890 forty-four members received payments and that only five of these
were post-1885 members.

[3] For an admirable account of the machinery and personnel of the party at
the time of the 1885 election see C. Cruise O'Brien, op. cit., ch. IV, V.

repeated here.[1] But it is necessary to stress that the fact that the conservatives, after a brief dalliance with Parnell, had rejected the principle of Irish self-government, while Gladstone had accepted it even at the cost of splitting his party, had a vitally important consequence. This was that Parnell's freedom to manoeuvre was again limited and in a most significant fashion. He claimed to stand for the idea of 'independent opposition'— that is to say, he conceived of an Irish party independent of all others, opportunist in its attitude, allying itself now with one party now with another, according to whichever came nearer meeting the Irish demand. The cardinal importance of the first home rule crisis was that after 1886 this policy of balance was no longer possible. Or rather, it was possible only for limited objectives. A land act or a housing act, or some other similar measure, might come from either English party, for either English party might find it politic to concede such legislation. But on the fundamental issue of home rule there was, after 1886, no choice. Home rule could only be obtained from the liberals, which meant in effect that the liberal alliance had become absolutely essential to the Irish parliamentary party, for there was virtually no alternative. How devastating a price the party would have to pay for the continuance of that alliance the events of 1890-1 were to show.

This, however, was yet well in the future. The defeat of the home rule bill and the return of the unionists to power in the summer of 1886 failed to weaken the alliance. On the contrary, events in Ireland and the unionist reaction to them soon tended to strengthen it. Renewed agricultural depression was rapidly converting the judicial rents fixed in and after 1881 into rack rents which the tenants were finding more and more difficult to pay. Ignoring alike the reports of its own observers, the findings of the Cowper Commission and constructive proposals by Parnell, the government neglected to take effective action. The Irish response was the Plan of Campaign, published in *United Ireland* in October 1886.[2] It was a device for collective bargain-

---

[1] See Hammond, *Gladstone and the Irish nation*, ch. xix–xxvi; C. Cruise O'Brien, *Parnell and his party*, ch. vi.

[2] *United Ireland*, 23 Oct. 1886. The document was unsigned, but is generally held to have been the work of Timothy Harrington. See C. Cruise O'Brien, op. cit., pp. 201–2.

ing on individual estates. Where a landlord refused to lower his rents voluntarily the tenants were to offer him a reduction. If he declined, they were to pay him no rent, but instead to contribute to an 'estate fund' the money they would have paid the landlord if he had accepted their proposal. And if he decided to fight by prosecuting and evicting the tenants it would be used for their maintenance and protection. Should the 'estate fund' not be sufficient, then the resources of the National League were to be called upon. One of the earliest and most publicised struggles developed on the notorious Clanricarde estate in Galway, but the movement spread rapidly and, though peaceful settlements were reached in some places, in others—notably in Tipperary—the conflict was bitter and prolonged.[1]

Thus, although in August 1887 the government belatedly passed a measure to ease the position of the tenants, it was faced by then with a full-scale agitation. In this agitation Parnell took no share. This may partly have been due to ill-health and partly to the claims his affair with Mrs O'Shea was making upon him at that time. But aside from this, the bulk of the evidence suggests that he looked very much askance at the whole undertaking.[2] In a striking speech to the Eighty Club in May 1888 he declared that he had known nothing about the launching of the Plan, but that if he had he would have advised against it. He pointed out, however, that after Dillon and O'Brien (the leaders of the agitation) had been arrested in February 1887 he could not disavow it, though he *had* stipulated that he and the parliamentary party should not be implicated, that the Plan should be confined to estates already affected and that moderation should be used.[3] Given his past experience with

[1] Subsequently John Dillon estimated that on 60 estates a peaceful settlement had been reached by 1888; that by 1890 the tenants had won a victory on a further 24 estates; that on 15 the landlords had triumphed and the tenants broken away from the Plan; and that on 17 the struggle was still in progress in 1892 (*Report of the evicted tenants' commission*, pp. 420–2 (C 6935), H.C. 1893, xxxi. 552–4).

[2] Healy, *Letters and leaders*, i. 266; Davitt, *The fall of feudalism*, pp. 517–8; R. B. O'Brien, *Parnell*, ii. 190–1.

[3] *F.J.*, 9 May 1888. For O'Brien's account of the interview with Parnell at which the leader explained his attitude see W. O'Brien, *Evening memories*, pp. 177–87. The interview in fact took place in December 1886, not February 1887, that is, before Dillon and O'Brien had been arrested (Morley, *Gladstone*, iii. 370–1).

the Land League and his subsequent emphasis on the liberal
alliance, it was natural enough that he should view with anxiety
a new agrarian movement which was only too likely to add to
his difficulties as a parliamentary leader. There were obvious
dangers in a situation where prominent members of the party
such as Dillon, O'Brien, Harrington and John Redmond were
active in a movement from which their chief stood aloof. But
any tendency towards discord which might have resulted was
checked by the two-fold pressure exerted against the Plan by
Rome and by the government. The latter, as was to be expected,
reacted to the situation by passing a coercion act. This act was
so severe that before long more than twenty members of the
Irish parliamentary party had been imprisoned under it. In
such circumstances, differences within the movement were
inevitably overshadowed by the need for united action against
the common enemy. The disapproval of the Pope was more
serious and might well have led to grave complications. In
the event, while it did cool the enthusiasm of some of the
hierarchy, it provoked a remarkable demonstration by many
of the catholic M.P.s in the course of which they resolved that
'Irish catholics can recognise no right in the Holy See to interfere with the Irish people in the management of their own
affairs'.[1] In this firm attitude they received wide popular
support and the party emerged from the incident with its
prestige higher than ever.

So far as the general political situation was concerned the
Plan of Campaign had three major consequences, each of which
had a bearing upon the events of 1890-1. In the first place, it
created a grave financial problem, since the burden of maintaining the evicted tenants strained the financial resources of
the movement to the uttermost.[2] The result was that when the
party split in two in 1890 each side struggled desperately to lay
hands on whatever funds existed, so as to reap the credit for
relieving 'the wounded soldiers of the land war', thereby
creating an additional source of friction. Secondly, Arthur

---

[1] C. Cruise O'Brien, *Parnell and his party*, ch. vii.

[2] Between October 1889 and May 1890 a fund of £61,000 was raised for
the tenants. This was reopened in October 1890 and steps were taken to
launch a mission to the United States (*F.J.*, 7 Oct. 1890; C. Cruise O'Brien,
op. cit., pp. 230-1).

Balfour's régime of coercion created in England a wave of sympathy for its victims and was undoubtedly a major factor both in cementing the liberal-nationalist alliance and in turning the tide in the constituencies in favour of the liberals. Finally, the fact that Parnell did not take part in the Plan inevitably concentrated the limelight upon those of his lieutenants who did. The burden—and the glamour—of leadership fell mainly upon John Dillon and William O'Brien, and it is not too much to say that the immense influence they exerted at the time of the split was largely due to the courage and energy they had shown in the years of Parnell's semi-eclipse. Unfortunately, however, that influence had to be exerted from a distance, since, because of their activities in connection with the Plan, both men had sentences of six months' imprisonment outstanding against them in November 1890. The previous month, while on trial, they had escaped to France, and later to America, and could not land in England or Ireland without being immediately arrested.[1]

Had this semi-eclipse continued for long it might well have had serious consequences for Parnell's control of the movement. From such consequences he was saved by a development which at one time threatened to ruin him, but which ended by placing him at the very zenith of his popularity. The story of the charges made by *The Times* against the Irish leader and his party in its articles on 'Parnellism and crime' and of the forged letters upon which they were mainly based has been told so often that only the briefest reference to it is needed here. In March 1887 *The Times* began to publish articles which were designed to establish a connection between Parnell and Irish terrorism. The climax was reached the following month when it printed in support of its allegations the facsimile of a letter purporting to have been written by Parnell himself on 15 May 1882 and in which he appeared to have expressed his regret for having had to denounce the Phoenix Park murders.[2] In the house of commons Parnell denounced this letter as a forgery,[3] but a libel action taken against *The Times* by F. H. O'Donnell —who had been one of Parnell's earliest associates in parlia-

---

[1] For an account of their escape, see *F.J.*, 16 Oct. 1890.
[2] *The Times*, 18 Apr. 1887.
[3] *Hansard*, 3, cccxiii. 1226-31.

ment, but was so no longer—allowed counsel for *The Times* to develop the theme of 'Parnellism and crime' and to produce what appeared to be further incriminating evidence.[1] Parnell repeated his denials and asked that a select committee of the house of commons be appointed to inquire into the authenticity of the letters, suggesting that it should contain no Irish members, but should have the power to compel witnesses to be produced. This was refused by the government, which instead set up a special commission to investigate the allegations and charges that had been made, not only against members of parliament, but also against others, such as Michael Davitt, who had been closely associated with the parliamentarians in the days of the Land League.[2] What was intended, evidently, was nothing less than an inquisition into the whole history of the nationalist movement in the past decade. If any connection existed between Parnellism and crime the special commission would assuredly establish it.

The sequel is well known. The commission searched diligently during the winter of 1888-9 and unearthed a great deal of interesting information about a great variety of topics. But the crux of their investigation was the letters said to have been written by Parnell. Were they forged or were they not? Everything turned on the answer to that question. By February 1889 the answer was known. The Dublin journalist Richard Pigott, from whom the letters had originally been obtained, broke down in the witness-box under the merciless cross-examination of Parnell's counsel, Sir Charles Russell. Within a few days he confessed to having forged the letters himself, then fled the country and shot himself in Madrid. Although it was only a year later that the commission issued its report, the exposure of Pigott proved to be the turning-point. And when the long examination ended at last, it resulted in all essentials in an acquittal for the Irish leaders of the charges that had been brought against them.[3]

[1] *The Times*, 3–6 July 1888.

[2] *Hansard*, 3, cccxxviii. 575–82, 742–3, 1101–2, 1408–13, 1774–9; *Annual Register, 1888*, pp. 143–5.

[3] Though the judges did find that they had promoted an agrarian agitation and that crime and outrage had been committed by persons whom they had incited to practise intimidation. For the background and history of the special commission see especially, O'Brien, *Parnell*, ii, ch. xxi, and *Life of*

For Parnell this triumphant outcome was the crest of the wave, certainly so far as English opinion was concerned. From the time of Pigott's collapse the tide set powerfully in his favour and nothing seemed too good for him. He was acclaimed by the liberals in the house of commons, he was entertained by them at the Eighty Club, he was given the freedom of Edinburgh, he was invited to Hawarden to discuss with Gladstone the future of home rule. Indeed, during 1889 it was the fashionable thing to visit the special commission court and watch the Irish leader conducting his long-drawn-out duel with counsel for *The Times*, and especially with Sir Richard Webster who, by combining this function with that of attorney-general, symbolised aptly enough the government's' interest in the *cause célèbre*. There were signs, however, that Parnell's reputation was in danger of being over-inflated and some of his admirers were apt to lose their heads. Amongst them, surprisingly enough, was Gladstone's daughter Mary. After visiting the court in May 1889, she drew a portrait of the Irish leader which those who knew him well would have had some difficulty in recognising. 'Parnell's coolness wonderful', she wrote. 'He really exhibited all the fruits of the spirit, love, peace, patience, gentleness, forbearance, long-suffering, meekness. His personality takes hold of one, the refined, delicate face, illuminating smile, fire-darting eyes, slight tall figure.'[1]

It was perhaps natural under the circumstances that there should have been this extreme reaction in Parnell's favour, but it was dangerous, since it set him on a pedestal which no man could occupy for long and which he, of all people, was scarcely in a position to occupy at all. To idealise him in this fashion was to invite an equally violent recoil should he at any time fail to come up to expectations. And in fact, when confronted eighteen months later with the knowledge that Parnell and Mrs O'Shea

---

Lord Russell of Killowen, ch. xii; A. Thorold, *Life of Henry Labouchere*, ch. xiii, xiv; Hammond, *Gladstone and the Irish nation*, ch. xxix.

[1] Mary Gladstone, *Letters and diaries*, ed. L. Masterman, pp. 408–9. Her father's reaction, admittedly recorded after the split, was characteristic. 'I was never enthusiastic about him', he told Sir Algernon West, 'only enthusiastic against the foul measures taken to crush him.' (*Private diaries of Sir Algernon West*, ed. H. G. Hutchinson, p. 13.)

had been living together for years, Mary Gladstone's disillusionment was understandably bitter.[1] In this she was no doubt typical of many liberals who in due course woke with a shock to find that this legendary figure was after all only a man of flesh and blood, with his full share of ordinary human passions.

In another sense also the hero-worship of Parnell had a distorting effect upon the political situation. By bringing him back dramatically to the centre of the stage, the special commission helped to conceal the fact that, even though his leadership had remained unquestioned by the party since 1886, the actual conduct of affairs had fallen increasingly into the hands of his lieutenants. Superficially, the discomfiture of *The Times* might seem to have consolidated Parnell's position and it may well have strengthened his belief in his own invulnerability. But so far as the real exercise of power was concerned, the special commission had changed nothing. The more Parnell withdrew himself from the details of party government, the greater became the prestige of those upon whom fell the day-to-day burden of administration. Thus, between 1886 and 1890, several of his subordinates had achieved independent reputations which, while individually insignificant compared to Parnell's, collectively represented a very powerful influence within the party. Among these reputations four had by 1890 emerged as pre-eminent—those of John Dillon, William O'Brien, T. M. Healy and Thomas Sexton—and it was their combined weight which in the end was to turn the scales decisively against him.

Of the four, Dillon's was undoubtedly the most distinguished name, for he was the son of John Blake Dillon, one of the most famous of the Young Irelanders. John Dillon himself was born in 1851 and educated mainly at the Catholic University and the College of Surgeons. Medicine soon gave place to politics, however, and in 1875 he made an appropriate début by supporting the candidature of the veteran Young Irelander, John Mitchel, in the Tipperary election of that year. At that time Dillon's views were certainly extreme and, though he does not seem to have joined the fenian organisation, he was regarded by the police as fenian in his sympathies.[2] From the outset the

---

[1] 'He and she undefended, and he has lived this life of lies all these years. A heart-breaking revelation. "Blot out his name." ' (Mary Gladstone, *Letters and diaries*, p. 413.)   [2] C. Cruise O'Brien, *Parnell and his party*, p. 30.

land question was his special interest, and his first major campaign was the Land League agitation in the course of which he was twice imprisoned in Kilmainham. He first entered parliament in 1880 for county Tipperary, but in 1885 became member for East Mayo, a seat he was to hold until defeated by Mr de Valera in 1918.

Even without his family connections Dillon's abilities would certainly have brought him to the top sooner or later. He was intelligent, courageous and so hard-working that he more than once endangered his health. He was passionately sincere and this sincerity gained him the respect and admiration of his countrymen; even though not one of the more stirring or flamboyant orators of the party, he was always heard with attention. He was a great reader and a great buyer of books. He was widely travelled and in later years was conspicuous as one of the very few Irish members at Westminster to take an intelligent and well-informed interest in colonial and foreign affairs. Add to this great administrative capacity, and acute (though sometimes over-pessimistic) judgment, and it is clear that John Dillon possessed many of the attributes of an ideal party chairman. After the split he did actually fill this rôle for the anti-Parnellites for three years, and later still had the melancholy distinction of presiding over the liquidation of the Irish parliamentary party in 1918. With Parnell his relations were those of mutual respect, but scarcely of affection, since Dillon, like many men of high principle, was not an easy colleague, much less a subordinate. He was apt on occasion—as in 1881 and to a certain extent in 1887-9—to take a line of his own and could never at any time have been described as a docile second fiddle. Unfortunately for himself, he was also sensitive and fastidious to a degree, and, as he found when in his turn he was called upon to lead, in Irish politics to be thin-skinned is to be vulnerable indeed.[1]

During the 'eighties Dillon's name was frequently coupled with that of William O'Brien and, though their paths later diverged, they were for twenty years the closest of collaborators and friends. O'Brien was almost the same age as Dillon—he was born at Mallow in 1852—and he also was connected through

[1] *The Times*, 5 Aug. 1927; Justin McCarthy, *Reminiscences*, ii. 377–80; Stephen Gwynn in *D.N.B., 1922–30.*

his father with the Young Ireland movement, though his own youthful imagination, like Dillon's, was captured by the fenians. His family was not wealthy and although O'Brien received a fairly comprehensive education at a protestant secondary school and at the Queen's College, Cork, he had to combine the later stages of his studies with journalism on the *Cork Daily Herald.* Later, he joined the staff of the *Freeman's Journal* and made good so rapidly that when Parnell sought an editor for *United Ireland* he was chosen for that exacting and responsible post, even though still in his twenties.

Much of this militant newspaper was written by O'Brien himself who was absolutely devoted to his work, was quite fearless, and several times found himself in trouble with the police for his uninhibited attacks upon various aspects of English rule in Ireland. He was always a prolific writer—he had written two novels before he was twenty-one—and words flowed from him torrentially. But this, which nowadays makes him tiresome to read, was no disadvantage in an age when politicians had few competitors for the time and attention of the public. O'Brien soon became as potent a platform speaker as he was a journalist, and his speeches were famous in Ireland for the frenzy into which he worked himself and which often enough he succeeded in imparting to his audience.

As a personality O'Brien was one of the most attractive of all the Irish party. He was kindly, humorous, unselfish and had a spark of idealism in his nature which endeared him to the rank and file of nationalists. As a politician, however, although his popularity, enthusiasm and ability made him a useful force, he was not in the fullest sense a leader. Where Dillon inclined towards pessimism, O'Brien's fault was over-optimism. Fertile in ideas, once he had conceived a policy he tended to underestimate the obstacles in his way. He lacked judgment and was too volatile to inspire awe or obedience. But with Parnell his relations were almost always pleasant. Parnell had given him his chance both as a journalist and as a politician (he entered parliament in 1883) and he repaid him with little less than hero-worship. Parnell on his side seems always to have had a genuine affection for O'Brien.[1]

[1] The only biography is by Michael Macdonagh, who has also written a short article in the *D.N.B., 1922–30.* See also the various volumes of

The same could not be said of T. M. Healy, between whom and his leader there existed, even before the split, a deep anti-pathy. Healy was younger even than Dillon and O'Brien—he was born at Bantry in 1855. He had some education at the Christian Brothers' school at Fermoy, but at thirteen he was sent up to Dublin to earn his living. We next hear of him as a shorthand clerk in a railway office at Newcastle-upon-Tyne. This was in 1871, when he was only sixteen. Ten years later he was an established figure both in Ireland and in parliament. Something of this he may have owed to his family, for his uncle, T. D. Sullivan, owned and edited *The Nation* newspaper in Dublin; this relationship was later reinforced when Healy married Sullivan's daughter, but it would not in itself have led to his extraordinarily rapid advance. For that he had mainly to thank his own brains, his flair for journalism and an infinite capacity for hard work.

It was, however, T. D. Sullivan who first opened the door for him by appointing him a parliamentary correspondent for *The Nation*. Healy's weekly articles were very favourable towards the Parnellite group and soon he too became a Parnellite. In 1880, impressed by his ability, Parnell sent for him to help him in the closing stages of his American and Canadian tour. On their return, Healy at once began to make a name for himself both as an organiser and as a speaker and was almost immediately returned to parliament as member for Wexford. The very next year he had a brilliant success in carrying an amendment to the land act of 1881—the famous 'Healy clause' safeguarding tenants' improvements from rent demands. This was only the beginning of his parliamentary reputation, for in years to come his knowledge of procedure, quick wit and ready tongue were to make him one of the ablest debaters in the house—though he always remained a debater rather than an orator of the first rank.

In the course of his meteoric rise Healy had shown remarkable qualities. His wide reading, phenomenal memory and intense application were such that he contrived to qualify as a barrister and build up a considerable practice even while consolidating his position in parliament. His vivid, ironic speeches had made him a powerful force with Irish audiences, while his acute

O'Brien's own reminiscences, especially *Recollections, Evening memories, An olive branch in Ireland*, and *The Parnell of real life*.

tactical sense—perhaps second only to Parnell's—had secured
him a place in the inner circle of the party. But there was a
reverse side to the picture. He was quick-tempered, his wit, if
brilliant, was apt to be barbed, and though he was devotedly
loyal to his family and friends, he could be a very bitter enemy.

His relations with Parnell were complex. At the outset he had
acted as the leader's private secretary, but this phase ended—
according to Healy's own subsequent account—in 1881 when
he and some others came upon evidence which seemed to indicate that Parnell had been involved in an affair with a barmaid.[1]
This may have weakened his admiration for Parnell as a man,
but it did not prevent him from working with him politically.
It was not until February 1886 that an open breach occurred
between them, when Healy and Biggar did their utmost to
prevent Parnell carrying Captain O'Shea as his candidate for a
by-election at Galway. Mrs O'Shea had then been Parnell's
mistress for several years and Healy and Biggar, not to mention
other members of the party, had come to know of the fact.[2]
How much they knew, or how long they had known it, it is still
impossible to say precisely, but there seems little doubt that
both Healy and Biggar regarded Parnell's action at Galway as
dictated by the exigencies of his liaison with Mrs O'Shea.[3] On
this occasion—the only one before 1890 when his public and

[1] T. M. Healy, *Letters and leaders of my day*, i. 107–10; M. Davitt, *The fall of
feudalism in Ireland*, p. 348. Davitt identifies this incident with the O'Shea
affair, but Healy is quite clear that this was not so.

[2] Wilfrid Scawen Blunt, the poet, apparently knew in February 1886 that
Mrs O'Shea had been Parnell's mistress and suspected she still was. At that
time he noted in his diary (12 Feb. 1886) that 'nobody seems to know the
true reason for Parnell's action' (W. S. Blunt, *The land war in Ireland*, p. 28).
A few months later, however, on his first visit to Ireland, he found there was
'secret talk' of this aspect of the Galway episode (ibid., p. 459).

[3] Henry Harrison, *Parnell, Joseph Chamberlain and Mr Garvin*, pp. 155–7, has
suggested that another possible motive for Parnell's support of O'Shea's
candidature may have been a desire to meet the wishes of Joseph Chamberlain, who at that time was anxious that O'Shea should obtain a seat. For
detailed consideration of this point see C. Cruise O'Brien, *Parnell and his
party*, ch. vi; T. W. Moody, 'Parnell and the Galway election of 1886',
I.H.S., ix, no. 35 (March 1955). For a suggestion that in October or November 1885 some at least of the Irish party knew of the love affair, see the letter
from Henry Labouchere to Chamberlain published by C. H. D. Howard,
'Joseph Chamberlain and the Irish "central board" scheme, 1884–5', in
I.H.S., viii, no. 32, p. 329, *n.* 25 (September 1953).

his private life converged—Parnell crushed the opposition ruthlessly, but obviously the episode marked out Healy as a potential enemy. Even before then, indeed, Healy seems to have been restive under Parnell's neglect of the party, for in 1885 we find him assuring Henry Labouchere, the radical M.P., that the real leadership was in the hands of Dillon, O'Brien, Justin McCarthy and himself.[1] Parnell, for his part, would scarcely have been human if he had not since 1886 nursed a deep hostility against his rebellious follower. He did not allow any hint of this to appear in public, but it is at least suggestive that Healy, though one of the ablest lawyers in the party, was not among counsel for the defence at the special commission—an exclusion which he not unnaturally resented, the more so as he had originally been led to believe that he would be offered a brief.[2] Even more suggestive is the fact that when Parnell met John Morley at Brighton in November 1890, the latter found him 'very benignant' towards his lieutenants in general, with the specific exception of Healy.[3] In the circumstances it was hardly surprising that when the crisis came, this deep, mutual antagonism should have risen to the surface and that the struggle within the Irish party should at times have seemed to have resolved itself virtually into a duel between the two men.[4]

Though very different in gifts, the last member of the quartette, Thomas Sexton, in some ways resembled Healy. Like him he was largely self-educated; like him he was a railway clerk in his early days; and like him he first made his mark as a contributor to *The Nation*—he became a leader-writer in 1867 when only nineteen. Indeed, it was Healy who first brought him to Parnell's notice. In 1880 he entered parliament as a Parnellite and before long also began to take a prominent part in the land agitation, being amongst those imprisoned in Kilmainham in 1881. Sexton was in the great tradition of parliamentary oratory

[1] A. Thorold, *Life of Henry Labouchere*, p. 251.

[2] Healy, *Letters and leaders*, i. 287–94; M. Davitt, *The fall of feudalism in Ireland*, p. 543.

[3] Gladstone papers (B.M., Add. MS 44,256, ff. 65–6), John Morley to Gladstone, 13 Nov. 1890.

[4] For Healy's biography see the obituary in *The Times*, 27 Mar. 1931; the article by Joseph Hone in *D.N.B.*, *1931–40*; Liam O'Flaherty, *T. M. Healy*; M. Sullivan, *No man's man*; Healy's own memoirs, *Letters and leaders of my day*.

and was held by some to be second only to Gladstone, though others thought his speeches far too long. Long they certainly were, but they displayed extraordinary mastery of detail and a real feeling for language. In addition, Sexton was reckoned the outstanding financial expert in the party—a reputation which seems to have been fully justified. However, able as he was, he could not by any stretch of the imagination be considered a potential leader, and this for two reasons. One was that, like so many of his colleagues, he was abnormally sensitive to criticism. The other was that he was solitary in his habits to the point of eccentricity. Unmarried, he lived entirely to himself, admitting none of his colleagues to intimacy. A party which had chafed repeatedly at Parnell's frequent disappearances was hardly likely to choose another recluse as his successor and, to be fair, there is no evidence that even Sexton himself considered that it should.[1]

(5)

While each of these four had his individual failings, they were all undeniably men of exceptional ability who, in any Irish government, would certainly have been prominent. Yet, in Parnell's party, despite their gifts, they remained subordinates and before 1890 the idea that any one of them might compete with him for the leadership would have seemed grotesque. Up to the very last moment Parnell, though disdaining the most elementary precautions, had to all appearances preserved an effortless ascendancy over his followers. They might grumble at his absences, complain of his inaction, even engage in the land agitation independently of him, but in the last analysis he was still 'the chief'.

Part—though not all—of this ascendancy Parnell no doubt owed to his past achievements. There were, it is worth recalling, very few leading men in the party—Dillon, J. J. O'Kelly and John Barry were three of the more obvious exceptions—who had had a significant political life of their own before being swept into Parnell's movement. And although a number had shared

[1] For Sexton's biography see his obituaries in *The Times* and the *Irish Independent*, 2 Nov. 1932; the article by Joseph Hone in *D.N.B.*, *1931–40*; and Justin McCarthy, *Reminiscences*, ii. 381–7.

with him the burden of the vital transition period between 1879 and 1882, the most important decisions had been made to all intents and purposes by him alone. Whenever negotiations or discussions had to be undertaken, it was Parnell and Parnell only with whom English political leaders dealt. He might consult with his lieutenants, and he might allow them a free rein in the house of commons, but his conception of leadership was that the ultimate responsibility for policy-making at the highest level always rested with himself.

As we have seen, this conception was extremely irksome to the more ambitious of the party and such episodes as the Galway election or—in a rather different way—the Plan of Campaign showed that their subservience had its limits. That there were not more demonstrations of this kind was due, to some extent at least, to the clumsiness of Parnell's English opponents. When Irish members were imprisoned under coercion acts and harsh measures were taken to crush the land agitation; when the power of Rome was invoked against the movement; when a great newspaper sought to incriminate the leader and the party by the most sordid means and when a unionist government lent itself to the intrigue with thinly-disguised relish—when these things were part of the very fabric of their lives, then the only honourable course for the Parnellites was to close their ranks and face each new peril as a devoted, loyal and united party.

It would, however, be wrong to suppose that Parnell's followers practised these virtues solely because the exigencies of politics compelled them to do so. If they accepted Parnell's leadership as completely as they did, it was not merely because he, as head of the party, had borne the brunt of English hostility. Nor was it merely because they regarded him as the embodiment of the home rule cause. It *was* this, but it was also something more. It was, at bottom, because they had come under the spell of his strange and powerful personality. What precisely it was about Parnell that fascinated his contemporaries has been debated from that day to this, and no completely satisfying answer has yet been given. Nearly everyone, of course, acknowledged his political ability—his grasp of the possible, his tenacity and patience, his power of concentration on the matter immediately in hand. Most of his one-time liberal allies praised him highly for these qualities, even where they failed to understand him in other ways. John Morley, for example, though ultimately disillusioned, was immensely impressed by him.[1] Asquith, who saw much of him at the special commission, considered him one of the three or four men of the century.[2] And Gladstone called him 'a political genius'[3] and 'the most remarkable man I ever met'.[4] Even Joseph Chamberlain, his arch-enemy at the last, admitted that he was a great man, though he added that he also thought him unscrupulous.[5]

These were the estimates of Englishmen, who knew him only as a political friend or foe. Those of his Irish followers who saw him at close quarters were in a better position to know what he was like as a man. Some were devoted to him, some grew to detest him, but all agreed that he was a phenomenon unique in their experience, and they recorded with insatiable interest whatever struck them most about him.[6] They commented, for example, on his good looks and especially on his brilliant eyes; they noted anxiously his pallor and the changes wrought in his appearance by the ill-health of his later years; they were intrigued by his love of physical exercise, by his fondness for children and animals, by his personal frugality and by his gift for silence; they were amused by his superstitions, by his tendency to appear in tweed suits on the most inappropriate occasions, by his scientific hobbies, by his indifference to literature and what they took to be his ignorance of Irish history—though this last may not have been so great as they imagined.[7] In short,

[1] *The Times*, 27 Oct. 1891; John Morley, *Recollections*, i. 236–49.

[2] Earl of Oxford and Asquith, *Fifty years of parliament*, i. 187–9.

[3] Morley, *Recollections*, i. 236.

[4] In conversation with R. Barry O'Brien in January 1897 and recorded by the latter in his *Parnell*, ii. 357.

[5] R. B. O'Brien, *Parnell*, ii. 131. Chamberlain was interviewed by Barry O'Brien in February 1898.

[6] The composite picture of Parnell in this and succeeding paragraphs is derived from many contemporary sources, of which the chief are R. B. O'Brien, *Parnell*; William O'Brien, *Recollections*, *An olive branch in Ireland*, *Evening memories*, and *The Parnell of real life*; Justin McCarthy, *Reminiscences* and *The story of an Irishman*; T. P. O'Connor, *The Parnell movement*, *The life of Charles Stewart Parnell*, and *Memoirs of an old parliamentarian*; T. M. Healy, *Letters and leaders of my day*; Michael Davitt, *The fall of feudalism in Ireland*; T. D. Sullivan, *Recollections of troubled times in Irish politics*; Katherine Tynan, *Twenty-five years : reminiscences*.

[7] It is perhaps worth pointing out that the library at Avondale was well equipped with books on Irish history in the seventeenth, eighteenth and

they were fascinated alike by his remoteness from their world and by the thread of paradox which seemed to run through his whole life. He was, after all, an aristocrat leading a predominantly middle-class party; he was a protestant at the head of an overwhelmingly catholic movement; he was a landlord, yet one of the most powerful enemies of landlordism; above all, he, who seemed cut out to be a man of action, had staked everything upon constitutional methods. It is not altogether unreasonable to suppose that this very quality of being different may well have been one of the things that contributed most to his hold upon his party.

Perhaps also—and again paradoxically—he owed something to the fact that his aloofness was physical as well as mental. Throughout his career he was essentially a solitary figure, and often a mysterious one, appearing and disappearing, going his own way and keeping his own counsel. In the early days, when he was trying to balance between the right and left wings in Ireland, this was probably inevitable, and later of course his own uncertain health and the claims of Mrs O'Shea accounted for the long and unexplained absences that baffled his followers. He had never been a sociable man and privacy no doubt suited his own inclinations. But he may also have felt—rightly or wrongly—that his public position demanded it and that it was no bad thing if a certain amount of divinity should hedge even a parliamentary leader. It was occasionally said—perhaps because of this—that Parnell treated his party as inferiors and that to some he was not even civil. There seems little or no trustworthy evidence to support such a charge. He could be brusque certainly, and both in speech and writing he was brief and to the point. He did not suffer fools gladly and his anger was not pleasant to encounter. But even those who in the end differed most sharply from him recalled that he was habitually affable, courteous and a man of great personal charm. This was

nineteenth centuries. How many of these Parnell had actually read, it is of course impossible to say, but there are frequent references in his speeches to the Volunteer movement of the eighteenth century and to various aspects of life in nineteenth-century Ireland. The Avondale library was sold on 14 Aug. 1901 and the auctioneer's catalogue contains a useful guide to the contents. Copies of the catalogue are in the National Library, Dublin, and also in the possession of Professor T. W. Moody, of Trinity College, Dublin, to whom I am indebted for this reference.

the verdict equally of William O'Brien, of Justin McCarthy and of T. M. Healy.[1]

Of course very few of the Irish members ever got close enough to see this side of him. For the party as a whole his chief attraction was probably his attitude towards England, and more particularly his behaviour in the house of commons. Permanently in a minority, pledged to accept no office and with only a limited interest in parliamentary business, most of the rank and file must have found the atmosphere at Westminster unfamiliar, frustrating and, often enough, unfriendly. In Parnell they had a leader who was not only not intimidated by the house of commons, but supremely indifferent both to its censure and its praise. What made this triumph over a hostile environment so remarkable to Irish eyes was that the man who achieved it used none of the traditional Irish arts. He was not eloquent, he was not emotional, he was not even witty. He made no appeal to the sympathies of his hearers, struck no attitudes, indulged in no extravagances of speech or gesture. Apparently unmoved by the storms which raged round him at every phase of his career, he gave the impression of being somehow outside the battle, even while most deeply committed to it. Everything he did—from calculated caution to no less calculated audacity—seemed to be directed by a cold and subtle intelligence, completely at home in politics and never carried away by the excitements or rigours of the game.

Yet those who saw him only as an aloof, imperturbable figure moving the pieces dispassionately about the chess-board, missed the most significant thing about him—which was that his celebrated control was not inborn, but had only been achieved by stern self-mastery. The more perceptive of his contemporaries realised something of this when they stressed his nervousness, his distaste for public speaking, his dislike of noise and large crowds. He had overcome these disabilities (almost fatal for a politician) by the exercise of relentless will-power and all who came in contact with him testified to the strength of that will-power. What was less clearly understood, however, was that Parnell was not only a man of extreme

[1] W. O'Brien, *The Parnell of real life*, pp. 40–60; Justin McCarthy, *Reminiscences*, ii. 91–2; T. M. Healy, 'The rise and fall of Mr Parnell' in *The New Review* (March 1891), iv. 196–7.

nervous energy, but was also a profoundly passionate man. Passionate in his love for Mrs O'Shea, which was no mere intrigue, but something vital to his existence; passionate also in his appetite for power and in his pride of leadership. Until the last year of his life these fires were banked and there was little on the surface to show that they existed. In 1890, however, when the O'Shea divorce case precipitated the final crisis, they erupted with a suddenness and violence which threatened to consume everything he had ever stood for, and did in fact end by consuming the man himself.

II

THE O'SHEA AFFAIR

~~~~~~

(1)

THE STORY of the triangular relationship between Parnell and
the O'Sheas, although it only began to emerge fully into the
light of day when Captain O'Shea filed his petition, had by then
run a long and tortuous course. Parnell had first met Katharine
O'Shea in the summer of 1880.[1] At that time he was leading a
strenuous and, socially at least, a lonely life. In the spring he
had come back from an exhausting American tour only to fling
himself into a general election campaign. No sooner was that
over than there was urgent work to be done in parliament, and
also in Ireland where the Land League agitation was spreading.
Parnell lodged in rooms when in London, but most of his days
and nights were spent at the house of commons; he was living
under great pressure and his health was far from good.[2] From
this existence, drab and hectic by turns, Mrs O'Shea offered
him an avenue of escape, and it is scarcely surprising that he
seized upon it eagerly. Although past her first youth—she was
the same age as Parnell—and the mother of three children, she
was a handsome, assured woman of the world with great

[1] Not the autumn, as suggested by counsel for O'Shea in the divorce court.
Parnell's first letter to Mrs O'Shea is dated 17 July 1880 and in her book she
shows clearly that it was summer when they met (Katharine O'Shea,
Charles Stewart Parnell: his love story and political life (first edition, 1914, hereafter cited as O'Shea), i. 136).

[2] O'Shea, i. 138–40.

35

vitality and considerable charm. They appear to have been attracted towards each other almost from their first meeting, though politics kept Parnell away from her for most of that summer. By the autumn, however, he was already writing to her as 'my own love'.[1]

She had then been married to Captain O'Shea for thirteen years, their last child having been born in 1874. O'Shea himself had been born in Dublin in 1840 the only son of a well-to-do solicitor who appears to have been an over-indulgent father.[2] The son, Willie (as he was generally called), was educated at Oscott College and was put down for Trinity College, Dublin; but, since he entered the 18th Hussars at the age of eighteen, the university can scarcely claim—or be blamed for—having much influenced the formation of his character. For some years he led the normal life of a subaltern in a crack cavalry regiment, spending a great deal of money and differing from his fellows perhaps only in that he spoke both French and Spanish fluently, having relatives in both those countries. He was still in the army when he met his future wife, but before they were married he had sold out with the rank of captain. The girl he married was the youngest of the thirteen children of Sir John Page Wood, who had formerly been chaplain to Queen Caroline, but whose last years were spent in the country parish of Rivenhall. The family was not wealthy, though it had distinguished connections. One of Katharine's uncles, Lord Hatherley, had been for a time Lord Chancellor in Gladstone's first ministry, and one of her brothers was Sir Evelyn (later Field-Marshal) Wood, V.C.

It soon turned out that O'Shea, having run through large sums of his father's money, was hard put to it to provide for a wife and family. He owned some land in Ireland,[3] but it was not valuable and he turned his energies to business, becoming interested in enterprises that often took him abroad for long periods at a time. These, however, failed to prosper and from early in their married life the couple were in constant financial difficulty, from which they were periodically rescued by Mrs

---

[1] O'Shea, i. 153, Parnell to Mrs O'Shea, 17 Oct. 1880.

[2] There was also a daughter; for the details of Captain O'Shea's origins and family see O'Shea, i. 25–8, 54–5; *D.N.B.*, second supplement (1912), article by S. Fryer.

[3] C. Cruise O'Brien, *Parnell and his party, 1880–90*, p. 16.

Benjamin Wood, Katherine O'Shea's rich 'Aunt Ben', who was to play a vital, though passive, rôle in their destinies. It was apparently this aunt who helped them with the expense of the children and who, having observed Captain O'Shea's prolonged absences (on one occasion he was in Spain for eighteen months trying—as usual without success—to manage a sulphur-mine), at length offered in 1874 to buy a house for her niece close to her own. She did in fact buy Wonersh Lodge, near Eltham in Kent, and from then on it became Katharine O'Shea's home. The only condition attached to the gift was that she should be on hand to act as the old lady's companion, but this was no great hardship, for there was a strong vein of domesticity in Mrs O'Shea's character which life with the captain had done little to satisfy. He, for his part, settled into rooms in London (paid for, according to Mrs O'Shea, by her aunt), coming only at intervals to Eltham to see his children and occasionally to take them to the local Roman Catholic church.[1] Mrs O'Shea later maintained that the arrangement whereby she lived at Eltham and her husband in London marked a real, if informal, separation.[2] Informal it had to be, for her aunt, who in some things was very strict, would not have tolerated an open breach. It is a question, indeed, how far she was aware that even a partial split had occurred, for not only did O'Shea appear spasmodically at Eltham, but Katharine herself went up to London from time to time to act as hostess for him at small dinner-parties he was in the habit of giving at Thomas's hotel in Berkeley Square.

Such was the situation when Parnell met Mrs O'Shea for the first time. Ironically enough, the meeting came about primarily as a means of furthering O'Shea's political ambitions. In 1880 he became, with the O'Gorman Mahon, a member of parliament for county Clare. To launch himself upon his new career he sought to ingratiate himself with his new colleagues, and especially with Parnell whose star was so obviously in the

[1] The O'Sheas were Roman Catholics and the marriage was, therefore, a 'mixed' one. Mrs O'Shea did at one time receive some instruction in the Roman Catholic faith but this ended, by her own account, in 'abrupt revolt against all forms and creeds' (O'Shea, i. 102).

[2] O'Shea, i. 108–23; Henry Harrison, *Parnell vindicated: the lifting of the veil*, pp. 118–29.

ascendant.[1] Consequently, the personnel of the dinner-parties began to change, business-associates giving place to Irish politicians. Justin McCarthy, Richard Power and Colonel J. P. Nolan are mentioned as having been guests from early on, but Parnell himself had persistently refused or ignored his invitations until the day came in the summer of 1880 when Mrs O'Shea herself confronted him face to face in Palace Yard at Westminster.[2] Thereafter, as we have seen, the affair went ahead very rapidly. But as soon as we attempt to trace its history in any detail we run at once into a major difficulty. This is the fact that while the proceedings in the divorce court gave one version of what happened, Mrs O'Shea herself (or Mrs Parnell as she then was), in the months immediately after Parnell's death gave a very different account to Henry Harrison, one of the youngest and most devoted of Parnell's followers; and what she told him he supplemented from his knowledge of her private papers, gained while he was helping her to set her affairs in order. It has to be borne in mind that Harrison only published his record in 1931, forty years after his conversations with Parnell's widow, and that public opinion at the time of the divorce was formed entirely by what was revealed in the course of the trial. We need go no further than the report of the court proceedings to explain the revulsion of feeling against the Irish leader which took place immediately the verdict had been given in O'Shea's favour. But if we wish to pass beyond the immediate effects of the case upon the political situation, and to consider the bearing of the whole affair upon our judgment of Parnell himself as a man, then Harrison's interpretation cannot be ignored.

The fact that the case did not come on until November 1890, nearly a year after the petition had been filed, left plenty of time for legal manoeuvring on both sides. One consequence of this was that when the trial opened it was found that various allegations had been made against O'Shea, the chief of which were that he had connived at his wife's relationship with

---

[1] But cf. O'Shea's own version in conversation with E. T. Cook of the *Pall Mall Gazette* after the divorce trial: 'You must remember I had taken him up when he was a pariah and none of his own class would have a word to say to him' (J. Saxon Mills, *Life of Sir E. T. Cook*, p. 107).

[2] O'Shea, i. 135.

Parnell over a long period and that he had committed adultery with her sister, Mrs Steele. These allegations were not pressed; indeed, so far from pressing them, the respondent and co-respondent did not even defend themselves against the original grounds alleged by Captain O'Shea. Mrs O'Shea's counsel held only a watching brief and Parnell was not represented at all. But the fact that counter-charges had been entered allowed Captain O'Shea to go into the witness-box and dwell at length on the way in which he had been systematically deceived for many years. His counsel, Sir Edward Clarke, was able to buttress his client's story by calling evidence which seemed to show conclusively that the deception had been not only prolonged, but squalid and degrading.[1] It was shown that Parnell had on occasion used false names, that he had taken houses in these false names, and that 'three or four times' he had only escaped detection by Captain O'Shea by climbing out of a room by a fire-escape and presenting himself a few minutes later at the hall-door as if he had just come to pay a call. This last allegation was actually based on a thoroughly untrustworthy piece of evidence—the uncorroborated story of a single maid-servant.[2] It could scarcely have stood up to serious cross-examination but, since there was no cross-examination, it was allowed to go uncontradicted and was a factor affecting not merely the issue of the trial (it impressed itself very vividly upon the judge), but the disgust felt by the public at large. In the circumstances a verdict for O'Shea was inevitable. He was awarded a decree *nisi* with custody of the children under sixteen; costs were to be paid by the co-respondent and by the respondent if it should be found that she had a separate estate.

What made the disclosures of the trial so devastating was that Parnell himself, at intervals since the petition had first been filed, had assured various people that he would emerge from the affair with his honour intact. He had even given an interview to the *Freeman's Journal* in which he asserted that the proceedings against him had been set in motion in the interest of *The Times* so as to prejudice his libel action then pending against that newspaper—a clear hint to Ireland, eagerly taken up in the

[1] *The Times*, 17 and 18 Nov. 1890.
[2] Evidence of Caroline Pethers, caretaker of No. 8 Medina Terrace, Brighton (*The Times*, 17 Nov. 1890).

editorial columns of the *Freeman's Journal*, that this was yet
another tory device to ruin the home rule cause. In this same
interview, with for him unusual expansiveness, Parnell also
stated that O'Shea had always been aware that he (Parnell)
had been constantly at Eltham in his absence from 1880 to
1886 and that since 1886 O'Shea had known that Parnell
constantly resided there from 1880 to 1886.[1] This was a very
remarkable assertion and it is curious that it did not attract
more attention at the time. In addition to this public statement,
Parnell had spoken to Davitt and written to William O'Brien
and T. P. Gill in the most reassuring terms.[2] Davitt, indeed,
claimed that he had been the first person to tell Parnell what
O'Shea's case was going to be. He asserted further that Parnell
had told him to go back to Ireland and tell his friends that he,
Parnell, was going to emerge from the ordeal 'without the
slightest stain on my name or reputation'.[3] There is no proof of
Davitt's claim to be familiar with the details of O'Shea's case,
but it is beyond question that he considered he had received
from Parnell the strongest possible assurances, and there was no
limit to his disillusionment when the verdict showed—or
seemed to show—that Parnell had been misleading him. One
of those to whom he repeated what Parnell had told him was
the influential English journalist, W. T. Stead, and the latter's
subsequent hostility to Parnell derived largely from the way in
which, as he saw it, Davitt had been deceived. As Stead wrote
to Gladstone: 'This is not an affair of adultery, but an affair
of confidence, and no man can evermore have confidence in

[1] *F.J.*, 30 Dec. 1889. The prolonged silence in Ireland about the divorce
from then until November 1890 is a remarkable indication of the trust most
people still had in Parnell. The liberal leaders too were silent—even in their
private correspondence there is little comment—but in this they merely
followed the late Victorian practice of separating private and public conduct
until forced to do otherwise. For another instance see R. Jenkins, *Sir
Charles Dilke*, pp. 222–3, 231.

[2] Gill Papers, Parnell to Gill, 31 Dec. 1889—letter not in Parnell's hand
but signed by him; William O'Brien, *Evening memories*, p. 466, and *The Parnell
of real life*, p. 157; Michael Davitt, *The fall of feudalism in Ireland*, p. 637; W. S.
Blunt, *My diaries*, i. 218–9, conversation with T. P. Gill on 7 Mar. 1896, in
which the latter remarked that 'Parnell had a complete case in defence
against O'Shea. O'Shea having connived throughout and profited in a
money way'.

[3] *The Times*, 28 Nov. 1890.

Parnell.'[1] John Morley, again, had also seen Parnell, only a few days before the trial, and had been assured by him that 'the other side don't know what a broken-kneed horse they're riding' and that there was absolutely no question of anything that would cause his disappearance from the scene.[2] Morley had written that very day to Harcourt that he had heard Sir Edward Clarke had 'some terribly odious material',[3] but presumably he was reassured by Parnell, for on November 13 he wrote to Gladstone his opinion that the Irish leader would emerge triumphant.[4]

For Parnell to have given these assurances in the foreknowledge that what would actually happen in court would be the very opposite would have been tantamount to planning his own political suicide. It is difficult to believe that he was not perfectly sincere in what he said, and that even a week before the trial came on he was not completely confident as to the outcome. To understand why he was so confident and why his plans went awry at the last moment, it is necessary to have the key to the inner history of the whole affair. Contemporaries did not have this key, for it is only since Henry Harrison published his *Parnell vindicated* in 1931 that it has become the common property of historians. It is true that the evidence Harrison collected does not always bear the weight of the conclusions he based upon it. Nevertheless, the theory he put forward goes far to explain what baffled so many people at the time—the contrast between Parnell's utterances *before* the trial and the sorry figure he cut in the testimony given *at* the trial.

The theory rests on the fundamental proposition that, despite what was said in the divorce court, Captain O'Shea was not a deceived husband but had, on the contrary, connived at the relationship between his wife and Parnell. This was the central theme of the conversations which Harrison had with Mrs Parnell at Brighton in the months after Parnell's death.[5] Her story was that although neither she nor anyone else had told

---

[1] F. Whyte, *Life of W. T. Stead*, ii. 20; *Review of Reviews* (Nov. 1890), ii. 600–2.

[2] John Morley, *Recollections*, i. 253–4.

[3] A. G. Gardiner, *Life of Sir William Harcourt*, ii. 82.

[4] Gladstone Papers (B.M., Add. MS 44,256, ff. 63–5), John Morley to Gladstone, 13 Nov. 1890; Morley, *Gladstone*, iii. 429.

[5] Henry Harrison, *Parnell vindicated*, pp. 118–29 and pp. 167–80.

O'Shea in so many words of her relations with Parnell—except once, when she let it out in the middle of a stormy scene—he not only knew, but actually encouraged her in the affair, at least at the outset.[1] This, it seems, did not prevent him from becoming jealous very quickly, and in her opinion this jealousy was at the root of a quarrel between the two men which occurred in 1881. In the course of this quarrel O'Shea sent a challenge to Parnell. The challenge was not refused, but a reconciliation was patched up and the threatened duel did not take place. But—so Mrs Parnell told Harrison—the significant aftermath of the episode was that while she agreed to maintain the façade of a marriage which had long ceased to have any inner reality, O'Shea on his side promised to leave her her freedom. Parnell, she added, himself made no promises to anyone, but was prepared to accept the situation created by the *dénouement* of 1881. He disliked the whole arrangement, and wanted to claim her openly as his wife, already privately regarding her as such, but he consented to bow to her wishes in the matter. He did nothing, however—and she emphasised this—either directly to deceive O'Shea, or to enter into any kind of bargain or negotiation with him.[2] Such, in brief, was Mrs Parnell's version of the affair. The question is—how far can it be proved to be the right one?

So far as the events of 1881 are concerned, Mrs Parnell's account given to Harrison rests only upon her word—there is no documentary evidence for it. Later, when her own book appeared in 1914, the brief passage devoted to the duel episode seemed to contradict what she had told Harrison. She said, for example, that Parnell, while accepting O'Shea's challenge, had explained to O'Shea that he must have some means of communicating with the government, that Mrs O'Shea had kindly undertaken the office for him, and that he trusted O'Shea would not object to his meeting her after the duel. A little further on she added that O'Shea then felt he had been too hasty and 'merely made the condition that Mr Parnell should not stay at Eltham'. In her book this is immediately followed by the statement that from the date of this quarrel 'Mr Parnell and I were one without further scruple, without fear and without

[1] Henry Harrison, *Parnell vindicated*, pp. 123–4.
[2] Ibid., pp. 171–2, 179–80.

remorse'—but nothing is said to indicate that O'Shea then *knew* that they were one.[1] Is this account any more firmly based than the account she gave Harrison? If anything, it is even more dubious, partly because it too is undocumented and partly because—as is clear from the preface—the book was written in close consultation with her son, Gerard O'Shea, who had been devoted to his father and was anxious above all to safeguard that father's reputation.[2]

There remains a third version of the episode—that given in the divorce court by O'Shea's counsel, Sir Edward Clarke. His rendering of it differs in some particulars from that given in Mrs O'Shea's book—in such matters, for example, as the date of the quarrel and the manner in which the challenge was conveyed. He too, however, alleged that some kind of assurance or explanation was given to O'Shea on Parnell's behalf—his assertion was that Parnell had met Mrs Steele and had told her that there were no grounds for O'Shea's suspicions and that in future he would not see Mrs O'Shea.[3] But this account also is curiously indefinite, for no evidence in support of this statement was produced. Yet one can hardly doubt that if the evidence had existed it would have been prominently paraded, as helping to fix the perfidy of the co-respondent as far back as 1881. It is odd, also, that although Mrs Steele, to whom Parnell's statement was supposed to have been made, was actually in the witness-box, she was asked no questions whatever about this matter. We are left then with this conclusion—that there are three versions of the quarrel in 1881, not one of which is properly documented or to be accepted without reserve. We may admit that O'Shea's suspicions were aroused—all the accounts agree on that—but how they were lulled, or to what extent, these are questions which must remain open.

(2)

Can we be any more precise with regard to 1882? This was

[1] O'Shea, i. 190.

[2] The book was written in her old age and contains a number of inaccuracies. Being written under O'Shea influence it was naturally concerned to show that the captain had been, as he had appeared in the divorce court, a deceived husband. For a detailed criticism of the book's shortcomings, see Harrison, *Parnell vindicated*, pp. 218–39.

[3] *The Times*, 17 Nov. 1890.

undoubtedly one of the vital years in the whole tortured history of the affair. In its early months Parnell was a prisoner in Kilmainham, and had been since the previous October. Captain O'Shea was busily engaged as a political intermediary shuttling to and fro between London and the prison in Dublin. Mrs O'Shea was expecting a baby, which was born in February and died two months later. What sort of interconnection can be established between these various facts? There are two clues. One is that the daughter born in February was Parnell's child. In Mrs O'Shea's book—written, it will be remembered, under the eye of Gerard O'Shea—she says in the clearest terms that it *was* Parnell's and she prints letters that he wrote her from Kilmainham which show beyond doubt that he took it to be his and that he was extremely anxious about her health.[1] Yet, in this same book which provides so much evidence about the paternity of the child, there occur two extraordinary statements that on the face of it would seem to indicate the real father to have been O'Shea. In one passage, speaking of the period between Parnell's arrest in October and the birth of the baby in February, she says that O'Shea became solicitous for her health and wished to come to Eltham more often than she would allow. 'He thought February would seal our reconciliation, whereas I knew it would cement the cold hatred I felt towards him, and consummate the love I bore my child's father.'[2] There is a strong implication here that O'Shea thought the child to be his. But stronger even than this is the second passage which occurs later, when she describes how the child lay dying, and how she feared it would be dead before Parnell could see it:

> Willie [i.e. O'Shea] was very good; I told him my baby was dying and I must be left alone. He had no suspicion of the truth, and only stipulated that the child should be baptised at once—urged, thereto, I think, by his mother and sister.[3]

Now, if these passages are placed alongside the letters Parnell wrote Mrs O'Shea from Kilmainham, they give the impression that each man believed himself to be the father of the child. And this in turn confronts one with the unpleasant hypothesis that in that case Mrs O'Shea must have been living with both her husband and Parnell in the early summer of 1881 when the

[1] O'Shea, i. 220–1, 225, 229, 237.   [2] Ibid., i. 210.   [3] Ibid., i. 244.

child was conceived. This hypothesis is, indeed, so unpleasant that Harrison rejects it utterly, and has put forward instead the theory that, since her book was written under O'Shea influence, it was necessary—if the story told in the divorce court were to be substantiated—to have evidence indicating, not that O'Shea *was* the father of the child, but that he *believed* himself to be so. In the divorce court itself the whole matter was handled with extreme caution. O'Shea did not mention the birth in 1882 at all, and his counsel contented himself with saying merely that after the birth of Carmen O'Shea in 1874 'no child was born until February 1882, when a child was born which died soon after its birth'.[1] Harrison suggests that the passages in Mrs O'Shea's book are deliberately designed to buttress the position O'Shea took up in the divorce court and are not a true description of the state of affairs in 1882.[2] Every feeling of charity or honour prompts one to accept this contention. Yet the historian has to record, with a detachment impossible for Harrison, who had known Mrs O'Shea and had a deep sympathy for her as Parnell's widow, that it remains only a theory. However plausible it may be, however much one may wish to be convinced by it, it lacks positive proof. We still cannot say with absolute authority which was true—the story she told Harrison after Parnell's death, or the story she gave—or was induced to give—in her old age, more than twenty years later.[3]

But there is a second clue to the events of 1882. On April 10 Parnell was released from Kilmainham on parole to attend the funeral of a nephew in Paris. On his way there he went to Eltham, where Mrs O'Shea put his dying child into his arms.[4] Next day, as he passed through London, he told O'Shea that he had been to Eltham.[5] Returning from Paris, he went again to Eltham and telegraphed to O'Shea that he was there.[6] By O'Shea's own testimony at the special commission which enquired into the charges made by *The Times* against the Parnell movement, Parnell stayed at Eltham for several days;

[1] *The Times*, 17 Nov. 1890.   [2] Harrison, *Parnell vindicated*, pp. 222–5.
[3] It should, however, be noted that Herbert Gladstone, who knew O'Shea fairly well, but admittedly wrote much later, was very definite that the O'Sheas were living together in 1882 (*After thirty years*, pp. 303–4).
[4] O'Shea, i. 245.
[5] *Spec. comm. proc.*, i. 344, evidence of Captain O'Shea.
[6] *Spec. comm. proc.*, i. 345.

in fact, they were there together discussing the political situation.[1] Again, according to Mrs O'Shea, when Parnell was finally released from Kilmainham on May 2 he came once more to Eltham.[2] And on the following Sunday, the Phoenix Park murders having occurred in the meantime, O'Shea went to the then home secretary, Sir William Harcourt, to demand police protection for Parnell and for himself—protection, significantly, which was to be provided both at Eltham and at O'Shea's London lodging in Albert Mansions.[3]

Now it seems clear from this not only that Parnell was at Eltham when O'Shea was absent, not only that O'Shea was aware of this fact, but that he was aware of it because Parnell himself had told him. In the divorce court, naturally, these inconvenient facts had to be glossed over. Thus, while O'Shea admitted that Parnell had gone to Eltham when released on parole, he made it seem that the Irish leader had been trying to see him 'and, finding I was not there, came up to Victoria Street'.[4] Again, O'Shea could not deny that Parnell had visited Eltham on his second release from prison, but he gave the impression that Parnell had only appeared there at his invitation. This, of course, was the obvious line for O'Shea to take. His counsel was able to produce plenty of evidence that Parnell had been often at Eltham in 1882, that Mrs O'Shea had been with him late at night, and that they had even been overheard talking together in dressing-rooms and bedrooms. It was essential for O'Shea to show that he was, as his counsel described him, 'entirely ignorant' that this was going on. He was bound, therefore, to insist that though he knew Parnell had visited Eltham, he believed those visits to be quite innocuous and intended either as a means of finding O'Shea himself or of discussing political business with him.

At one point, however, in his divorce-court evidence O'Shea contradicted his own statement before the special commission. On the latter occasion he had testified that Parnell, on returning from Paris, had gone to Eltham and telegraphed to him to join him there. In the divorce court, on the other hand, he swore that Parnell, on his way back from Paris, had stopped at the Grosvenor hotel and had departed thence to Kilmainham.

---

[1] *Spec. comm. proc.*, i. 346.   [2] O'Shea, i. 262.
[3] *Spec. comm. proc.*, i. 353–4, 381.   [4] *The Times*, 17 Nov. 1890.

This may only have been a lapse of memory on his part, but to Henry Harrison, disbelieving as he did O'Shea's story at the divorce trial, it indicated an intention of lying in order to deceive the court. Harrison advances as further evidence of O'Shea's duplicity a remark the latter made in the divorce court when he said: 'I was never there when he (Parnell) was there. It was not within my knowledge that he was visiting my wife there.'[1] If this referred to Eltham, as Harrison implies, it was an obvious lie. But the report of the trial, although a little ambiguous, suggests very strongly that this remark applied, not to Eltham, but to a house in Brighton which Mrs O'Shea had for a few months in 1882. Indeed, to assume—as Harrison tends to do— that O'Shea was telling the truth about Eltham at the special commission and lying about it in the divorce court, is scarcely justified, since Harrison himself has shown that some other parts of the captain's testimony at the special commission were unreliable.[2] But, even if we make this assumption, and suppose that O'Shea was correct in what he swore before the special commission about Parnell's visits to Eltham in 1882, this still does not prove that he *knew* that when Parnell was there Mrs O'Shea was his mistress. Granted they were at Eltham together in O'Shea's absence, and that he was aware of this, the fact remains that no absolutely conclusive evidence has emerged to show that O'Shea realised then and there how far things had gone between them.

But, although the evidence may not be conclusive, it is certainly suggestive. In fact, taking the birth of the child in February and the coming-and-going at Eltham in April and May together, it is hard to see how Captain O'Shea can have remained in ignorance. In order to accept his assertion in the divorce court that he was still in the dark in 1882 we have to believe not only that he and Parnell were sharing Mrs O'Shea's favours in 1881, but also that in 1882, although he knew Parnell was at Eltham in his absence, he failed to realise the implications of the fact—and this despite his furious jealousy the year before. We may well feel that Harrison's theory, even if not proved to the hilt, places less strain upon the imagination than O'Shea's statement in the divorce court, made upon oath though it was.

[1] Harrison, *Parnell vindicated*, p. 313.   [2] Ibid, pp. 314–9.

When we turn to the years after 1882 the difficulty of believ-
ing O'Shea's story is increased. It is increased, above all, when
we read that in his evidence in court he stated that 'my daughter
Clare was born in March 1883' and that 'our youngest child'
was born in November 1884.[1] For, if anything in this whole
complex affair is clear and certain, it is that these two children
were not O'Shea's but Parnell's. Harrison found them accepted
as such when he was in Brighton in 1891, and he has preserved
a letter written to him in after years by Norah O'Shea, the
second child of the O'Shea marriage, in which she refers to the
children as Parnell's.[2] Even O'Shea's own counsel in the
divorce case, when later he came to write his memoirs, described
them as 'unquestionably' Parnell's daughters.[3] Indeed, he went
so far as to distinguish between them and the first child—the
one that died after two months—by describing O'Shea as
'mistakenly' supposing himself to have been the father of the
latter.[4] Now, if it was hard enough to believe that O'Shea was
mistaken in 1882, how much harder it is to be asked to accept
that he was equally mistaken in 1883 and 1884. For, if his
divorce court story is true, and if he genuinely believed these
two daughters to be his, then it can only follow that Mrs
O'Shea deceived both her husband and her lover not once but
three times and that she contrived to maintain the deception
over a period of three years.[5]

Nothing of this, of course, was allowed to come out in the
divorce court and Captain O'Shea's claim to be the father of the
two youngest children was not questioned. His counsel was thus
able to skate without difficulty over what might have been the
very thin ice of the years 1883 and 1884. Indeed, he was able to
do much more than that and produce for each year what
seemed to be damning evidence. Thus, the notorious 'fire-

---

[1] *The Times*, 17 Nov. 1890.
[2] Harrison, *Parnell vindicated*, pp. 215–6, letter dated 1 Feb. 1921.
[3] Sir E. Clarke, *The story of my life*, p. 291.   [4] Ibid., p. 286.
[5] It is significant that Mrs O'Shea's book makes no mention of the existence
of these two daughters even though they were the best possible proof of the
reality and completeness of that 'love-story' her book was intended to
portray. It is difficult to resist Harrison's conclusion that they were omitted
from the book because to recognise that they were Parnell's would be inconsistent with the story told in the divorce court (Harrison, *Parnell vindicated*,
pp. 220–5).

escape' episode was attributed to the winter of 1883-4, and
Captain O'Shea was shown as having protested in 1884 both to
his wife and to Parnell about the scandal that was likely to arise
if Parnell persisted in visiting Eltham in his absence.[1] If, however, the story Mrs Parnell told Harrison had been presented
in court, these protests would have been given a very different
interpretation. They would have been held up, not as the
natural reaction of an indignant husband threatened with the
break-down of his marriage, but as an angry warning that the
terms of the 'agreement' of 1881 were not being observed, and
that if Parnell and Mrs O'Shea could not be more discreet, he
would have no option but to intervene. But, where a case *might*
have been made, there was only silence; and Sir Edward
Clarke was unmolested as he methodically added what appeared
to be proof after proof to his demonstration of the long-drawn-
out and deliberate perfidy of the Irish leader.

Counsel's task, however, became much more difficult when
he approached the period 1885-6, for during these years the
relationship between Parnell and O'Shea underwent a decisive
and permanent change for the worse. Up to the summer of 1885
the captain, who had an unquenchable, but quite unjustified,
confidence in his own capacity as a negotiator, still hoped for
political advancement by acting as a link between Joseph
Chamberlain and Parnell in connection with the former's
scheme for a measure of local self-government for Ireland.[2]
With the collapse of that scheme and the onset of the general
election in the autumn, signs of serious tension began to appear,
and O'Shea's letters to his wife about this time show traces of
deep hostility to Parnell.[3] The latter, having failed to find an
English seat for O'Shea, ended—as we have seen—by forcing
him upon the Galway constituency in Ireland, even though
O'Shea refused to take the parliamentary pledge and despite
the intense hostility of members of the Irish party.[4]

If either man still had any illusions about the other—which
was doubtful enough—the Galway election must certainly have

[1] *The Times*, 17 Nov. 1890.

[2] 'Documents relating to the Irish "central board" scheme, 1884-5', ed.
C. H. D. Howard in *I.H.S.* (Mar. 1953), viii. 237–63; C. H. D. Howard,
'Joseph Chamberlain, Parnell and the Irish "central board" scheme, 1884–
5', in *I.H.S.* (Sept. 1953), viii. 324–61.

[3] O'Shea, ii. 90, 92.   [4] See above, pp. 38–9.

shattered them. Yet it is curiously difficult to determine precisely when the irrevocable break between them occurred. At the special commission O'Shea himself declared that he had been on friendly terms with Parnell 'until June 1886—May or June 1886'.[1] In the divorce court he simply said, in answer to a persistent juror, that his suspicions of his wife and Parnell were first aroused in 1886.[2] But she, on the other hand, alleged that O'Shea's connivance in her relations with Parnell lasted from 1880 until 'the spring of 1886'.[3] When asked at the special commission what changed his attitude towards Parnell, O'Shea replied that before the division on the second reading of the home rule bill 'certain things came to my knowledge . . . which absolutely destroyed the good opinion I had hitherto held of Mr Parnell'.[4] He was not pressed as to what the certain things were, but it is known that he did not vote on the second reading of the home rule bill—the division was taken on June 7—and that he resigned his seat immediately afterwards.[5] Clearly, the critical period lies somewhere between the spring of 1886 and the ending of the home rule debate on June 7. Within that period something happened which may help to date the rupture between the two men a little more exactly. This was the fact that one day in May, Parnell, who was then actually living at Eltham, became involved in an accident with a market-gardener's cart when returning from London. Since he was a key political figure at the time anything that happened to him was news. Accordingly, there shortly appeared in the *Pall Mall Gazette* a paragraph entitled 'Mr Parnell's suburban retreat' and informing its readers that the Irish leader usually lived at Eltham during the parliamentary session.[6]

The publication of such a statement in a newspaper so widely read could not be ignored. O'Shea was immediately stirred to action and telegraphed his wife to know the meaning of it. She replied dismissing the report as an invention by Healy and his friends to annoy O'Shea, and attributing it to spite on account of his success in the Galway election. A letter from Parnell to her, explaining his presence in the neighbourhood by the fact that he had had horses stabled near Bexley Heath and

<hr>

[1] *Spec. comm. proc.*, i. 343.   [2] *The Times*, 18 Nov. 1890.
[3] *The Times*, 17 Nov. 1890.   [4] *Spec. comm. proc.*, i. 367.   [5] Ibid., i. 362.
[6] *Pall Mall Gazette*, 24 May 1886.

regretting that she had been troubled in the matter, was produced in court and contemptuously described by Sir Edward Clarke as 'invented for the purpose of setting Captain O'Shea's suspicions at rest'. Asked if he had in reality accepted his wife's assurances in May 1886, O'Shea made the baffling reply: 'Well, yes, but I had found out something which had nothing to do with the matter, and I desired her again before I went abroad to have no communication with Mr Parnell.'[1] We do not know what that 'something' was (though it has been the subject of ingenious speculation by Harrison[2]), or even if it ever existed outside O'Shea's imagination, but we do know that later in the year, when writing to W. T. Stead in angry denial of a report that Parnell had been staying with him at Eltham, O'Shea said categorically: 'The fact is that I have had no communication whatsoever with Mr Parnell since May.'[3] It seems, therefore, that the decisive break probably came about the end of May, though whether the cause of it was the *Pall Mall Gazette* paragraph, a political difference, or the mysterious 'something' which O'Shea did not elaborate, was not made any clearer by the proceedings at the special commission or in the divorce court.

(3)

The fact that the break came then, however, did not mean that O'Shea ceased to keep a vigilant eye upon his wife. Several times subsequently during 1886 newspaper rumours involved him in embarrassment and drove him to demand explanations. Thus, in July, August and September he wrote either protesting about the rumours that were circulating or forbidding her to have any further communication with Parnell.[4] Despite this, in

[1] *The Times*, 17 Nov. 1890.

[2] Harrison, *Parnell vindicated*, pp. 267–81. Harrison's guess—he calls it a 'legitimate surmise'—was that O'Shea may at that time have learnt from one or other of the liberal ministers that the cabinet was aware of the nature of the relationship between himself, his wife and Parnell; in Harrison's view, once O'Shea realised this fact he would have realised also that he could have little to hope for in future from the liberal party, and that in effect he was a spent force, politically speaking. This is a plausible theory, but it is no more than a theory.

[3] O'Shea, ii. 219, letter dated 19 Dec. 1886.

[4] *The Times*, 17 Nov. 1890. See especially the letter dated 25 Sept. 1886,

October the *Sussex Daily News* was able to report that Parnell had been staying with Mrs O'Shea at Eastbourne. Again there was an urgent telegram from Captain O'Shea, again there was a denial from his wife. On this occasion, however, as Sir Edward Clarke admitted, his client's suspicions 'were not altogether allayed'.[1] Yet, when in December 1886 the *Pall Mall Gazette* published another paragraph, this time stating that Parnell was visiting Captain O'Shea at Eltham,[2] O'Shea, after asking that the statement should be contradicted, personally assured W. T. Stead (the editor) that he was perfectly satisfied that the relationship between his wife and Parnell was one to which he could take no objection whatever. This interview, which Stead with some reason described as 'one of the most curious that I have ever had', took place on 20 December 1886. It seems that O'Shea came to Stead's office, complained about the recent rumours, and asked Stead to interview him. Stead's account—and he was famous for his accuracy—was that O'Shea had declared that the difference between Parnell and himself was purely political and had nothing whatever to do with Mrs O'Shea. Stead then mentioned that he had seen a report in an American newspaper which described Parnell as living at Eltham. O'Shea's reply to this was so emphatic, and so different from what the evidence in the divorce court indicated to have been his real attitude in 1886, that it is worth reproducing:

Believe me, there is not a word of truth in the story. Mr Parnell has never been at Eltham since our difference, and notwithstanding all these rumours, there has never been the least cause for me to suspect my wife. . . .[3]

We will postpone for the moment the question which has obviously to be answered—why Captain O'Shea went out of his way to give the editor of an important newspaper a totally false picture of the situation—and merely note, as Stead duly noted when the divorce court proceedings were published, how completely untrustworthy the transaction showed him to be. Meanwhile, the newspaper paragraphs continued into 1887 and whenever he noticed them O'Shea always reacted in the same where he writes 'in the interests of Gerard, Norah and Carmen', but—significantly—does not mention the children born in 1883 and 1884.

[1] *The Times*, 17 Nov. 1890.
[2] *Pall Mall Gazette*, 18 Dec. 1886.
[3] *Review of Reviews* (Nov. 1890), ii. 599–601.

way as before—making his protest and receiving the usual dis-
claimers. His counsel naturally took the line that O'Shea's
reactions were the normal ones of a husband who cannot be
quite certain that he is being deceived, but jumps to defend his
honour the moment an ugly rumour comes to his ears.
Harrison's interpretation of these events is, of course, very
different. He maintains that O'Shea was quite prepared to let
things remain as they were so long as publicity was avoided.[1]
But that whenever the press penetrated the not very efficient
screen of secrecy put up by Mrs O'Shea and Parnell, he was
bound to make his protest—for two reasons. First, because if he
did not he would lie under the imputation of having a too
accommodating sense of honour. And secondly, because if
affairs so developed as to oblige him to take divorce proceedings,
it was essential for him to have evidence which would show that
whenever his suspicions had been aroused he had made his
protest and received satisfactory assurances.[2] On this hypothesis,
the frequent changes of residence by Parnell, and his use of
false names, can be explained as necessary evasions not of
O'Shea but of the press; indeed, as evasions which were as
necessary to O'Shea as to him.

The importance of the interview with Stead is that it helps in
some measure to support this hypothesis. If O'Shea was a
genuinely deceived husband, then his periodic protests were at
least in character. He might appear gullible in allowing himself
to be put off so often with specious excuses and denials, but at
least it could not be said that he had not taken the kind of action
which a man of honour should take. And if he had stopped
there his behaviour would have been perfectly intelligible and
consistent. But, typically, he over-reached himself and went
just one step further than he need have done. It was not enough
for him to register his protest as the rumours came out. He
must also go to the editor of the *Pall Mall Gazette* and assure

[1] Harrison, *Parnell vindicated*, pp. 281–7.
[2] This may be why in 1887 Sir Charles Dilke heard from P. A. Chance,
an Irish nationalist M.P., that O'Shea *was* going forward with the divorce
and that Parnell had 'no defence possible' (Dilke Papers, 'Diary', 13 Feb.
1887, B.M., Add. MS 43,927). Later, when recording this in his memoir,
Dilke added: 'I have never known what was the reason of the immense
delays which afterwards occurred' (Dilke Papers, 'Memoir', 13 Feb. 1887,
B.M., Add. MS, 43,941).

him in the most uncompromising terms that there was no ground for them. Temporarily, no doubt, he achieved his objective. Stead could scarcely call him a liar to his face—indeed, in his account of the interview, he says he had 'no option but to believe' O'Shea's statement. But the divorce proceedings show this statement to have been manifestly untrue. If, then, O'Shea was really protesting vigorously to his wife and Parnell at the very time he was assuring Stead there was nothing to protest about, the inference is unavoidable that the interview with Stead was designed to throw him off the track. But if O'Shea was a genuinely deceived husband why should he want to throw Stead off the track? Should he not rather exert himself to know the truth, however unpleasant it might turn out to be? Suppose, however, he was not a *deceived* but a *conniving* husband? In such a case he had every reason to want to baffle the press. Protesting against rumours was all very well, but the more there were, the more difficult for him to go on conniving. Better far, he might argue, to go to the fountain-head and stop the flow of rumours altogether.

It is still true, however, even when all is said, that the hypothesis of O'Shea's connivance remains a hypothesis. In judging that enigmatic character we are confronted by two alternatives. Either he was a simple-minded but excessively indulgent husband—and what we know of his career does not suggest that either of these epithets is particularly appropriate—and was vilely deceived. Or else he covered his tracks so skilfully that to this day no solid, irrefutable evidence exists to prove in black and white that he knew of the relationship and connived at it. We say there is no solid and irrefutable evidence—but if the facts marshalled in the preceding pages mean anything, they point overwhelmingly to connivance. Perhaps the fairest summing-up of this most complex and difficult problem is to say that we cannot prove when and how O'Shea came to know of the love of Parnell for his wife, but that we can show that to remain ignorant of it for eight years required on his part a capacity for ignoring unpleasant facts so superhuman as to be beyond belief.

But further, we have also to accept that if O'Shea was a deceived innocent, then his wife was so faithless as to be capable of leading both him and her lover each to think that he was the father of the children born in 1882, 1883 and 1884. The view taken here is that this question of paternity is the pivot of the whole matter. If Mrs O'Shea did betray both men, then indeed anything is possible and much of the difficulty in accepting O'Shea's divorce-court story disappears. But if she did not, then O'Shea's story is almost impossible to credit. Now Parnell, when he met and fell in love with Katharine O'Shea, was no moon-struck youth, but a very experienced leader whose judgment had already been proved in the endlessly complicated politics of the time. He was a proud and sensitive man, and would surely have been quick to notice any coolness or double-dealing on the part of the woman he loved. It is scarcely imaginable that such a man could have been deceived not once but three times. On the contrary, we know that so far from his suspicions having been awakened, his love for Mrs O'Shea never wavered, and, if any-thing, became more passionate as the years went on. As for her, though many faults have been laid at her door, it has never been suggested that she did not love Parnell, and she herself has recorded in her book—written as it was under O'Shea auspices —that years of neglect and quarrels had killed her love for O'Shea long before she met Parnell. From February 1882 (when Parnell's first child was born), she says, she could not bear to be near her husband.[1] It seems impossible, therefore, that she could have brought herself to live with him in 1883 and 1884 and have given him grounds to suppose that the children born in those years were his. In the circumstances, the conclusion that O'Shea was in the fullest sense a conniving husband is irresistible.

But, it may be asked, suppose O'Shea did accept such an ignoble rôle, what was his motive for doing so? Or—to put it crudely—what was it that he got out of the arrangement up to 1889, but ceased to get in that year? For part of the time, possibly, he may have hoped for political advancement, since he undoubtedly had high ambitions, which at one stage did not stop short of the chief secretary's office.[2] He might well feel that it would be to his interest to have, not only close political con-tact with Parnell, but also a hold over him such as the threat to expose the latter's secret relationship with his wife would give him. Up to 1886 O'Shea *was* extremely active in political

[1] O'Shea, ii. 85.　　[2] O'Shea, ii. 209, O'Shea to his wife, 4 May 1885.

negotiation, but, as we have seen, his break with Parnell in the spring of that year effectively closed this avenue to him. The political incentive, therefore—though it may have been a valid one until he resigned from parliament—does not cover all the facts of the case, since a further three and a half years elapsed before he took the first steps in the direction of divorce.

The motive for his prolonged acquiescence which Mrs Parnell gave Harrison was very different. She emphasised the fact that the captain was chronically short of money and that, apart from the fact that his separate establishment in London was paid for by Mrs Wood, he received various presents from the old lady.[1] The year after this story was told to Harrison we find O'Shea himself explaining to Chamberlain that from 1880 to the year of Mrs Wood's death his income averaged £2,500, 'irrespective of any present from Mrs Wood who allowed my former wife about £4,000 a year; but often, and especially in 1882, I was in want of money, owing to political expenses and, if you will, extravagant personal outlay, and I certainly pressed my former wife to keep her aunt up to her promises'.[2] But apart altogether from what O'Shea got, and what his wife got, there was the prospect of what they might expect to get when Mrs Wood died.

According to Mrs Parnell the triangular relationship first became regularised in 1881,[3] at which time Mrs Wood was already eighty-eight years old. It was a reasonable assumption that she would not live very long and that 'appearances' would have to be kept up only for a short time. This assumption was completely falsified by the fact that she did not die until 19 May 1889.[4] So long as she lived not only did the O'Sheas have to wait for their legacy, but while they waited they walked on a razor's edge. If she realised the true state of affairs, there would be an end of the fortune they expected to inherit, for there could be little doubt as to how she would react when she found out that her favourite niece—though admittedly neglected by her husband—had been living in adultery for a long period under the roof which she herself had provided. Much of the almost intolerable tension of the situation sprang from this

[1] Harrison, *Parnell vindicated*, pp. 122, 179, 191–2.
[2] J. L. Garvin, *Life of Joseph Chamberlain*, ii. 399, *n*. 1. O' Shea to Chamberlain, 30 Mar. 1892.
[3] Harrison, *Parnell vindicated*, p. 125.   [4] *The Times*, 21 May 1889.

simple fact—that it had to endure so long. Yet, if the risks were great, so was the ultimate prize. How great we may gather from a letter O'Shea wrote to Chamberlain in November 1888. Explaining that his wife was under a written engagement not to communicate directly or indirectly with Parnell, and that the latter was under a written order not to do so with her, O'Shea continued:

> I dare say a great many people have some notion of the state of affairs, but I am most anxious for my children's sake that nothing about it should actually be published, because a very large fortune for them may depend upon its not coming into print.
>
> I believe Mrs Wood of Eltham is worth £200,000 or more, all left to them and . . . Mrs O'Shea's relations would use any weapon to change her will.[1]

It is true that O'Shea, in this same letter, went on to disclaim any personal interest in the inheritance, but it is immaterial whether he wanted it for his children or for himself. The essential point is that he *had* an interest in the expected legacy and that this was a strong motive to induce him to remain silent for so long about the relations between his wife and Parnell.

Such, at any rate, was the explanation Mrs Parnell gave Harrison and it certainly accounts very convincingly for the captain's behaviour during the crucial year, 1889.[2] Mrs Wood, as we have seen, died in May of that year. It turned out that she had left practically all her great wealth to Mrs O'Shea, her sole beneficiary of any consequence. But she had left it to her in such a way that it could not apparently be the subject of any claim by her husband, nor brought within the scope of her marriage-settlement.[3] It seemed, in short, that O'Shea had waited so long to no purpose. It is not surprising that he reacted violently. He was not the only one to do so, however, for a whole group of Wood relations conceived that their legitimate expectations had been frustrated, and were resolved to contest the will. It was only the most recent of several such testaments and it was an obvious manoeuvre to suggest that it had been made under the influence of Mrs O'Shea and that, in justice,

[1] Garvin, *Life of Chamberlain*, ii. 397–8, O'Shea to Chamberlain, 3 Nov. 1888. Later, 13 Oct. 1889, O'Shea wrote that the fortune consisted of £145,000 in Consols and some land in Gloucestershire (ibid., ii. 399).

[2] Harrison, *Parnell vindicated*, pp. 178–80.   [3] Ibid., p. 187.

the fortune should be divided among the various claimants. To these claimants Captain O'Shea decided to attach himself. We know from a letter of his to Chamberlain that he had determined on this course by October 1889, and that he was considering whether he should not take 'some strong action' in what he called 'the other business', by which, presumably, he meant his wife's relationship with Parnell.[1]

It is easy to see how the disappointment over the will might at one and the same time goad O'Shea into action to dispute the terms of the bequest and remove the main obstacle to his commencing divorce proceedings. Once he was committed to the probate case, the divorce was a strong card for him to play. The natural defence for Mrs O'Shea in the matter of the will was that the money had been left to her as her aunt's favourite niece, loved and trusted by her. If, however, it could be shown in court that this favourite niece had been deceiving her aunt for over eight years, much of her moral standing would be destroyed. After he had made up his mind to play this card O'Shea did not waste time. On October 19, very properly for a catholic in his position, he called on Cardinal Manning and expressed his intention of applying for a divorce. When the cardinal asked for proof of Mrs O'Shea's infidelity, O'Shea produced a transcript of a *Pall Mall Gazette* paragraph.[2] There was a prolonged pause while the cardinal reflected, and also, it may be, while he consulted others.[3] Then, on November 26, he wrote to O'Shea deprecating a separation and apparently arguing that there was insufficient evidence. It seems also—to judge from O'Shea's indignant reply on November 27—that the cardinal had suggested that O'Shea had delayed a long time before taking this step and hinted further that a 'pecuniary argument' was involved. Both these suggestions O'Shea emphatically denied, and there followed more exchanges of letters and at least one interview. The outcome was that O'Shea grew increasingly impatient and ended by concluding that the

[1] Garvin, *Life of Chamberlain*, ii. 399, O'Shea to Chamberlain, 13 Oct. 1889.

[2] O'Shea, ii. 221–2. In this account the paragraph is dated 14 May 1886, but this is a misprint for 24 May 1886—the latter was the date mentioned in the divorce court.

[3] Or so O'Shea believed (Blanche E. C. Dugdale, *Life of Arthur James Balfour*, i. 182–3, O'Shea to Balfour, 26 Dec. 1889; O'Shea, ii. 223; Sir E. Clarke, *The story of my life*, pp. 283–4).

cardinal was trying to screen Parnell.[1] For our immediate purposes, however, Manning's attitude is less important than the fact that the length of the negotiations helps to explain why O'Shea did not take his final step until December. The last letter from him to Manning that we know of is dated December 17. One week later the petition for divorce was filed.

(4)

Clearly there is at least a strong presumption—especially in view of the timing of O'Shea's actions during 1889—that, despite his repudiation to Cardinal Manning of any 'pecuniary argument', the money motive was a powerful factor affecting his behaviour. Was there any other factor which might similarly have influenced the timing of the divorce? We have to remember that Parnell himself, who up to this had preserved an Olympian detachment from all this intrigue and counter-intrigue, stated in December 1889 that he regarded the divorce petition as having been brought in the interest of *The Times*, in order to weaken his position in his libel action against that newspaper.[2] So far as is known Parnell never expanded this statement, but Henry Harrison later improved on it, alleging that the bringing of the divorce at the particular moment chosen was dictated primarily by political considerations, and was in fact a device deliberately used by what he calls 'the Chamberlain-O'Shea combination' to retrieve the disaster to the unionist cause of the miscarriage of the special commission.[3] How far can this assertion be proved?

It is certainly true that by 1889 relations between Parnell and Chamberlain were far from friendly. By Chamberlain's own admission he did his best in 1888 to persuade members of the government to appoint a royal commission to enquire into the charges brought by *The Times* against the Irish leader, and when the bill to set up the special commission was being debated in parliament he intervened very effectively.[4] That

[1] Garvin, *Life of Chamberlain*, ii. 401, O'Shea to Chamberlain, 30 Dec. 1889. The correspondence with Manning, or rather O'Shea's side of it, is in O'Shea, ii. 221–7.

[2] *F.J.*, 30 Dec. 1889. See above, p. 39.

[3] H. Harrison, *Parnell, Joseph Chamberlain and Mr Garvin*, pp. 201–24.

[4] Garvin, *Life of Chamberlain*, ii. 386–7, Chamberlain to Mary Endicott (his

59

same summer, before this bill had passed, there was an open clash between the two men, Parnell accusing Chamberlain of using Irish members to do work he was afraid to do himself, and also of betraying cabinet secrets. This was at once denied by Chamberlain, but a bitter controversy developed between them over the 'central board' scheme of 1885, in which Captain O'Shea had been an intermediary. Too unreliable an intermediary, indeed, for Chamberlain to be able to make the crushing retort he would have wished, and in the end it was Parnell who stood his ground and Chamberlain who had to moderate his tone.[1]

This clash was symptomatic of a deeper antagonism. For Irishmen Chamberlain was 'the man who killed home rule',[2] and for Parnell in particular he was the confidant of Captain O'Shea. For Chamberlain, on the other hand, Parnell was the living embodiment of home rule, and home rule was the rock upon which his own career was in danger of foundering. It was home rule which had separated him from the liberals and thrust him into the political waste-land where he was now trying desperately to re-orientate his course. The failure of the 'Round-table conference' with his former colleagues in 1887,[3] and Chamberlain's own support for the government's Irish coercion act of that year, virtually closed the door upon any return to the liberal party.[4] It was scarcely feasible yet for him to pass into the unionist camp, for his 'unauthorised programme' of 1885,

fiancée), 10 and 24 July 1888. But, in the relevant chapter (written in 1892) of his political memoir, Chamberlain wrote that he had privately urged the government to meet Parnell as far as possible in the matter. 'The great object seemed in my opinion to have a full enquiry and at the same time to avoid the appearance of pressing hard upon a political opponent . . . As, however, the government desired to appoint a commission in preference [to the parliamentary committee suggested by Parnell] I supported it in the house' (Joseph Chamberlain, *A political memoir, 1880–92*, ed. C. H. D. Howard, p. 283).

[1] *The Times*, 2, 6 and 13 Aug. 1888; Chamberlain, *A political memoir, 1880-92*, ed. C. H. D. Howard, pp. 158–9; Garvin, *Life of Chamberlain*, ii. 388–92; Harrison, *Parnell, Chamberlain and Mr Garvin*, pp. 169–93.

[2] The phrase was said to have been used by Parnell himself (R. B. O'Brien, *Parnell*, ii. 158).

[3] Joseph Chamberlain, *A political memoir, 1880–92*, ed. C. H. D. Howard, ch. ix; Garvin, *Life of Chamberlain*, ii. 278–96; Gardiner, *Life of Harcourt*, ii. 16–38.   [4] Garvin, *Life of Chamberlain*, ii. 301–3.

with its attacks upon property and privilege, was still likely to be held against him.[1] But certainly, if the time ever came for an alliance with the unionists, nothing would commend him more in those circles than to do what he could to break up the liberal-Parnellite combination. We have seen that, by his own account, he contributed something to the setting of the scene for the special commission. The special commission itself revealed that he had done more than this. One of the first witnesses to be called on behalf of *The Times* was none other than Captain O'Shea. It emerged that when *The Times* had sought for Captain O'Shea's services, it had applied for them through Chamberlain.[2] Further, it appeared that when in 1885–6 Captain O'Shea himself had been making certain investigations about material which might prove damaging to Parnell, it was with Chamberlain's help that he enquired at the Home Office for information gathered by various people in Paris and elsewhere.[3] In view of the close connection which thus undoubtedly existed between O'Shea and Chamberlain up to and including the period of the special commission, the question inevitably arises—did this connection persist into the period of the divorce-court proceedings?

To this question Henry Harrison has given an emphatic affirmative. In support of this affirmative the most 'direct' (as he calls it) evidence is a recollection written down many years later by Sir Alfred Robbins, who, at the time of the divorce, had been the London correspondent of the *Birmingham Daily Post*. Robbins recorded that a month after parliament had risen in August 1889, 'I was asked by one on the inside of the liberal-unionist "machine" whether Parnell would be politically ruined by a divorce, the then recent Dilke instance being given as a precedent, and Captain O'Shea, it was added, being willing to take proceedings.'[4] Robbins, though, as he says, instinctively detesting a political manoeuvre of this kind, pointed out the risk in view of the recent Pigott collapse, and doubted whether the unionist managers 'who were indicated to be wavering' would

[1] For the 'unauthorised programme' see Garvin, *Life of Chamberlain*, ii. ch. xxvii.

[2] *Spec. comm. proc.* i. 357; Michael Davitt, *The fall of feudalism in Ireland*, p. 632.

[3] *Spec. comm. proc.* i. 362–4; Harrison, *Parnell, Chamberlain and Mr Garvin*, p. 158.　　　　　[4] Sir A. Robbins, *Parnell: the last five years*, pp. 132–3.

find that it would pay. We are not told who was the liberal-unionist on the inside of the machine, nor who were the unionist managers, but when we reflect upon the fact that it was a liberal-unionist newspaper which Robbins represented, and that Joseph Chamberlain always attached great importance to the party machine or 'caucus' which had its stronghold in Birmingham, it is hard to avoid the suspicion that such grave issues can scarcely have been discussed in such a quarter without some word of it at least reaching the great man himself. It must, however, remain a suspicion, for nothing has been established directly linking Chamberlain with the query put to Robbins.

Is there any other evidence which may help to connect 'the Chamberlain-O'Shea combination' with the divorce? We know that O'Shea kept Chamberlain informed of the state of his affairs during this period and we have already seen that in October 1889 he had written to Chamberlain that he was considering moving in 'the other business'.[1] To this letter Chamberlain replied sympathetically, though assuring O'Shea that, as he never listened to scandalous reports about his friends, he knew no more than what O'Shea himself had told him. However, he added, such things could not be hushed up and 'I am not sure that the boldest course is not always the wisest'.[2] A few months later, after the petition had been filed, Chamberlain wrote that 'any further hesitation would have given rise to an accusation of complacency under an injury which no honourable man can patiently endure'.[3] Harrison dismisses these as 'show-letters', and argues that as Chamberlain had known of the affair ever since 1882, they were designed to protect his position in case it ever became necessary for his correspondence with O'Shea to be published.[4]

This raises the question of how far Harrison is correct in stating that Chamberlain became aware of the liaison as early as he says he did. According to Sir William Harcourt's biographer, Harcourt came to know of it while home secretary in Gladstone's 1880–5 ministry[5] From a memoir by Sir Charles Dilke

[1] Garvin, *Life of Chamberlain*, ii. 399.
[2] Ibid., ii. 400. Chamberlain to O'Shea, 14 Oct. 1889.
[3] Ibid., ii. 401. Chamberlain to O'Shea, 10 Jan. 1890.
[4] Harrison, *Parnell, Chamberlain and Mr Garvin*, pp. 205–7.
[5] Gardiner, *Life of Harcourt*, ii. 81–2.

we learn that Harcourt passed his information to the cabinet
when they were discussing the Kilmainham 'treaty' at a meeting
on 17 May 1882. At this meeting, it seems, Harcourt remarked
that the 'treaty' would not be popular 'when the public discovered that it had been negotiated by Captain O'Shea, "the
husband of Parnell's mistress".[1] As originally published, this
entry in the memoir was somewhat abridged, but Harrison
inspected the manuscript in the British Museum and has filled
the gap. Dilke's record, then, continued: 'He (Harcourt) informed the cabinet that he knew that in the previous year
(1881) O'Shea had threatened Parnell with divorce proceedings, and that it was only Mrs O'Shea's discovery of adulterous
relations of her husband which had put him in her power: and
that O'Shea had shut his eyes and made the best of it . . .'[2] Then
follows the end of the sentence, which was published in Dilke's
biography: '. . . but that after this it would hardly "do for the
public" for us to use O'Shea as a negotiator.'[3] This account,
based as it is on Dilke's memoir, is open to two objections,
though these are not insuperable. One is that Dilke himself was
not in the cabinet (though he was a junior minister), and the
other is that there was no cabinet meeting on May 17. These
objections have been met ingeniously by Harrison. First, he
says, though Dilke was not in the cabinet, Chamberlain was.
The two men were very close friends at the time, and Dilke himself has recorded that his memoir was written from information
chiefly supplied by Chamberlain and that Chamberlain had
seen and agreed to the record.[4] Harrison has established the
date at which Chamberlain saw the memoir as 1890-1, and he
has produced detailed evidence of the closeness with which he
examined the document and the scrupulousness with which
Dilke noted a difference of recollection between them (on a
matter which had no connection with the cabinet of May 17).[5]
The inference here is obvious—that Dilke's account of what

[1] S. Gwynn and G. Tuckwell, *Life of Sir Charles Dilke*, i. 445.
[2] Harrison, *Parnell, Chamberlain and Mr Garvin*, p. 49. While this book was
in the press I have verified Harrison's account from Dilke's memoir (B.M.,
Add. MS 43,936, ff. 110-11), and from the diary on which the memoir was
apparently based (B.M., Add. MS 43,924, ff. 81-7).
[3] Gwynn and Tuckwell, *Life of Sir Charles Dilke*, i. 445.
[4] Ibid., i. 439.
[5] Harrison, op. cit., pp. 41-54.

happened at the cabinet was derived from what Chamberlain had told him and that therefore Chamberlain must have been there in person. As for the second objection, that no cabinet was held on the date in question, Harrison has pointed out that from time to time informal meetings of cabinet ministers were held, but that since they *were* informal, they were not always known either to the press or to the public at large. The meeting of May 17, he suggests, may have been just such an occasion.[1]

At all events one thing is clear—when Chamberlain read this passage some eight or nine years later he did not dispute its accuracy. It seems reasonable to suppose, therefore, that as early as 1882 he had become aware of the existence of the Parnell-O'Shea triangle. That the matter was attracting the attention of the liberal leaders at the time appears to be beyond dispute. For example, when a few days after this so-called cabinet Gladstone received his first letter from Mrs O'Shea and consulted Earl Granville, the latter, in replying, noted: 'She is said to be his mistress.'[2] This suggests that Gladstone himself might not have been at the meeting of May 17—if he had been, it would scarcely have been necessary for Granville to draw his attention to Parnell's relations with Mrs O'Shea. But whether he was there or not, he certainly did not encourage conversation on the subject, for when Granville's nephew, George Leveson Gower, mentioned it to him in connection with the Kilmainham treaty, he was severely snubbed for his pains. 'You do not mean to ask me to believe', he recollected the prime minister saying, 'that it is possible a man should be so lost to all sense of what is due to his public position, at a moment like the present, in the very crisis of his country's fortunes, as to indulge in an illicit connection with the wife of one of his very own political supporters, and to make use of that connection in the way you suggest?'[3]

It is impossible to say for certain if Gladstone did believe it there and then, but his agile mind must have found it hard to resist certain speculations when, the very next month, he had his first meeting with Mrs O'Shea. Of that meeting she later

[1] Harrison, *Parnell, Chamberlain and Mr Garvin*, pp. 49–51.

[2] J. L. Hammond, *Gladstone and the Irish nation*, p. 670. The original of Granville's letter, in the Gladstone Papers (B.M., Add. MS 44,174, f. 127) is dated simply May 24. However, in the context, there seems little doubt that Hammond is correct in assigning it to 1882.

[3] W. S. Blunt, *My diaries*, ii. 280–1, entry for 25 Oct. 1909.

wrote: '. . . he knew before the conclusion of our interview, and allowed me to know that he knew, what I desired that he should know—that my personal interest in Parnell was my only interest in Irish politics.'[1] It is true that her account has been severely criticised by Gladstone's son Herbert,[2] but the fact remains that to a man of the world—such as Gladstone undoubtedly was—Mrs O'Shea's appearance on the scene, coming so soon after Granville's comment, must have been almost irresistibly suggestive.

The indications are, then, that by 1882 some, at least, of the cabinet knew of the affair and that almost certainly Chamberlain was among them. And even if Chamberlain—appearances to the contrary—did not learn of it then, he received at least one other hint when Labouchere wrote to him (probably in October or November 1885) that Parnell was or was supposed to be the lover of O'Shea's wife.[3] There is also a reference in one of O'Shea's own letters which seems to point in the same direction. In December 1889, when writing to Arthur Balfour (then chief secretary for Ireland) of his decision to move for a divorce, O'Shea enclosed a letter from Chamberlain who, he said, 'is acquainted with the facts'.[4] It is not known what was in Chamberlain's letter, but it is interesting that, as late as December 1889, he should still have been close enough to O'Shea to write an explanatory letter of this kind for him. And while 'the facts' with which Chamberlain was acquainted *may* only have been imparted to him by O'Shea on the eve of the divorce proceedings, and *may* have been restricted to what O'Shea told him, this argues a lack of awareness, almost a naïveté, on his part which would have been most untypical.

But if it is true that Chamberlain knew—or even had good grounds for suspecting—that Parnell was Mrs O'Shea's lover

[1] O'Shea, i. 270.

[2] Viscount Gladstone, *After thirty years*, pp. 295–306. When Mrs O'Shea's book came out in 1914, John Morley, who was in a better position than most to know Gladstone's mind on the matter, was asked if Gladstone *had* known of the relationship and replied: 'I dare say he did' (J. H. Morgan, *John, Viscount Morley*, p. 87).

[3] C. H. D. Howard, 'Joseph Chamberlain and the Irish "central board" scheme, 1884–5' in *I.H.S.* (Sept. 1953), viii. 329, *n*. 25.

[4] Blanche E. C. Dugdale, *Life of Arthur James Balfour*, i. 182–3.

long before the divorce proceedings were set in motion, does this prove Harrison's contention that Chamberlain's letters to O'Shea in 1889 were 'show-letters'? It may be so, but it does not follow conclusively. At least one other explanation is possible. It is just conceivable that Chamberlain, while himself in possession of the secret, was not aware until O'Shea actually nerved himself to take proceedings, quite how much the latter had previously known of the affair or for how long. No one, after all, is anxious to have to tell a deceived husband of his deception. In such circumstances Chamberlain, however much he might have known beforehand, was hardly likely to write to O'Shea, when the latter informed him of his decision to move, that he was only astonished that he had not taken action long ago. Admittedly, in view of the close relations between the two men, this is an extremely unlikely explanation. Nonetheless, it *is* a possible one, and therefore it certainly cannot be said that Harrison's conclusion follows inescapably from his premises.

But suppose Harrison was right and that these were 'show-letters'. Would that necessarily prove that O'Shea and Chamberlain were in combination and that the divorce was engineered as a political high-explosive to blast the liberal-nationalist alliance to pieces? The verdict must surely be that the case, though plausible and skilfully argued, is not proven. Harrison has certainly produced a number of facts which are interesting, even suggestive—e.g. the parts played by Chamberlain and O'Shea in the special commission, the evidence of Sir Alfred Robbins, the O'Shea-Chamberlain correspondence of 1889[1]— but he has not unearthed any conclusive documentary evidence to show that the two men, or either of them, planned to use the

[1] Harrison also quotes Sir Edward Clarke's later reminiscence (*The story of my life*, pp. 284–5), of the curious fact that when O'Shea sought out a solicitor to prepare his case he went first to Joseph Soames, who had been solicitor for *The Times* in connection with the special commission, and was then sent by Soames to another solicitor who turned out to be the son of Mr Justice Day, one of the judges at the special commission. Harrison sees in this fresh evidence of the liaison between Captain O'Shea and the group associated with *The Times's* campaign against Parnell (*Parnell vindicated*, pp. 145–6), but it proves nothing, except perhaps that O'Shea was extraordinarily insensitive to appearances if he really thought Soames a suitable person to act for him. Ultimately, under Clarke's guidance, O'Shea's case was transferred to other and less compromising hands.

divorce in the way he has said it was used. No doubt, from a unionist viewpoint, it was highly convenient that it came when it did. But that is a very different thing from proving that it came when it did because Chamberlain and O'Shea acted together, acted from political motives, and acted in furtherance of some deep-laid unionist conspiracy. It is, of course, likely enough that even if such a scheme had been hatched, no evidence of it would have been put on paper—or allowed to survive if committed to writing—because of the disastrous consequences if it ever came to light. If this is what happened then we shall probably never know the truth. But all that can be said in the present state of our knowledge is that while it is legitimate to regard *The Times* forgeries as a deliberate attack upon Parnell, the divorce-case—although it succeeded brilliantly where the earlier blow failed—has not been shown to have been designed cold-bloodedly as a political weapon. Or, in other words, that while O'Shea's action had immeasurable political consequences, he himself had quite adequate personal reasons for taking it, whether or not he received any other prompting.[1]

(5)

Now at last, perhaps, we can attempt to explain why Parnell assured so many people before the case opened that he would come out of it unsullied. Obviously, if the facts of O'Shea's connivance were as set out above, there was plenty of evidence

[1] There is a possibility—though a faint one—that the Chamberlain Papers might hold a clue to these matters, but at the time of writing they are not open to inspection. The Balfour Papers are another possible source, but they too cannot be seen at present. Probably, however, they would yield nothing, for Mrs Dugdale has printed a reply from Balfour to O'Shea's letter informing him of the pending divorce which indicates—as was indeed to be expected—that he was not concerned with what O'Shea had to tell him (*Life of Balfour*, i. 182–3). The records of *The Times* were investigated by Henry Harrison near the end of his long crusade in vindication of Parnell. He has described in a booklet (*Parnell, Joseph Chamberlain and The Times*) what he found there, but makes no mention of anything new relating to the divorce question. Had such material existed, he would no doubt have made the most of it. Since writing the above I have been informed by the librarian of *The Times* Library that there is no material relevant to this point in the Library.

to prevent the latter from winning his suit. But Parnell, in giving his assurances, apparently meant, not merely that he could block O'Shea's petition, but that he could turn the tables on him. The key lay in the captain's high financial expectations which—as we have seen—had been thwarted by Mrs Wood's will. According to what Mrs Parnell subsequently told Harrison, she was certain O'Shea could be bought off. She said that if she had been able to find £20,000 to give him *she* could have divorced *him*.[1] And we do not have to rely for this figure upon her testimony alone. O'Shea's own counsel has recorded that his client told him that he could have £20,000 if he abandoned the suit, and Sir Edward Clarke himself thought that the other side believed 'down to the last moment' that O'Shea would not appear in court.[2] However, as Harrison truly observes, since the will upon which Mrs O'Shea's fortune depended was being contested by other claimants, her potential wealth was in jeopardy and she was not a good prospect for a loan.[3] The money was not forthcoming and so the case went to court. It is of course possible that she was mistaken, and that if the money had been available O'Shea might still have refused it, either because he was not prepared to barter what remained of his self-respect in this crude fashion, or even, conceivably, for political reasons. But the fact that Mrs O'Shea not only hoped to raise the money, but also reckoned that her husband could be in effect bribed into doing what she wanted, goes far to explain Parnell's optimism before the trial began. Is not the most reasonable explanation of what he said to Morley and others that he believed up to the last moment that O'Shea would withdraw and that in the end it would be Mrs O'Shea who would get the divorce?[4] For, even if they had been obliged to wait for some months before obtaining the divorce, until a new case could be prepared in which the rôles of the husband and wife would be reversed, O'Shea's eleventh-hour withdrawal in November 1890 would still have been a triumph, complete and dramatic enough to have satisfied Parnell

---

[1] Harrison, *Parnell vindicated*, pp. 128–9.

[2] Sir E. Clarke, *The story of my life*, pp. 289–90.

[3] Harrison, *Parnell vindicated*, pp. 150–1.

[4] This appears to have been Sir Edward Clarke's view also (*The story of my life*, p. 290).

and to have vindicated him in the eyes of his friends and followers.

This, at any rate, seems the most reasonable way of accounting for Parnell's attitude on the eve of the disaster. It does not, however, account for one other feature of the trial which mystified many people at the time, and which still mystified Harrison when he looked back on these events forty years later —the series of allegations made against Captain O'Shea. These, it will be remembered, included the assertion that he had connived at and condoned his wife's relationship with her lover, and also the even more startling statement that he, O'Shea, had committed adultery with her sister, Mrs Anna Steele. No one has ever fathomed quite why this latter plea was entered and Mrs Parnell herself shied away from the subject when discussing the divorce with Harrison in 1891. Mrs Steele's explanation—given in court—that the charge arose out of a quarrel between the two sisters over Mrs Wood's will may well be the correct one. Harrison, who thought the introduction of such an allegation unwise and unnecessary, attributed it to the fact that Mrs O'Shea had quarrelled with her best legal adviser, Sir George Lewis (he once described her as 'a very charming lady, but an impossible one') and planned her own strategy in her own amateurish way.[1] The other pleas—of connivance and condonation—can perhaps be justified as constituting a weapon to be used against the captain if, at any time during the trial, circumstances necessitated the blocking of his suit. But if the intention really were for Mrs O'Shea to divorce her husband the obvious course was to concentrate upon his alleged adulteries and to leave questions of connivance or condonation severely alone. That the words were allowed to appear in the first place was probably due to Mrs O'Shea's reluctance to abandon all hope of fighting the case. Indeed, she told Harrison the following year that she would really have preferred that there should have been no divorce because of the injury she feared it might do to Parnell.[2]

[1] Harrison, *Parnell vindicated*, pp. 108, 146–9. If, as Mrs Parnell asserted to Harrison (ibid., p. 140), proof of some seventeen infidelities by Captain O'Shea had been assembled for use, then the charge against her sister was indeed unnecessary.

[2] Ibid., p. 129. In her book Mrs Parnell also stressed her anxiety that the

In the end, as we have seen, these allegations were not pressed. And the reason they were not pressed was because—whatever Mrs O'Shea may have wished or intended—Parnell himself was determined that there should be a divorce, even if it was the captain who divorced his wife and not the other way round. She described vividly to Harrison how impossible it was to persuade Parnell to contest the case, and when she published her book in after years she told the same story.[1] Parnell's attitude from first to last had been perfectly consistent. He had always wanted to make her his wife in the public eye, as he had always considered her to be in their private life, and hitherto he had refrained only out of deference to her wishes. But now that things had come to a crisis, he would not lift a finger to prevent a decision. In the final outcome it was O'Shea's willingness to risk his connivance being proved, against Parnell's passionate wish to take Mrs O'Shea as his wife. The sequel showed that O'Shea had nothing to fear.

We may conclude, then, by suggesting that Parnell's confidence on the eve of the trial was based on the assumption that O'Shea could be bought off. Once it appeared that this could not be done—either because there was no money or because O'Shea had his own reasons for not putting himself on sale—there was nothing for it but to let the case go by default. And in the result, as we have seen, O'Shea was awarded his decree *nisi* and the custody of the children under sixteen. This last was a bitter blow to Parnell who was rumoured, even before the trial, to have sought legal advice as to whether there was any European country to which he could take Mrs O'Shea and the two children born in 1883 and 1884, and where he could retain custody of the children despite the order of an English court.[2] So badly did he take the decision that Mrs O'Shea's counsel, Sir Frank Lockwood, who had to bear the brunt of his displeasure, described him as 'so wild and peculiar in his manner as to show signs of madness'.[3] The loss of the children, however, was an inevitable consequence of his determination to have the

case should be fought, adding that her counsel, Sir Frank Lockwood, begged her to get Parnell to allow him to do so (O'Shea, ii. 158).

[1] Harrison, *Parnell vindicated* pp. 128–9; O'Shea, ii. 158–61.
[2] Sir E. Clarke, *The story of my life*, pp. 290–1.
[3] Lord Askwith, *Lord James of Hereford*, p. 220.

divorce at any price. What further price would be asked of him in terms of his career, of his private happiness, of life itself, he had soon to learn.

III

WAR OF MANOEUVRE

~~~~~~

(1)

THE NEWSPAPERS which on the morning of Monday, 17 November 1890 carried the first instalment of the divorce proceedings, published also Parnell's usual letter to the members of the Irish parliamentary party, summoning them to assemble on November 25 for their customary meeting at the beginning of a new session of parliament.[1] This was a clear indication that, so far as he was concerned, the divorce suit was an incident in his private life which had no bearing whatever on his public position. How far either Irish or English opinion would agree with him remained to be seen.

The first news from Ireland at least was cheering. The main nationalist newspaper—the *Freeman's Journal*—took the line that what mattered most was the political future, and that it was for the Irish, not the English, people to decide whether or not Parnell's continuance in the leadership would jeopardise that future. The paper's own view was that there could be no 'swapping or changing' of leaders. 'We would not if we could. We could not if we would.'[2] The same day that this article appeared the central branch of the Irish National League met in Dublin and thus provided an opportunity for some of the leading men in that organisation to express their views on the situation. The chair was taken by John Redmond and several

[1] *F.J.*, 17 Nov. 1890. [2] *F.J.*, 18 Nov. 1890.

other members of parliament were there; most of these—though not all—subsequently remained faithful to Parnell and it has been conjectured that they were sent by him to guide the meeting.[1] However this may be, a resolution pledging support to Parnell was enthusiastically passed, and there seemed no shadow of any kind.

Two days later there was a bigger and more important meeting at the Leinster Hall, Dublin, which was to loom large in future controversies and to be a source of embarrassment to some of those present for a long time to come. The chair was taken by the Lord Mayor (Alderman E. J. Kennedy) and many members of the parliamentary party were present. Although one of the main purposes of the gathering had originally been to help the evicted tenants, this inevitably faded into the background and the proceedings were dominated by the burning question of the hour—would Ireland stand by Parnell or repudiate him? To this question the meeting seemed to give a decisive answer. The vice-chairman of the party, Justin McCarthy, in proposing a resolution of support for the leader, not only made the already familiar distinction between Parnell's private and public life, but also hinted that the private life might not turn out in the end to be so blameworthy as appeared on the surface.[2] It is true that off the platform he was not so optimistic and foresaw a time of crisis ahead,[3] but he allowed none of this to appear in his speech and his resolution was certainly firm enough to please even the most exacting Parnellite. It ran as follows:

That this meeting, interpreting the sentiment of the Irish people that no side issues shall be permitted to obstruct the progress of the great cause of home rule for Ireland, declares that in all political matters Mr Parnell possesses the confidence of the Irish nation and rejoices at the determination of the Irish parliamentary party to stand by their leader.[4]

It was in seconding this speech that T. M. Healy made one of the most celebrated speeches of his career. It was not a long speech, for he was only just recovering from an attack of typhoid

[1] C. Cruise O'Brien, *Parnell and his party*, p. 286. [2] *F.J.*, 21 Nov. 1890.
[3] J. McCarthy and Mrs Campbell Praed, *Our book of memories*, p. 256.
[4] In actual fact, the parliamentary party had not yet had a chance to give any indication of whether they would stand by, or throw over, their leader.

fever and was still very weak, but it was an extremely able one and was very warmly received. His argument was that the issue of Parnell's leadership was essentially an Irish issue, and that in deciding it Irishmen must not be influenced by English opinion—'for Ireland and for Irishmen, Mr Parnell is less a man than an institution'. It would, he said, be 'criminal' to surrender him at the first breath of opposition and he fiercely criticised a recommendation which had already come from a certain quarter (he meant Davitt) that Parnell should retire. But, though he ended with the famous warning 'not to speak to the man at the wheel', it would be wrong to dismiss his speech as a simple and unconditional endorsement of Parnell's leadership. Far more typical of his real attitude was his answer to the hypothetical question—might not support of Parnell indicate servility on the part of his followers? Healy's answer was vehement: 'Servile to Mr Parnell! Who is servile to him? I am no man's man but Ireland's; and if I stand here to-night, as I gladly do, to second this resolution, I do so, not for the sake of Parnell as an individual, but for the sake of Ireland as a nation.' One further passage near the end was ominous because it suggested what the meeting in the enthusiasm of the moment clearly did not take in, that his report for Parnell was subject to certain reservations. After saying that he would abide by the national party and the national leader, he continued:

Let me, however, say this—that while we owe a duty to Mr Parnell, Mr Parnell owes a duty to us. We have stood by Mr Parnell: Mr Parnell must stand by us. He, too, as we have to consider our position, let him consider his, and as we are acting with sole thought to the interests of Ireland, so we may fairly demand that in every act and determination and resolution of his, he shall act with equal singleness of purpose.[1]

The resolution supporting Parnell was passed unanimously, and that this was so was certainly due in part to a cable from the United States which was read out early in the proceedings. It was signed by John Dillon, T. P. Gill, Timothy Harrington, William O'Brien and T. P. O'Connor and it was an unequivocal declaration for Parnell. These men, together with T. D. Sullivan, had gone to America a few weeks previously on a

[1] *F.J.*, 21 Nov. 1890.

mission to raise funds for the evicted tenants and their absence from the scene while the crisis was developing at home contributed greatly to the difficulties of the situation.[1] When the divorce case was being tried all the delegates were hard at work collecting money and addressing meetings in different American cities. The news from home at once put them in a very awkward position. Their mission was soon thrust on one side and it was not long before they suspended their tour until they could confer amongst themselves. They were bombarded with letters and cables from Irish-Americans, some violently for Parnell, others clamouring for his retirement. They were pestered day and night by reporters who lurked in the corridors of their hotels, ready to pounce on them if they so much as attempted to leave their bedrooms. Worst of all, they were starved of accurate news from home, having to rely upon the sensational accounts in the newspapers, which left them very little the wiser. Their first reaction to the news was an instinctive gesture of loyalty to their leader. Dillon was reported on Sunday, November 16—while the divorce case was in mid-course—as having said that Parnell's retirement was impossible in the existing state of affairs.[2] A few days later four of the delegates —Dillon, O'Brien, Gill and T. P. O'Connor—were interviewed and all expressed themselves in favour of Parnell.[3] Then, when they had all converged upon Buffalo, they found a cable from John Redmond and Dr Kenny asking for their support. The Leinster Hall meeting was imminent and they had very little time for discussion. And at this point the first sign of division among them began to appear. T. D. Sullivan, who, through his control of *The Nation* newspaper and his relationship to T. M. Healy, was an influential figure, took the view that the moral offence of Parnell's adultery made him impossible as a leader and he therefore refused to associate himself with any move on Parnell's behalf.[4] The cable of confidence in the leader which

---

[1] The mission had been launched in Dublin early in October (*F.J.*, 7 Oct. 1890).

[2] *F.J.*, 17 Nov. 1890.

[3] *F.J.*, 20 Nov. 1890.

[4] Ironically, *The Nation* in its issue of 22 Nov. 1891 took the line that it was the duty of every Irishman to rally to the political leadership of Parnell, though it expressed sorrow and disappointment at his moral lapse. Subsequently, of course, it took up the orthodox anti-Parnellite position.

aroused such enthusiasm in Dublin thus went without Sullivan's signature.[1]

T. D. Sullivan was one of the few who did not allow themselves to be swept away by the strong tide of support for Parnell, but there were others who felt as he did and who carried even greater weight. From two very different sources—the church on the one hand, and Michael Davitt on the other—the reaction against Parnell had already begun to gather way. So far as the former was concerned, however, the position was peculiarly difficult. The Irish bishops were not likely to condone Parnell's offence, and on moral ground alone they would have had a good case for breaking with him. But they would have to be extremely careful how they acted, since whatever they did would be certain to have political repercussions, and there was an obvious danger of raising the old spectre of clerical interference if they exerted too open an influence upon the Irish parliamentary party. The ideal solution, from their viewpoint, would be for Parnell's followers to repudiate him on moral or political grounds (or both) on their own responsibility and without any kind of ecclesiastical advice or pressure. It was, therefore, preferable that for the time being, however great the provocation, the bishops should make no public pronouncement. It is curious that Cardinal Manning, who normally steered a skilful course through all Irish shoals and shallows, seems not to have realised their predicament. On November 19 he wrote twice to Dr W. J. Walsh, archbishop of Dublin, about the 'supreme disaster' of the divorce case. In his second letter he urged that 'the most *vital* friends of Ireland' considered that if the Irish leadership remained unchanged 'the bishops, priests and people of Ireland will be seriously affected in the judgment of all English friends, or the chief of them'. Significantly, he added not only that he was sure of 'the judgment and feeling of Rome' on the matter, but that there was now a great opportunity for the bishops to regain control of the movement:'. . . if ten years ago the bishops and priests had spoken and acted together, the movement would not have fallen into the hands of laymen.'[2] To Manning, apparently, the fact that the crisis

[1] William O'Brien, *An olive branch in Ireland*, pp. 11–14.
[2] Sir Shane Leslie, *Henry Edward Manning : his life and labours*, p. 436; P. J. Walsh, *William J. Walsh, archbishop of Dublin*, pp. 408–9.

might split the Irish national movement in two was less important than that it offered the Irish church a golden opportunity to reassert itself.

The theocratic argument, though seductive, was perilous, as no-one knew better than the leaders of the hierarchy in Ireland. Dr Walsh passed this letter to Archbishop Croke, who replied that while he did not go so far as Manning, who seemed to think that Parnell's retaining the leadership meant ruin, it would certainly cause serious damage. For himself, he was finished with Parnell: 'His bust, which for some time has held a prominent place in my hall, I kicked out yesterday.' Nonetheless he recognised the delicacy of the position. Writing as he did shortly after the Leinster Hall meeting (his letter was dated November 22) he realised that the support for Parnell manifested there, together with the attitude of the press, had created a difficult situation. If only the laymen had not plunged in so precipitately a temporary retirement for Parnell might have been arranged. 'But now, really, I fear things must be allowed to take the direction given them by the Irish members—come what may.'[1]

This letter is interesting on two counts. First, because it indicates that so far as Archbishop Croke was concerned, a temporary retirement by Parnell would at that stage have been sufficient. And, secondly, because it shows that the archbishop himself did not see his way to interfere directly. Others of the hierarchy, however, were anxious for more direct action. For example, Dr Gillooly, bishop of Elphin, wrote within two days of the divorce court decision that it was an emergency that called for a meeting of the standing committee of the bishops. 'Our silence', he added, 'would be interpreted and quoted by the party leaders as an approval of the policy they have adopted.'[2] And later, when the meeting of the Irish parliamentary party was imminent, he suggested that it would be well 'to communicate our views to some of our M.P.s *before* Monday next, in order to influence the decision of that day, as we have the best possible right to do'.[3] Another prelate, Dr B.

[1] Walsh, *William J. Walsh*, pp. 409–10.
[2] Walsh Papers, Dr J. Gillooly to Archbishop Walsh, 19 Nov. 1890.
[3] Walsh Papers, Dr J. Gillooly to Archbishop Walsh, 28 Nov. 1890; the same day Dr J. Donnelly, bishop of Clogher, also wrote in favour of a meeting of the standing committee.

Woodlock, bishop of Ardagh, who had, as he admitted, thought at first that the divorce suit would end, like the Pigott forgeries, in a triumph for Parnell, also urged strongly that the standing committee should be summoned.[1] While hopeful that Gladstone would be equal to the crisis, he asked indignantly: 'Are we to allow him and a lot of nondescript ministers to proclaim the laws of Christian morality, while we are *canes muti, non volentes latrare*?'[2] He agreed all the same with Dr Walsh that it would be better not to intervene publicly 'if we can get our M.P.s to do their duty'.[3]

And this in fact was the course the archbishop followed, for, although refraining from public action, he did move behind the scenes. On November 23 he saw Dr J. E. Kenny, whom he knew to be close to Parnell, and urged upon him that the leader should voluntarily retire. Next day he wrote Kenny a letter intended to be shown to Parnell, again stressing the wisdom of retirement. 'The question', as he put it, 'now really is this, whether we are to have things go on unchanged or to have home rule in our life-time. Both cannot be combined.'[4] Later, when he had to answer charges that the bishops had kept silent during the early stages of the crisis, he was able to point to this letter as evidence to the contrary,[5] but the fact remains that, so far as the public was concerned, the meeting of the party took place on November 25 without any open influence having been exerted either by the two archbishops or by any of the hierarchy.

If the bishops were reticent, the same could not be said of Michael Davitt. At the time of the divorce he was editing the *Labour World*, a paper designed for the English working-classes, and with his knowledge of the latter, together with his reputation in Ireland and among the Irish overseas, he could be a formidable enemy or an invaluable ally. Unfortunately, as we have seen, he was one of those whom Parnell had assured that there was nothing dishonourable in the divorce case. When the trial came, with its apparently damning disclosures and its

[1] Walsh Papers, Dr B. Woodlock to Archbishop Walsh, 25 Nov. 1890.

[2] Walsh Papers, Dr B. Woodlock to Archbishop Walsh, 26 Nov. 1890.

[3] Walsh Papers, Dr B. Woodlock to Archbishop Walsh, 27 Nov. 1890.

[4] Walsh, *William J. Walsh*, p. 410. It is not clear from this letter if, at this stage, Dr Walsh had made up his mind about whether the retirement should be permanent or temporary.

[5] *Insuppressible*, 13 Jan. 1891.

verdict for O'Shea, his indignation boiled over. In his impetu-
ous fashion he rushed into print, declaring that the crisis had
been brought about by Parnell himself and that both Irish and
British home rulers had a right to expect him to deliver their
cause from 'the deadliest peril by which it has yet been assailed'.
There could be no two opinions, he wrote, as to what his course
should be:

> He is urged by the highest considerations that could appeal to a
> leader to efface himself, for a brief period, from public life, until the
> time which the law requires to elapse before a divorced woman can
> marry enables him to come back, having paid the penalty which the
> public sentiment rightly inflicts for such transgressions as his.[1]

And on the same day that this article appeared he wrote to
Archbishop Walsh in language of despair: 'Is he going to force
himself and his paramour upon Ireland at the expense of home
rule? . . . If he appears next Tuesday at the opening of parliament as the *newly elected leader* of the Irish people, good-bye for
this generation to home rule and God help Ireland.'[2]

Both in the vehemence of his language and the prescience of
his forecast Davitt was virtually alone at that date, and even he
went no further than to demand a temporary retirement. So far
as the parliamentary party, and the wider public beyond them,
were concerned, everything would depend upon the line Parnell
himself would take when the party met in London on November
25. So far he had given no inkling of his intentions and it might
turn out that he was prepared to sacrifice himself for the common good, accepting the loyalty of his supporters as a graceful
tribute to his services. Or it might even be that he would still
be able to justify himself and confound his critics. Had he not
at the outset described the divorce proceedings as a continua-
tion of *The Times's* vendetta against him?[3] After all, when the
Pigott forgeries had first appeared things had looked black
enough. But Parnell had said they were not genuine and he had
been right. Now he had said that he would not suffer dishonour
in the divorce court. Might he not, appearances to the contrary,
be right again? To men who had followed their leader through
great vicissitudes of fortune, who had watched him bring home

---

[1] *Labour World*, 20 Nov. 1890, quoted in *F.J.*, 21 Nov. 1890.
[2] Walsh, *William J. Walsh*, p. 408.   [3] *F.J.*, 30 Dec. 1889.

rule, as it seemed, almost within their grasp, the habit of loyalty was overwhelming. And it was strengthened by the crudity and violence of certain sections of English opinion in the week between the verdict and the meeting of the party. When a Methodist minister, for example, publicly denounced Parnell as 'the most infamous adulterer of the century' and when he wrote that if the Irish people deliberately accepted such a man as their leader they were morally unfit for self-government, pride of race combined with loyalty to the individual to induce them to turn a united front to such attacks.[1]

(2)

Unfortunately for Parnell these cries of outraged morality sounded very differently in English ears. To the leaders of the liberal party, drawing so much of their strength from Wales and from the industrial north, 'the non-conformist conscience' was a factor that had to be seriously considered. Nor was it the only factor. English catholicism, too, was roused by the 'revelations' of the divorce court and Cardinal Manning lost no time in pressing Gladstone to act. On November 21 he wrote to Gladstone that Parnell could not be upheld as leader. He had heard (from W. T. Stead) that Archbishop Croke was for Parnell's retirement. 'If Archbishop Walsh agrees, I think it will be done. But it rests more with you more than with any man. If you say, "Do not fetter my freedom of action and take away my strength by putting the cause of Ireland in opposition to the feeling and instinct of England and my chief supporters", Mr Parnell would retire from leadership and still give all aid, as before, to the Irish cause.'[2]

In fact, by the time Gladstone received this letter his mind

[1] The minister was the Reverend Hugh Price Hughes, quoted in M. Macdonagh, *The home rule movement*, p. 199.

[2] Gladstone Papers (B.M., Add. MS 44,250, ff. 296–7), Manning to Gladstone, 21 Nov. 1890; Leslie, *Manning*, pp. 436–7. On the same day Gladstone also had a letter from Lord Acton in which Acton said that he had thought the Parnell case doubtful at first, because attacks on private character ought to be kept out of politics. 'But it will not do to act as if the moral question were not the supreme question in public life and, in a sense, the *vera causa* of party conflict' (Gladstone Papers (B.M., Add. MS 44,094, f. 142), Acton to Gladstone, 21 Nov. 1890).

had already moved far along the road it was to travel for the remainder of the struggle. Apart from the sense of outrage felt by religious people, he had also to bear in mind the atmosphere of the day. It was an age when the social conventions were strictly observed—or, perhaps more accurately, when open breaches of them were severely punished. Secret liaisons might, and did, exist, but if they came to public notice they spelt ruin. Involvement in the divorce court, especially, was assumed to be fatal to any public man. Thus Gladstone would have to reckon with the impact upon the constituencies of an alliance with a man who had flouted one of society's most rigid rules. But the position was even worse than this, for the alliance with Parnell had as its objective the setting up of a separate parliament in Ireland. And if that objective were to be achieved at all, it would certainly not be helped by the knowledge that the prospective head of a new Irish government had not only been through the divorce court but had—apparently—been revealed as having practised over many years a peculiarly squalid deception. It needed little imagination to see how joyfully the unionists would throw themselves upon this exposed flank of the liberal-nationalist alliance.[1]

In these circumstances, it was asking more than flesh and blood could bear to demand of the liberal rank-and-file that they should struggle on towards home rule with the electoral mill-stone of Parnell about their necks. Already they had endured much for the cause. Ireland had split them asunder. English reforms had been put on one side and the party had gone into the wilderness because of home rule. Hitherto, Gladstone's spell had held them and they had remained faithful to his ideal of an Irish settlement. And they had had their reward. As the unionist régime of coercion in Ireland had continued year by year, English opinion swung once more on to the liberal side—and the swing could be measured in the constituencies. By the end of 1889, the by-elections which had been contested had resulted in one gain for the government and twelve for the liberal opposition.[2] During 1890 the tide continued to flow towards the liberals and as recently as October of

---

[1] The leading article of *The Times*, 18 Nov. 1890, gives a very fair sample of how avidly the unionist press seized their chance.

[2] *The Times*, 29 June 1892.

that year their candidate had won the Eccles by-election on the issue of conciliation *versus* coercion in Ireland.[1] These victories promised a resounding success at the next general election and it was hardly to be expected that English liberalism, by espousing the cause of a discredited Parnell, would consent to fight this election with one hand tied behind its back. Conveniently, moral indignation and political expediency alike seemed to point to the exit of the Irish leader.

As the date for the hearing of the suit had approached there had naturally been some speculation amongst the liberal leaders about its outcome. As early as November 4 Gladstone was writing apprehensively to Arnold Morley, the liberal chief whip, that he feared the worst,[2] though after John Morley had seen Parnell at Brighton a few days later he had—as we have seen—been able to report more reassuringly that the Irish leader had brushed aside the notion that the divorce proceedings would have any effect upon his public position.[3] Then on November 15 came the first devastating day of the trial. It was no wonder that when Gladstone next wrote to John Morley— on November 16—he was plainly mystified. 'What could he mean by his language to you?'[4] Morley, in his reply to this, gave it as his own opinion that Parnell would continue to lead 'with the fullest support from his colleagues and from the constituencies'. He added that when he was last in Ireland he had talked the matter over with Dillon:

His view was clear; that so far as Ireland was concerned, the proof of the charges would make no difference in P.'s authority, *provided* there was no disclosure of nauseous details. Whether the story now told comes within this proviso, I do not undertake to determine; but I am pretty sure that the Irish will stomach it, tho' no priest will be able to go on to a platform with him for a long time to come.[5]

Morley himself evidently thought that Parnell's best chance

---

[1] Morley, *Gladstone*, iii. 428. In 1890 the liberals lost one more seat, but gained four; in 1891 they gained a further five, and in 1892 one more before the general election took place. The total for the whole parliament during which ninety-seven by-elections were contested (excluding Ireland), was thus twenty-two liberal gains and two unionist gains, leaving the liberals a gain on balance of twenty seats (*The Times*, 29 June 1892).

[2] Morley, *Gladstone*, iii. 429. [3] See pp. 40–1 above. [4] Morley, *Gladstone*, iii. 429.

[5] Gladstone Papers (B.M., Add. MS 44,256, ff. 72–3), John Morley to Gladstone, 17 Nov. 1890.

was to retire, though he had little hope that he would do so. As he wrote to Earl Spencer: 'It is a sad mess isn't it? P. is going to stand to his guns as if nothing had happened—and I don't see he has any chance save total disappearance. Mr G., however, thinks that *now* the pope may come down upon him more effectively than before.'[1]

It so happened that on November 20 and 21 the annual meeting of the National Liberal Federation was to be held at Sheffield, and this gave an opportunity of judging the reaction of the constituencies to the divorce proceedings. But the fact that the meeting would be followed in four days by the opening of parliament meant that the liberal leaders had to make up their minds very quickly. Effectively, this meant that Gladstone, Sir William Harcourt and John Morley must agree upon a policy. Harcourt had good claims to succeed Gladstone in the leadership, and Morley was virtually certain to be chief secretary for Ireland in the next home rule government. They were an oddly assorted pair for, though close friends, their temperaments and outlooks were very different. Harcourt was bluff, genial and outspoken—but behind this deceptive façade he concealed an acute and subtle mind. Loyalty to Gladstone had so far kept him staunch to home rule, but he could scarcely be described as one of its most devoted adherents and, as we shall see, his fidelity soon showed signs of cracking under the strain. Morley, on the other hand, could never have been mistaken for anything but the intellectual he was. He had come late into public life (in 1883, when he was forty-five years old) after a brilliant career as a man of letters and a political journalist, and though ambitious, he was too sensitive and too ready to take offence for the rough-and-tumble of politics, in which Harcourt, by contrast, delighted. However, Morley stood in a peculiarly close relationship to Gladstone, and he was also—after Gladstone—the Englishman most trusted by the leading members of the Irish parliamentary party. Gladstone, for his part, was now close on eighty-one years of age and lingered in politics only to complete his Irish mission. And Gladstone, even by November 17, doubted that Parnell could be upheld.[2] Soon he was faced

[1] Spencer Papers, John Morley to Earl Spencer, 17 Nov. 1890.
[2] Gladstone Papers (B.M., Add. MS 44,094, ff. 137–40), Gladstone to Lord Acton, 17 Nov. 1890; Hammond, *Gladstone and the Irish nation*, p. 632.

with a plea for advice from Morley who, with Harcourt, was to speak at the National Liberal Federation meeting. On November 19 he replied that 'abstractedly' it was for the Irish to decide and that for the moment English liberals must watch and wait. He added, echoing a phrase he had already used to Lord Acton, that he kept repeating to himself 'in the interior and silent forum' the words 'it'll na dae'.[1]

Morley and Harcourt duly went to Sheffield and made two very flat and non-committal speeches. They found, however, as they reported to Gladstone, that feeling against Parnell was strong and they had the greatest difficulty in restraining the president of the Federation, Dr Robert Spence Watson, from saying so publicly.[2] Harcourt's letter to Gladstone of November 22 was especially emphatic and Gladstone's reply to him on the day following is of particular interest, since it laid down the policy that was to guide him during the next vital days. After saying that he hoped to see Harcourt, John Morley and Arnold Morley in London the following afternoon, he suggested that Justin McCarthy should be asked if he, Gladstone, were to expect any communication from Parnell, instancing as a precedent Parnell's offer to resign in 1882 after the Phoenix Park murders.[3] He had, he said, observed 'the profound movement of the public mind' in the last week, and he continued:

The effect of that observation, corroborated by counsel with my friends, is to convince me that the continuance of Mr Parnell in the leadership of the Irish party at the present moment would be, notwithstanding his splendid services to his country, so to act upon British sentiment as to produce the gravest mischief to the cause of

[1] Morley, *Gladstone*, iii. 431–2; copy in Gladstone's hand in Gladstone Papers (B.M., Add. MS 44,256, ff. 75–6); Hammond, *Gladstone and the Irish nation*, pp. 632–4. From Morley Gladstone heard in reply that W. T. Stead was going 'to raise his fiercest whoops' against Parnell, on the ground that the latter was now utterly unworthy. Stead had told him (Morley) of Davitt's fury at being deceived and that Cardinal Manning had already expressed his views 'in quarters where it is proper that they should be first known' (Gladstone Papers (B.M., Add. MS 44,256, ff. 79–80), John Morley to Gladstone, 19 Nov. 1890).

[2] Morley, *Recollections*, i. 256–7; Gardiner, *Life of Harcourt*, ii. 83-4.

[3] It appears that, in the privacy of his family circle, Gladstone made no secret of the fact that he was expecting Parnell to resign not merely the leadership but his seat as well (Mary Gladstone, *Letters and diaries*, ed. L. Masterman, p. 413, entry under 22 Nov. 1890).

Ireland; to place those who represent the party in a position of irremediable difficulty; and to make the further maintenance of my own leadership for the purposes of that cause little better than a nullity.[1]

There followed two days of intense activity behind the scenes. On Sunday, November 23, McCarthy had a visit from Henry Labouchere, the influential radical M.P. and proprietor of the periodical *Truth*. Labouchere said he had been sent by Harcourt and Morley and that they all thought Parnell should retire for a time. Would a letter of advice to him from Gladstone have the desired effect? McCarthy was a little vague in his reply and confessed he had no means of getting in touch with Parnell. The best he could do was to give the address of the club to which Parnell's secretary, Henry Campbell, belonged. He did, however, make it clear that the Irish party could not throw Parnell over, but that if the initiative came from him to retire for the present, 'that would be quite a different thing'.[2] That same night John Morley succeeded in having a talk with Henry Campbell, who informed him that on the previous Friday (that is, the day after the Leinster Hall meeting) Parnell had seemed to be in a yielding mood, mainly out of consideration for Gladstone.[3]

The next day, November 24, Gladstone came up to London and stayed—as was his custom at this time—with Stuart Rendel in Carlton Gardens. That afternoon Lord Granville, the two Morleys and Harcourt visited him and they considered what they ought to do. Harcourt, in his brisk, stand-no-nonsense fashion, was all for Gladstone writing direct to Parnell and telling him bluntly that, apart altogether from the political aspect, the immorality of his conduct had made him unfit to continue as leader. Gladstone, however, would have none of it. A leader of a party, he said, was not a judge of morals. 'It would make life intolerable.' On the other hand, it seems clear that he was more impressed than ever by the clamour of the nonconformists. Rendel, who met him on his arrival at Euston, told Morley a few years later that on his way from the station Gladstone 'at once broke out in the carriage and declared that

[1] Gardiner, *Life of Harcourt*, ii. 84–5.
[2] McCarthy and Praed, *Our book of memories*, pp. 256–7.
[3] Morley, *Recollections*, i. 259.

Parnell was impossible, that the country and the party, and in particular the non-conformists, would never endure any maintenance of political relations with him'.[1] However, in their conference in the library of Rendel's house, they eventually agreed that when McCarthy called he should be asked to communicate with Parnell and, Morley recalled later, 'I understood it was to be in the terms of Mr Gladstone's letter to Harcourt, including the passage about Mr Gladstone's own leadership'.[2]

At this point McCarthy arrived and Gladstone went upstairs to speak to him. Since McCarthy's actions during the next twenty-four hours had a very direct bearing on the tragic course events were soon to take, his account of this interview—written that same night—is important:

> He (Gladstone) spoke with chivalrous consideration of Parnell's 'splendid and unrivalled services to Ireland', but told me very sadly that his remaining in the leadership now means the loss of the next elections and the putting off of home rule until the time when he (Gladstone) will no longer be able to bear a hand in the great struggle to which he has devoted the later years of his life. He spoke with intense feeling and earnestness. He said he would not write this to Parnell himself, because it might seem harsh and dictatorial and might hurt Irish feeling: but he authorised me to convey his views to Parnell when I see him. This will not be until to-morrow. It was a momentous interview—well-nigh tragic in its tone. It touched me deeply. I have written to Parnell asking him to decide nothing as to himself until he sees me in the house, and have sent the letter to the house on the off-chance of his going or sending there early to-morrow . . . I am much perturbed . . . all depends upon to-morrow.[3]

To McCarthy this interview was clearly a severe shock, though even so, as the sequel showed, he seemed not to have grasped its full implications; in this he is perhaps not entirely to blame, for with Gladstone the habit of circumlocution was so deeply ingrained that he was never an easy man to understand, and was likely to be more difficult than ever when feeling his way in

---

[1] F. E. Hamer (ed.), *The personal papers of Lord Rendel*, p. 126, note of conversation with Morley made by Rendel on 2 Nov. 1895.

[2] Morley, *Recollections*, i. 259–60; Lord E. Fitzmaurice, *Life of the second Earl Granville*, p. 499.

[3] McCarthy and Praed, *Our book of memories*, p. 258.

a delicate and complex situation. When his visitor had gone, Gladstone rejoined the group in the library and reported that, while McCarthy did not know where Parnell was, he hoped to see him next day and would privately show him a short, concise letter which he, Gladstone, was to prepare. John Morley, in his account of the scene, adds that when they left the house Gladstone had already drafted the letter.[1] It is not clear whether McCarthy ever received this letter, though Parnell three times asserted subsequently that he did do so,[2] and after Parnell's death one of his followers, Pierce Mahony, repeated the assertion.[3] McCarthy, through all the controversies that followed, neither denied nor admitted having got it, though after Parnell's death he did write to the press explaining that what Gladstone had told him he had told Parnell, viz., that the latter's retention as Irish leader would mean the loss of the general election; but, added McCarthy, he did not know that Gladstone contemplated retiring from the liberal leadership if Parnell remained.[4]

However this may be, the liberal leaders did not rely on one means of communication only. Before leaving Carlton Gardens they decided that Gladstone should write a letter to John Morley which the latter should show to Parnell if, as he expected, he met the Irish leader next morning. Then, having wrung from a reluctant Mrs Gladstone permission for her husband to

[1] Morley, *Recollections*, i. 260. Gladstone, interviewed by Barry O'Brien in January 1897, confirmed that he *had* written the letter (R. B. O'Brien, *Parnell*, ii. 366–7).

[2] In an interview in Dublin on 10 Dec. 1890, in a speech at Kells on 16 Aug. 1891 and in a letter to the press the next day (*F.J.*, 11 Dec. 1890, 17 and 18 Aug. 1891).

[3] *Pall Mall Gazette*, 14 Nov. 1891.

[4] *Pall Mall Gazette*, 9 Nov. 1891. Hammond, *Gladstone and the Irish nation*, p. 640, states that the letter *was* given to McCarthy, but he does not give his authority. Gladstone, in the interview quoted in footnote 1 above, assumed McCarthy had received it, but had no evidence that he had in fact done so. Contemporary press reports are of little help, since they constantly confuse the letter to McCarthy with the more important letter to Morley. Even less helpful is McCarthy's own account given to Barry O'Brien 'later', when he said not only that Gladstone had not asked that Parnell should resign— which may have been true—but that the liberal leader had not requested him to convey anything to Parnell, which was clearly wrong (R. B. O'Brien, *Parnell*, ii. 247). O'Brien does not give the date of this account or say whether it was oral or written.

dine that evening at Arnold Morley's house in Stratton street, they departed. When they met again at the dinner-table Gladstone handed John Morley his draft letter. Morley saw at once that Gladstone had omitted the cardinal point—that if Parnell remained at the head of the Irish party then his own leadership of the liberal party would become 'almost a nullity'. Gladstone, though afterwards admitting that he thought this was to have been a post-script ('what a post-script to be sure!' is Morley's comment) agreed then and there to insert the all-important passage in the body of the letter. In its final form it closely resembled the letter to Harcourt quoted above, except that it referred to Gladstone's interview with McCarthy and stated that the latter had been told of Gladstone's conclusion that Parnell's continuance 'at the present moment' in the leadership 'would be productive of consequences disastrous in the highest degree to the cause of Ireland'. The letter also stated that Gladstone had given his views to McCarthy in confidence, not to be disclosed to his colleagues generally if he found that Parnell contemplated spontaneous action— but that, if Parnell did not so act, he had asked McCarthy to lay his views before the Irish party when they met on the morrow.[1]

Up to this point Gladstone, though acting in haste and at the last moment, had been extremely correct and circumspect. Parnell being inaccessible, he had made his attitude plain to the vice-chairman, Justin McCarthy. McCarthy was much at home in liberal circles and it was a reasonable assumption that he, if anyone, would be in a position to impress upon Parnell the serious strain the divorce court proceedings had put upon the liberal-nationalist alliance. But even if McCarthy failed him, Gladstone still had a second string to his bow in his letter to Morley. Both from that letter and from the interview with McCarthy it is clear that Gladstone realised something of the delicacy of Parnell's position. He was convinced that the Irish leader should retire, but realised that it would be dangerous to press him too hard. Parnell might perhaps be helped in his decision by an insight into Gladstone's mind, but he was a proud man at the crisis of his career, and his pride must be

[1] Morley, *Gladstone*, iii. 436–7; *Recollections*, i. 260–1; Hammond, *Gladstone and the Irish nation*, pp. 638–40, 647–8.

tenderly handled. Plainly, Gladstone staked all upon the
personal touch. Everything, in the last resort, depended upon
one or both of his emissaries making contact with Parnell.

(3)

The next morning—the day of the opening of the new session
of parliament and of the Irish party's meeting—John Morley
heard by telegram from Campbell that he had not been able to
reach Parnell.[1] Morley went at once to McCarthy and found
that he had not been able to see him either. After lunch, therefore, Morley went to Carlton Gardens where he found Gladstone 'eager and agitated', having just heard from Arnold
Morley that McCarthy had in the end seen Parnell and learnt
that the latter was resolved 'to stand to his guns'.[2] Thus vanished
the last chance the liberal leaders had of influencing Parnell
before the crucial meeting of the Irish party. All they could do
now was to wait anxiously upon events.

The Irish members assembled in Committee Room Fifteen at
a quarter to three, three-quarters of an hour later than their
usual time.[3] The minutes of the party are brief and to the point
in their description of this momentous occasion. The chair was
taken by Richard Power, the senior whip. Thereupon Thomas
Sexton moved, and Colonel J. P. Nolan seconded, the re-
election of Parnell as chairman for the coming session and the
motion was passed with acclamation. Parnell, having then
taken the chair, thanked the party for re-electing him and
proceeded to refer briefly to the verdict of the divorce court.
The minute-book summarises what he had to say in these terms:

He asked his friends and colleagues to keep their lips sealed as his
were on this subject until the time came when he could speak freely

[1] Rumours—and in the absence of proof they must remain rumours—
circulated later that Campbell boasted that he had prevented Morley from
meeting Parnell (Healy, *Letters and leaders*, i. 342; T. P. O'Connor, *Memoirs
of an old parliamentarian*, ii. 206). It was even rumoured that Mrs O'Shea
intercepted a letter from John Morley to Parnell (A. Robbins, *Parnell, the
last five years*, p. 159).

[2] Morley, *Recollections*, i. 262.

[3] *F.J.*, 26 Nov. 1890. This bears out Parnell's assertion in the following
August that Morley was wrong in thinking the time of the meeting had been,
as he put it, 'accelerated' (*F.J.*, 18 and 19 Aug. 1891).

on the topic. When that time came they would find their confidence in him was not misplaced. He would not further allude to the matter beyond once more asking them to keep their lips closed in reference to that topic.[1]

This account is so bare and matter-of-fact as to be suspect. Could Parnell really have expected his followers to be satisfied with such a delphic utterance? These men had come to the meeting racked by the most fearful anxieties. For a week past there had been a torrent of comment in press and pulpit, much of it hateful and malicious, but some of it coming from responsible and respected sources. Moreover, even if their church had not yet spoken publicly, they could not but be aware of the likely attitude of the bishops. And although that morning's *Freeman's Journal* assured them that Gladstone's opinion had no doubt been taken and would greatly influence Parnell's decision, they must have realised that the divorce catastrophe threatened their alliance with the liberal party.[2] That very morning a leading liberal newspaper had carried the plain warning that Parnell 'ought to know that for thousands of his English supporters there are higher considerations than party politics, and that neither for him nor for any man will they condone a distinct violation of the moral law'. And it added ominously: 'Having made careful enquiries from the best sources of information, we are enabled to tell Mr Parnell that if he continues to lead the Irish party, home rule cannot be carried.'[3] In the face of such pressure the re-election of Parnell by his party was an act of great faith and one which they might well expect him to reciprocate by letting them into his confidence.

It seems that he did actually say a little more than the minutes recorded and that the meeting took a slightly different course from that already described. Later that day Donal Sullivan wrote an account of the proceedings to his nephew T. M. Healy, who was still not well enough to leave Dublin. Sullivan reported that after the motion to re-elect Parnell had been put to the meeting, Jeremiah Jordan (a protestant and Captain O'Shea's successor as a member for Clare) appealed to Parnell to retire—even if only for a month. This suggestion was received

[1] Dillon Papers, 'Minutes of the Irish parliamentary party', 25 Nov. 1890.
[2] *F.J.*, 25 Nov. 1890.
[3] *Daily News*, 25 Nov. 1890.

in silence. Then, wrote Sullivan, Parnell rose 'amidst cheers and cheers again. I noticed Justin (old and young[1]), John Barry, William Abraham, P. J. Power, W. J. Lane and Maurice Healy did not cheer'. According to Sullivan, Parnell made a long speech denying that he had ever accepted O'Shea's hospitality or that O'Shea had ever been his friend, asking the party for their confidence and saying he would not surrender.[2]

The interest of this letter, written as it was on the actual day, is that it resembles very closely the account which Sullivan published in the *National Press* a year later and which purported to be based on notes taken as the speech was delivered.[3] If Sullivan's two versions of the speech are even approximately correct, it can have held small comfort for those who heard it. Some, perhaps, had expected from Parnell's confident assurances when the petition was first filed in December 1889 that there must be an explanation honourable to their leader and that the squalid details uncovered in the divorce court could somehow or other be disposed of. Others, again, seem to have anticipated that when they elected Parnell he would treat their vote for him as a gesture of appreciation for his past services and would then gracefully withdraw.[4] But all they had been told in effect was that Parnell and O'Shea had not been friends—which cannot have been news to very many of them. Thus, although they had begun the meeting by demonstrating their loyalty to their leader, when they emerged again into the busy corridors of the house they were further than ever from a solution.

Meanwhile, Gladstone's letter, which was to have made it all plain, was still in John Morley's pocket, and Morley was still to have his interview with Parnell. This took place soon after the

[1] McCarthy's son, Justin Huntly McCarthy, like his father a well-known novelist in his day, was also a member of the party.

[2] Healy, *Letters and leaders*, i. 322–3. Henry Harrison, who was also present, recalled many years later that Parnell had described O'Shea as 'my bitter and unrelenting enemy' (*Parnell vindicated*, p. 10).

[3] *National Press*, 21 Nov. 1891. Sullivan was a journalist by profession.

[4] 'We all expected it', wrote Sullivan to Healy in the letter already quoted. In his published narrative of 1891 Sullivan asserted that *The Standard* of that morning had declared that Parnell would retire if elected, and that this had influenced many of the Irish party who believed the statement to have been inspired by J. M. Tuohy, London correspondent of the *Freeman's Journal* (*National Press*, 21 Nov. 1891).

Irish meeting ended, and we have a vivid account of it from Morley, made 'at the time'.[1] As they walked towards Gladstone's room, Parnell told him he had been re-elected chairman. Morley said he was sorry to hear it, as he had a communication to make which might still make a difference. He then read out the famous letter. 'As he listened', wrote Morley, 'I knew the look on his face quite well enough to know that he was obdurate.' In vain Morley urged on him that to defy British opinion was to court ruin at the next general election, in vain he suggested that retirement now did not mean that Parnell could not come forward a year later:

He answered, in his slow, dry way that he must look to the future; that he had made up his mind to stick to the house of commons and to his present position in the party until he was convinced, and he would not soon be convinced, that it was impossible to obtain home rule from a British parliament; that if he gave up the leadership for a time, he should never return to it; that if he once let go, it was all over.

It was impossible to shake him. Though Morley noticed that he was paler than usual, he remained calm and resolute to the end. With that strange detachment he so often displayed, and which was part of his strength, he observed that of course Gladstone would have to attack him and that he expected it—Gladstone would have a right to do so. But Gladstone himself, when he saw Morley shortly afterwards, was dumbfounded and could hardly believe what Morley told him. And, in the shock of the moment, he made a grave decision. He 'burst out' that they must publish his letter to Morley at once. The latter, playing for time, protested that it was too late and that they really ought to consider before taking such a step. They went into the house and were presently joined by Harcourt, who had been for brutal measures from the start. Then and there they decided that the letter must be published and Morley, seeing Parnell in his place, sent him a message to come and see him. As they walked up and down the lobby, Morley told him of their intention. ' "Yes", he said amicably, as if it were no particular

---

[1] Morley, *Gladstone*, iii. 439–41. Morley errs slightly in saying that it was a little after three when he saw Parnell. It was in fact nearer four, since the Irish meeting did not end until 3.45 (*The Times*, 26 Nov. 1890; *F.J.*, 26 Nov. 1890).

concern of his. "I think Mr Gladstone will be quite right to do that; it will put him straight with his party".[1]

It might almost seem from this casual reply that Parnell failed to understand the significance of this new turn of events. Yet it needed no deep penetration to realise that what was happening was certain to put the loyalty of his party to an excruciating test. Ever since 1886 they had been taught, Parnell himself had taught them, to look to the liberals for salvation. The liberal alliance had become the foundation of the whole movement for home rule; without it, there could be little hope for the future. But if the liberal alliance were so essential, and if the party were forced to choose between it and the leader, many would consider the cause more precious than the fate of the individual, however well-loved and respected that individual might be. Men would choose differently no doubt, and many extraneous factors would influence them—temperament, past history, personal dealings with Parnell. But if enough of them were convinced that the choice really lay between Parnell and home rule, there could be little doubt of the result.

The business of choosing would have been painful enough even under the most favourable circumstances, but the decision to publish the letter was certain to make it far more difficult. Gladstone, like everyone else involved in the crisis, was under great strain and of course, as Parnell himself realised, he was above all anxious 'to put himself straight with his party', but even this can scarcely excuse the haste with which he acted. His own explanation is not very convincing. 'When', he wrote, 'we found that Mr McCarthy's representation had had no effect, that the Irish party had not been informed, and that Mr Morley's making known the material parts of my letter was likewise without result, it at once was decided to publish the letter. . . .'[2] The obvious comment which this invites is that, though Parnell himself might have been quite unaffected when Morley read the letter to him, the Irish party had a right to know its contents and to decide in privacy whether or not to

[1] Morley, *Gladstone*, iii. 439–41; Hammond, *Gladstone and the Irish nation*, pp. 643–4.

[2] Morley, *Gladstone*, iii. 444–5, note made by Gladstone, 28 Nov. 1890. This shows T. M. Healy to have been in error in stating that Gladstone, 'under the impression that McCarthy had read his letter to the party', published its text that evening (*Letters and leaders*, i. 323).

take back the confidence they had just bestowed on their leader. The key to the whole delicate situation was privacy. Once the letter was published, the matter appeared in a very different light. What in private might have seemed a reasonable, indeed necessary, communication from one partner in the home rule alliance to the other, could in the glare of publicity be all too easily represented as an arrogant attempt by the leader of a great English party to dictate to the Irish members what they should do and what they should not do. Inevitably, national pride was deeply wounded and the emotional tension immeasurably heightened. For those who could pierce through the mists of passion to the realities of the situation, the publication of the letter created a position of almost intolerable embarrassment. They might feel that if home rule was everything that mattered, then Gladstone was more important to them than Parnell, but, with Gladstone's letter public property, they could not fail to realise that in siding with the liberals they laid themselves open to the charges of submitting to English interference and of abandoning their own leader.

From the Parnellite viewpoint also, the publication of the letter was disastrous. Without it, some of Parnell's more moderate supporters might possibly have been brought to agree to the suggestion of a limited or temporary retirement by Parnell, which up to that time was all that most people seemed to demand of him. But once the letter was in print, their personal loyalty to their leader was engaged and they were led into the intransigent position of standing by Parnell at all costs. Parnell, for his part, needed no encouragement to go his own way, but he would not have been human if the demonstrations of some of those nearest him had not steeled his purpose to turn an impassive front to all attempts at manoeuvring him into resigning the chair to which he had just been re-elected.

Most of the Irish members seem to have learnt of the contents of Gladstone's letter about dinner-time.[1] Thunder-struck, some of them were for having another meeting that night, and a number did assemble about nine o'clock. But it was not a formal meeting—there is no record of it in the party minutes—and Parnell did not attend it. Those who wanted a formal meeting, however, busied themselves in obtaining signatures to a

[1] *F.J.*, 27 Nov. 1890; R. B. O'Brien, *Parnell*, ii. 250.

requisition that one should be called. Thirty-one members signed, and the meeting was fixed for the next day at two o'clock.[1]

When the party assembled, John Barry moved the resolution 'That a full meeting of the party be held on Friday to give Mr Parnell an opportunity of reconsidering his position'. This was seconded by Dr Andrew Commins and Parnell rose to reply. His speech was brief and made it quite clear that he had no intention of reconsidering his position. He had been unanimously re-elected by the party and it was for the party to shoulder the responsibility for reversing its decision. There followed numerous speeches on both sides of the question. Those who pleaded with Parnell to retire based their case partly upon the importance of preserving the liberal alliance, and partly on the argument that if the liberals lost the next general election the plight of the evicted tenants would be disastrous. Parnell's supporters, on the other hand, seem to have contented themselves largely with urging him not to yield to liberal dictation. The meeting was inconclusive and it was finally agreed to adjourn until the following Monday. In the meantime the whips were to send a cable to T. P. Gill in America so that he could inform his fellow-delegates of the situation at home; this cable was only to be sent after it had been seen by Parnell and by Barry and Commins—proposer and seconder of the original resolution.[2]

From the point of view of those who wanted a speedy decision this meeting was a distinct set-back. Not only had it revealed that Parnell was not going to make things easy for his opponents by retiring gracefully, but the fact that it had adjourned until Monday would give him time in which he might attempt to influence Irish opinion in his favour. Indeed, the editorial of that morning's *Freeman's Journal* had already pointed the line that Parnellites should take. It was that Ireland had 'with one voice' declared that Parnell should continue to lead her and

[1] *National Press*, 23 Nov. 1891; *F.J.*, 27 Nov. 1890. The latter source asserts that the number of signatures was thirty-eight, but this is incorrect. The party minutes of 26 Nov. 1890 list the names of thirty-one signatories.

[2] Dillon Papers, 'Minutes of the Irish parliamentary party', 26 Nov. 1890. No reporters were admitted to the meeting, but a statement was subsequently issued to the press which was substantially the same as what was recorded in the minutes (*F.J.*, 27 Nov. 1890).

that Gladstone's letter had 'violated the principle of independent opposition—the hinge on which the Irish party turns'.[1]
The implication was clear—unity must be preserved so that
Parnell could continue to balance between English parties as he
had done in the past. That the circumstances of the past were
very different from those of the present was easy to overlook in
the heat of the moment. But the debate had also shown that
there was a strong body of opposition to Parnell headed by some
of the senior men in the party (e.g. John Barry, Thomas Sexton
and Arthur O'Connor) and well equipped with arguments
difficult to answer. Moreover, the speed with which the reaction
had taken shape was in itself ominous.

Both sides now began to organise feverishly for what they
assumed would be the decisive struggle on Monday, December
1. Parnell's opponents sent an urgent wire to Healy and that
powerful reinforcement arrived in London on Thursday,
November 27.[2] The next evening he wrote to his wife that in a
few hours Parnell was to issue a manifesto 'to crush both ourselves and the Gladstonians'. To counter this, he said, he had
drawn up a requisition for a meeting of the party to condemn
the issue of any declaration intended to overawe or influence
the party's debate on the coming Monday.[3] This meeting duly
took place and in Parnell's absence Justin McCarthy took the
chair. A resolution was proposed declaring that any member of
the party who by speech or writing attempted to influence or
overawe the deliberations of the adjourned party meeting,
would be acting in breach of the understanding as to the purpose of the adjournment—which was to give time for communicating with absent colleagues. Parnell's supporters at once
moved that no meeting of the party should be held at which he
was not present. Healy agreed that they ought to adjourn, if
they could be assured that he would be present later. They
adjourned accordingly until nine o'clock, but as the house rose

[1] *F.J.*, 26 Nov. 1890.

[2] Healy, *Letters and leaders*, i. 326. Healy in his memoirs says that he only
received the wire on Thursday and did not reach Westminster until Friday.
This was an error of recollection, for one of his own letters to his wife is dated
November 27 (Thursday) and written from the house of commons. Sir
Henry Lucy (*Diary of the Salisbury parliament, 1886–92*, p. 319) noted his
presence on November 27.

[3] Healy, *Letters and leaders*, i. 326–7, letter to his wife, 28 Nov. 1890.

at eight they were denied the use of a room, and in the words of the minutes: 'The adjourned meeting therefore fell through.'[1]

On the Parnellite side the main hope was centred upon a manifesto which the leader was believed to be preparing. This was to be his supreme justification and until its contents were known it was impossible to tell which way the fortunes of war would go. He might even at this late hour redeem himself and offer a convincing explanation to his fellow-countrymen as to why they should hold to him and ignore Gladstone's warnings. He might be able to do this, or he might not—only the document itself could reveal which. For him—with the liberals in full cry, the unionists triumphant, and signs of division evident within his own party—it was a decisive moment. Much depended upon the manifesto.

[1] Dillon Papers, 'Minutes of the Irish parliamentary party', 28 Nov. 1890, It seems to have met again briefly on Saturday morning, but informally. since the proceedings were not entered in the minutes. It does not appear to have achieved anything (*F.J.*, 1 Dec. 1890).

IV

THE PARNELL MANIFESTO

(1)

THE MEETING of the Irish party on Wednesday, November 26 had shown Parnell what until then he may possibly have under-estimated, the strength of the opposition against him, once it had begun to seem as if the choice lay between Gladstone and himself. Outwardly he had remained as cool and resolute as ever and—as Sexton told Healy—if an intelligent foreigner had entered the room he would have imagined that the entire party was being tried for adultery, with Parnell as the judge.[1] But when he returned to Mrs O'Shea that night he warned her there would be a fight and that it was going to be 'tough work'. Then and there, she says, he absorbed himself in the preparation of his manifesto.[2] He intended it to be primarily a counter-blast against Gladstone and against some of his own colleagues. So much, at any rate, he told McCarthy when the latter visited him on Thursday. The vice-chairman found him 'very friendly, sweet and affectionate to me', but set upon issuing the manifesto without delay. McCarthy managed to persuade him to hold it back for twenty-four hours until he, McCarthy, could once more see Gladstone.[3] It seems that on Friday he had two inter-

[1] Healy, *Letters and leaders*, i. 326, Healy to his wife, 27 Nov. 1890; Viscount Esher, *Journals and letters*, ed. M. V. Brett, i. 146.   [2] O'Shea, ii. 161–3.
[3] McCarthy and Praed, *Our book of memories*, p. 259, McCarthy to Mrs Praed, 28 Nov. 1890.

views with Gladstone, one of them—so he afterwards said—at Parnell's request. What precisely the liberal leader said at these interviews is not known, but apparently he spoke of home rule in such a way as to leave no doubt in McCarthy's mind that when he read the manifesto he would certainly contradict it.[1] And McCarthy, for his part, came away from these meetings determined that unless something quite unexpected happened, he would vote against Parnell on Monday, all ties of friendship notwithstanding.[2]

On Friday night, before sending the manifesto to the press, Parnell called together a few members of the party on whom he felt he could rely—among them the Redmond brothers, J. J. O'Kelly, Edmund Leamy, Colonel J. P. Nolan and Dr J. G. Fitzgerald.[3] Before he began to read the document Parnell asked that McCarthy be brought to the house to hear it and when he had arrived the reading commenced. The manifesto was long, but it fell fairly obviously into four sections.[4] The first was a strong attack on Gladstone for attempting to influence the Irish party in the choice of its leader. The opening phrases were ominous, for they referred to 'the integrity and independence of a section of the Irish parliamentary party having been apparently sapped and destroyed by the wire-pullers of the English liberal party', and a little later to 'the English wolves now howling for my destruction'.[5] It was not difficult for his hearers to imagine the effects of language such as this upon English opinion, but the harsh note struck at the outset continued inexorably to the end.

The second and most important section of the manifesto was devoted to what purported to be an account of certain details of the home rule settlement that the liberals proposed to introduce if they won the next election. These details were said to

[1] *Pall Mall Gazette*, 14 Jan. 1891; *F.J.*, 16 Jan. 1891.

[2] McCarthy and Praed, *Our book of memories*, p. 261.

[3] R. B. O'Brien, *Parnell*, ii. 257. D. Sullivan, 'The story of room fifteen' in *National Press*, 24 Nov. 1891, states that some subsequent opponents of Parnell besides McCarthy were also there.

[4] The text of the manifesto will be found in Appendix I, pp. 320–6 below.

[5] Some published versions omitted the word 'apparently', but Parnell later confirmed that it should have been included (*F.J.*, 4 Dec. 1890; R. B. O'Brien, *Parnell*, ii. 258, *n.* 1).

have been imparted to Parnell by Gladstone himself at Hawarden the previous December. They concerned four topics and may be briefly summarised as follows:

1. Parnell alleged that Gladstone and the liberals were resolved to retain the Irish members at Westminster, but to reduce them from 103 to 32.

2. Gladstone was reported as having said that the settlement of the land question would be attempted by the imperial parliament on the lines of the land purchase bill of 1886, but that he would put no pressure on the liberal party to adopt his views. 'In other and shorter words', wrote Parnell, 'that the Irish legislature was not to be given the power of solving the agrarian difficulty, and that the imperial parliament would not.'

3. Control of the Irish constabulary, Gladstone was alleged to have stated, would have to remain under imperial authority for an indefinite period, though the funds for maintaining, paying and equipping it would be compulsorily provided from Irish sources.

4. Finally, said Parnell, Gladstone had suggested that the right of appointing the judiciary (from supreme court judges to resident magistrates) should be retained in the hands of the imperial authority for ten or twelve years.

Of these four propositions the first, relating to the retention of the Irish members at Westminster in reduced numbers, was obviously the key one. Parnell's comment on it was that so long as the land, the police and the judiciary were outside Irish control, it would be essential to retain the full number of Irish members at Westminster. To consent to any reduction in their numbers would be to repeat Grattan's error in disbanding the Volunteers before victory had been achieved. However, said Parnell, to conciliate English opinion, he had agreed to the withholding from the Irish parliament of full control over the police and the judiciary, though he had protested at the absence of 'any suitable prospect of land settlement'. But, he asserted, so far as Irish representation in parliament was concerned, he had been told that, pending the general election, 'silence should be absolutely preserved with regard to any points of difference on the question of the retention of the Irish members'.

The third section bore all the appearance of a tactical manoeuvre, and an obvious one at that. It was an attempt to fasten on the liberals and on John Morley in particular (himself alleged to be under pressure from Labouchere) the responsibility for Parnell's having attacked the unionist land purchase bill of the previous session.[1] 'I think this was false strategy', Parnell admitted, 'but it was strategy adopted out of regard to English prejudices and radical peculiarities.' What he really meant—as the sequel was to show—was that he was now resuming his freedom of action on the land question and was preparing the way for a campaign in support of the unionist measure, which had been re-introduced that session.

Finally, in the last paragraphs of the document, Parnell took up the subject of the interview he had had with John Morley shortly before the divorce proceedings came on—the interview at which he had assured Morley that those proceedings would not lead to his disappearance from the scene. We know from Morley that in the course of their conversation he had asked 'guilelessly' if it was out of the question that Parnell should take the post of chief secretary in the next liberal ministry—to which Parnell had made the expected reply that it *was* quite out of the question that he or any of his party should join the government. Morley had then mentioned the difficulty of finding a seat for one of the Irish law officers in a liberal administration and—according to him—Parnell had promised that when the next general election came he would do his best to get one for him.[2] In the manifesto this casual—but private—conversation appeared as 'a remarkable proposal' not merely that Parnell himself or one of his colleagues should become chief secretary, but also that it would be desirable to fill one of the Irish law offices 'by a legal member of my party'. This ingenious account of the interview allowed Parnell not only to deal a side-blow at Healy (whom few would have much difficulty in recognising as the 'legal member' in question) but also to demonstrate the principle of independent opposition in action. 'I told him', he wrote, 'amazed as I was at the proposal, that I could not agree

[1] If Parnell had really acted under pressure he had certainly acted with great vigour, even going to the almost unprecedented lengths (for him) of writing an article on the subject in the *North American Review;* the article is summarised in *Review of Reviews* (July 1890), ii. 36.

[2] Morley, *Recollections*, i. 252–3. In a letter to Gladstone reporting this interview Morley wrote: 'He would find an Irish seat for one of your Irish law-officers *at* the general election, but not before' (Gladstone Papers (B.M., Add. MS 44,256, f. 69), John Morley to Gladstone, 15 Nov. 1890).

to forfeit in any way the independence of the party or of any of its members.' It was, he added, a proposal 'based upon an entire misconception of our position with regard to the Irish constituencies and of the pledges which we had given'.

One other topic he and Morley had discussed at Brighton had been the future of the Plan of Campaign estates. Morley's version—noted down the morning after their talk—was that he had asked Parnell if the Campaign tenants did not expect to be reinstated the day after the general election. To which Parnell had replied that if the tories lost the election the landlords would know the game was up—an optimistic assumption which Morley made it clear he did not share.[1] But to this also Parnell in the manifesto gave his own interpretation. According to him, Morley had said that when the liberals came back to power it would be impossible for them to do anything for the evicted tenants by direct action and that it would be impossible for the Irish parliament, under the powers to be conferred on it, to help them either. He, Parnell, only mentioned this, he said, because it had been urged as a reason for his expulsion that unless the liberals came back to power at the general election the Campaign tenants would suffer. On the contrary, he now asserted, the liberals proposed no direct action for these people whereas he pledged himself to see that they would not be neglected.

He ended by recalling that sixteen years previously he had conceived the idea of an Irish parliamentary party independent of all English parties. He contended that in the ten years since he had begun to lead the party it had remained independent, and that if it continued independent in the future it would win home rule. Those who supported him, he declared, were not endangering the cause—but, even if the peril threatened by the liberals (he meant the loss of the general election) were to be realised, 'I believe that the Irish people throughout the world would agree with me that postponement would be preferable to a compromise of our national rights by the acceptance of a measure which would not realise the aspirations of our race'.

(2)

Such was the famous counter-stroke to Gladstone's letter.

[1] Morley, *Recollections*, i. 253.

From first to last it was an extraordinary document. On the face of it, it seemed improbable that Gladstone had said what he was represented to have said, or that he could possibly have tied his hands in advance by laying down such precise details about legislation which was bound to be controversial when debated in parliament and on which it was essential that he should have the greatest possible freedom of movement. Especially was it hard to credit that he should have spoken in such a brusque and unhelpful fashion about the land question, since his whole record showed that he had long been of all men the most convinced that the settlement of the land problem went hand-in-hand with, if it did not actually precede, the establishment of home rule. As for the future of the Irish members at Westminster, it was of course an open issue and must obviously depend upon the extent of the powers conceded to an Irish parliament. But to represent the liberals as being unanimous in taking up a doctrinaire attitude on the mystic number of thirty-two was to strain belief almost beyond breaking-point.

But even if every word in the manifesto were true, and it was an exact record of what Gladstone had said, two comments have still to be made. One is that this was a highly private and confidential matter which should only have been divulged by mutual consent of the two parties concerned; or alternatively, that if Parnell had felt that he was being asked to listen to proposals which fell too far short of the Irish demand, he should have ended the interview at once and declined to enter into any vow of secrecy. And the other comment is that, so far from being outraged by these proposals, Parnell went straight from Hawarden to Liverpool, where he spoke in the most adulatory terms of the liberal leader and urged the English people to lend their aid in winning 'the great battle I trust we are on the eve of entering upon'.[1] And not only did he speak like this in public, but he left his Liverpool host in no doubt that he was extremely pleased with his trip to Hawarden. When the manifesto appeared, that gentleman wrote at once to Gladstone in obvious bewilderment, reporting that when Parnell had stayed with him he had shown himself 'very much impressed with his visit to you, and your cordiality, but more than all with the

___

[1] *The Times*, 20 Dec. 1889.

thoroughness of your proposals in regard to Ireland which went really further than he could have expected from any great English statesman, and that they meant a most satisfactory solution'.[1] Why did he speak thus of Gladstone if he had just received from him such lame proposals as to home rule? And why, if these proposals were really so defective, had he not taken his own colleagues into his confidence and disclosed to them this new development which, if he had stated it correctly, was so obvious a threat to the cause?

These questions were to be asked many times in the days that followed, and they were to loom large in the debates which the party resumed in Committee Room Fifteen on December 1. As we shall see presently, the answers he then gave—that the talks were confidential, that the proposals were not final, that he wanted to give Gladstone time to reconsider his position—were not very convincing and certainly did not mollify his critics. In a sense, however, it is less important to know why he had kept silence for so long than why he had broken it when and how he did. The timing of the manifesto is in itself a sufficient answer to the first of these problems. Obviously, so long as his leadership of the Irish party was unquestioned by the liberals, he was in a position to re-open negotiations about home rule—either on the basis of the Hawarden conversations or on some other lines—if and when he pleased. But the moment it became clear that liberal opinion would no longer tolerate him as an ally, and that the loyalty of his own party was in danger of cracking under pressure, the position was abruptly changed. From his viewpoint, not only did the hostility of the liberals absolve him from any discretion he might still have felt bound to observe concerning his visit to Gladstone, but the very fact that his party was wilting under that hostility made it necessary for him to regain the initiative as quickly as possible. And since the Irish party was to meet again on December 1 he had to deliver his counter-stroke before then.

This, however, does not explain the most important question —why the manifesto took the form it did. Why was it phrased

[1] Gladstone Papers (B.M., Add. MS 44,511, f. 199), E. Evans to Gladstone. The letter is dated 28 Nov. 1890, but this should be 29 Nov. 1890, as it contains a reference to the manifesto, which only appeared on the morning of Nov. 29.

in terms so bitter and uncompromising as to make any hope of reconciliation between him and his former allies impossible? Some contemporaries, naturally, saw it as the reaction of a man goaded into fury and striking out wildly in all directions.[1] Almost certainly they were wrong. Parnell may well have felt personal resentment against Gladstone—in the near future he was to use very offensive language about 'the grand old spider' —but he was not normally a man who allowed his political judgment to be clouded by emotions of that kind. Indeed, we have already seen that he had told Morley that he expected Gladstone to attack him and that he faced with equanimity the prospect of the letter to Morley being published. Moreover, the manifesto was not dashed off in the heat of the moment. On the contrary, Parnell spent long hours and much thought in the writing of it. He never used words lightly and we may be sure that whatever was in the document was there for a purpose. That purpose may be deduced from the fact that, while the manifesto dealt in detail with the alleged short-comings of the liberals in the matter of home rule, it said nothing whatever about his own appearance in the divorce court. What he was attempting, in reality, was a diversion on the grand scale. Strategically, it was vital for him to make the coming conflict turn on something else besides the divorce case which, with the upsurge of English opinion, had become dangerous ground. The Hawarden conversations and his interview with Morley at Brighton gave him the avenue of escape he needed, for they might allow him to direct attention—for a time at least—away from the question of his own fitness for leadership towards the broader question of what shape the next home rule bill should take. And, given this purpose, it must be admitted that his position was skilfully chosen. The topics mentioned in the manifesto as having been discussed with Gladstone were not only of urgent importance to Irishmen, but had all been controversial issues in 1886 and issues on which the liberals had ever since been very reluctant to commit themselves.

By 1889 this reluctance had become so marked as to be a source of embarrassment, which the unionist speakers eagerly

[1] 'Mr Parnell seems to have resolved that if he falls he will drag the home rule cause and the cause of the people and tenants of Ireland with him' (*Daily News*, 29 Nov. 1890).

exploited in their platform campaign that autumn.[1] Partly perhaps to counter the effects of this bombardment, and partly to ascertain the views of some of his former colleagues before the expected visit of Parnell, Gladstone held an informal conference at Hawarden. The topic that exercised them most seems to have been the thorny problem which had so vexed them during the crisis of the first home rule bill—the future of the Irish members at Westminster. Earl Granville, writing to Earl Spencer who was unable to attend the conference, explained that Gladstone, John Morley, Harcourt and Lord Ripon were all against announcing any definite scheme of home rule and went on to give one very good reason why this should be so—they were divided on the question of what to do with the Irish members:

With regard to the Irish M.P.s (he wrote) Gladstone was at first inclined to the admission of all to the imperial parliament, but only on imperial subjects—but he came round to the opinion that it would be better not to limit the questions. He, Ripon and Morley are for diminishing the number.

Harcourt is for no diminution either in number or subjects. He believes we shall want them for a liberal majority. It is not clear that Parnell would consent to a diminished number, though he does not object to their total exclusion.[2]

Spencer himself seems to have inclined towards Harcourt's view, for two days later at Stockton, while disclaiming any intention of discussing the details of a home rule bill, he admitted that it seemed inevitable that the Irish members must be retained in the imperial parliament, and that there seemed no middle course between total exclusion or retaining them as they were.[3] Harcourt, however, was evidently worried at the prospect of finding himself in a minority on this issue and letters from him flew in all directions. Not only did he write to Gladstone explaining his position, but he sent copies of the letter to both Spencer and Granville. In a covering note to the

[1] *Annual Register*, 1889, pp. 197–260. Probably the most irksome critics of the liberals were their former bed-fellows, Joseph Chamberlain and Lord Hartington. For two typical examples of their speeches at this time see *The Times*, 3 Oct. 1889 (Chamberlain at Newcastle) and 5 Oct. 1889 (Hartington at Stirling).

[2] Spencer Papers, Earl Granville to Earl Spencer, 22 Oct. 1889.

[3] *The Times*, 25 Oct. 1889; Gladstone Papers (B.M., Add. MS 44,314, f. 7), Earl Spencer to Gladstone, 8 Nov. 1889.

latter he expressed himself with his usual vigour: 'My clear conviction', he wrote, 'is that to commit ourselves to anything of the sort [i.e. a reduction of the Irish members] would be a fatal and irretrievable error.'[1]

The liberal leaders were thus in a confused state of mind when Parnell arrived at Hawarden in December 1889. However, it seems from a note Gladstone made at the time that he was prepared to discuss with his visitor a variety of topics, including land purchase, the supremacy of the imperial parliament, judicial appointments (though he only mentions judges 'of the superior courts') and financial relations.[2] But the most immediate and urgent subject was the question of the Irish members. And on this—according to a secret memorandum on the conversations which he himself wrote and circulated to his former cabinet colleagues—Gladstone's report was as follows:

> I may say, however, that we were quite agreed in thinking that the real difficulty lies in determining the particular form in which an Irish representation may have to be retained at Westminster. We conversed at large on the different modes. He has no absolute or fore-gone conclusion.
>
> He emphatically agreed on the wisdom and necessity of reserving our judgment on this matter until a crisis is at hand.[3]

This, evidently, is a memorandum of a discussion, not of a decision, and it would indeed have been foolish to expect these conversations to solve all problems, though they did at least seem to show—in Spencer's phrase—'good temper and moderation to rule in Mr C. S. P.'s heart'.[4] Gladstone, for his part, seems to have been well satisfied, and noted in his diary that Parnell 'was certainly one of the very best people to deal with that I have ever known'.[5] The anger and disillusionment of the

[1] Spencer Papers, Sir W. Harcourt to Earl Spencer, 25 Oct. 1889; Granville Papers (P.R.O. 30.29, box 29A), Sir W. Harcourt to Earl Granville, 27 Oct. 1889. And to John Morley he wrote, 'from the point of view of a liberal majority we can't afford to diminish the force of the Irish members' (Harcourt Papers, Sir W. Harcourt to John Morley, 27 Oct. 1889).

[2] Hammond, *Gladstone and the Irish nation*, pp. 619–21.

[3] Gladstone Papers (B.M., Add. MS 44,773, f. 171), Gladstone memorandum, 23 Dec. 1889.

[4] Granville Papers (P.R.O. 30.29, box 22A), Earl Spencer to Earl Granville, 29 Dec. 1889. But he added: 'Whether the divorce suit will affect him or not I know not. I wonder it has not been taken before.'

[5] Hammond, *Gladstone and the Irish nation*, p. 605.

liberals may, therefore, be imagined when Parnell published in his manifesto what they could only regard as a completely distorted version of the conversations. As might have been expected, it was Harcourt who erupted most violently and on the very day the document appeared he dashed off heated letters to Granville, Spencer and Gladstone. Two things in particular aroused his anger. One was Parnell's assertion that Gladstone had said it was 'the unanimous opinion' of his colleagues and himself that the Irish representatives should be reduced from 103 to 32. So far from this being true, as Harcourt reminded both Granville and Spencer, he had protested vigorously against any such idea.[1] The other concerned a different, but no less delicate matter, and on this he wrote as follows to Gladstone:

Since seeing you I have observed a statement in Parnell's manifesto which I think requires to be specially traversed and contradicted, viz. that you stated that you would 'renew the attempt to settle the land question by imperial legislation *on the lines of the land purchase bill of 1886*'.

This assertion uncontradicted will have a most injurious effect upon our friends. They or most of them had fondly hoped that the land bill of 1886 was dead and buried. They know that the principal cause of the disaster of 1886 was to be found in the proposals of that bill and it will alarm them beyond measure to suppose that you have it in your mind to propose again 'a measure on the same lines'.[2]

Parnell, had he been able to see this letter, would no doubt have derived a certain sardonic satisfaction from the evidence it gave of his enemies being at cross-purposes amongst themselves. But any advantage he might have gained from these liberal differences was more than off-set by the anger he aroused among them, both by the language of the manifesto and by his breach of confidence in publishing it at all. However much they might disagree on land purchase, or on the future of the Irish members at Westminster, they could at least unite in condemning Parnell. This was so obvious a consequence of his action

[1] Granville Papers (P.R.O. 39.29, box 29A), Sir W. Harcourt to Earl Granville, 29 Nov. 1890; Spencer Papers, Sir W. Harcourt to Earl Spencer, 29 Nov. 1890.

[2] Gladstone Papers (B.M., Add. MS 44,202, f. 41), Sir W. Harcourt to Gladstone, 29 Nov. 1890.

that it is impossible to believe that the Irish leader had not foreseen it. He must have known that his account of the Gladstone and Morley conversations would be challenged—as indeed it immediately was—by both men and that his violation of secrecy would make it virtually impossible for them to act with him ever again. One can only suppose that he himself had already come to the conclusion that, after the publication of Gladstone's letter, the breaking-point in the liberal alliance, at least so far as he was concerned, had already been reached. If that were so, then their anger at his manifesto would be—for him—an irrelevant factor in the situation, or rather, its only relevance would be to make it easier for him to resume his full freedom of action and to put into operation once more the principle of 'independent opposition'. If this *was* the explanation of his indifference to liberal feelings, it follows that he must have based his strategy upon the hypothesis that the 'independent opposition' of 1885 was still possible in 1890. This was the hypothesis which he spent the rest of his life trying to prove. From the start, however, it was extremely unlikely that he would be able to carry the senior members of his party with him. To men on the spot like Healy and Sexton, or to Dillon and O'Brien in America, the brutal and abrupt reversal of the whole trend of nationalist policy, which was what the manifesto seemed to portend, was the signal that Parnell had become politically impossible.

To whom then did he seek to appeal? The answer which suggests itself—and which his subsequent career seems to bear out—is that he was already laying his plans for an appeal to the country over the heads of the party. It is important to remember that up to the time he issued the manifesto the news from Ireland had been predominantly favourable. He had received enthusiastic assurances of support from the Irish National League and from the *Freeman's Journal*, and he may well have felt that this represented a fund of loyalty upon which he could draw to an unlimited extent. And it was significant that when the party met on December 1 the main effort of his supporters was devoted to trying to secure an adjournment until members should have gone to Ireland and consulted their constituents. If the people remained loyal, therefore, the fact that the liberals and many of his own party would be alienated by the manifesto was, comparatively, of less importance, for it was not primarily directed at them. It was, rather, a key move in the campaign to transfer the struggle from London to Ireland, from a party mesmerised by liberal 'wire-pullers' to a country still deemed to be loyal to 'the chief' and whose deep-rooted suspicions of all English parties might yet again be whipped up into a frenzy.

Time alone would tell whether or not this long-term policy would be successful. The more immediate consequences of Parnell's action appeared to be utterly disastrous. It was little wonder that McCarthy was horrified when he heard the manifesto read out and declared at once that he disapproved of every word of it. It was, he said, offensive to the party's liberal allies and he objected particularly to the phrase 'English wolves'. Parnell refused absolutely to change this and, as there seemed nothing more to be said, William Redmond took the disconsolate vice-chairman home.[1] Upon the liberals the effect was no less devastating. Gladstone read the manifesto next day before breakfast and told his host, Stuart Rendel, that it was an astounding document. 'It was', Rendel recorded, 'a professed revelation of four modifications of home rule, said to have been definitely proposed by him to Parnell at Hawarden. The singular thing was that Parnell had utterly mis-stated every one.'[2] Representatives of the press soon gathered and Gladstone settled down to write a detailed denial of Parnell's assertions. The inevitable Morley appeared and Harcourt also looked over the letter of denial before it was sent off. 'I told you so, I told you so', he could not refrain from saying.[3]

In his version of the conversations Gladstone, while traversing Parnell's statements in detail, was at pains to emphasise that all that had passed between them had been suggestions for discussion—there had been no proposals. 'The conversation between us', he wrote, 'was strictly confidential and in my

[1] R. B. O'Brien, *Parnell*, ii. 266–7; T. P. O'Connor, *Memoirs of an old parliamentarian*, ii. 216.

[2] F. E. Hamer (ed.), *The personal papers of Lord Rendel*, p. 75, from a note made by Rendel the same day.

[3] Ibid., p. 76. Before giving his letter to the news agencies, Gladstone allowed E. T. Cook of the *Pall Mall Gazette* and Professor J. Stuart of *The Star* to see it. In his diary of that day Cook wrote that as Gladstone came up to speak to him he 'looked very brisk and flowing over with a kind of battle glee' (J. Saxon Mills, *Sir Edward Cook*, pp. 110–1).

judgment, and as I understood in that of Mr Parnell, to publish even a true account of it is to break the seal of confidence which alone renders political co-operation possible.'[1] Morley was equally emphatic in his declarations, taking special care to deny that he had said either that a liberal government would do nothing by direct action for the evicted tenants, or that it would be impossible for an Irish parliament to do anything. On Morley, indeed, this latest turn of events had had a most depressing effect, for he had had a high opinion of Parnell. 'His conduct', he wrote to Spencer, 'in repeating confidential talk from Mr G.'s dinner-table and from mine reveals an infamy of character which I had never suspected.'[2] Harcourt, by contrast, though angered by the manifesto, had always had fewer illusions about the Irish leader and his wrath was mingled with relief. 'The blackguardism of the man is now patent to the world', he wrote to his wife on the day the manifesto appeared. And he added: 'I feel some satisfaction in remembering that I have never shaken hands with him.'[3] Even the political consequences, he considered, might not turn out to be wholly disastrous. As he wrote to Spencer: 'It is well we should have found out in time what sort of man we had to deal with in case the responsibility for action had ever devolved on us. We may have better men to deal with hereafter, we can't have worse ... what will be the future of the nationalist party is dark enough, but it is plain that we have saved the English liberal party, which was the paramount consideration. My own belief is that Mr G. is stronger to-day in Great Britain than he was before the row.'[4]

(3)

The English reaction to the manifesto was easy enough to predict. From the point of view of the balance of power within the Irish party, the reaction of the delegates in America was more immediately important. It will be remembered that these delegates—with the exception of T. D. Sullivan—had cabled

[1] *The Times*, 1 Dec. 1890. A letter from Morley appeared in the same issue.
[2] Spencer Papers, John Morley to Earl Spencer, 1 Dec. 1890.
[3] Gardiner, *Life of Harcourt*, ii. 87.
[4] Spencer Papers, Sir W. Harcourt to Earl Spencer, 1 Dec. 1890. He wrote in similar terms to John Morley a week later (Gardiner, *Life of Harcourt*, ii. 89).

their support of Parnell to the Leinster Hall meeting. Subsequent events—and particularly the news of Gladstone's letter, which they saw in the papers on November 26—began to suggest to some of them that they might have been too precipitate. According to Harrington, Dillon's view of the situation was considerably changed by the Gladstone letter.[1] On the same day that they learnt of the letter T. P. Gill heard from Dr Kenny and J. J. Clancy that it had not been before the party when it met on November 25 and that the position was most serious.[2] There followed frantic cabling between the members of the delegation, dispersed as they were among several American cities. The outcome was that they agreed to meet at Cincinnati to decide what they ought to do.[3] From Harrington's diary we can deduce that the first faint division between himself and his colleagues was beginning to appear. He travelled with Dillon to the rendezvous and they talked of little but the crisis. Harrington, under pressure, admitted that while he would be prepared to join the others in a private expression of opinion to Parnell that he should retire temporarily, nothing would induce him to put any public pressure upon him.[4] At Cincinnati they found more cables awaiting them, including one from Parnell urging them to suspend judgment until they had seen his manifesto. Perhaps even more regarded was one from Sexton and Healy which ran:

Large majority including foremost members will vote resignation, otherwise general election lost, campaigners ruined, dissolution inevitable if Parnell maintained. Envoys supporting majority means practical unanimity.[5]

Almost immediately Harrington found himself drawn into argument with his colleagues. Sullivan, he says, 'was only too glad' of an opportunity for getting rid of Parnell. O'Brien too, with whom he had a heated exchange, was all for immediate

[1] Harrington Papers (N.L.I., MS 2195), 'Diary', 26 Nov. 1890.
[2] Gill Papers, cable from Kenny and Clancy to Gill, 26 Nov. 1890.
[3] Ibid., cables from William O'Brien to Gill, and from Dillon and Harrington to O'Brien, 26 Nov. 1890; Dillon Papers, cable from Gill to Dillon, 26 Nov. 1890; *F.J.*, 27 Nov. 1890.
[4] Harrington Papers (N.L.I., MS 2195), 'Diary', 27 Nov. 1890.
[5] Ibid., 28 Nov. 1890; Gill Papers, cable from Parnell to Dillon and O'Brien, 28 Nov. 1890, and from Healy and Sexton to ?, 27 Nov. 1890.

action, but Dillon intervened and persuaded the other four delegates to agree to a private wire being sent to Parnell urging him to retire in favour of McCarthy. This, it appears, was signed by all except Harrington.[1]

Next day the manifesto was before them and upon five out of the six delegates the effect was catastrophic. They united in condemning it as a breach of faith which would make it impossible for Gladstone ever to work with Parnell in the future, and both Dillon and O'Brien declared at once that on no account would they serve under him again. Harrington now found the gulf opening before his feet, and his distress is movingly recorded in his diary.[2] Anxiously they discussed the position and eventually decided to send a counter-manifesto announcing their break with Parnell. As a preliminary move they despatched a cable home which was signed by all save Harrington and which stated that they had read the manifesto with the deepest pain. 'It convinced us that Mr Parnell's continued leadership is impossible.'[3] That day they travelled to Chicago and it was from there that on Sunday November 30 they launched their counter-manifesto. They began by explaining that their decision to break with Parnell had been forced on them by the document which he himself had produced in his own justification. They were, they said, repelled by 'the method in which, ignoring the origin of the present calamitous situation, Mr Parnell endeavours to fasten responsibility for it upon Mr Gladstone and Mr Morley . . .' It was true that violent attacks had been made upon Parnell, but his own language in his manifesto had been 'lamentable'. It was nonsense, they declared, to say that Gladstone's letter was an attempt to dictate to the Irish party, for the very basis of the alliance with the liberals was that the latter should adopt the programme to obtain which the Irish party had been formed. The implication was clear— in the eyes of the American delegates, so long as the liberals held

---

[1] Harrington Papers (N.L.I., MS 2195), 'Diary', 28 Nov. 1890; Gill Papers, copy of cable to Parnell, 28 Nov. 1890. The entry in Harrington's diary says that the retirement was to be 'temporary', but this word does not appear in the copy of the cable in the Gill Papers.

[2] Harrington Papers (N.L.I., MS 2195), 'Diary', 29 Nov. 1890. But privately he noted that he still felt that Parnell's giving way voluntarily 'would on the whole be the best way out of the difficulty'.

[3] *The Times*, 1 Dec. 1890.

to this programme, the alliance was an honourable one and involved no subservience. And they ended on a note uncompromising enough to satisfy even the most extreme of Parnell's opponents. 'Mr Parnell', they wrote, 'has entered upon a rash and fatal path, upon which every consideration of Ireland's safety, as well as of our own personal honour, forbids us absolutely to follow him.'[1] Harrington, for his part, also broke silence on that melancholy Sunday and gave an interview to three pressmen who were waiting for him outside his bedroom door. He took what was already becoming the orthodox Parnellite line—that the unity and independence of the party mattered above everything else and that these both depended upon Parnell continuing to lead it.[2]

There can be no doubt that the outspoken declaration against him by all but one of the American delegates was one of the most serious reverses Parnell had yet suffered. Given the prestige of Dillon and O'Brien, and it stood far higher than that of any other of Parnell's lieutenants, their repudiation of him, apart from any effect it might have upon the waverers, was exactly the cue which the leaders of the opposition needed. Now they could mass their forces for Parnell's overthrow without the fear that in doing so they would find themselves isolated from the men whose names carried the greatest weight in the country. Later events were to show that for Dillon and O'Brien rejection of Parnell did not necessarily mean acceptance of everything his enemies might do or say, but this does not alter the fact that at the crucial moment—on the eve of the party meeting—those enemies had received an invaluable reinforcement. They might split the party by attacking Parnell, but with Dillon and O'Brien to all appearances on their side, they had good reason for thinking that when the great divide came all that would be left to Parnell would be a deluded and insignificant minority.

But even apart from this there were signs that a force more

[1] *F.J.*, 1 Dec. 1890.

[2] Harrington Papers (N.L.I., MS 2195), 'Diary', 30 Nov. 1890. The report of the interview is in a newspaper-cutting pinned to a page of the diary. It is from an American paper (unnamed) and bears the date Chicago, 30 Nov. 1890. In the course of the interview, referring to the divorce, Harrington asserted that under other conditions a better defence might have been made against the charges.

powerful than any that Dillon and O'Brien could command was to be thrown decisively into the scale against Parnell. On the day Gladstone's letter became common knowledge— November 26—W. M. Murphy, a Dublin business-man who in the party was usually aligned with the Healy-Sullivan group, wrote to Archbishop Walsh pointing out that the interval between then and the party meeting on Monday would be used by Parnell to strengthen his hands and that his opponents 'should get some support from home in this crisis'.[1] The archbishop, however, was far too skilful a diplomatist to charge blindly into the fray and give Parnell an opportunity to raise the cry of episcopal interference. On the contrary, virtually ignoring Murphy's plea, the statement he issued to the press on November 28 was extremely guarded, though it did contain a veiled hint to the party to watch what they were about on December 1; for the decision then taken, he said, might put upon the bishops 'the duty of considering whether, or how far, it will be in our power to continue in future to place in the Irish parliamentary party that confidence which, as a body, we felt justified in placing in it in the past'.[2] Nonetheless, the last paragraph of his statement reminded his readers of 'certain events of not very remote occurrence' (the Pigott forgeries) and suggested that they were not yet in a position to form a final judgment on the divorce case.

Publicly, therefore, the archbishop still held his hand. Privately, however, he was beginning to move. Writing that same day to Cardinal Manning, he mentioned that he had called a meeting of the standing committee of the Irish bishops for December 3. This, as he pointed out, could give no colour to any charge that the bishops would be directly influencing the party in its deliberations, but of course the fact that the meeting had been called would be bound to have a strong effect. 'We cause no embarrassment by pressure. But we make it known that after their decisive act we meet to see how it affects us and our priests and people.'[3]

It was later to be held against the bishops by the Parnellites that they delayed so long before giving any public indication of

[1] Walsh, *William J. Walsh*, p. 413.
[2] Ibid, p. 414; *F.J.*, 29 Nov. 1890.
[3] Leslie, *Manning*, p. 438.

their views.[1] Looking back upon the crisis in longer perspective, we can see that their cautious policy was a wise one. From their point of view, the best solution of the whole tangle would have been for Parnell to have retired voluntarily at the very outset, and it was certainly not for them to increase his difficulties. Failing a voluntary retirement, the next best solution would have been for the party to have come to a decision without any outside intervention. But Gladstone's letter had of course constituted just such an intervention and touched off a whole chain of reactions. And when Parnell's manifesto appeared as a culmination of that chain, silence was no longer a virtue but a danger. Accordingly, Archbishops Croke and Walsh agreed speedily upon joint action. The former sent a telegram (intended for publication) to Justin McCarthy which left no doubt about his views. 'All sorry for Parnell', it began, and continued, 'but still in God's name let him retire quietly and with good grace from the leadership.' If he did not do so, Dr Croke prophesied all manner of ruin, including the possible break-up of the party, the crushing of the evicted tenants and the indefinite postponement of home rule.[2]

Archbishop Walsh's intervention took the form of an interview given to the Central News Agency. He explained that he had so far withheld comment because of the assurance Parnell had given Davitt that his reputation would be unsullied by the divorce proceedings. Parnell's continued silence seemed to shatter that assurance. Then followed the significant part of his statement:

. . . if the Irish leader would not, or could not, give a public assurance that his honour was still unsullied, the party that takes him or retains him as its leader can no longer count on the support of the bishops of Ireland. In speaking as I have spoken, I confine myself almost exclusively to the moral aspect of the case. If Mr Parnell can set himself right I raise no question as to the probable political results of yesterday's political manifesto. That is a political matter and I leave it to be dealt with by those who are the accredited representatives of the Irish people in the political affairs of the country. But . . . I cannot but look upon the issuing of that document as an act

[1] E.g. Parnell's speech at Limerick, and Archbishop Walsh's rejoinder (*F.J.*, 12 and 13 Jan. 1891).
[2] *F.J.*, 1 Dec. 1890; Walsh, *William J. Walsh*, p. 416.

of political suicide. It will bring disaster upon Ireland unless those whose duty it is to guard her interests are now faithful to their trust.[1]

This by itself would certainly have had a powerful influence upon many in the Irish party. But that same day, to make assurance doubly sure, he wrote in the most unequivocal terms to T. M. Healy. 'The leadership, I take it, is practically vacant. If there was any doubt, or room for doubt, on that point up to this, there will, I trust, be none to-morrow.' He added that Healy might make any use he wished of the letter, short of publishing it.[2]

Such then was the position after a fortnight of the most extraordinary ups and downs of fortune. As the crisis passed through each successive phase it seemed to become only more complex and the hope of reconciliation more distant. With a breathtaking speed and completeness the familiar landmarks of political life had been obliterated and it was impossible to tell what the end would be. The forces combined against the Irish leader were formidable, but his name and personality, however discredited in some circles, still counted for much, and his opponents were far from under-estimating the importance of the Parnell legend. But had the legend survived the hammer-blows of the last fortnight? Could he even at this late hour exert his old spell and recall his party to their accustomed docility? To these questions the events of the next few days were to provide a dramatic answer.

---

[1] *F.J.*, 1 Dec. 1890. [2] Walsh, *William J. Walsh*, p. 416.

V

COMMITTEE ROOM FIFTEEN

(1)

WHEN THE IRISH parliamentary party assembled in Committee Room Fifteen at noon on Monday, December 1, Parnell's position, though not hopeless, was certainly serious. To all appearances his manifesto had fallen flat and had served not merely to widen the breach with the liberals, but to bring into the open against him powerful opponents such as Dillon, O'Brien and the two archbishops. Though no vote had yet been taken by the party, it was already clear that there was a very strong group working actively against his continuance as leader, and even T. M. Healy, by no means prejudiced in Parnell's favour, was taken aback at the bitterness he found in some quarters when he arrived in London.[1] On the other hand, Parnell could be sure of the devotion of a considerable number of followers (though precisely how many was still in doubt) and he could count upon the support of the major nationalist newspaper, the *Freeman's Journal*, even if, as it eventually turned out, the other important paper, *United Ireland*, was for a time unreliable. Again, although it was impossible to tell whether in the country at large the habit of loyalty to 'the chief' would be able to withstand the shocks of the past fortnight, the indications were that the National League would be on his side.[2]

[1] Healy, *Letters and leaders*, i. 327, letter to his wife, 28 Nov. 1890.
[2] Many of the telegrams read to the party at the meeting of December 1

From Parnell's point of view, therefore, the best strategy would be to divert the party from a direct attack upon his leadership until he could fight in more favourable circumstances. This meant, in effect, until he could transfer the struggle from London, with adverse liberal influences ever present, to Dublin or to Ireland at large where he might hope to appeal in broad and simple terms to the emotions of his hearers. His antagonists, once they had made up their minds that they would not serve under him again, naturally wanted to bring matters to a decision as quickly as possible. The longer the dispute continued the heavier the strain upon the liberal alliance and the greater the temptation to the tories to take advantage of their opponents' embarrassment by a snap dissolution of parliament.

The arena in which this struggle was fought out was a spacious oak-panelled room looking out across the Thames from an upper floor of the house of commons. In the centre was a large horse-shoe shaped table. Parnell sat at its head with Justin McCarthy on his right and Henry Campbell on his left. Beyond McCarthy were his son, Justin Huntly McCarthy, Thomas Sexton, T. M. Healy and several others who were to oppose Parnell, though sitting amongst them was J. J. O'Kelly, one of his strongest supporters. On Parnell's left, beyond Campbell, was a group of prominent 'Parnellites' including the old fenian, John O'Connor, Edward Harrington of the *Kerry Sentinel* and J. J. Clancy, prominent in the Irish Press Agency. Further down the table opponents and followers of Parnell were mingled, as they were at other tables scattered round the room, except in one corner by a window where some of his most implacable enemies were grouped—among them John Barry, another old fenian, and Arthur O'Connor.[1]

The only reporters allowed to attend the debates were the team provided by the *Freeman's Journal*. There were five of them

were from branches of the National League and were enthusiastically in favour of Parnell (*F.J.*, 2 Dec. 1890; *The Times: the Parnellite split*, p. 35). It was Healy's view that the branches were being 'worked' against Parnell's opponents by D. J. Hishon and Dr J. E. Kenny (Healy, *Letters and leaders*, i. 332, letter to his wife, 2 Dec. 1890). He voiced this opinion later in the debate, but withdrew it when vehemently contradicted by Dr Kenny (*F.J.*, 5 Dec. 1890). In fact the National League remained Parnellite throughout the split, though naturally it lost many of its members.

[1] M. Macdonagh, *The home rule movement*, pp. 207-8; *F.J.*, 3 Dec. 1890.

under the direction of J. M. Tuohy and considering that the proceedings lasted on occasion for ten or eleven hours, with only short adjournments for meals, their achievement was a remarkable one and was recognised as such by their fellow journalists.[1] During the debates T. M. Healy made a complaint that the reports as they appeared in the *Freeman's Journal* were 'cooked' in favour of Parnell and this was later repeated by Donal Sullivan, who was one of the secretaries of the party and who, in November 1891, published an account of the proceedings in Committee Room Fifteen.[2] It is of course true that the editorial policy of the *Freeman's Journal* was favourable to Parnell, but that this bias extended to the reporting of the debates has yet to be proved. At any rate it is noteworthy that the party itself accepted the *Freeman's Journal* day-to-day accounts as the official reports, for the minutes, normally written in a secretary's hand, consist, from the afternoon of December 1 to the evening of December 6 inclusive, entirely of cuttings from the *Freeman's Journal*.[3] Moreover, it is easy to check whether or not the reports were censored before being printed because, as the debates proceeded, the *Freeman's Journal* staff took it in turn to dictate their shorthand notes to reporters of the *Press Association* who waited in the corridor outside. In this way many other newspapers were able to describe fully what went on in Committee Room Fifteen.[4] Thus, even if the editorial staff of the *Freeman's Journal* had been tempted to falsify the reports for the sake of influencing opinion in Ireland, it would be simple to detect the falsifications from other newspaper accounts. But in fact, comparing the *Freeman's Journal* with *The Times*, which had no reason to love Parnell, and the liberal *Daily News*, which through Justin McCarthy had 'anti-Parnellite' connections, the reports, apart from a few verbal differences and the natural tendencies of the English newspapers to abbreviate some of the less important speeches, are in all essentials alike. The same, indeed, may be said of Donal Sullivan's version which, though

[1] M. Macdonagh, *The home rule movement*, p. 209, *n*. Their names were Thomas Harrington, Charles Ryan, Michael Macdonagh, Ernest Hobson and Timothy O'Riordan.

[2] *F.J.*, 4 Dec. 1890; *National Press*, 27 Nov. 1891.

[3] Dillon Papers, 'Minutes of the Irish parliamentary party', 1 to 6 Dec. 1890.

[4] M. Macdonagh, *The home rule movement*, pp. 208–9.

it too shortens some of the speeches and differs in some details from the reports in the *Freeman's Journal*, corresponds closely with those reports on the major issues.[1]

When the proceedings began on December 1, seventy-three of the eighty-five members of the party were present.[2] For the first hour the meeting was conducted in private and the party minutes indicate that the time was mainly taken up by the reading of telegrams from various sources—including the initial declaration against Parnell by five out of the six party members then in America—and by a discussion as to whether or not the press should be admitted. After having decided to allow the *Freeman's Journal* reporters to attend, the meeting adjourned for lunch.[3] When they resumed there was more reading of messages for and against Parnell and this provoked a sharp argument as to whether or not to read the second and more explicit declaration against Parnell by their colleagues on the American mission, which was in some of the morning papers, though not in all, and which had arrived so recently that Justin McCarthy, to whom it was addressed, had not had time to go home and see if the original was there. The reading of it was

[1] Sullivan's account first appeared in the *National Press* in ten instalments between 21 Nov. and 5 Dec. 1891; it was subsequently published as a booklet entitled *The story of room fifteen*.

[2] Their names were: W. Abraham, J. Barry, A. Blane, G. Byrne, H. Campbell, P. A. Chance, J. J. Clancy, A. Commins, T. J. Condon, M. Conway, W. J. Corbet, J. Cox, D. Crilly, J. Dalton, J. Deasy, T. A. Dickson, Sir T. Esmonde, J. Finucane, Dr J. G. Fitzgerald, J. C. Flynn, P. J. Foley, Dr J. Fox, E. Harrington, H. Harrison, L. P. Hayden, M. Healy, T. M. Healy, J. Jordan, Dr J. E. Kenny, M. J. Kenny, D. Kilbride, E. F. V. Knox, W. J. Lane, E. Leamy, M. McCartan, J. McCarthy, J. H. McCarthy, P. Macdonald, W. A. Macdonald, Sir J. M'Kenna, J. G. S. MacNeill, J. R. Maguire, P. Mahony, B. C. Molloy, J. Morrogh, W. M. Murphy, J. Nolan, Col. J. P. Nolan, J. F. X. O'Brien, P. J. O'Brien, A. O'Connor, J. O'Connor, T. O'Hanlon, F. A. O'Keefe, J. J. O'Kelly, C. S. Parnell, J. Pinkerton, P. J. Power, R. Power, T. Quinn, J. E. Redmond, W. H. K. Redmond, W. J. Reynolds, J. Roche, T. Sexton, J. D. Sheehan, D. Sheehy, E. Sheil, J. Stack, D. Sullivan, Dr C. Tanner, J. Tuite, A. Webb.

The following were absent: J. Dillon, T. P. Gill, T. Harrington, W. O'Brien, T. P. O'Connor, T. D. Sullivan (all in America); J. L. Carew, J. Gilhooly, R. Lalor, J. Leahy and Col. the O'Gorman Mahon (all ill); and P. O'Brien in prison. One seat—North Kilkenny—was vacant.

[3] Dillon Papers, 'Minutes of the Irish parliamentary party', 1 Dec. 1890. From lunch-time onwards the record in the minute-book consists of the *Freeman's Journal* reports of the debates.

postponed until the next day and the meeting turned to consider questions of procedure. Parnell maintained that this was
an adjourned meeting from the previous Wednesday and that
they still had before them John Barry's motion 'that a full
meeting of the party be held on Friday to give Mr. Parnell an
opportunity of re-considering his position'. Since this motion
had been proposed on Wednesday, November 26, the Friday to
which it referred was clearly intended to be November 28.
Parnell, however, held that the Friday intended was Friday,
December 5. Barry thereupon offered to withdraw his resolution,
but Parnell would not allow this, though he was prepared to
consider amendments. Two were forthcoming. One was from
Colonel J. P. Nolan who moved that the question of the chairmanship be postponed until members had had an opportunity
of ascertaining in person the views of their constituents and
until the party could meet in Dublin. The other, which had
been planned the day before in Arthur O'Connor's rooms, was
put forward by William Abraham (one of the handful of
protestants in the party) and was simply to the effect that
Parnell's chairmanship of the party be now terminated.[1]
Parnell, amid some laughter and applause, ruled that the latter
was out of order and the debate proceeded on the basis of
Colonel Nolan's amendment.[2]

(2)

These preliminary exchanges were enough to show that
Parnell—though he claimed to be following the standing orders
of the house of commons, as was customary at meetings of the
Irish party—was going to use his powers as chairman to the full.
At the outset, however, the dangers of this were not apparent.
There was a good case for an exhaustive survey of the situation
before any vital decision was taken and in fact for two days the
debate was carried on at a high level with considerable dignity
and restraint.[3]
Of the many speeches that were made during those two days,
the opening ones on each side were the most important. After

---

[1] Healy, *Letters and leaders*, i. 328–9, letter to his wife, 30 Nov. 1890; Donal
Sullivan, 'The story of room fifteen', in *National Press*, 25 Nov. 1891.
[2] *The Times: the Parnellite split*, p. 40.   [3] *F.J.*, 2 and 3 Dec. 1890.

Colonel Nolan had briefly proposed his amendment and Sir Joseph M'Kenna had seconded it, Thomas Sexton rose to speak. What he had to say might be a major factor in determining the waverers, for his speech in support of Parnell the previous Tuesday had helped to determine the party's attitude and had even, in the opinion of some, strengthened Parnell's will to remain at the head of the party.[1] For him, it soon appeared, a rapid decision was urgent, chiefly on the grounds that liberal members of parliament were finding it difficult to meet their constituents and that unless the Irish party faced its responsibility the alliance with 'the liberal democracy of Great Britain' might be broken up. Moreover, the fear of a tory counter-stroke overshadowed his mind. 'How if a dissolution finds us with the question undetermined, with England excited, with large classes of persons enraged by the present condition of affairs, with our own country torn into wars and factions?' Much of his speech was devoted to condemning Parnell's manifesto and he indignantly denied that any section of the Irish party was subservient to English radicals such as Labouchere and Stuart.[2] The movement now on foot to secure Parnell's retirement from the chair was no hole-and-corner conspiracy, but arose amongst men who had shared Parnell's burden from the early days, men whose advice he had sought in the past, men who had held the party together 'at times when you were not in their midst'. As for the integrity of the party, which Parnell had asserted had been undermined: 'Integrity is not unconditional acceptance of the views of any man. Independence is not submission to the will of any man. We are your colleagues, Mr Parnell, but we are not your slaves.' At the end of his long and studiously moderate speech Sexton spoke in moving terms of his affection for his leader and of his regret at having to ask him to retire 'for a period at least' from the leadership.[3]

He was followed by John Redmond who, like Sexton, was one of the most polished orators of the party. He had still to win his

[1] Healy, *Letters and leaders*, i. 322–3, D. Sullivan to Healy, 25 Nov. 1890.

[2] Henry Labouchere, M.P., proprietor of the journal *Truth*, and Professor J. Stuart, M.P., editor of *The Star*. Parnell interrupted Sexton's speech to single them out by name.

[3] *F.J.*, 2 Dec. 1890; M. Macdonagh, *The home rule movement*, pp. 209–10.

main reputation, but his speeches in Committee Room Fifteen
and after established him as one of the most formidable of
Parnell's supporters and probably helped to prepare the way
for his ultimate succession to the leadership of the Parnellite
wing after Parnell's death. At the outset he seized upon an
assertion that Sexton had made during his speech—that the
decision as to the chairmanship was a matter of party organisation and that there was no need for an appeal to the constituencies. Redmond had no difficulty in demonstrating the hollow-
ness of this argument.[1] The question at issue in reality was the
leadership of 'the Irish race throughout the world' and it was,
he said, 'heart-breaking' that such a question should be discussed in the context of the liberal alliance. Sexton had attached
the greatest importance to that alliance and had in effect asked
the party to sacrifice Parnell to preserve it. But, said Redmond,
'. . . where we are asked to sell our own leader to preserve an
alliance, it seems to me that we are bound to inquire into what
we are getting for the price we are paying'. Here, Parnell interjected: 'Don't sell me for nothing. If you get my value, you
may change me to-morrow.' Redmond went on to develop what
later became the stock theme of Parnellite orators all over the
country—that to sacrifice Parnell to save the liberal alliance
was to sacrifice the independence of the Irish party. And was
the alliance worth-while after all? If what Parnell had written
in his manifesto was true—and he, Redmond, was prepared to
take Parnell's recollection of the Hawarden interview as more
accurate than Gladstone's—then the home rule bill the liberals
would produce would be 'a sham and a fraud on the nationalist
aspirations'. And, he added, if the party lost its independence
its American supplies would be cut off and the evicted tenants
would be endangered. After expressing the hope that the crisis
would not bring 'the terrible curse of disunion' upon the
country, he sat down.[2] His speech had been powerful, eloquent
and transparently sincere and was interrupted many times by
loud applause.

[1] Redmond himself undertook that if the party came to a decision hostile
to his view then, before supporting Parnell further, he would resign his seat
and consult the wishes of his constituents. He did not in fact do this, but
when Parnell died he resigned his own seat in order to contest his dead
leader's seat in Cork.

[2] *F.J.*, 2 Dec. 1890.

He was followed at once by T. M. Healy, the most brilliant debater in the party, the man with the quickest and most bitter tongue and the only survivor (now that Biggar was dead) of the partnership which had headed the revolt of February 1886. When Healy rose to speak, although his intimates knew what he felt, he had made no important public utterance since his speech in support of Parnell at Leinster Hall nearly a fortnight previously. He was now faced with the need to reconcile that speech with a demand that Parnell should retire, and was at the same time still suffering from the after-effects of typhoid.[1] He had already made up his mind that Parnell must go and his natural nervous irritability at having to make a difficult speech was probably increased by his belief that on his arrival in London Parnell had deliberately cut him.[2] He began moderately and well. He opposed the motion for delay because he doubted if delay would allow them to know more of Parnell's mind than they already knew from his manifesto. As for adjourning to Dublin—Dublin had been so neglected in the past as a place for meetings of the party that the proposal to meet there now seemed a 'somewhat novel proposition'. 'The ends are judgment—not that judgment should be given in a particular locality.'

He passed on to take up the charge that in asking Parnell to resign they would be said to be yielding to English clamour. He pointed out that when the home rule bill of 1886 was introduced, the Irish party abated some of their demands 'to conciliate English opinion'. That bill had not given the Irish parliament control of the police and the judiciary and it had, originally at least, contemplated the total exclusion of *all* the Irish members from Westminster.[3] Yet, though in 1886 they all (including Parnell) accepted such proposals as adequate, now in 1890 Parnell declared himself horrified at Gladstone's treatment of these same topics in their conversations at Hawarden. This, however, had not prevented him from going straight to

[1] Healy, *Letters and leaders*, i. 330. Dr J. E. Kenny, a fiery Parnellite, who looked after Healy in his illness, later told Dillon that Healy was only half-recovered when he came to London (Dillon Papers, J. E. Kenny to Dillon, 13 Dec. 1890).

[2] Healy, *Letters and leaders*, i. 324.

[3] Though on 10 May 1886 Gladstone offered to reconsider this, it was then too late (Hammond, *Gladstone and the Irish nation*, pp. 512–4, 525–31).

Liverpool and speaking enthusiastically of Gladstone despite 'the terrible secrets entrusted to him at Hawarden', secrets which he had not imparted to his colleagues. So far so good. Healy had clearly and forcefully made his point that Parnell was being inconsistent. Unfortunately, but characteristically, he yielded to the temptation to go just that one step further which was certain to provoke his antagonist. Asking if Gladstone had really abandoned his position of 1886, he said, '. . . if the Hawarden interview be the capital matter on which Mr Parnell bases himself in his manifesto, why, I say, were these false words uttered at Liverpool? Either Mr Parnell at Liverpool was false, or his manifesto was false'.

Parnell at once intervened. 'I will not stand an accusation of falsehood from Timothy Healy', he said, 'and I call upon him to withdraw.'

Out of respect to the chair Healy did withdraw the offending remark and turned to explain his own attitude in the crisis. He had gone to Leinster Hall and pronounced for Parnell 'in the face of English clamour'. Why did he change afterwards? He did not change 'until it was shown that he (Parnell) had left himself no foothold upon which he could help Ireland through the medium of the English people'. Why, asked Healy rhetorically, did he defer to English opinion, why did they all do so in 1886? His answer is an important insight into how he and others like him regarded this whole problem and it is worth quoting at length:

We were willing to do so because we were led by Charles Stewart Parnell, and he was able so to abate the passion and the recollection of wrong and of centuries of suffering on the part of Ireland as to insure this acceptance, almost without an exception, by every body of representatives of the Irish nation. Ireland possessed neither armies nor fleets. Having neither armies nor fleets we are bound to rely upon constitutional and parliamentary methods. There is no hope, there was no hope, for Ireland until Mr Parnell succeeded in obtaining from Mr Gladstone the promise of a home rule settlement. He did it in consultation with English opinion, abating many of our demands, forgetting much of our wrongs and sufferings, and when we to-day calculate from the expression of English opinion that, not in units or in tens of thousands, but millions, the voters of the liberal party have declared themselves against Mr Parnell and declared that the result of the mischief which will result to Ireland by his continuance in the leadership must be fatal to the hopes of our country, I found myself upon the hard necessities of the case, and while I would rather, if I could, prevent this cataclysm in the party . . . I say that the necessities of Ireland are paramount.

The best thing Parnell could have done, said Healy in conclusion, would have been to retire, even if only temporarily, when the party had met on the previous Tuesday. Or, at the least, why did he not then take the party into his confidence and reveal what he had to say about Gladstone's attitude at Hawarden? Why were several days allowed to pass 'and then, not the party, but the entire world, learn of this event for the first time'? They had maintained Parnell for many years, not only on account of his services but because of the great value of his name. But let them now keep him as leader and of what value would his name be? 'I say to Mr Parnell, his power is gone. He derived that power from the people. We are the representatives of the people.' For his part, Healy would vote for retirement.[1]

It was an extremely able speech, logical, well-argued, fastening unerringly upon the weak points in Parnell's case. And as if he realised that this was likely to be the most serious indictment he would have to face, Parnell himself rose to speak next. Although only three speeches had so far been delivered, the main lines of conflict had already been drawn. It was plain that Parnell's opponents were going to concentrate upon the argument that they were having to choose between their leader and home rule. Hitherto they had discussed the matter on the political rather than the moral level and had sedulously avoided the divorce case. For them, the decisive events were Gladstone's letter to John Morley and Parnell's manifesto which, taken together, made it virtually impossible that Parnell could ever again work with the liberal party. And, as both Sexton and Healy made clear, the maintenance of the liberal alliance was the key-stone of their entire policy. The Parnellite case, on the other hand—as Redmond stated it—was quite simply that the independence of the Irish party was the paramount consideration. If they got rid of Parnell now and the liberal party came back to power in the future, Gladstone would have the Irish party in the hollow of his hand—it would, Redmond had said, be 'a discredited and powerless tool of the liberal party'. As for

[1] *F.J.*, 2 Dec. 1890.

the conflict between Parnell's and Gladstone's recollections of the Hawarden conversations, it was of course a corollary of the principle of independent opposition that one must accept the Irish rather than the English leader's version.

This still left the further question unanswered, why Parnell did not take the party into his confidence when he found—if he found—Gladstone's assurances defective. It was to this question that Parnell in his speech primarily addressed himself. But first he delivered a broadside against Healy. 'Mr Healy has been trained in this warfare. Who trained him? Who saw his genius first?[1] Who telegraphed to him from America to come to him and gave him his first opportunity and chance?[2] Who afterwards got his first seat in parliament for him . . .? That Mr Healy should be here to-day to destroy me is due to myself.' Then, turning on his opponents at large, he castigated them for their performance at Leinster Hall. He had not asked Healy to second the resolution of support for him. He had not asked McCarthy to go over to Dublin and say he had secret information which would put a different complexion on hidden events. And where was Sexton at that time? 'Where were you all? Why did you encourage me to stand forward and maintain my leadership in the face of the world if you were not going to stand by me?' An observer of the scene has said that all through this passage he was labouring under deep emotion and struggling to keep his passion under control. It flared out once more, however, in an almost incoherent allusion to John Barry (though he did not mention him by name), 'the leader-killer who sharpens his poniard to stab me as he stabbed the old lion Isaac Butt, in the days gone by'.[3]

At last he came to deal with the question of the Hawarden conversations. He had not told the party about them, he said, because his interview with Gladstone was a confidential one, not to be communicated to any of his colleagues. 'My responsi-

[1] A possible answer might have been T. D. Sullivan, who brought Healy from an obscure clerkship in Newcastle-upon-Tyne to become a London parliamentary correspondent for *The Nation* (Healy, *Letters and leaders*, i. 56).

[2] The reference is to Parnell's American tour in 1880 (Healy, *Letters and leaders*, i. 79; R. B. O'Brien, *Parnell*, i. 205–6).

[3] It was John Barry who had taken the lead in replacing Butt by Parnell in the presidency of the Home Rule Confederation of Great Britain in 1877 (*F.J.*, 29 Aug. 1877).

bility', he continued, 'was enormous. Was I by a single stroke, without giving any time or opportunity to Mr Gladstone to consider his position, to denounce him on account of a half-completed programme?' The reason he had not exposed the Hawarden conversations in his Liverpool speech was because none of Gladstone's proposals had been definite or final and the principal one—concerning the future of the Irish members at Westminster—might be subject to further revision. To the eye of faith this might have seemed a convincing explanation, but to many in his audience it was scarcely likely to be satisfactory. Even if Parnell had in fact committed the elementary and most untypical error of binding himself to secrecy in such a vital matter, his story that Gladstone might undergo a change of heart and that therefore he said nothing to discourage him, did not agree well with the very precise, not to say abrupt, language the liberal leader was represented in the manifesto as having used. Furthermore, the timing of the manifesto was in itself enough to make it suspect, for there could hardly be any doubt that it had been provoked by Gladstone's letter to John Morley. Yet, though this was true, it was not the whole truth and events were to show before the week was out that the manifesto was less a counter to the Gladstone letter than a skilful attempt to divert attention away from it.

Some inkling of this Parnell allowed to appear towards the end of his speech. John Redmond had spoken earlier of an incident that had occurred during the week-end just past and Parnell now gave an expanded version of it. Admitting there was a difference of recollection between Gladstone and himself about their conversations, he had proposed to McCarthy that he, McCarthy, should obtain from Gladstone, Harcourt and John Morley letters declaring that in the event of the liberals returning to power a home rule bill would be proposed under which control of the police would be given to an Irish executive responsible to an Irish parliament; that effective power to settle the Irish land question would also be included in the bill; and that both these provisions would be regarded as vital. Before McCarthy went on this mission Parnell told him that if these concessions were made he would retire from public life. McCarthy had then gone to see Gladstone whose response had been entirely negative. The proposition had also been laid before Harcourt—who, as Parnell reminded his hearers, was probably the future leader of the liberal party—and Harcourt had replied that under no circumstances would he give any promises whatever to the Irish party.[1] The moral Parnell drew from this episode was simple—'there is not a single one of the lot to be trusted unless you trust yourselves'. And, after breaking very uncharacteristically into a quotation ('To thine own self be true') he ended on this note: 'If I am to leave you to-night I should like to leave you in security. I should like—and it is not an unfair thing for me to ask—that I should come within sight of the promised land.'[2]

He was followed by Justin McCarthy, anxious to explain and justify the part he had taken in these transactions. He confirmed that he had—very reluctantly—gone to Gladstone and Harcourt, but had not succeeded in seeing Morley. Gladstone had told him that Parnell was 'absolutely mistaken' in his account of the Hawarden interview and that they had parted in general agreement as to the basis of a home rule bill, though they differed about details. McCarthy then went on to say that Gladstone had stated that he could only negotiate with the elected leader of the party and therefore could not negotiate with him. Consequently he was unable to sign any document or give any message. As to Harcourt, he had not said what Parnell reported him as saying—that he would make no promise of any kind to any Irish member. But what he had said was that, as a result of the manifesto, 'he would not give me or anybody else any assurance in writing or by word of mouth that was to be brought in any way under the notice of Mr Parnell'.[3] And that was the whole story. Before concluding, McCarthy reproached Parnell for keeping the Hawarden conversations from the party and for making too light of his mistake. In doing

---

[1] The interview with Gladstone and Harcourt was on Sunday, November 30 (Spencer Papers, Sir W. Harcourt to Earl Spencer, 1 Dec. 1890; statement of John Redmond and letter of Justin McCarthy, *F.J.*, 15 and 16 Jan. 1891; Gardiner, *Life of Harcourt*, ii. 88).

[2] *F.J.*, 2 Dec. 1890; M. Macdonagh, *The home rule movement*, p. 212.

[3] Harcourt's version was that McCarthy had proposed that he, Gladstone and Morley should sign a letter binding themselves to certain terms proposed by Parnell, this letter to be kept an inviolable secret. 'I did not attach any importance to Mr Parnell's pledge of secrecy.' See his letter to the Press Association in *F.J.*, 3 Dec. 1890.

so, he extracted from Parnell the only admission of error he had yet made, when he said, with an ingenuousness which cannot have deceived many: 'I am perfectly willing to admit that I was to blame in that, but I am glad I have told it all now, before the mischief was done.' To which McCarthy rejoined: 'Speaking for myself, the whole transaction seems to me to have betrayed from the beginning a vital error of judgment!' ('Hear, hear', from Parnell).

There was no point in discussing further the question of the abortive negotiations after McCarthy had spoken, but that it should have been mentioned at all was interesting, because it revealed that the very day Parnell's manifesto was issued he had begun his attempt to manoeuvre the liberal party into a false position by placing on them the onus of having to refuse guarantees to the Irish party on subjects about which most Irishmen felt strongly. The manoeuvre had failed in the first endeavour, but its potentialities were far from exhausted and much more was to be heard of it in the days ahead.

Meanwhile the debate continued and as the hour grew later and the strain heavier tempers began to be frayed. One Parnellite, Edward Harrington, seemed determined to be provocative in the taunts he threw at the opposition. 'If I find men here to-night', he said, 'whom neither five-line whip, nor forty-line whip would bring to the house for a critical division, if I find such men here to-night ready to lap up the blood after the decapitation takes place, I am forced to give them credit for no very high motive.' Another of Parnell's followers, M. Conway, became involved in a futile altercation with Sexton, asserting that Sexton had told him when they were coming over on the boat together that he knew that Gladstone was about to issue a manifesto threatening to retire if Parnell were not thrown over by the Irish party. Knowing what we do of the history of Gladstone's letter, we can sympathise with Sexton's indignant reply that this was 'pure imagination, pure invention'. Next, Conway turned violently on Healy for the change in his attitude since the Leinster Hall meeting. Why did he not support Parnell now? 'Because', interjected Healy, 'he is useless for any purpose.' After some further speeches, Alexander Blane pointed out that Parnell had been in the chair for eleven hours. The adjournment was then moved and after a sharp clash between Parnell and Healy as to whether or not the motion had been properly put, they parted just before midnight, to meet again at noon the next day.

Nothing had been determined at the end of this long meeting except that the party was bitterly divided, that the voting might be close and that the fight would probably be long-drawn-out. However, even Healy, who had emerged as Parnell's most formidable opponent, considered that discussion was necessary and wrote that same night to Archbishop Walsh that it was only fair that everyone should have a chance of putting his views on record. As for himself: 'In my life I never spent so awful a time, and I am harassed body and soul.'[1] Writing to his wife, he admitted that Parnell's conduct in the chair had been dignified. 'Even in his reply to me, considering what I had said, there was nothing to complain of.'[2]

(3)

The second day's debate began with the reading from one of the morning papers of the full text of the second declaration against Parnell issued by all the Irish delegates in America except Timothy Harrington.[3] This gave rise to a long and sometimes acrimonious discussion as to which members of the party had been in communication with the delegates and it was not until the afternoon that the main debate was resumed. Once again it turned largely upon the kind of relationship which should exist with the liberal party. J. J. O'Kelly, one of the most important of Parnell's followers, put the point very forcibly that, important as the liberal alliance might be, the liberal power to give home rule was limited by the power of the house of lords to veto it. As for surrendering Parnell: 'The moment that you give away your chief for one reason under foreign pressure, you lay down a rule by which the political life of the next man who leads you is rendered insecure.' On the other hand, the opposite view was put by M. J. Kenny. It was all very well to talk of an independent Irish party, but an independent

[1] P. J. Walsh, *William J. Walsh*, p. 418.
[2] Healy, *Letters and leaders*, i. 331, letter to his wife, 1 Dec. 1890.
[3] Text in *F.J.*, 2 Dec. 1890; the second day's debate is reported in *F.J.*, 3 Dec. 1890.

Irish party in the house of commons could never of itself win home rule. 'You are bound to enter into an alliance with some English party before you can ever obtain home rule for Ireland.'

Always they came back to the same dilemma, the dilemma which had faced Parnell himself in 1885 and which had in effect ended his period of independent opposition. The choice of constitutional agitation as against revolutionary conspiracy had brought with it the necessity to manoeuvre between English parties at Westminster. And this sooner or later involved choosing between those parties. But once the conservatives had determined—as they had determined in 1886—that home rule was a threat to the empire and that the union must be maintained, nothing was left to the Irish party but an alliance with the liberals. The most striking thing about the debates in Committee Room Fifteen was that they showed that neither side had really learnt the lesson of the events of 1886. Parnell's opponents admitted that the liberal alliance was essential to them, but maintained that this did not affect the independence of the Irish party. In so far as the party remained a separate entity and its members continued to refrain from accepting place or office from either liberals or conservatives, this was true enough. But where they were mistaken was in confusing institutional independence with independence of strategy. What they failed to see was that though they might exist as a separate party with their own organisation, their freedom of action was inevitably limited by the hard fact that only the liberals could give them home rule.

This much, at least, could be said for them—that since 1886 they had realised that the liberal alliance *must* be cultivated, even if they had not perceived the full implications of that alliance. Parnell's supporters, on the other hand, seemed to have learnt nothing since 1886, and could not see that to cling to the policy of 'independent opposition' was to doom the party to sterility. Thus, the argument advanced near the end of the debate by Henry Harrison that Gladstone's action had cleared the way for the Irish party to resume its policy of holding the balance between liberals and conservatives, was fallacious because it assumed that—*on the issue of home rule*—there was any longer a balance to be held. Once the conservatives had turned their backs on the whole concept of home rule, the essential pre-condition for a successful policy of balance had automatically disappeared.

Not all the speakers concentrated on this fundamental problem, though the best of them never strayed very far from it. The only other theme of comparable importance was the bearing of the divorce case upon the crisis and it was noticeable that, although it had been avoided in the earlier speeches, several speakers referred to it on the second day.[1] Arthur O'Connor, J. F. X. O'Brien, T. A. Dickson and Jeremiah Jordan all spoke of it as having influenced their attitude, though Jordan was the only one who could claim to be thoroughly consistent, since he had made the divorce the ground of his solitary opposition to Parnell on the day of his re-election to the chair.[2] It is, however, fair to add that at least one other speaker, J. F. X. O'Brien, who considered that after the divorce-court proceedings Parnell's leadership was 'intolerable and a disgrace', would have opposed his re-election at the outset on those grounds had he not believed that Parnell would retire of his own accord.

Eventually, after more speeches which did little but cover the same ground over and over again the time came to vote on Colonel Nolan's amendment. It was late in the evening and the room, which had no gas or electricity, was only dimly lit by candles and oil-lamps placed here and there on the tables. Parnell rose to put the question. 'All in favour, say "aye".' Loud cries of 'aye' from his supporters. 'Those to the contrary, say "no".' Shouts of 'no'. 'I think the "ayes" have it', said Parnell. Amid ironic laughter this ruling was challenged and Parnell himself, holding a list of names, went through it alphabetically. At the end he announced that the noes were 44 and the ayes 29, so that the noes had it by a majority of 15. The declaration was received in silence and the meeting adjourned.[3]

---

[1] On the first day one of the protestant members—E. F. V. Knox—had referred to it in terms of deep disapproval (*F.J.*, 2 Dec. 1890). A further theme which deeply concerned many members was the effect of the controversy upon the fortunes of the evicted tenants. David Sheehy's speech on the first day was mainly devoted to this question, but in this he was exceptional. Most of the principal speakers were preoccupied—as they were bound to be —with the primary issue of Parnell and the liberal alliance.

[2] Healy, *Letters and leaders*, i. 322, Donal Sullivan to Healy, 25 Nov. 1890.

[3] M. Macdonagh, *The home rule movement*, pp. 214–5; *F.J.*, 3 Dec. 1890.

(4)

This vote, though everyone realised its significance as indicating the relative strength of the two groups, was far from decisive. Parnell, as his opponents were well aware, was determined to fight on and his resources were by no means exhausted.[1] The next day, Wednesday, the party spent an hour and a half in secret session and an impatient public had to wait until Friday morning before the events of Wednesday and Thursday were revealed. What had happened was that one of Parnell's supporters, J. J. Clancy, had put forward a proposal by which it seemed just possible that the unity of the party, the liberal alliance and Parnell's self-respect might all yet be saved. In introducing it he insisted that the crucial factor in the situation was Gladstone's letter of November 24. If it was true that it was this letter which had turned the scale in the minds of many members of the Irish party, it was essential that they should find out what was in Gladstone's mind in the matter of home rule. 'Mr Gladstone made the situation, he could end it.' If they could bring him to give satisfactory assurances on the two vital topics of the land and the police, then he, Clancy, had authority for saying that Parnell would retire from the leadership. He then read his amendment, which was as follows:

That in view of the difference of opinion that has arisen between Mr Gladstone and Mr Parnell as to the accuracy of Mr Parnell's recollection of the suggestions offered at Hawarden in reference to suggested changes in and departures from the home rule bill of 1886 on the subject of the control of the constabulary and the settlement of the land question, the whips be instructed to obtain from Mr Gladstone, Mr John Morley and Sir William Harcourt, for the information of the party, before any further consideration of the question, what their views are in relation to these two vital points.[2]

This amendment was read in the absence of Parnell. He was now sent for and while he was coming Sexton suggested that the proposition was so grave and weighty that they should adjourn

[1] Healy, *Letters and leaders*, i. 331–2, letter to his wife, 2 Dec. 1890. 'It is now evident that we shall have a big fight in the country afterwards.' That same evening a meeting of the National League in Dublin had asserted its faith in Parnell with the greatest enthusiasm (*The Times: the Parnellite split*, pp. 122–5; *F.J.*, 3 Dec. 1890).
[2] *F.J.*, 5 Dec. 1890.

until next day in order to consider it. When Parnell entered and took the chair, Sexton renewed his request for an adjournment, but also asked two pertinent questions. First, who was to pronounce on the adequacy of the liberal assurances—would Parnell allow a majority vote of the party to do so? And secondly, if they were given and found adequate would Parnell then retire voluntarily from the leadership of the party? When he sat down, Healy rose impulsively and speaking 'with strong emotion' (as the official report described the scene) said that if Parnell felt able to meet the party on these points he would be the first to call him back as leader of the Irish race 'at the very earliest moment possible, consonant with the liberties of his country'. After Sexton had spoken in like manner Parnell replied briefly that he too needed time for consideration. And so it was agreed to adjourn until Thursday.[1]

Looking back, it is difficult to see why this offer produced such a sense of relief, such a recrudescence of hope, amongst Parnell's opponents. They had Justin McCarthy's word for it that Gladstone would treat only with the accredited leader of the party. And they had Gladstone's declaration that if Parnell continued as leader, his own leadership of the liberal party would become 'almost a nullity'. Putting these two facts side by side, was it likely that the new manoeuvre would be any more successful than the old? But distance lends a clarity that was impossible to those who met in Committee Room Fifteen with the future of their entire movement still in the balance. The vote of the previous evening, though a victory for Parnell's opponents, was yet far from overwhelming. It behoved the leaders of the opposition to walk warily. Undeniably it was tempting to approach Gladstone, and if hard and fast promises could be got from him that would be a great gain. It could be argued, also, that while Gladstone was justified in refusing McCarthy, who came to him in no official capacity, he would be bound to pay more attention to the whips if they presented themselves armed with the authority of a resolution unanimously and enthusiastically endorsed by the entire Irish party. Above all, they had been given to understand that Parnell would retire if satisfactory assurances were obtained. True, he had not yet admitted that he would allow the satisfactoriness of these assurances to be

[1] *F.J.*, 5 Dec. 1890; R. B. O'Brien, *Parnell*, ii. 278-9.

settled by a majority vote of the party, but at least he had not rejected the proposal out of hand. Looked at in this light, the action of the majority in agreeing to an adjournment is intelligible. Clancy's amendment may have been only a straw, but the alternative to it was so terrible that men were not to be blamed if they clutched at it in desperation.

When the party reassembled on Thursday it very soon appeared that a night's reflection, so far from making Parnell more amenable, had made him more difficult to deal with than ever. It was rumoured that he had intended to resign but that Mrs O'Shea had stiffened his determination to persist.[1] There is no direct evidence of this and it seems her own inclination was rather for them to forget the world and be forgotten. 'But then', she says, 'I knew that he would not forget; that he would come at my bidding but that his desertion of Ireland would lie at his heart; that if he was to be happy he must fight to the end.'[2] And fight he did. He began by stating firmly that he could not surrender any part of his responsibility:

My responsibility is derived from you to some extent, to a large extent, but it is also derived from a long train of circumstances and events in which many of you, and I speak to you with great respect, have had no share. My position has been granted to me, not because I am the mere leader of a parliamentary party, but because I am the leader of the Irish nation. . . And you, gentlemen, know, and I know, that there is no man living, if I am gone, who could succeed in reconciling the feelings of the Irish people to the provisions of the Hawarden proposals.

It was a proud claim proudly made, but to those of his hearers who were set on his retirement and who, the day before, had been almost persuaded that he was on the verge of a magnanimous gesture, it must have sounded a note of doom. He went on to say that before they asked him to surrender this responsibility the party itself should, for both his and the constituencies' benefit, declare its opinion in regard to the two questions of the land and the police. He then read out a resolution which he wished them to pass:

That, in the opinion of the Irish parliamentary party, no home rule bill will be satisfactory or acceptable to the Irish people which

[1] Donal Sullivan in *National Press*, 28 Nov. 1891.   [2] O'Shea, ii. 162.

will not confer the immediate control of the Irish police on the executive responsible to the Irish parliament; and secondly, which does not confer upon the Irish parliament full power to deal with the land question.

If the party agreed to this resolution, and if it were found that the liberal assurances corresponded with the demands embodied in the resolution, then he would resign from the chairmanship of the party. And he had a second resolution to propose which was to the effect that the party should appoint a sub-committee consisting of the whips[1] and of five members each from the majority and minority of those who voted on Colonel Nolan's amendment; and that this sub-committee should select from among themselves three delegates from each side to seek an interview with Gladstone, Morley and Harcourt to find whether their views accorded with those of the party on the points at issue, and whether they would agree to embody those views in their projected home rule bill and regard them as vital to it.

These two new proposals changed the ground completely. Apart from the fact that the second blandly ignored the vote of Tuesday night, by giving each side equal representation on the sub-committee and on the delegation, the first resolution substituted concrete demands for Clancy's much vaguer amendment, which had proposed simply that the liberals be asked 'what their views are with regard to these two vital points'. For Parnell this new manoeuvre, if it were accepted, would have two possible advantages. First, by it he would commit his party to making certain practical demands—*devised by him*—in connection with the home rule bill contemplated by the liberals. Or, in other words, he bound them to accept *his* view of what was an adequate price to get for throwing him over. And, if the liberals responded satisfactorily, he would be able to withdraw from the leadership in triumph rather than disgrace, having demonstrated his ability, even at the very moment of his eclipse, to exact valuable concessions from his enemy.

But would the liberals respond satisfactorily? It was extremely probable that they would not. And this was where the

[1] The whips were J. Deasy, Richard Power and L. Carew (Dillon papers, 'Minutes of the Irish parliamentary party', 25 Nov. 1890). Of these, Deasy had voted against Nolan's amendment and Power for it. Carew was absent but ultimately declared for Parnell.

manoeuvre would give Parnell his second advantage. For if they refused his terms the pre-condition of his resignation had lapsed, he still remained leader and the battle had still to be fought. Fought, moreover, with the additional argument on his side that the liberals, having attempted to enforce his retirement, had refused to do anything which might make it easier for him to go. It may be argued, of course, that in putting forward proposals which were almost certain not to be accepted by Gladstone and his colleagues, Parnell was giving fresh cause for anger to those in his own party who were pressing for his deposition and who were likely to lose no time in attacking this latest example of his delaying tactics. And indeed, if the leadership of the party had been all that was at stake, Parnell's action might well seem calculated to destroy any hope he might still have had of retaining that leadership. He was too shrewd a politician, however, not to have realised that that hope was already very slender. Not only had the vote taken earlier in the week revealed how formidable was the opposition ranged against him, but the newspapers of that very Thursday morning carried the long-awaited declaration of the standing committee of the Irish Roman Catholic hierarchy which, as was to be expected, denounced him as unfit to be the Irish leader—and denounced him, not on political grounds, 'but simply and solely on the facts and circumstances revealed in the London divorce court'.[1] This declaration was undoubtedly a great access of strength to the majority in the party and must in any event have made his survival as chairman more unlikely than ever.

But beyond the party lay the constituencies and it is the essential key to Parnell's speeches and behaviour from the time he issued his manifesto onwards to realise that he never forgot that he was—as even Healy had said the previous day—'the leader of the Irish race'. Thus he might be defeated within the ranks of the party, but he could still appeal over the heads of the

[1] *F.J.*, 4 Dec. 1890. During the week of the debate, Archbishop Walsh's main source for what was happening in London seems to have been W. M. Murphy, M.P., who sent him at least ten telegrams in six days. One of these ('Nothing can save the country from internecine conflict like strong and decisive pronouncement from the bishops now') was sent on the evening of the day on which the pronouncement was made (Walsh Papers, Murphy to Walsh, 3 Dec. 1890).

party to the people. Admittedly, the declaration of the standing committee of the hierarchy would affect the people as well as the party—but for that very reason some simple, yet powerful, rallying-cry was needed to counteract the hostile influence of the church. The charge of 'liberal dictation' met that need admirably, and it had already formed the staple of pro-Parnell speeches in the early days of the debate. If it could now be shown that the liberals had refused to give satisfaction as to the land and the police, the emotional force of this rallying-cry would be greatly strengthened. In London it was easy to point to the unreasonableness of expecting Gladstone to reveal his hand in advance on such important topics. In Ireland, where men knew little of the matter except that they wanted the land and hated the police, there was clearly much capital to be made out of the refusal of the liberals to discuss these things.

In the meantime, however, Parnell's manoeuvre was not un-naturally greeted by his opponents as an intolerable evasion of the issue. It was not surprising that when Healy followed Parnell the two clashed almost at once. Healy said that Parnell was in effect refusing to submit himself to the judgment of the party. Parnell replied that this was 'an entire misrepresentation of his speech'. Healy then tried to pin him down to accepting the majority decision as to whether the liberal assurances were satisfactory. Parnell rejoined that he would stand or fall by his own proposal. 'Then', said Healy, 'you will fall, Mr Parnell.' Upon which there were ironical cries from the Parnellites of 'Crucify him', and 'Away with him', which drew heated accusations of blasphemy from their opponents. Healy, continuing his speech, grew angrier and more emphatic. It was clear, he said, that their debates were a waste of time since, when a decision had been taken, Parnell was determined to defy it. He turned then to justify the liberal alliance, seeking to show that Parnell himself, as recently as June of that year, had spoken enthusiastically about it. What broke off that alliance, he asked? Whereupon Parnell, Colonel Nolan and Dr Fitzgerald simultaneously exclaimed that it had been broken off by Gladstone's letter. Healy, yielding to the temptation to deliver a deadly counter-thrust, flared out that the alliance had perished 'in the stench of the divorce court'. Concluding, he maintained that nothing had happened since Parnell had praised the liberal alliance in June to make him, Healy, change his mind about Gladstone or turn back 'into that course of hatred towards the English people out of which you led me'. Parnell, he said, was a Frankenstein who, having created the party, was able and determined to destroy it. 'If you, sir', he said, 'should go down, you are only one man gone. Heads of greater leaders have been stricken on the block before now for Ireland (Colonel Nolan—"Not by their own friends, not by their own allies") and the Irish cause remained. The Irish people can put us down, but the Irish cause will remain always.'[1]

Healy was followed by John Redmond who described his speech as a string of insults and 'the worst-tempered and most hysterical speech that was ever delivered by a man in the position of a leading politician'. He warned the meeting that Parnell must be satisfied as to the views of the majority on the subjects of the land and the police before he could surrender his responsibility. If he were driven out without proper guarantees the Irish race would be torn in two. At length, when there seemed little hope of any kind of agreement being reached, Sexton contrived to bridge the gap. Not less than Healy—but much more moderately—he defended the liberal alliance, stressing that only with the good-will of the liberals could they hope for a home rule majority at the next election. Anything that threatened to weaken the liberals was, therefore, a menace to the Irish cause. Events had shown that Parnell's continued leadership would be just such a menace. Parnell was not indispensable— no man was. Turning to the point at issue, he urged Parnell not to move his resolutions. After some exchanges between the two Parnell agreed not to do so. 'All I have to say', he interposed, 'is that if you take these proposals to the liberal leaders, and if you say that the answer of the liberal leaders upon these two points is satisfactory to you, and if you decide that it is so satisfactory by resolution, it will be satisfactory to me.'[2]

Clancy's amendment therefore held the field and a committee was appointed consisting of Parnell, McCarthy, Sexton, Healy, John Redmond and Edmund Leamy to take the necessary steps to obtain the views of Gladstone, John Morley and Harcourt on the two topics of the control of the police and the settlement of the land question. The amendment itself was then

[1] *F.J.*, 5 Dec. 1890. [2] *F.J.*, 5 Dec. 1890.

put to the meeting and passed with only P. A. Chance and the implacable John Barry dissenting.[1] In so far as Parnell's more concrete demands upon the liberals were thus excluded from the terms of reference of the deputation, the outcome of the debate was a set-back for him. On the other hand, when the committee met to appoint the delegation which was to interview the liberals, it decided to give the two sections of the party equal representation. The delegates chosen were Sexton, T. M. Healy, John Redmond and Leamy, and Parnell could rely upon the two last-named to make sure that, if the liberals did offer concessions, those concessions would be satisfactory to him; while the fact that the party had agreed to send a deputation at all and that the entire controversy had—if only for the time being—been diverted from the question of Parnell's leadership to that of the projected home rule settlement, was in itself a considerable tactical success.[2]

(5)

Much, however, depended upon the liberal reaction. The day following the passing of Clancy's amendment—that is, Friday, December 5—was one of much coming and going, shrouded for the most part in secrecy. It was only on Saturday, when the delegates made their full report, that the party at large learnt precisely what had happened.[3] After Thursday's meeting the whips wrote to the three liberals asking them to meet the delegation. Harcourt and Morley both replied that Gladstone was the leader of the party and that any interview should be with him alone, while Gladstone himself declined to consider the matter 'with a selection of my friends and former colleagues which has been made neither by me, nor by the liberal party of this country'.[4] He was, indeed, at that very time being urged by Harcourt to reserve absolute freedom of action. Harcourt was

[1] The wording of the amendment was the same as that given above, p. 135, except that in its final form it added the names of the committee to the whips who alone were designated in the original version.

[2] Healy, writing to his wife next day, said he was convinced Parnell was tricking them, but 'we should be open to condemnation if we failed to take every step to try to keep the party together' (Healy, *Letters and leaders*, 1. 334).

[3] *F.J.*, 8 Dec. 1890.   [4] *F.J.*, 8 Dec. 1890.

afraid that the deputation's having been agreed to at all was a sign that Parnell was reasserting his supremacy. 'They are not waiting for you to make peace for them', he wrote, 'they have signed it already and at your expense. It is all what they call on the race-course a "put-up job" and they are supping together like actors who have been murdering one another on the stage for the amusement of the audience.'[1] The upshot was that Gladstone received the delegates next day by himself. Sexton then read him a statement of the points about which the Irish party wished to be reassured. Gladstone in his turn read from a memorandum the gist of which was that while he was always ready to confer with Irish members on questions affecting their country, 'such a conference was barred when it was sought for the declared purpose of determining a question of recollection as to the Hawarden conversation'. Redmond asked whether, if this barrier were removed, the discussions might proceed? Gladstone replied that in that case he would regard the matter as if the barrier had not existed; as they left the room he added that he would not have much difficulty in speaking about the police.[2]

Momentarily baffled, the delegation retired to consult Parnell, McCarthy and the whips and it was decided to call a private session of the party for that (Friday) afternoon. At that meeting Clancy's amendment was rescinded and another one passed in its place.[3] This later amendment omitted all reference to the Hawarden conversation and simply empowered the same four delegates to seek a conference with Gladstone to ascertain the liberal intentions with regard to certain details connected with the settlement of the Irish land question and the control of the police. It was proposed by John Redmond and seconded by Sexton and the only dissentients were again John Barry and P. A. Chance. The whips then wrote once more to Gladstone seeking a further interview. He, however, in the interval had conferred with members of his own party, and replied that he did not see that anything was to be gained from a further

[1] Harcourt Papers, Sir W. Harcourt to Gladstone, 4 Dec. 1890 (copy in Harcourt's hand). [2] *F.J.*, 8 Dec. 1890.
[3] The correct text of this amendment is in *F.J.*, 6 Dec. 1890; the version in *F.J.*, 8 Dec. 1890, is in fact a simple repetition of Clancy's original amendment.

conference.[1] He pointed out that his letter of November 24 had referred to the question of the leadership and had no proper connection with the subject of home rule.

We have arrived at the conclusion that I cannot undertake to make any statement of our joint intentions on them or on any other provisions of a home rule bill in connection with the leadership of the Irish party. When the Irish party shall have disposed of this question, which belongs entirely to their own competence, in such a manner as will enable me to renew the former relations, it will be my desire to enter without prejudice into confidential communication such as has heretofore taken place . . . upon all amendment of particulars and suggestion of improvements in any plan for a measure of home rule.[2]

Thus was the door bolted and barred. Parnell's manoeuvre had been brought to nothing by the stern determination of the liberals not to negotiate with the Irish party until the leadership issue had been settled. A modern historian, usually sympathetic to Gladstone, has criticised the action of the liberal leaders in this phase of the crisis, and indeed it must be said that their attitude was very unyielding.[3] There were, however, serious obstacles in the path of the proposed concessions and it is not surprising that they proved insuperable. For one thing, Gladstone himself was under heavy pressure to resist the Irish demand. Harcourt, as we have seen, had begged him to cut the matter short and Cardinal Manning also urged him to refuse all discussion.[4] Again, the liberal leaders had been so convinced

---

[1] Harcourt, in notes which are undated but appear to have been made at the time, indicates that Gladstone would like to have communicated his personal opinions on the land and police questions to the delegates, but that he (Harcourt) and John Morley protested. Gladstone, he says, 'rather resisted', but ultimately yielded. According to Harcourt the draft of Gladstone's final letter to the delegates was drawn up by John Morley, Samuel Whitbread and Harcourt himself. Before the letter was sent Spencer, Granville, Herschell, Trevelyan and Shaw Lefevre had been summoned to Gladstone's room in the house of commons. 'All unanimous that no pledges of any kind shall be given' (Harcourt Papers, 'Notes dictated by W.V.H. to L.H. on Parnell crisis, 1890'). [2] *F.J.*, 8 Dec. 1890.

[3] Hammond, *Gladstone and the Irish nation*, pp. 660–4.

[4] Gladstone Papers (B.M. Add. MS 44,512, ff. 45–6), Sir W. Harcourt to Gladstone, 3 Dec. 1890; Gladstone Papers (B.M., Add. MS 44,250, ff. 303–4), Cardinal Manning to Gladstone, 5 Dec. 1890; A. G. Gardiner, *Life of Harcourt*, ii. 88–9; Hammond, *Gladstone and the Irish nation*, p. 663, *n.* 1.

by Parnell's manifesto that he was utterly untrustworthy that they can scarcely be blamed for refusing to have anything to do with the Irish party while he was still at its head; and the fact that the only vote so far taken in Committee Room Fifteen had shown him to be in a minority was a further inducement to wait until he was safely out of the way. Finally—as Parnell knew and as Gladstone knew that he knew—they were by no means at one on how to deal with the land question and they would certainly have been embarrassed if they had had to commit themselves to any definite policy on it at such short notice.[1]

All the same it was a great misfortune that so little effort was made to meet the Irish demands. Those demands might have been inadmissible or they might not—only a conference could have revealed which. If a conference had been held and if it had turned out to be impossible to give the desired assurances, Gladstone could at least have claimed that he had made a serious attempt to help his allies out of their difficulty. On the other hand, if it had proved feasible to make concessions, then there would have been a chance that the unity of the Irish party might yet have been saved, that Parnell's peaceful retirement might have been secured and much of the bitterness of the next few months avoided. Further, if the liberals had been able to give the kind of pledge for which they were asked, they would have forced Parnell's hand. For either he would have been obliged to acknowledge that the assurances were satisfactory and withdraw as he had promised, or else would have been reduced to a merely factious opposition which might very well have cost him the support of his more moderate supporters; indeed Healy, who served on the delegation to Gladstone with John Redmond and Edmund Leamy, seems to have believed at the time that if Gladstone had given an effective guarantee and Parnell had tried to evade it, they would no longer have stood by him.[2]

These, however, are the might-have-beens of history. The reality was very different. Both sections of the Irish party recognised that Gladstone's refusal was the signal for the struggle to begin again and one of them at least intended that it should not

[1] Gladstone Papers (B.M., Add. MS 44,256, ff. 63-4), John Morley to Gladstone, 13 Nov. 1890.

[2] Healy, *Letters and leaders*, i. 334, letter to his wife, 5 Dec. 1890.

last long. Late on Friday night, after it was known that the negotiations had failed, Healy and Sexton went to Parnell and urged him to bow to the necessity of the case. He replied that he would take the night to consider. On the Saturday morning they returned to him and he told them that he owed a responsibility to Ireland and could not retire. They warned him that the majority would not endure further obstruction and, if no decision was reached during the day, would withdraw from the meeting; no doubt their anxiety was sharpened by the realisation that parliament was due to rise for the Christmas recess the following Tuesday and that if they had not brought the debate to a close by then they might be faced with the prospect of continuing it in Dublin. Parnell, however, was adamant, though he shook hands agreeably enough as they left, 'if', as he remarked, 'it is to be for the last time'.[1]

Very soon the signs of rupture began to appear. After the report on the failure of the negotiations had been read to the party two members rose simultaneously to propose motions. One was William Abraham, whose course of action had been agreed upon in advance by Parnell's opponents, and whose intention was to move the motion he had tried in vain to move at the beginning of the week—that Parnell's leadership be terminated.[2] The other was John O'Connor, who wished to move a resolution calling the attention of the Irish people to the fact that Gladstone had refused to state his views on home rule until the party had first removed Parnell from his chairmanship. Parnell called on O'Connor—his own supporter—but so tense had the atmosphere become that this ruling created immediate pandemonium. Abraham, trying to read his motion, could not be heard, and passed the paper on which it was written to Justin McCarthy. Parnell, who had been on his feet calling loudly for O'Connor to be heard and declaring angrily that until they deposed him he would have obedience to the chair, snatched the paper from the hands of the unoffending McCarthy. It even

[1] Healy, *Letters and leaders*, i. 336; Morley, *Gladstone*, iii. 451; D. Sullivan, 'The story of room fifteen' in *National Press*, 1 Dec. 1891.

[2] Donal Sullivan, 'The story of room fifteen' in *National Press*, 2 Dec. 1891. Healy, later in the debate, claimed that Abraham had risen before O'Connor and should have been called first. In fact the two men rose so nearly together that even an impartial chairman might have found it difficult to decide which should have priority.

seemed to some as if his self-control had so far left him that he would strike the vice-chairman, and John Redmond and Leamy hurried to restrain him. The uproar continued all around them and John Barry could be heard calling Parnell 'a dirty trickster'. Gradually the clamour died down as men came to their senses and realised how far the party had slid into anarchy. John O'Connor was allowed to read his motion and proceed with his speech. In the course of it Parnell could be seen apologising to McCarthy who apparently received his remarks in good part.[1]

But the calm thus restored was not to last for long. John O'Connor in his speech said that if the party rejected Parnell it would in effect be placing itself under Gladstone's leadership. Arthur O'Connor interjected that Gladstone was not a member of the party. What followed can best be described as it appeared in the *Freeman's Journal*:

Mr J. Redmond: 'The master of the party' (cheers and counter-cheers).
Mr T. M. Healy: 'Who is to be the mistress of the party?' (cries of 'shame', noise, several members calling out remarks which could not be distinguished in the uproar).
Mr W. Redmond: 'They must be very badly off when they go to arguments like that.'
A voice: 'It is true.'[2]

Parnell, on hearing Healy's remark, rose once more in fury and this time it did seem as if he would strike his opponent. A few of Healy's friends gathered round him and Arthur O'Connor, to ease the tension, called out: 'I appeal to my friend the chairman.' Parnell replied with passion: 'Better appeal to your own friends. Better appeal to that cowardly little scoundrel there

[1] The above description is based on the report in *F.J.*, 8 Dec. 1890; Michael Macdonagh's eye-witness account in *The home rule movement*, pp. 217–9; Donal Sullivan's report in 'The story of room fifteen', *National Press*, 2 Dec. 1891; *The Times: the Parnellite split*, pp. 175–8. In a letter written just after the scene described above, W. M. Murphy probably expressed the views of many anti-Parnellites when he said: 'While acknowledging his enormous services in bringing the question to its present position, if we got home rule with his power unimpaired we should only be exchanging British parliamentary rule for the autocracy of a man who has proved himself to be filled with some of the worst passions of human nature' (Walsh Papers, Murphy to Archbishop Walsh, 6 Dec. 1890).   [2] *F.J.*, 8 Dec. 1890.

who dares in an assembly of Irishmen to insult a woman.'[1] The moment passed and Parnell with a violent effort restrained himself, but the final impossible word had been said. The discussion continued a little longer. John O'Connor's speech was seconded by J. J. O'Kelly. William Abraham then asked leave to move his original resolution as an amendment to O'Connor's motion. Parnell replied that this could not possibly be considered an amendment and ruled it out of order. After another sharp clash between Parnell and the irrepressible Healy and short speeches from Arthur O'Connor and Edmund Leamy, the debate was at last closed by Justin McCarthy.

> I see no further use [he said] carrying on a discussion which must be barren of all but reproach, ill-temper, controversy and indignity, and I will therefore suggest that all who think with me at this grave crisis should withdraw with me from this room.[2]

He then left the room, followed by forty-four of his colleagues, including his son Justin Huntly McCarthy who said that though he had voted for Parnell before and would have done so again, now that a decision had been taken by the majority he felt he must go with them.

This occurred at half-past four in the afternoon. When the last of his opponents had gone, a few of Parnell's supporters made brief speeches, but time was limited, for the serjeant-at-arms had not been able to let them have the room beyond five o'clock. In putting a motion to adjourn the meeting Parnell spoke once more, and spoke less to the little circle of devoted followers grouped around him, than to the wider public which he must now attempt to win over by every means in his power:

> I wish to say in putting this resolution that the men who have deserted from our party this evening have deserted on the eve of the day when we were about to return to our own country and that these men, while clamouring for a decision, clamoured for that decision because they dreaded the lightning of public opinion in Ireland. . . . It was this Irish opinion they wished to stifle, that they have recoiled from; and it was this Irish opinion they fled from when they fled from this room this evening. Gentlemen, we have won to-day. Although our ranks are reduced in numbers, I hold this chair still.

[1] M. Macdonagh, *The home rule movement*, pp. 220–1; *F.J.*, 8 Dec. 1890.
[2] *F.J.*, 8 Dec. 1890; M. Macdonagh, *The home rule movement*, p. 222.

. . . They left this room because their position here was no longer tenable. They saw they had arrayed against them that great force to which we all must bow—that great force without which none of them would ever have come here. And recognising that, they stand to-day in the most contemptible of all positions—the position of men who, having taken pledges to be true to their party, to be true to their leaders, to be true to their country, have been false to all these pledges.[1]

For Parnell, evidently, the breaking of his party was far from being the end of all things. The note of defiance in his speech was unmistakable and it was clear that the fight would go on.

[1] *F.J.*, 8 Dec. 1890. Those who remained with Parnell were: A. Blane, G. Byrne, H. Campbell, J. J. Clancy, M. Conway, W. J. Corbet, J. Dalton, Dr J. G. Fitzgerald, E. Harrington, H. Harrison, L. P. Hayden, Dr J. E. Kenny, E. Leamy, W. A. Macdonald, Sir J. N. M'Kenna, J. R. Maguire, P. Mahony, Colonel J. P. Nolan, J. Nolan, J. O'Connor, J. J. O'Kelly, R. Power, T. Quinn, J. Redmond, W. Redmond, E. Sheil.

Those who left the room were: W. Abraham, J. Barry, P. A. Chance, A. Commins, T. J. Condon, J. R. Cox, D. Crilly, J. Deasy, T. A. Dickson, Sir T. Esmonde, J. Finucane, J. C. Flynn, P. J. Foley, J. F. Fox, M. Healy, T. M. Healy, J. Jordan, M. J. Kenny, D. Kilbride, E. F. Knox, W. J. Lane, M. M'Cartan, Justin McCarthy, J. H. McCarthy, P. Macdonald, J. G. S. MacNeill, B. C. Molloy, J. Morrogh, W. M. Murphy, J. F. X. O'Brien, P. J. O'Brien, A. O'Connor, F. A. O'Keefe, J. Pinkerton, P. J. Power, W. J. Reynolds, J. Roche, T. Sexton, J. D. Sheehan, D. Sheehy, J. Stack, D. Sullivan, Dr C. Tanner, J. Tuite, A. Webb.

It is not clear whether T. O'Hanlon and J. Nolan were present on this occasion or not, though the former is not listed and the latter is. Both, however, were, and remained, Parnellites.

VI

THE RIFT WIDENS

~~~~~~~~~~~~~~~~~~~~~~~~~~~~~~~~~~~~

(1)

ALTHOUGH we can see now that the rupture of the party in Committee Room Fifteen was a decisive event in the downfall of Parnell, this was by no means obvious at the time. Even though a majority had declared against him it was far from certain how their action would be received in the country. And while they had the church with them, and could reasonably look to Dillon and O'Brien for support, they had no organisation, no daily newspaper, and scarcely any funds. It was, therefore, essential for them to put themselves on a war footing without delay and the moment they left Committee Room Fifteen they began to plan their first moves. Having assembled in another room in the house of commons, they immediately passed a resolution 'that Mr Parnell's chairmanship of the party is hereby terminated'. Next, they proceeded to elect Justin McCarthy as sessional chairman in his place, at the same time arranging for a committee to be elected when they met again on Monday, December 8, this committee 'to exercise jointly with the chairman the powers and discharge the functions hitherto attached to the chairmanship of the party'. Before separating, all forty-five of them signed a declaration in which they announced their continued devotion to the principle 'that the Irish party is, and always must remain, independent of all other parties', and asserted that they would never consider any proposal for a home rule settlement 'except such as satisfies the aspirations of the Irish people'.[1]

Later that evening they met informally in Arthur O'Connor's rooms and elected a further committee, this time to launch a new national daily newspaper in Ireland.[2] The committee consisted of Justin McCarthy, T. A. Dickson, W. M. Murphy, John Barry, T. M. Healy, Thomas Sexton and John Morrogh. Nearly all of these had business experience and Murphy and Morrogh were probably among the wealthiest members of the party. Justin McCarthy, though certainly no business-man, had valuable contacts with the newspaper world, while Healy could be relied on to supply both organising and journalistic ability. But even more important than producing a newspaper was the problem of financing the party, for more than half those who had followed McCarthy out of Committee Room Fifteen (twenty-eight to be precise) were, in greater or lesser degree, dependent upon grants from party funds.[3] Since the normal grant was £200 per head per annum,[4] and since at the time of the split the credit balance in the Irish Parliamentary Fund (from which these grants were usually made) was only £76 1s. 5d., the position was very grave.[5] It eased a little when it was found that a sum of £1,000 was available as a partial repayment of money originally advanced from the Parliamentary Fund to a special account concerned with the evicted tenants, but even so those present at the meeting of December 6 hastened to contribute what they could to meet the most pressing needs of the moment. Newspaper reports reckoned the total of this subscription at £1,020,[6] but the treasurer's books indicate

[1] *F.J.*, 8 Dec. 1890; *The Times: the Parnellite split*, pp. 187–8.

[2] Healy, *Letters and leaders*, i. 338–9, in a letter to his wife gives the impression that this meeting took place on Sunday, but the newspaper reports place it definitely as the evening of Saturday, December 6.

[3] J. F. X. O'Brien (N.L.I., MS 9231), 'Ledger of the Irish parliamentary fund, 7 Dec. 1890–6 Apr. 1896', p. 80.

[4] F. S. L. Lyons, *The Irish parliamentary party, 1890–1910*, p. 205.

[5] J. F. X. O'Brien Papers (N.L.I., MS 9230), 'Cash-book of the Irish parliamentary fund, 7 Dec. 1890–6 Apr. 1896'; (N.L.I., MS 9231), 'Ledger of the Irish parliamentary fund, 7 Dec. 1890–6 Apr. 1896', p. 169, balance-sheet for the period 7 Dec. 1890–31 Dec. 1891. T. M. Healy, in a letter to his wife of 7 Dec. 1890 (*Letters and leaders*, i. 338), estimated the majority's resources at £1,200, but in doing so he was probably including the £1,000 diverted from the special (evicted tenants) account.

[6] *F.J.*, 8 Dec. 1890; *The Times: the Parnellite split*, p. 189. Justin McCarthy,

that in fact the amount raised in this way, not merely at that meeting but during the whole of December, was only £448 1s. 0d.[1]

Before the meeting broke up one further step was taken which, while it did not add to the resources of the majority, at least prevented Parnell from increasing his—an obvious tactic in view of the fact that fourteen of his followers also were dependent upon grants.[2] For some years past there had existed in Paris a sum of money consisting largely of investments in American securities. There were apparently two accounts—a 'general' comprising money lodged in 1882, and a 'special' derived mainly from American subscriptions in aid of the Irish parliamentary party and dating from 1886.[3] It was the latter—the 'Paris fund' (or 'funds')—that now became a bone of contention between Parnellites and anti-Parnellites. It is difficult to be sure exactly how much money was involved, for contemporary estimates varied greatly. Davitt—who, however, was not familiar with the later history of the fund—believed it had

writing to Mrs Praed, put the figure at £1,200, but he was probably confusing this with the amount they had in hand, that is, the balance of £76 1s. 5d. from the old fund, plus the £1,000 from the evicted tenants' account (McCarthy and Praed, *Our book of memories*, p. 268). The figure of 'over £10,000' mentioned by Healy to his wife in the letter already quoted (*Letters and leaders*, i. 338) is so wide of the mark as to suggest a misprint.

[1] J. F. X. O'Brien Papers (N.L.I., MS 9230), 'Cash-book of the Irish parliamentary fund, 7 Dec. 1890–6 Apr. 1896'. Even by the end of June 1891, so J. F. X. O'Brien reported to John Dillon, the amount raised by subscription from party members only totalled £637 1s. 0d. (Dillon Papers, J. F. X. O'Brien to John Dillon, 9 Aug. 1891). For further details of the general financial situation, see Appendix II.

[2] C. Cruise O'Brien, *Parnell and his party*, p. 328.

[3] Harrington Papers (N.L.I., MS 8930), copy of affidavit of Justin McCarthy, 28 Apr. 1892, in *Kenny and others v. McCarthy and others*. It is not clear how much the general account was worth in 1890, but in 1887 it appears to have been only just over £2,000. If Healy was right in his later contention that Parnell between 1882 and 1890 made grants from it to the National League or to needy members of the party as occasion warranted, it was probably not very large by the time of the split (Harrington Papers (N.L.I., MS 8930), Munroe and co. to J. G. Biggar, 2 July 1887; copy of affidavit of T. M. Healy, 26 Apr. 1892, in *Kenny and others v. McCarthy and others*). It seems that the money in the general account was not finally released from Paris until 1899 (Harrington Papers, B. F. Hawksley (solicitor) to T. C. Harrington, 11 Nov. 1899).

originally amounted to £32,000.[1] Healy's estimate (made, like Davitt's, at the time of the split) was £42,000,[2] but in William O'Brien's recollections (admittedly, twenty years later) the figure of £50,000 is mentioned.[3] Parnell himself did not help matters by giving two different totals—£40,000 and £46,000—in the course of a single speech. This speech was made near the end of his life and he did not make it clear whether the figures he quoted represented the amount at the split, or only at the time he was speaking.[4] We do know, however, that when the fund was finally released from Paris in 1894 it totalled £39,000.[5] Since at least £8,000 was withdrawn during 1891 it follows that the total in December 1890 cannot have been less than £47,000.[6] Indeed, if we also take into account the heavy legal expenses between 1891 and 1894, it is quite possible that O'Brien's figure of £50,000 may not have been so wide of the mark after all. Until the death of J. G. Biggar in February 1890, the fund had been lodged in his name and those of Parnell and Justin McCarthy. Now that the two survivors were in opposite camps the natural policy for each was to ensure that the other should not have access to the money. The initiative was seized by the majority section when at their meeting of December 6 they decided to send J. F. X. O'Brien and Arthur O'Connor to Paris to restrain the bankers from releasing any of the money at Parnell's demand.[7] A week later it was announced that they had secured a temporary injunction from the French courts directing Messrs Munroe (the American bankers with whom the fund was lodged) not to set free any part of it without the consent of all concerned.[8] It was not in fact until after Parnell's death that effective steps were taken to bring the dispute to a close and even so there was long and costly litigation before the

[1] Interview in *F.J.*, 9 Dec. 1890.

[2] Healy, *Letters and leaders*, i. 338, letter to his wife, 7 Dec. 1890.

[3] W. O'Brien, *An olive branch in Ireland*, p. 47. In 1886 the fund had actually reached £52,400 (Harrington Papers (N.L.I., MS 8930) copy of affidavit of J. F. X. O'Brien, 27 Apr. 1892 in *Kenny and others v. McCarthy and others*).

[4] *F.J.*, 14 Sept. 1891, speech at Listowel, 13 Sept. 1891. A few months earlier he had given yet another figure, £43–44,000 (*F.J.*, 1 June 1891).

[5] Dillon Papers, memorandum by Davitt, 23 Oct. 1894, the day after the fund was released from Paris.

[6] For the withdrawals in 1891 see ch. x below.

[7] *F.J.*, 8 Dec. 1890; Healy, *Letters and leaders*, i. 338.

[8] *The Times*, 15 Dec. 1890.

rival parties agreed jointly to disburse the money to the evicted tenants.

On Monday, December 8, the anti-Parnellites met again and elected the committee which was for all practical purposes to be their governing body. It comprised William Abraham, John Dillon, T. M. Healy, William O'Brien, Arthur O'Connor, T. P. O'Connor, David Sheehy and Thomas Sexton. At this meeting also it was decided that Justin McCarthy should issue a manifesto to the Irish people justifying the action of those who had taken the momentous decision to break away from Parnell.[1] This document, when it appeared, attempted to lay the responsibility for the crisis squarely upon Parnell. It explained that Parnell had done nothing to repel the charges made against him and that the party had only re-elected him partly out of gratitude for past services and partly 'in the desperate hope that his leadership might yet be reconciled with the safety of our cause'. That hope, said McCarthy, had soon had to be abandoned and the party had had to consider whether their duty bound them to Parnell or to Ireland. The answer could not be in doubt. Their allegiance must be to Ireland, not to one man. And when Parnell's manifesto—'that fatal document' McCarthy called it—was published it clearly made further co-operation between him and Gladstone impossible. Which, said McCarthy in effect, made Parnell impossible for them. And McCarthy, while denying indignantly that he and his friends had submitted to dictation from Gladstone, made it clear that in their view the fate of home rule depended on the liberal leader. 'We remind Mr Parnell', he said, 'that the men whom he now assails . . . are the men who, when Mr Parnell left the party derelict, still preserved its integrity, maintained its independence, fought the battle of their country inch by inch, never uttered a word against the leader who had left them to struggle as best they could without his aid.'[2]

(2)

Both sides, however, were well aware that meetings in London and manifestoes issued from London were no substitute for action in Ireland. And in Dublin at least the preliminary

[1] *F.J.*, 9 Dec. 1890.   [2] Ibid., 11 Dec. 1890.

sparring had begun even before the debates in Committee Room Fifteen had properly got under way. Thus on December 1 a number of Parnell's supporters had met at the National Club, Rutland square—thenceforth the headquarters of Dublin Parnellism—and had passed a resolution calling for the establishment of a committee 'to uphold Mr Parnell as leader of the Irish people'. On December 3 this took shape as the Parnell leadership committee and before long similar bodies appeared in other centres.[1] Nor were the anti-Parnellites behindhand. About the same time they formed a national committee to organise the opposition to Parnell, and by the middle of the month had received the public support of Archbishop Walsh.[2] A few days later they were in a position to hold their first general meeting. W. M. Murphy was in the chair and he claimed that the national committee in the three weeks of its existence had attracted 3,000 members—the published list included members of parliament, priests, professional men, and men active in various branches of local administration.[3] Archbishop Walsh in a letter to Murphy continued to press for more and yet more local organisation, which he saw as the key to the situation. Indeed, he warned him that, without such organisation, the anti-Parnellites would have little alternative but to surrender to Parnell.[4]

All this was only the prelude to the arrival of the leading figures on each side. On the night of December 9 Parnell and Healy both left London by the same train and arrived in Dublin next morning—Healy to be assaulted in the streets and Parnell to receive a rapturous welcome.[5] The latter's first task was to re-establish his control over *United Ireland*, the newspaper which had been started in 1881 expressly as a vehicle for Parnell's own ideas and policies and which had been edited from the beginning by William O'Brien. During his enforced absence from the country in 1890 O'Brien had left as his deputy Matthew Bodkin, a barrister by profession, but with considerable journalistic

[1] *F.J.*, 2 and 4 Dec. 1890; *United Ireland*, 20 Dec. 1890. For an indication of the way these Parnell leadership committees had spread see the comprehensive list of 88, excluding Dublin, in *F.J.*, 24 July 1891.

[2] '*Suppressed*' *United Ireland*, 15 Dec. 1890.   [3] *Insuppressible*, 23 Dec. 1890.

[4] Archbishop Walsh to W. M. Murphy, 26 Dec. 1890. I am indebted to Miss Eva Murphy for permission to make use of this letter.

[5] *F.J.*, 11 Dec. 1890; Healy, *Letters and leaders*, i. 340.

experience. Upon Bodkin, therefore, had fallen the immediate responsibility for the line taken by the paper in the confusing weeks that followed the divorce case. In his issue of November 22 he had adopted an orthodox pro-Parnell position, but a week later he had begun to waver.[1] Then came Parnell's manifesto and the repudiation of it by the Irish delegates in America, including, of course, William O'Brien. Parnell, anticipating what was likely to happen, wired from London on December 2 that the leading article in the next issue must be submitted to him before it was printed. The same day a cable arrived from O'Brien instructing Bodkin that if the party voted for Parnell he should hand over the paper to anyone authorised by him, but that if the vote went against Parnell he should 'let *United Ireland* strenuously support our views and permit nobody to interfere'. This was shortly followed by a second cable from O'Brien ordering Bodkin to support the views of the delegates in America, unless the party decided otherwise, but to avoid the use of unkind language towards Parnell.[2] Since a majority voted against Parnell on Colonel Nolan's amendment on December 2 Bodkin saw his way clear. He ignored Parnell's demand and on December 6 came out strongly on the anti-Parnellite side.[3]

Such was the position when Parnell arrived in Dublin. He lost no time in proceeding with a group of his supporters to the offices of *United Ireland*, followed by the excited crowd which gathered round him constantly in Dublin at this time. When Bodkin returned to the offices after breakfast, he found Parnell and some of his followers in the editor's room. Parnell told him that he was dissatisfied with the previous issue and that he was dismissing him. Bodkin denied he had any legal right to do so, whereupon Edmund Leamy intervened to say that Parnell had appointed *him* editor. Parnell then ordered Bodkin to leave the room, which he refused to do. At this point, by Bodkin's own account, a mob invaded the office and threatened him. Bowing to superior force, he agreed to leave.[4] Or, as one of those who

[1] *United Ireland*, 29 Nov. 1890. See for example the leader entitled 'In agony'.

[2] Ibid., 6 Dec. 1890.

[3] See especially the articles entitled 'Ireland or Parnell' and 'To the old guard'.

[4] *'Suppressed' United Ireland*, 13 Dec. 1890—this was a facsimile of the

took part in the operation put it more picturesquely: 'I went up to Matty Bodkin. "Matty", says I, "will you walk out, or would you like to be thrown out?" and Matty walked out.'[1]

This, though spectacular, was only a secondary objective. The main purpose of Parnell's visit was to address a great meeting of his supporters at the Rotunda that night. This was the first time he had had an opportunity of speaking to his fellow-countrymen in Ireland since the verdict in the divorce court and it was certain to be an important occasion. Some insight into the frame of mind in which he approached this meeting can be got from a long interview he gave during the day to Tracy Grieves, London correspondent of the *New York World*. The most significant things about the interview were that Parnell showed himself even more hostile to Gladstone than before, if that were possible, and that he held out no prospect whatever of reconciliation with his enemies. He explained his long silence about the Hawarden interview by saying that he could not reveal Gladstone's proposals while any hope of obtaining better terms remained. Asked why he had then revealed these terms in his manifesto, he replied: 'Because Mr Gladstone's letter meant the breaking-off of negotiations with me. He appealed to the Irish party as my judge, and consequently as my successor. It was, therefore, necessary for me, doubtful as I was of the stability of the party and its capacity for negotiation, to impart my knowledge to Ireland.'

This interpretation of his action may have satisfied his followers, but it is hard to see how it can have gained him many converts. Apart from the provocative references to Gladstone and the disparaging remarks about his own former followers, it failed to explain convincingly how he, the leader of an independent party, had allowed himself to be manoeuvred into a position where he had felt obliged to keep silent about proposals vitally affecting his colleagues and of which he himself disapproved. Even if it was true that the resistance of the party *had*

edition which was seized by Parnell and was printed with the aid of *The Irish Catholic* and *The Nation* (M. McD. Bodkin, *Recollections of an Irish judge*, pp. 174–5).

[1] R. B. O'Brien, *Parn.* ⟨⟩ ⟨⟩ ⟨⟩. Katharine Tynan, *Twenty-five years: reminiscences*, p. 325, attributes the remark to John Clancy, the sub-sheriff of Dublin and an ardent Parnellite.

been undermined by Gladstone's letter, there had been a period of eleven months between the Hawarden conversations and the appearance of that letter during which Parnell had given no sign that he considered the party unworthy of his confidence. That was the time—it could reasonably be argued—when he might have sought their advice, or at least that of the leading members, as he had done when the home rule proposals of 1886 had come before him.[1]

It seemed, however, from the rest of the interview that he had no intention of conciliating those party members who opposed him. He looked, he said, to a general election for a solution—the constituencies would decide. He made no effort even to play for the support of Dillon and O'Brien. Asked if their return would mend matters, he said they might have helped before the 'secession':

> But it is now too late. Mr Gladstone's obstinacy on the one hand, and the ignorance and inexperience of so many members of the party on the other, had produced the catastrophe. I was at all times willing to compromise, as my acceptance of Mr Clancy's amendment proves, an acceptance which would have involved my retirement had Mr Gladstone given the assurances the Irish party required. But these assurances were not given, and my persecution by the party was still persisted in. Messrs Dillon and O'Brien, instead of taking up the position of mediators, took sides against me from the first, and so lost the opportunity of successful intervention. In any event, their intervention would now be too late.[2]

Considering that he himself in private had already informed O'Brien of his willingness to meet him, that two of his own closest followers, John Redmond and Dr Kenny (though possibly unknown to him) had cabled urgently to the delegates in America begging them to come to Paris for consultation, that the *Freeman's Journal* had also advocated such a course, and that on the very day of Parnell's arrival in Dublin it had published O'Brien's decision to go to France, this was reckless language.[3]

---

[1] For the procedure in 1886 see T. M. Healy's speech in Committee Room Fifteen on December 4 (*The Times: the Parnellite split*, pp. 145–7).

[2] *F.J.*, 11 Dec. 1890.

[3] Gill Papers, cable from Parnell to W. O'Brien, 8 Dec. 1890, cables from John Redmond to T. P. Gill, 29 Nov. 1890, and from John Redmond and Dr Kenny to W. O'Brien, 9 Dec. 1890. Both the latter cables were marked

It has to be remembered, however, that Dublin was fiercely Parnellite and that when Parnell was there he tended to over-estimate his strength. Certainly, the reception he got that night did nothing to disillusion him. After a torch-light procession through streets thronged with his supporters, he came at last to the Rotunda where he received a tumultuous welcome. His speech was eagerly received, though it threw no fresh light on the situation. He took the now familiar line that it was Glad-stone—and more particularly Gladstone's letter—that was responsible for the crisis. The core of his argument was the need for absolute independence of all English parties, though there was a passage in his speech which suggested that even this might not be enough.

I have not misled you. I have never said that this constitutional movement must succeed. I have never promised you absolute suc-cess, but I have promised you this, that if you trust me, I will do all that mortal man can do to perform it. What is the position? We stand at the parting of the ways. . . . It is an issue which means the life or death of the constitutional movement . . . if Ireland cannot win upon this line within the constitution, she can win upon no other line within the constitution, and if our constitutional movement of to-day is broken, sundered, separated, discredited and forgotten, England will be face to face with that imperishable force which to-night gives me vitality and power, and without which we are broken reeds. . . . And if Ireland leaves this path upon which I have led her . . . I will not for my part say that I will not accompany her further.[1]

But Dublin was not Ireland, and he dared not linger there. First, he had to go to Cork and defend himself before his con-stituents, who were likely to be divided amongst themselves since his fellow-member for the city was T. M. Healy's brother Maurice.[2] And beyond Cork loomed another and greater ordeal. The vacancy in North Kilkenny caused by the death of

private and the second was 'from ourselves alone', so this manoeuvre may have been unknown to Parnell (*F.J.*, 8 and 10 Dec. 1890).

[1] *F.J.*, 11 Dec. 1890. For a vivid eye-witness account see Katharine Tynan, *Twenty-five years: reminiscences*, pp. 325-7.

[2] Parnell's opponents had busied themselves in setting up a national com-mittee in Cork about the same time as the similar organisation was being formed in Dublin (*Cork Examiner*, 9 Dec. 1890 and letter from Archbishop Walsh to W. M. Murphy, 26 Dec. 1890 referred to above).

E. P. M. Marum before the split had still to be filled, and already the anti-Parnellite whip, John Deasy, had moved the writ for the by-election.[1] It was inevitable that this contest would be regarded as a trial of strength between the two wings of the party and would be fought on the sole issue of Parnell's leadership. It would be the first clash in Ireland between Parnell and his opponents and the gaze of the whole country would be fixed upon that narrow, concentrated stage.

On the morning of Thursday, December 11 he set off for Cork but not before he had added another detail to the legend fast gathering round his name. The previous night, taking advantage of the concentration of Parnellite forces round the Rotunda, his opponents had contrived to reoccupy the offices of *United Ireland*. Learning of this, Parnell, on his way to Kingsbridge station, drove with Dr Kenny from the latter's house to the premises, determined to recapture them. The door was locked in his face and no answer made to his knocking. From near-by his supporters brought crowbars, and while Parnell himself seized one and thundered at the main door, another group forced an entry through the area. Presently the door yielded and he and his followers burst in just as the other storming party rushed up from the basement. There was a moment's confusion when the two groups collided and seemed likely to set upon each other by mistake, but then they surged upstairs.[2] The building had been evacuated through a back entrance, the resistance of a small rearguard was easily overpowered, and when an excited crowd saw Parnell appear at a window—pale, dusty and dishevelled—*United Ireland* was his again.[3] It had

---

[1] *F.J.*, 9 Dec. 1890. Marum had died on 21 Sept. 1890 (*Annual Register, 1890*, pp. 183–4).

[2] One of the basement party, D. J. Hishon, was in fact injured by mistake by those who broke in the door (*F.J.*, 12 Dec. 1890). It was alleged in '*Suppressed*' *United Ireland*, 15 Dec. 1890, that it was Parnell himself who struck Hishon, but this is not established. '*Suppressed*' *United Ireland* was the name under which Bodkin brought out a temporary paper on 13, 15 and 16 Dec. 1890. The Parnellites then took legal action to prevent him using the name *United Ireland* in his title, and the paper then appeared as *Insuppressible*. It continued to function until 24 Jan. 1891 when it ceased under circumstances described in ch. vii below.

[3] *Evening Telegraph*, 11 Dec. 1890; *F.J.*, 12 Dec. 1890; '*Suppressed*' *United Ireland*, 15 Dec. 1890; R. B. O'Brien, *Parnell*, ii. 294–6; Katharine Tynan, *Twenty-five years: reminiscences*, p. 328.

been an extraordinary and ominous episode, a moment of intense passion when long-suppressed anger at last found relief in action.

In Cork he had a stirring reception. Crowds met him when he arrived, escorted him about the city and thronged the broad street outside the Victoria hotel where he had his headquarters. Here his main speech followed much the same line as he had taken in Dublin and was to take again many times in the months to come. He told his audience that they need not fear the loss of 'this trumpery bill of Gladstone's'. He had, he said, a good opinion of 'this Grand Old Man':

> ... but never in the palmiest days of Gladstone and his reputation for Ireland could I dismiss from my mind for one single instant the possibility that Gladstone and Ireland might again be in conflict and that the duty might once more fall to my lot to come amongst you and lead you.[1]

It began to seem as if he were harking back to the pre-Kilmainham days, to the time when he had to make a reputation as an independent leader tied to no party. His provocative remarks about Gladstone recalled his Wexford speech of 1881,[2] and suggested that, in his revulsion from the liberal alliance, he was rebelling against the whole constitutional movement he had done so much to create. It was in Cork also that he took up again a theme which had already figured in his Rotunda speech and of which more was to be heard in the days ahead. At the Rotunda he had appealed to the working-men of Dublin 'for the recruits in the grand army of Irish nationality which I hope to lead in the near future'. In Cork one of his speeches was mainly devoted to the interests of the workers and he declared that he would do all he could for them. It was as if he had already realised that, with the majority of the party against him, he would have to face the hostility of a considerable section of the monied and professional classes and must seek his allies wherever he could find them.[3]

[1] *United Ireland*, 13 Dec. 1890.
[2] R. B. O'Brien, *Parnell*, i. 308–10.
[3] A recent analysis of the party at the time of the rupture in Committee Room Fifteen suggests that the business element and the lawyers were largely—though not exclusively—against Parnell (C. Cruise O'Brien, *Parnell and his party*, pp. 327–8).

From Cork Parnell went straight to Kilkenny. It is important at this point to remember that he—and, indeed, his opponents also—had been under continuous strain for nearly three weeks. Long hours of debate in Committee Room Fifteen, followed by the overnight crossing to Dublin; the hectic scenes in that city; the tedious train journey to Cork with personal appearances at every station; the meetings and the speeches there—all these things made severe demands upon a man whose health was delicate. Throughout this winter, Mrs O'Shea later recalled, he suffered considerable pain from rheumatism in his left arm.[1] So long as he was near at hand, in London or Brighton, she was able to keep some watch over him, but in Ireland it was very different. Feverish meetings in stuffy, over-crowded rooms were often followed by long drives in open side-cars with little or no protection from the weather—weather which that winter was often atrocious. Constantly, in the descriptions of Parnell's appearance at this time, there are references to his extreme pallor.[2] At Cork his host, M. J. Horgan, was much concerned about his health and Parnell seemed to him near the end of his tether.[3] And a few days later when Barry O'Brien saw him at Kilkenny he thought he looked a dying man.[4] He had, or seemed to have, amazing resilience and his will-power was inexhaustible. But he was living at such a pace that no constitution, however strong, could stand it indefinitely.

In Kilkenny he was faced with a difficult situation. Before the split in the party had developed very far, a nationalist candidate had been adopted by a routine county convention presided over by John Redmond.[5] He was Sir John Pope-Hennessy, who had recently retired from a distinguished, if controversial, career as a colonial governor, but whose record as a politician it needed a long memory to recall.[6] He had, however, been

[1] O'Shea, ii. 163.

[2] M. Macdonagh, *The home rule movement*, p. 213; O'Shea, ii. 162; R. B. O'Brien, *Parnell*, ii. 296.

[3] R. B. O'Brien, *Parnell*, ii. 297.

[4] Ibid., ii. 300. On December 11 he wrote to Mrs O'Shea admitting that he was feeling ill (O'Shea, ii. 180-1).

[5] *Kilkenny Journal*, 29 Nov. 1890.

[6] He had been returned to parliament for King's County in 1859 as a

approved by Parnell as a suitable candidate apparently on McCarthy's recommendation.[1] On the very day that Parnell arrived in Ireland the newspapers announced that Pope-Hennessy had declared against him, chiefly on the grounds that the catholic hierarchy had condemned his leadership.[2] Anticipating this, Parnell had previously asked Barry O'Brien if he would stand as his candidate. O'Brien agreed reluctantly, Parnell promising to pay his expenses, though it was understood that if he could find a man who would pay his way better he should take him. Such a candidate was eventually found in Vincent Scully, a wealthy Tipperary landlord and a leading figure in the Munster and Leinster bank. Characteristically, Parnell, having decided on Scully as his candidate, allowed O'Brien to travel to Kilkenny, leaving it to Dr Kenny to inform him when he got there that he was no longer Parnell's choice, but that he was expected to help to get Scully elected.[3] Fortunately he agreed to do this and his narrative of events is an important source for the history of the election from the Parnellite point of view.

Early though Parnell was in the field, his opponents were there before him, as David Sheehy and Denis Kilbride—both specialists in the affairs of the evicted tenants—had arrived in Kilkenny on December 10. They were speedily followed by other anti-Parnellite members of parliament and by the powerful—though independent—ally, Michael Davitt. Davitt later described how the campaign was planned by himself and T. M. Healy. The constituency was divided into districts and several members of parliament were assigned to each district. Davitt himself, with John Deasy and the excitable Dr Tanner, held a roving commission, while T. M. Healy, his brother Maurice and P. A. Chance were based on Kilkenny town.[4] The Parnellites,

'catholic conservative' and had interested himself in Irish economic and educational questions before beginning his career as a colonial governor in 1867 (*The Times*, 8 Oct. 1891; *D.N.B.*).

[1] *F.J.*, 28 Jan. 1891, speeches of T. Harrington and Dr J. E. Kenny. As early as January 1890 McCarthy had referred to the possibility of Pope-Hennessy entering the house of commons as one of the Irish party (McCarthy and Praed, *Our book of memories*, p. 212).

[2] *F.J.*, 10 Dec. 1890; this issue also contained a strong letter of support for Pope-Hennessy from the archbishop of Cashel.

[3] R. B. O'Brien, *Parnell*, ii. 289–90, 298–9. [4] *Insuppressible*, 27 Dec. 1890.

after an initial unfortunate experience in trying to work through a committee, adopted the same plan as their opponents, and since they too tried to mobilise every available member of their party, the number of M.P.s in the constituency was very large.[1] Most of the principal antagonists had arrived in Kilkenny by December 12 and since the polling-day was fixed for December 22 their efforts had to be compressed into a very short space of time. It is not too much to say that in that ten days the rift opened in Committee Room Fifteen was so widened that no sane man could anticipate any prospect of ultimate reconciliation. It was a continuous nightmare, rising steadily to a crescendo of bad-feeling, bitterness and actual violence. The attention of the entire country was focused upon Kilkenny. What happened there was reported in the most minute detail, and lost nothing in the telling, so that what had been quietly and reasonably debated a week or so earlier was now bandied to and fro in the heated and distorting atmosphere of the hustings, to the lasting damage alike of the unity and the prestige of the party.

Each side lost no opportunity in putting its case to the electorate over and over again. The arguments used were those that had been used in Committee Room Fifteen and may therefore be very briefly summarised. Parnell's thesis was that he had come to Kilkenny to vindicate the principle of independent action. 'This is the principle we have got to fight [for]—it is home rule for Ireland free from outside interference of anybody, and if you can't be trusted to choose your own leader, pray what can you be trusted to do?'[2] And again, a couple of days after: 'I will only say at present that the issue before you is whether you will carry out your own wish and your own opinion in the choice of your member, or whether you will be dictated to by Englishmen.'[3] And once more, at Johnswell a week later, he spoke in language reminiscent of earlier years when he warned his hearers not to repeat Grattan's mistake in disbanding the Volunteers before his final objective was achieved. 'We to-day

---

[1] Estimated at seventy by Healy, *Letters and leaders*, i. 341.

[2] *F.J.*, 13 Dec. 1890, speech at Kilkenny on the night of his arrival on Friday, December 12.

[3] *United Ireland*, 20 Dec. 1890, speech at Tullaroan, on Sunday, December 14.

will not give up our weapons until we are sure that we shall have a parliament worthy of the aspirations of our nation—until we are sure that we shall have an assembly able and willing to look after the interests of every class amongst our countrymen.'[1]

The thesis of independent opposition was an easy one for the electorate to understand and—invested with all the glamour of Parnell's still formidable prestige—it was certain to have a wide appeal. His opponents' task, on the other hand, was in some ways more complicated. They had to insist not only that the party must be governed by majority rule and that the chairman must be subject to that rule like everyone else, but also that the crisis had its origin in Parnell's own misconduct, which had made it impossible for the liberals to work with him. And since their case was in essence that it was only from the liberals that home rule could be obtained, they found themselves in the disagreeable position of having to put it to the voters that the choice lay between Parnell and home rule. As Davitt asked early on in the contest: 'Were they prepared to sacrifice home rule for one man's ambition and allow an insolent dictator to destroy the hopes built up in the last twelve years?'[2] And these hopes, as he pointed out on another occasion, depended for their fulfilment upon 'the democracy' of Great Britain which Parnell, he suggested, had done little to interest in the Irish cause.[3]

These were already well-worn arguments and had earlier been debated with moderation. Moderation, however, was the first casualty of the Kilkenny election. Inexorably a bitter, personal note crept into the speeches. Each side used it and the more it was used, and the worse the things that were said, the more hopeless became the chances of ultimate reunion. Healy, especially, showed no compunction in alluding to the divorce-court proceedings. At the very outset he referred twice in one speech to Mrs O'Shea, and the same evening said what it must have been in his mind to say for a long time past—that he had told his colleagues before that the time to have checked the

[1] *F.J.*, 22 Dec. 1890, speech at Johnswell, 21 Dec. 1890.

[2] *Insuppressible*, 17 Dec. 1890, speech at Ballinakill, 16 Dec. 1890.

[3] *F.J.*, 13 Dec. 1890, speech at Kilkenny, 12 Dec. 1890; *Kilkenny Journal*, 17 Dec. 1890, speech at Freshford, 14 Dec. 1890. See also Sexton's temperate statement of the anti-Parnellite case in *Insuppressible*, 20 Dec. 1890.

danger was at the Galway election in 1886. And he was reported as declaring: 'That was the time to strangle this intrigue, and if his late lamented friend [J. G. Biggar] was alive they knew what side he would take . . . The party had only known of the affair by rumour, and could not accept it as true, but he knew, and Mr Biggar knew, the true facts in connection with the Eltham intrigue . . . they knew he [Parnell] was prostituting a seat in parliament to the interests of his own private intrigues.'[1] And at Castlecomer, two days later, he repeated the charge that Parnell had put O'Shea into the Galway seat in 1886 'as the price of his wife'.[2] Such language could only have the effect of provoking Parnell into a fury of blind retaliation. Speaking at Freshford on Sunday, December 14 he repudiated the notion that the issue was a personal one. 'If I had ever made my position in Irish politics and in Irish public life a personal question, the miserable gutter-sparrows who were once my comrades would not be in a position to come here to-day. . . . But I will not waste my time and breath upon such miserable scum.'[3] This, however, did not prevent him in later speeches moving from the general to the particular. Thus, Dr Tanner was a 'cock-sparrow', Davitt a 'jackdaw', and Justin McCarthy 'a nice old gent for a tea-party'.[4]

Davitt for his part was no less unsparing in his language. In the midst of the conflict he wrote as follows in his *Labour World*, a newspaper intended primarily for that 'British democracy' whose importance he was so anxious to impress upon the Kilkenny electors:

All that Mr Parnell's worst foes have ever said of the man he has more than justified. His tactics in Ireland now are the crowning disgrace of his career. False to friends and false to country, he now stands revealed as a tyrant the most unscrupulous that ever rode roughshod over the hopes and sentiment of a nation. Let the end be what it may, Mr Parnell is for evermore impossible as a leader of a united Irish people. Well may it be asked: 'Is Mr Parnell mad?' That there are evidences of insanity in his actions no one can doubt.

[1] *F.J.*, 13 Dec. 1890, speeches at Freshford and Kilkenny, 12 Dec. 1890.
[2] *Kilkenny Journal*, 17 Dec. 1890, speech at Castlecomer 14 Dec. 1890: *The Times*, 15 Dec. 1890 has 'as the price of his wife's shame'.
[3] *F.J.*, 15 Dec. 1890.
[4] Ibid., 17 and 22 Dec. 1890, speeches at Castlecomer and Kilkenny on 16 and 20 Dec. 1890.

But surely all who follow him are not tainted with madness? Surely the Irish race will not allow this man to wreck their hopes.[1]

This rivalry between Parnell and Davitt was one of the most striking and tragic aspects of the campaign.[2] To anyone who reflected on the history of the past twelve years the fact that these two men should now be deadly enemies was an over-whelming proof of how deep the split in the national movement had gone. And when on the same day both were involved in mob violence and injured as a result, the degradation of Irish politics seemed complete. The trouble occurred because both sides decided to speak at the same time at Ballinakill on December 16. A scuffle took place between the two parties and Davitt received a severe blow from a stick. Parnell expressed his regret at what had happened and both groups moved on to Castle-comer. There a misunderstanding arose as to an offer, which Parnell thought had come from Davitt and Davitt claimed had come from the opposite side, that the two men should speak from the same platform. Parnell scornfully referred to this incident in his speech at Castlecomer (it was on this occasion he called Davitt a jackdaw) and he was much interrupted. Both sides recognised Castlecomer with its mining population as a vital district and it soon appeared that it was strongly anti-Parnellite. Parnell's attacks upon Davitt aroused the resent-ment of the crowd and as he drove away from the meeting the brake upon which he was sitting was showered with mud and slaked lime. All the occupants were covered and he himself was hit in the eye.[3] Subsequently there was some dispute as to whether it was lime or flour that was thrown. Healy, for example, later asserted that it was flour,[4] and at the time Parnell's telegrams of reassurance to Mrs O'Shea were held to prove that he had escaped undamaged.[5] On the other hand, admittedly sixty years after the event, Henry Harrison, who was beside Parnell when the incident occurred, assured the present

---

[1] Quoted in *F.J.*, 19 Dec. 1890.

[2] That shrewd tactician Healy recognised that having Davitt on their side made all the difference to the anti-Parnellites (*Letters and leaders*, i. 343, letter to his brother, 15 Dec. 1890).

[3] The events of December 16 are reported in *F.J.*, 17 Dec. 1890; *Daily News*, 17 Dec. 1890.

[4] Healy, *Letters and leaders*, i. 345–6.   [5] *Insuppressible*, 31 Dec. 1890.

writer emphatically that it *was* lime which was thrown and that if Parnell had not shut his eyes in time he might have been badly hurt.[1] As it was he suffered only minor injury and a good deal of discomfort.

(4)

The duel between Davitt and Parnell, however, was not confined to exchanges of abuse and to exhibitions of rowdyism by their respective partisans. Underlying these surface manifestations there was a deeper and more serious conflict resulting from the fact that at Kilkenny, for the first time for many years, different sections of Irish opinion were openly ranged on different sides. Ironically, in this situation the rôles of the two men were strangely reversed. Twelve years earlier, when the 'new departure' was being worked out, it had represented for Davitt a very real break with his fenian past.[2] Having made the break and having given his support to Parnell's policy, Davitt had remained completely loyal to the 'new departure' and had done nothing to damage the broad national movement into which Parnell had gathered the most diverse elements of Irish life—ex-fenians, clergy, farmers, tenants, shop-keepers and middle-class professional men. It may be imagined, therefore, with what bitterness he saw Parnell making what he, Davitt, believed to be a reckless appeal to the young men of the country to desert the constitutional movement and return to the paths from which the 'new departure' had offered a prospect of escape. Speaking on December 21, Davitt condemned Parnell's appeal to the 'hill-side men'[3] and to the fenian sentiment of the country. It would, he said, be 'a piece of criminal folly for him or any

---

[1] The reasonably impartial account in the *Daily News*, 18 Dec. 1890, suggests that mainly flour was thrown, but that Parnell was actually hit by a stone to which lime was attached.

[2] For the 'new departure', see pp. 6–7 above.

[3] It is one of the minor ironies of history that this expression—'hill-side men'—was apparently popularised, if not invented, by, of all people, Captain O'Shea. He used it at the special commission to describe what he called 'old nationalists' (he meant fenians), 'the men who thought the day might come when they could fight their country's battle on the hill-side against the British forces, and in the meanwhile objected to all outrages' (*Spec. comm. proc*, i. 371).

other man to ask the young men of Ireland to face the overwhelming might of England in the field. Mr Parnell himself
would be the last man to lead the way in this policy of madness
and desperation, and he was only making the appeal in the
hope of snatching a victory in North Kilkenny.'[1]

That such an appeal was being made on behalf of Parnell,
even if not actually by him, seemed beyond dispute. A few days
earlier there had appeared an 'appeal to the men of the hill-side'
issued in Parnell's name. From first to last it was an inflam-
matory document as the following brief extract will show:

> Will you give him up to the Saxon wolves who howl for his
> destruction? Or will you rally round him as your fathers rallied
> round the men of '98, and shout with a thousand united voices, 'No
> surrender! Hurrah for Charles Stewart Parnell, the leader of an
> independent Irish party, and down with the faction which would
> make Irish people the servants of a foreign power!'[2]

And if this were not enough, even John Redmond, among the
most level-headed of Parnell's followers, was to be found proclaiming that Parnell's fight was the same fight that had been
carried on for centuries. 'It was the same old fight that in the
old dark days was fought by the brave Irishmen on the hill-
sides, which was fought by other weapons in the days of the
Land League.'[3]

In the light of such speeches and in the face of Davitt's accusation, it became a matter of urgent importance for Parnell to
define his position in the clearest possible terms. He took the
opportunity of doing so at Kilkenny on Sunday, December 21
and his speech was undoubtedly one of the most important he
made during the entire election campaign. It was not a speech
calculated to reassure moderate opinion. True, he repudiated
the 'appeal to the hill-side men' and he denied that he had
promised to lead the young men against the armed might of
England. On the contrary, so long as he could lead an independent party in the English parliament, there was hope of
obtaining legislative independence by constitutional means.
And so long as such a party existed he would remain at its head.
Then, however, he struck a more defiant note:

---

[1] *Insuppressible*, 22 Dec. 1890; *F.J.*, 22 Dec. 1890.
[2] *Daily News*, 18 Dec. 1890.   [3] Ibid. 20 Dec. 1890.

But when it appears to me that it is impossible to obtain home rule for Ireland by constitutional means I have said this—and this is the extent and limit of my pledge, that as the pledge which has been accepted by the young men of Ireland, whom Michael Davitt in his derision calls the hill-side men—I have said that when it is clear to me that I can no longer hope to obtain our constitution by constitutional and parliamentary means, I will in a moment so declare it to the people of Ireland and, returning at the head of my party, I will take counsel with you as to the next step.

This, he said, had been his declaration in Cork in 1880 and he had not departed from it.[1] He continued:

... and if the young men of Ireland have trusted in me it is because they know that I am not a mere parliamentarian; that I can be trusted to keep my word to them to go as far as a brave and honest heart can go on this parliamentary alliance, and test it to the uttermost, and that when and if I find it useless and unavailing to persevere further, they can depend upon me to tell them so.[2]

These were ominous words. Indeed, if Parnell really meant what he said, it seemed as if he might end by turning his back on everything he had achieved in the previous ten years. As his speech indicated, an independent parliamentary party was for him the essential pre-condition of a constitutional movement. But the sting lay in that word 'independent'. Implicit in his

---

[1] His Cork speeches may in retrospect have seemed more fiery than they actually were. The most important of them were primarily concerned with the land agitation and with parliamentary obstruction; of course we cannot be sure that they were fully reported, though the accounts in the *Cork Daily Herald*, 5 Apr. and 4 Oct. 1880, are lengthy. However, Parnell had no need to hark back to 1880 to find speeches with revolutionary over-tones. As recently as 1889, at the height of the constitutional agitation and the 'union of hearts', he had told an Irish gathering that if they could not win home rule by parliamentary action, 'I for one would not continue to remain for 24 hours longer in the house of commons. . . .' He added that the parliamentary policy was 'a trial' and that he did not believe 'in the possibility of maintaining for all time an incorruptible and independent Irish representation at Westminster' (*F.J.*, 24 May 1889). For an acute analysis of the tactical considerations which may have prompted this particular speech see C. Cruise O'Brien, *Parnell and his party*, p. 234, *n.* 1. It is interesting that one of the first speeches he made in Ireland after the Kilmainham treaty should have been on similar lines (*F.J.*, 17 Aug. 1882).

[2] *F.J.*, 22 Dec. 1890; *United Ireland*, 27 Dec. 1890; R. B. O'Brien, *Parnell*, ii. 304–5.

behaviour since the start of the crisis had been the assumption
that the notion of independence was inseparable from that of
loyalty to him, whatever the pressure and whatever the cost. It
does not seem to have entered his head that reasonable men
might genuinely feel that there was a point beyond which their
loyalty should not be stretched and that this point was reached
when personal devotion was seen to involve the most deadly
risk to home rule. The trend of his argument was simple—but
devastating. The party would lose its independence if it finally
abandoned him under liberal 'dictation'. But a successful constitutional movement postulated an independent party. Therefore, if the party ceased to be independent, a constitutional
movement—at least on the existing lines—would become
impossible. Naturally, to those who, in the past decade, had
come to regard such a movement as the one hope of home rule,
and who saw in the liberal alliance the greatest achievement of
the parliamentary party, Parnell's Kilkenny speeches came as
a profound shock. And even though he repudiated violence, his
alternative was scarcely less desolating, for he seemed to offer
only the prospect of starting all over again from the position of
1880, but this time without the aid or sympathy of either of the
great English parties. Contrasted with this bleak doctrine,
Davitt's point of view was both more rational and more optimistic. He, who had risked more and suffered more than most
men in the struggle against England, having renounced physical
force—at any rate in the foreseeable future—was perfectly
consistent with the attitude he had taken up at the time of the
'new departure'. So that when he advocated the liberal alliance
and the need to work in harmony with the democratic masses in
Britain, it was the old fenian rather than the disillusioned
parliamentarian who struck the moderate note.

The issue, however, was complicated by a further factor. No-
one could have gone about the constituency during the struggle
without realising that the tremendous power of the priests was
being thrown into the scale against Parnell. It was all very well
for Davitt, when the election was over, to declare emphatically
'I would be the last man in Irish politics to stand dictation at
the hands of the priest-hood or any other class in political
matters',[1] but in this case circumstances were too strong for him;

[1] *Insuppressible*, 27 Dec. 1890, speech in Dublin, 24 Dec. 1890.

there may not have been 'dictation' but that there was influence seems inescapable. Barry O'Brien's assertion that the struggle at Kilkenny was in essence a repetition of the old clash between fenianism and the church was doubtless an over-simplification, but it contained a germ of truth.[1] No responsible pastor was going to allow his flock to be led away into wild courses if he could possibly help it, and every parish priest in the diocese had plentiful guidance from his superiors as to what was the right path to follow through the political jungle.[2] Not only had the standing committee of archbishops and bishops declared against Parnell on general grounds, but Archbishop Croke had written strongly in support of Pope-Hennessy's candidature, and the local bishop had issued a statement which, though the language was guarded, was in effect an appeal to the voters to support the anti-Parnellite candidate.[3] Parnell himself realised that he would have the priests against him and at one stage, learning that they intended to act as personation agents on polling-day, he contemplated a protest to the sheriff. His supporters tried in vain to make him see that, however undesirable the practice, they had the legal right so to act and that any such protest would fail. It was only when O'Brien put it to him that this would be 'drawing the sword on the whole order' rather than objecting to the action of any individual priest, and thus something impossible for a protestant to attempt, that Parnell saw his point and desisted.[4] In the event, the priests did act in this way[5] and one of Parnell's catholic supporters,

[1] R. B. O'Brien, *Parnell*, ii. 302–3, 305–6.

[2] There were one or two priests who stood out for Parnell, but the vast majority were against him. Two examples of Parnellite clergy were Fr J. Ryan who presided at his Kilkenny meeting of December 21, and Fr N. Murphy of Kilmanagh (*The Times*, 22 Dec. 1890; R. B. O'Brien, *Parnell*, ii. 306; *Daily News*, 20 Dec. 1890).

[3] *Insuppressible*, 13 and 16 Dec. 1890.

[4] R. B. O'Brien, *Parnell*, ii. 306–7. The most important function of personation agents in the Kilkenny election was to be present in the polling-booths when the illiterates declared to the returning-officer how they wanted to vote. For the procedure under the Ballot Act of 1872 see *Statutes, United Kingdom*, 35 and 36 Vict., c. 33, first schedule, part I.

[5] The special correspondent of *The Times*, who affected to view the election with sardonic detachment, recorded that on polling-day priests acted as personation agents in fourteen out of the fifteen polling-booths. He also reported, though without giving his authority, that in some districts as many

Timothy Harrington, who had flung himself into the fray immediately on his return from America, wrote angrily to William O'Brien of the part they were playing:

Kilkenny was the saddest sight I ever witnessed in Ireland. In every polling-booth in the division a priest sat at the table as persona-tion agent. The people were instructed to declare they could not read and the voters came in bodies with the priests [at?] their heads declaring they were catholics and would vote with their clergy.[1]

This, it must be said, was the view of an ardent Parnellite, soon himself to be deeply embroiled with the church over this very question of the priest in politics, and should properly be treated with reserve. We shall never know precisely the extent of clerical influence at Kilkenny. There was no petition to un-seat the successful candidate—perhaps because the Parnellites themselves had a far from unblemished record in the matter of mob violence—and so there was no official enquiry to elicit detailed evidence.[2] An outside observer, the correspondent of the liberal *Daily News* and therefore certainly not sympathetic to Parnell, at one time reported that 'all the priests of North Kilkenny are canvassers in the nationalist [he meant anti-Parnellite] cause'.[3] It is only fair to add, however, that in later reports he suggested that their main contribution lay rather in speaking at meetings and in giving facilities near their churches for anti-Parnellite gatherings.[4] Opinions might differ as to the form taken by clerical influence, but that such influence should have been exerted can scarcely in itself have been a matter for surprise. Given the facts of the case—a largely rural constitu-

---

as twenty-five per cent of the voters were declared illiterates (*The Times*, 24 Dec. 1890).

[1] Gill Papers, Harrington to William O'Brien, 27 Dec. 1890. An Irish-American correspondent of John Devoy's described to him a letter he had received (early in 1891) from J. J. O'Kelly in which O'Kelly said that the priests had smashed the movement. 'From what he (O'Kelly) saw at the Kilkenny elections (sic) he is pretty certain that P(arnell) will be beaten at the general elections just as badly as he was at Kilkenny. The priests have preached a regular crusade against them' (W. O'Brien and D. Ryan (ed.), *Devoy's post-bag*, ii. 317–8).

[2] The attack on Davitt at Ballinakill already referred to was one example of such violence. The rough reception given to Healy on his arrival at Kilkenny was another (*The Times*, 13 Dec. 1890).

[3] *Daily News*, 18 Dec. 1890.   [4] Ibid., 19, 20 and 26 Dec. 1890.

ency, the attitude of the hierarchy, the nature of Parnell's original offence, the opposition to him of so many leading men in the constitutional movement—it was morally certain that the priests, so far from shrinking from intervention, would regard it as their duty to use every effort to defeat Parnell and his candidate.

(5)

Polling took place on December 22. Parnell himself was well aware at the last that he would be beaten,[1] while, in the other camp, Healy a week earlier had forecast almost the exact margin of Pope-Hennessy's victory.[2] When the result was announced it was found that this margin was 1,165—Pope-Hennessy having obtained 2,527 votes against Scully's 1,362.[3] Naturally, Parnell's opponents hailed Kilkenny as a decisive triumph and some even seem to have believed that he himself would recognise it as such and give up the struggle.[4] If so, they were soon to be disillusioned. On the eve of the result he had told Barry O'Brien that he would fight on,[5] and in his speech after the declaration of the poll he repeated this promise publicly in no uncertain language. He would fight, he said, in every constituency, as opportunity served. Once again he recalled his declaration at Cork in 1880—that when it seemed to him hopeless to expect legislative independence from England by means within the constitution, he would call upon his colleagues 'to shake the dust off our feet upon the palace at Westminster' and return to Ireland to take counsel with the people. He continued:

I renew to you, men of Kilkenny, the pledge which I made to the citizens of Cork in 1880. . . . I will never allow my name and my authority to be used to tempt the people of Ireland into any hopeless struggle, either constitutional or otherwise, and when constitutional struggle, if it ever does (I don't say it ever will), becomes useless and unavailing, at that moment I will declare my belief to you and I will take your advice and be guided by your judgment.[6]

[1] R. B. O'Brien, *Parnell*, ii. 307.

[2] Healy, *Letters and leaders*, i. 342–3, letter to his wife, 15 Dec. 1890.

[3] *F.J.*, 24 and 25 Dec. 1890; Healy, *Letters and leaders*, i. 345–6; R. B. O'Brien, *Parnell*, ii. 308.

[4] *Insuppressible*, 24 Dec. 1890, leading article entitled 'Gloria in excelsis Deo'.

[5] R. B. O'Brien, *Parnell*, ii. 307.   [6] *F.J.*, 24 and 25 Dec. 1890.

Thus he ended the election as he had begun it, and although he took care to qualify his remarks in this as in other speeches, it was his assertions rather than his reservations that naturally attracted most attention. If Kilkenny was an important turning-point in the struggle—and there can be no doubt that it was—this was due partly to the fact that Parnell's public declarations indicated, more startlingly than most people in Ireland had yet had a chance to realise, the turn his mind was taking. It was almost as if the combined effects of physical and mental stress, disgust at what he felt to be the weakness of his followers, and hatred of Gladstone, had blinded him to political realities. Since 1882 he had committed the entire national effort to support of the constitutional movement and in doing so had captured the imagination of a great English statesman and the sympathy of a large section of the English people. To put all this in jeopardy, to sneer at Gladstone, to cast off with contempt the liberal alliance, to gird at his former colleagues because they clung to that alliance, seemed—to some of his contemporaries, at least—little short of madness.[1] It is indeed hard to understand how he can have imagined that he would find adequate support for this abrupt and breath-taking *volte face*. The inescapable fact, which he could not or would not understand, was that he no longer had—Ireland no longer had —the freedom of movement *within the constitutional framework* which had existed before the home rule campaign of 1886. Once the choice between English parties had been made, and once the English parties themselves had made up their minds, the pattern of future advance was clear. Any departure from that pattern could only mean at best a postponement of self-government; at worst it could bring effective parliamentary action to an end.

In Parnell's view, no doubt, either of these alternatives would have been preferable to the spectacle of an Irish party which, by jettisoning its leader at Gladstone's nod, exhibited its frailty

[1] For example, Davitt's article in the *Labour World*, quoted on pp. 166–7 above. Others besides Davitt expressed doubts about Parnell's sanity at this time. Thus, Earl Granville thought he was 'off his head' (Spencer Papers, Granville to Spencer, 20 Dec. 1890). And Cardinal Manning found his belief that Parnell was of unsound mind 'still more confirmed'. He considered that what he took to be Parnell's appeal to the hill-side men was 'the last scintillation' (Gladstone Papers, B.M., Add. MS 44,250, f. 306, Manning to Gladstone, 21 Dec. 1890).

to the world. Independence—identified as always with loyalty to him—remained for Parnell the key to the situation. With independence everything was still possible, even though it might be necessary to build again from the foundations. Without it there could be no future—or, at any rate, no future at Westminster. Kilkenny—and this was a further reason for its significance in the history of Parnell's fall—showed that when these arguments were put to the electors they were moved by powerful forces to reject them. Whether because of the church's condemnation of Parnell's moral lapse, or because they refused to abandon their belief that home rule could only be won from the liberals, or for both reasons together, a majority of voters had shown beyond question that their attachment to the constitutional movement remained unshaken. There was in fact only one section of opinion that was ready to follow Parnell enthusiastically on the grim trek back to the position of 1880. By spurning his own former colleagues, by alienating the church, by alarming sober and moderate men, he left himself with little option but to shape his course towards the fenians. How many of these rallied to him it is impossible to say, but it was observed that two of the most famous names of the old guard were to be found on his side. These were James Stephens, who had declared for him early in December, and John O'Leary, who wrote strongly in his support during the election.[1] True, Stephens and O'Leary were old men, no longer active in politics, and Stephens, in the eyes of many, had a disreputable past. They were, however, the living symbols of a tradition which had never accepted the constitutional approach to the Irish problems, but rather had cherished the dream of armed revolution. That the guardians of such a tradition should have thrown their weight behind Parnell so openly and so promptly was a storm-signal which no-one could fail to understand. Nor were they the only ones, for such influential fenians as Mark Ryan in London, and John Devoy, who could speak for many (though not all) Irish-Americans, were to be found on the same side.[2]

---

[1] *F.J.*, 3 Dec. 1890; *United Ireland*, 20 Dec. 1890; Katharine Tynan, *Twenty-five years : reminiscences*, p. 344.

[2] For Irish-American groupings see W. O'Brien and D. Ryan (ed.), *Devoy's post-bag*, ii. 316–7. For the support given to Parnell by London fenians see Mark Ryan, *Fenian memories*, pp. 148–56.

If Parnell realised the seriousness of his defeat, he allowed no trace of it to appear in his demeanour. He arrived back at Kingsbridge at night and the ever-faithful Dubliners greeted him as warmly as if he had won a great victory. He was escorted from the station to the Parnell leadership committee rooms in Rutland square in a vast procession with bands and banners and flaming torches. He stood up in his waggonette, a bandage covering his injured eye, his hair and beard ruffled—a wild, fierce figure. As they went through College Green, past the Bank of Ireland which had housed Grattan's parliament in other days, he flung out his arm and without speaking pointed to the building. The gesture was at once taken up by the crowd which received it with a deep roar of applause.[1] No speech could have declared so vividly his invincible determination to struggle on, let the end be what it might.

[1] *F.J.*, 24 and 25 Dec. 1890; M. Macdonagh, *The home rule movement*, pp. 226-7.

VII

AN AMERICAN INTERLUDE

~~~~~~

(1)

As THE BITTERNESS of the conflict between Parnell and his opponents deepened, and as that conflict spread into Ireland, the
attitude of the Irish delegates in America became a factor of
growing importance. We have seen already the eagerness with
which their views were awaited in Dublin, and by the party
when it met in London, and it is certainly no exaggeration to
say that their early telegram in support of Parnell helped to
determine the outcome of the Leinster Hall meeting, just as
their later denunciation of him contributed to the action of the
majority when they decided to repudiate his leadership. Once
the split in the party had become a recognised fact, it was
obvious that those who had not been directly involved in the
angry exchanges of Committee Room Fifteen were in a position
where they could exert a decisive influence. Distance, which had
so hampered the delegates in their appreciation of the difficulties
of the men on the spot, now proved to have its advantages. In
America it was possible to achieve a perspective denied to those
at home and to assume a degree of aloofness from either party
which allowed the delegates to consider, and ultimately to
attempt, a policy of reconciliation. And since this policy of
reconciliation remained the best hope of the country from
December 1890 until February 1891, it is essential to understand
the frame of mind in which the mediators approached their task.

Decisive though their utterances proved to be at critical points during the struggle, it is plain from their letters and diaries that they themselves were racked by constant anxiety as to what was the right course to follow. After they had all (except, of course, Harrington) sent off the pronouncement against Parnell which was read in full to the party on December 2 there was nothing they could do except wait for the result of the debate in Committee Room Fifteen. The strain was intense but, although Harrington differed from his colleagues, they were still on speaking terms and he was able to note down his impressions of them at close quarters. O'Brien's nervous temperament had apparently suffered worst from the crisis and he astonished Harrington by his vehemence and bitterness against Parnell's supporters. Dillon, on the other hand, was 'calm, unimpassioned but resolute, and I fear that no consideration will bring him and Parnell together again'.[1]

Dillon's reactions at this juncture were especially important in view of the grave decisions he was shortly to be called on to take, and it is fortunate for the historian that during these weeks he too kept a diary. From this diary it appears that while the fortunes of war in Committee Room Fifteen swayed this way and that, he was divided between reluctant admiration for Parnell's tactics, irritation at the blunders of his opponents, and the direst forebodings of the effects of the struggle upon the future of the Irish movement. At the very outset, impressed by the strength of the non-conformist reaction to the verdict of the divorce court, he had assumed that Parnell would go under.[2] But later, after Parnell had induced the party to seek guarantees from Gladstone, he inclined to the opposite view. After Clancy's amendment had been debated and passed on December 4, he wrote:

The compromise which has been adopted at this day's meeting is in my mind nothing other than a rat-trap skilfully set by P. and in which he now has his opponents securely caught. And it seems to me now that the only way out of the imbroglio is that Parnell should resume the lead, and all members of the party who can reconcile it to their conscience and honour to follow him should fall into line again.[3]

[1] Harrington Papers (N.L.I., MS 2195), 'Diary', 2 Dec. 1890.
[2] Dillon Papers, 'Diary', 23 Nov. 1890.   [3] Ibid., 4 Dec. 1890.

Evidently he expressed the same view to Harrington, for that very day the latter recorded that Dillon had said to him that the worst thing that could happen now would be for Parnell to retire, because the position would be absolutely hopeless for anyone else. Later, when they had heard definitely that Clancy's amendment had been adopted by the party, Dillon remarked that Parnell had put them all in a trap and caught them, a view which was apparently also shared by O'Brien.[1] Even two days later, before he knew that the negotiations had failed, Dillon was still divided between appreciation of Parnell's generalship and contempt for his opponents:

> This idiotic piece of tactics seems to me to have handed over the opposition bound hand and foot to Parnell. The question at issue is entirely changed, and the minds of people drawn to a new issue. . . Every fresh development only increases my admiration for the infinite political skill of Parnell, his power of planning a campaign, of *seeing* what ideas will take hold of the minds of the people, of diverting discussion from the real points in controversy. . .[2]

For a few days the delegates parted company, Harrington going to Detroit and the others to New York. On December 8, Harrington received a cable from Parnell requesting his return and on the next day he arrived in New York before setting out for Ireland.[3] He lost no time in meeting his fellow-delegates and found that in the interval William O'Brien had been in communication with Parnell and had arranged to go to France to confer with him.[4] By this time, of course, the split in the party had taken place and the situation was developing fast. On December 6, the very day the party broke in two, Justin McCarthy had cabled, asking for authority to add their names to the anti-Parnellite declaration.[5] But, with the prospect of a meeting with Parnell opening up before them, Dillon and O'Brien were anxious not to commit themselves irrevocably. On December 8 they issued a statement to the press in which

[1] Harrington Papers (N.L.I., MS 2195), 'Diary', 4 Dec. 1890.

[2] Dillon Papers, 'Diary', 6 Dec. 1890.

[3] Harrington Papers (N.L.I., MS 2195), 'Diary', 8 and 9 Dec. 1890.

[4] Ibid., 9 Dec. 1890; Gill Papers, cable from Parnell to W. O'Brien, 8 Dec. 1890; *The Times*, 10 Dec. 1890.

[5] Gill Papers, cable from Justin McCarthy to Dillon and W. O'Brien, 6 Dec. 1890; for the anti-Parnellite declaration see above, p. 154.

they said that they felt obliged to remain silent, though they admitted that they had cabled home approving of Justin McCarthy's election 'as chairman of the Irish party'.[1] Next day, however, the anti-Parnellites learnt that this approval had its limitations. In a further cable to Justin McCarthy, while declaring themselves in sympathy with the resolutions the anti-Parnellites had already passed, they added: '. . . we desire, as hitherto, to leave the responsibility to you, co-operating by methods we believe best to secure Mr Parnell's withdrawal, and the reunion of the party.'[2]

There can be little doubt, in view of the fact that O'Brien was even then making up his mind to go to France, that they meant by this to indicate that they held themselves free to negotiate direct with Parnell if such a course should seem to hold out any hope of a peaceful settlement. But with Parnell's arrival in Dublin on December 10, his seizure of *United Ireland* and his provocative interview with Tracy Grieves, the prospect of such a settlement seemed more remote than ever. That very day, indeed, Bodkin, in sending them news of his expulsion from the offices of *United Ireland*, urged them to issue a manifesto supporting the anti-Parnellite candidate for North Kilkenny.[3] The next day, spurred on by Parnell's second capture of *United Ireland*, he renewed his plea, and his cable—staccato and almost incoherent as it is—is worth reproducing, since it reflects so vividly the confusion and excitement of the time:

Resolute manifesto from you, Dillon, sorely needed. Parnell playing with you. Strikes foul blow while you hold your hands. Retook offices midnight. To-day Parnell himself broke in with crowbars assisted by O'Connor, Kenny, Leamy, Redmond and mob, police standing by. Old employees expelled. Rumours actively circulated that you, Dillon, coming round to Parnell. *Freeman, Telegraph*[4] blackguard, rousing mob. Country with us. Vigour and promptness win. *Suppressed United Ireland* appearing to-day, *Nation* office. Cable supporting paper. We shall denounce prostitution of the journal you

[1] *The Times*, 8 Dec. 1890; *F.J.*, 9 Dec. 1890.

[2] *F.J.*, 10 Dec. 1890. This cable was not dated, but it was read to the anti-Parnellite majority at their meeting of December 9; it was signed by all five of the delegates who had declared against Parnell.

[3] Gill Papers, cable from Bodkin to W. O'Brien, 10 Dec. 1890.

[4] The reference is to the *Evening Telegraph*, owned by the *Freeman's Journal* company.

founded and suffered for. Your instructions conduct paper literally obeyed. . . . Readdress all my letters any capacity *Nation* office.[1]

Under this provocation it was impossible for Dillon and O'Brien to remain silent. O'Brien replied at once to Bodkin deploring that the paper which for ten years had withstood all the assaults of Dublin Castle 'should receive the worst stab from the leader I all but worshipped', and adding he was proud to know that '*United Ireland* continues insuppressible'.[2] Then, together with the other delegates, he and Dillon set about drawing up a public statement which should be an adequate answer to what Parnell had said in his Dublin interview, yet which would still leave the way open for negotiation. They began by recalling that when they started their tour six weeks previously the Irish cause had been in the ascendant, the prospects of a liberal victory at the next general election had been good, and that all that had been needed was a fund to keep the evicted tenants going until the unionist government had fallen. The American tour had promised well, for some 200,000 dollars had been subscribed in the first two weeks.[3] Then had come the crash. Parnell, they said, argued that the change in the situation was due to treachery by Gladstone and to the corruption of the Irish parliamentary party. In fact, these imputations were side-issues, designed to distract attention from the real issue. 'That issue is whether it is humanly possible to win the general election under Mr Parnell's leadership.' They concluded that, given the circumstances, it would be impossible to win under him and they left their readers in no doubt that for them the importance of maintaining the liberal alliance was paramount. They were careful, though, to speak of Parnell himself with studied moderation and to refer appreciatively to his past services.[4]

The firmness of this manifesto, however, was deceptive, for they were in a most dejected frame of mind when they wrote it. They were all agreed that there seemed no course open to them

[1] Gill Papers, cable from Bodkin to W. O'Brien, 11 Dec. 1890.

[2] '*Suppressed*' United Ireland, 15 Dec. 1890. The cable was dated New York, December 11.

[3] It was reckoned that some £15,000 had been subscribed in the first nine days (*F.J.*, 14 Nov. 1890). John Morley estimated the total for the entire mission at £50,000 (Gladstone Papers (B.M., Add. MS 44,256, ff. 101-2), John Morley to Gladstone, 27 Dec. 1890).

[4] *F.J.*, 12 Dec. 1890.

but to resign, and Dillon's entry in his diary that night was despondent. 'The more I wrote, the more utterly hopeless I became of the situation.'[1] Part, at any rate, of this hopelessness seems to have sprung from the fact that while every step Parnell took made it more difficult for them to have anything to do with him, they disliked the attacks that had already been made upon him inside and outside the parliamentary party and were far from happy at the company they would have to keep if they joined in the general hue and cry. It was impossible to say this publicly, of course, but O'Brien opened his mind a little on the subject to Harrington before the latter returned to Ireland. Having visited both Dillon and O'Brien, Harrington described his impressions thus:

Both are much more conciliatory in tone than they have been and both strongly begged me to use my best endeavours to promote peace. . . . O'Brien impressed upon me to explain to Parnell how they deprecated the attacks upon him and hated finding themselves in association with Healy, Davitt and the bishops in those attacks, and that they will be most ready to entertain any proposal for peace he makes; but of course I can see that they hold that no terms are admissible if they do not include his temporary retirement from the chair.[2]

We do not know if they gave Harrington any more precise idea of what their terms would be—on the whole, it is unlikely that they did—but they could have done so had they wished, for the previous night they, together with T. P. O'Connor and T. P. Gill, met at the Hoffman House hotel to discuss what O'Brien's policy should be if and when he met Parnell in France. The peace terms which were then discussed were jotted down roughly by John Dillon on the hotel notepaper and this is the main source we have for the views of what might be called the moderate anti-Parnellite section at this critical stage.[3] From the notes of this discussion it is quite evident that they were

---

[1] Dillon Papers, 'Diary', 10 Dec. 1890.
[2] Harrington Papers (N.L.I., MS 2195), 'Diary', 12 Dec. 1890.
[3] Gill Papers, 'Memorandum for Paris negotiations', 11 Dec. 1890. There is a second version, also in Dillon's hand and of the same date in the Dillon Papers; it differs from the other version in a few details, but in all essentials it is the same. I have used the one in the Gill Papers, since it was this that O'Brien had with him when he met Parnell in France.

prepared to give Parnell very generous terms to secure his with-drawal. The particular concessions they were ready to make may be summarised as follows:

(1) Some acknowledgment was to be made of the informality of McCarthy's election and if Parnell wanted him re-elected (presumably they meant by a full party meeting) this was to be done.

(2) There should be some personal satisfaction for Parnell such as a public declaration or a resolution by the party enumerating the circumstances which might excuse or palliate Parnell's action; for example, the Leinster Hall meeting, the party vote,[1] Gladstone's hasty publication of his letter, and the tone of the press.

(3) An attempt should be made to get the two archbishops—Croke and Walsh—to retract their denunciations of Parnell.

(4) It should be suggested to Parnell that his personal influence would always be dominant, that his retirement would probably only be temporary, and that his return to the leadership would be welcomed under certain (unspecified) conditions.[2]

(5) Some special recognition should be given to Parnell in the negotiations with the liberals as to the terms of the home rule bill. It was to be proposed that he should share with the chairman of the party in all discussions on the provisions of such a bill.[3] It should be put to the liberals that this concession was called for by the state of Irish opinion, just as the retirement of Parnell was demanded by English opinion. It should be pointed out to them that Parnell as an independent critic would be much more dangerous and have greater power to wreck a home rule bill.

(6) If Parnell objected to the committee that had been elected to share the chairman's functions it could be 'thrown over-

---

[1] That is, the re-election of Parnell to the chair on November 25.

[2] Just before this clause, the MS in the Gill Papers has this passage crossed out: 'That he might nominate leader for six months or veto on election thereof.' The version in the Dillon Papers is more fragmentary, but it runs: 'Give P. nomination or veto on chairman for this year . . . discussion—agreed nothing can be done in this direction.'

[3] The MS in the Gill papers has at this point a pencilled insertion in Gill's hand in brackets, 'and other Irish legislation', with a note that these words were added at Boulogne on Parnell's suggestion. The MS in the Dillon Papers, while agreeing that Parnell was to share in discussion of the home rule provisions, adds that this could only be with the consent of Gladstone.

board',[1] or he might be offered the right to nominate on it an equal number of his supporters.

(7) Parnell was to remain president of the National League—the negotiations in France were to affect only the chairmanship of the party.

(8) Parnell was to be joint treasurer, with two others elected by the party, of all party funds—cheques to be signed by any two treasurers.

In many ways this is a most revealing document. It shows, above all, the lengths to which its authors were prepared to go to smooth the way for Parnell's retirement, even if it were only to be a temporary retirement. At this stage, apparently, they did not contemplate his resignation from anything except the chairmanship of the party, and were prepared to turn a blind eye to the inevitable complications which would result from deposing him from that office and yet leaving him, not only with a say as to the disposition of the party funds, but also at the head of the organisation (the National League) in Ireland. And not only that, but it was also to be in his power either to destroy the party committee outright or at least to neutralise it. From Parnell's point of view, with these strong points still in his possession, it would be a powerful temptation to fall in with such proposals, and no doubt the delegates in America felt they had to bait their hooks richly to catch so large a prize. But in doing so, they appeared to have attached too little importance to the fact that in conceding so much to Parnell they were certain to rouse the anger of his opponents. And this perhaps was where their absence in America told most heavily against them. If they had experienced the passion of Committee Room Fifteen, or the turbulence of Dublin, it would have been easier for them to realise that too many people were too deeply involved in the struggle for these large concessions to be lightly made. With such men as Healy, Sexton, Davitt and the two archbishops against him, Parnell would not readily be allowed to ride off with so many of the honours of war.

(2)

From another quarter, also, the line of policy marked out for O'Brien was open to objection. Although the delegates, like

[1] Both versions use this actual phrase.

everyone else, must have been well aware that Gladstone had more than once made it clear that he would not discuss home rule details in connection with the leadership question, this was precisely what they were proposing when they envisaged that Parnell should have special recognition in any negotiations about the terms of a home rule bill. It needed little insight to perceive that Parnell would be all too likely to seize upon such a proposition and make it an essential condition of his retirement. But obviously this was not something which they alone could give—it required the consent of Gladstone. In other words, there was a danger that they might find themselves in the position of having to put it to the liberal leader that Parnell would retire if he, Gladstone, agreed to his sharing with the chairman of the Irish parliamentary party in all discussions of the projected home rule settlement. It is hard to see how Gladstone in such circumstances could have avoided the conclusion that he was being confronted yet again with an attempt to link the questions of the leadership and home rule—an attempt to which he would presumably return, as before, a discouraging reply. Nothing shows so clearly the desperate importance which the delegates attached to Parnell's retirement as their willingness to commit themselves to a proposal of this kind, knowing as they did the strength of English feeling against the Irish leader, and understanding as they did the distrust and resentment of the liberals at the way in which Parnell had dealt in his manifesto with Gladstone's privately imparted thoughts on home rule.

They had, however, one further contingency to consider. If the negotiations broke down—indeed, whether they did or not —on what conditions would they contemplate remaining members of the Irish parliamentary party? From a hastily scribbled postscript to the notes which Dillon made of their discussions it seems that they were prepared to stay in the party if both Parnell and his opponents agreed to reasonable terms— by which, presumably, they meant either the terms they had just been discussing amongst themselves or their equivalent. If Parnell rejected the proffered compromise, their path would be clearer, but even so they decided that they would need to obtain from the anti-Parnellites some assurance that there would be a chance of continuing the American tour and of raising perhaps £60,000 in addition to the money already collected.[1] They would also want some proof that they could hold public meetings in Ireland and that popular hostility was directed against individuals rather than against the majority as such;[2] that there was a reasonable prospect of a party fund; that there was a possibility of 'spiking' the *Freeman's Journal*; and that the party would agree to take responsibility for the evicted tenants.

These conditions were admittedly hypothetical and at the time they were put on paper the chances of their ever being fulfilled were slender. The news from Ireland was always confusing and became more and more gloomy as the Kilkenny election got under way. Meanwhile, the delegation was breaking up rapidly and Dillon and O'Connor were soon to be left alone in America. On Saturday, December 13 William O'Brien, accompanied by his wife and T. P. Gill, sailed on the *Obdam* for France, while on the same day Harrington left for Ireland.[3] Just before O'Brien had sailed he and Dillon had yielded to the plea of T. J. Condon that they should send a message for the guidance of a meeting in connection with the evicted tenants shortly to be held in Tipperary. The line they took was that while they would like to have advised a truce in the struggle 'pending our efforts for an honourable reconciliation', as Parnell had challenged public opinion it was necessary to speak out. And they repeated what they had said before—'unless Mr Parnell can be induced to retire and end this hateful strife the inevitable result will be the loss of the general election'.[4] Once O'Brien had sailed, the responsibility for maintaining this line rested upon Dillon and O'Connor, and the difficulty of their task increased as the campaign in Ireland gathered momentum. Theirs was an unhappy position. On the one hand, Parnell's violent speeches were not calculated to impress them in his favour, while on the other hand the language used against him aroused their anger and disgust. However, from the purely political stand-point it was essential for their purposes that Parnell should be beaten

[1] This is the version in the Gill Papers. The MS in the Dillon Papers has 'Assurance of raising £30,000 in addition to amount already collected'.

[2] Both versions record that T. P. O'Connor queried this condition.

[3] *The Times*, 15 Dec. 1890. T. D. Sullivan left for home on December 17, arriving in Ireland on Christmas Day (*The Times*, 18 and 26 Dec. 1890).

[4] *The Times*, 13 Dec. 1890.

in Kilkenny, since only then would it be feasible to deal successfully with him in France. O'Brien might be a match for a Parnell
chastened by defeat, but a Parnell flushed with victory would
quite possibly ignore him altogether.

We find, therefore, at this time a contrast between Dillon's
public utterances and his private correspondence. In public he
continued to press for Parnell's retirement and indeed, considering a peaceful settlement was his aim, went near to over-playing
his hand. Thus, on December 15, he issued a statement in the
course of which, while hoping that good would come of the
prospective conference in France, he used words that were
likely to rankle:

> In the meantime, however, Mr Parnell has plunged Ireland into a
> conflict for purely personal ends, and has used language and base
> accusations, revolting to every free man, which, unless altered, show
> that he is unfit to be the leader of a nation aspiring to be free.[1]

Again, a few days later he and O'Connor issued an appeal to
the electors to vote for Sir John Pope-Hennessy on the grounds
that American aid would once more be given generously only
if Ireland showed herself united. 'Such unity', they said, 'can
only be secured by such an overwhelming victory in North
Kilkenny as will show Mr Parnell the futility of all further
opposition to the majority of his party and the will of his
country.'[2]

This was strong language, but it masked a deep, inner uncertainty. Even on the very day of O'Brien's departure, Dillon
sent a letter after him which showed that, while he might exhort
the Kilkenny electors to vote against Parnell, he had little love
for the methods used by the men on the spot. After commisera-
ting with O'Brien on the rigours of the voyage (the food on the
Obdam, he feared, would be appalling) he referred directly to
the election: 'Healy is maddening. And I expect Davitt will be
as bad. And it infuriates me to read of Parnell being hounded
down by the priests.'[3] The letters he himself was receiving from
home did nothing to ease his mind. From his own cousin,
Valentine Dillon, who had sided with Parnell, he learnt that
if at that moment an honourable compromise could be

[1] *F.J.*, 16 Dec. 1890.   [2] *Insuppressible*, 22 Dec. 1890.
[3] Gill Papers, Dillon to W. O'Brien, 13 Dec. 1890.

arranged, Clancy, Kenny and John Redmond among others would welcome it—provided it did not deal too harshly with Parnell. But his cousin added—what John Dillon himself was to find later—that the vehemence with which Parnell was being assailed made it very difficult for the moderate men on his side to enter into any kind of negotiations.[1] Also from Dublin, and written on the same day, came a long and affectionate letter from another Parnellite, Dr J. E. Kenny, reproaching him and O'Brien for taking their stand against Parnell so early and for ignoring the appeals of himself and Clancy and John Redmond. Dillon would have been shocked, he said, at the thirst to destroy Parnell which had been shown at the first meeting of the party after the publication of Gladstone's letter. It is an interesting side-light on the cross-currents of personal feeling at the time that for Kenny the villains of the piece were not Healy (whom he excused as being only half-recovered from his illness), but Sexton and John Barry. He admitted that Parnell's subsequent manifesto was provocative and said that if he had been present he would have urged him not to issue it, or at least not to include in it any reflections on the party's integrity. But, as he pointed out, Parnell's chief antagonists could not plead the manifesto as an excuse because they had defined their position before it had been written, or before anything had been heard of its being about to be published.[2]

No doubt Kenny was overwrought, as most men were on either side, but the picture he painted of the hostility towards Parnell shown by some of the leading men in the party could not be ignored. If such was really the temper of the anti-Parnellites who could control them, and what hope of compromise was there? No-one could seriously suppose that Justin McCarthy was the man to ride the whirl-wind. Too busy, too good-natured, too attached to his literary life, too much absorbed in his losing battle against old age and poverty, he was at that moment in the worst possible condition to bridle the passions of those who had elected him as their chairman. One of Dillon's correspondents had been to see him and reported that he was suffering from a heavy cold, his usual cheerfulness quite extinguished, and that he remained depressed throughout the

[1] Dillon Papers, V. B. Dillon to John Dillon, 13 Dec. 1890.
[2] Ibid., Dr J. E. Kenny to John Dillon, 13 Dec. 1890.

interview. He had been doubtful whether any compromise at all was possible and had declared that even if the majority consented to serve *with* Parnell in the future, they would never agree to serve *under* him.[1]

It is not surprising that with evidence of this kind before him Dillon's spirits should have sunk steadily lower. On December 17 he noted in his diary: 'I have not felt utterly beaten until now. . . . I do believe the game is up and unhappy Ireland must pass thro' the valley of death into which Parnell is dragging her.'[2] Next day he poured out his views in a long letter to O'Brien which contained the most complete analysis of the situation that he had yet made. It was an extremely pessimistic one. He had, he said, 'an absolute conviction that the situation is hopeless', and he still thought the best thing O'Brien and himself could do would be to resign, declaring that Parnell's action and the amount of support he had received had made it impossible either to retain the liberal alliance or to win the next election. Naturally, he was much preoccupied with how the Kilkenny struggle would affect the position. Suppose, he said, that Parnell, though beaten there, decided to fight on:

I believe that with private encouragement from him the fenian party would rapidly become once more formidable, and that a parliamentary party relying on the bishops and priests for support, and having Parnell and the extremists on its flank, would soon become utterly contemptible, and would be either at the mercy of the liberals, or would be obliged to break with Gladstone and the liberals and thereby fully justify Parnell's action and put themselves in a position from which *no* amount of explanation would ever extricate them.

I believe that in this event the election would be hopelessly lost. And it is quite possible that when the liberals saw that the election could not be won with home rule they might then throw over home rule at the last moment. And this again would fully justify Parnell in the eyes of the multitude.

Dillon, evidently, was not going to fall into the error of underrating the strength, or potential strength, of the Parnellite forces and if he was right in his estimate—the anti-Parnellites in Ireland would have denied that he was—then the logical con-

---

[1] Dillon Papers, Mrs Kate Rea to Dillon, 15 Dec. 1890.
[2] Ibid., 'Diary', 17 Dec. 1890.

sequence might well be, as he said, the ruin of the liberal alliance and with it the cause of home rule. But there was another possibility. Might not Parnell after all come to terms with O'Brien and agree to retire? Dillon considered this possibility also, but concluded that if Parnell retired without committing himself to a hearty support of the party, the end result would be just as bad:

I *very* much doubt whether the election could be saved. Harcourt, Fowler and that set will make a tremendous effort to get rid of home rule. And even if the Old Man should succeed in retaining it, there will be no more enthusiasm. The party will go into the election without heart. All cordial relations between our party and the liberals are hopelessly broken. None of P.'s supporters can go near an English meeting . . . and those of the party (i.e. the majority) who would still be welcome on English platforms will be afraid to go lest they should be singled out as the English section.

Consequently, his judgment was that the only hope of winning the general election on a home rule basis would be if Parnell retired and when retiring issued a strong appeal to 'the Irish race' to give a loyal support to the parliamentary party.[1]

Since Parnell's actions and words showed not the slightest indication that he intended to do anything of the sort, Dillon's pessimism—given his assumptions—had some justification, though it is only fair to add that it may partly have been the product of his physical condition. He was very far from well and the intense nervous strain of the crisis, coming on top of years of overwork, probably contributed to the acute dyspepsia from which he suffered in New York. As the days passed he spent more and more time in his hotel room, for although he had friends in the city there was nowhere, he wrote, where he could feel entirely at home.[2] Most of the time he felt sick and sluggish and whiled away the time reading Lowell's essays on Dante, Chaucer and Dryden. There was, indeed, nothing for him to do

[1] Gill Papers, Dillon to W. O'Brien, 18 Dec. 1890. T. P. O'Connor, who saw this letter before it was posted, wrote one himself suggesting that Dillon's anxieties about fenianism were exaggerated, but insisting that, so far as the situation in England went (about which he knew a good deal), any continuance of Parnell's leadership would be disastrous (Gill Papers, T. P. O'Connor to W. O'Brien, 19 Dec. 1890). See also W. O'Brien, *Olive branch*, p. 24. [2] Dillon Papers, 'Diary', 29 Dec. 1890.

except record in his diary the loneliness, sickness and utter frustration in which he spent the miserable Christmas of 1890.[1]

His colleague, William O'Brien, was in a more cheerful frame of mind. From the *Obdam* he wrote hopefully to Dillon that he felt their early firmness with Parnell was bearing fruit, and that he was turning to them for salvation:

> Now I am wholly convinced that an understanding with him is *our* only salvation also, if the country is to be held together. . . . It is pretty clear P. will do what we want, and on the other hand we ought to make it plain . . . to all concerned that we will not tolerate any attempt to hunt P. down like a wild beast. . . . Let *nothing* tempt us to join in any howl for his destruction. If we smash his men, we will be smashed ourselves.[2]

This was a change from the bitter and disillusioned O'Brien who had so shocked Harrington in the early days of the crisis, but there was no great mystery about the transformation. O'Brien was always adept at convincing himself that events were shaping themselves to his design, always ready to read between the lines the kind of message he wanted to see there. His argument was simple. The more the anti-Parnellites raged against their former leader, the more likely his defeat at Kilkenny, the more amenable to reason he might become. This was not perhaps a very profound analysis of Parnell's psychology, but it allowed O'Brien to approach his task in better spirits than he would otherwise have done. When, therefore, he arrived at Boulogne on a bitterly cold Christmas morning, his attitude was one of restrained optimism. And this was fortunate, for the situation that awaited him was baffling and complex beyond his worst anticipations. He was soon to need all the optimism he could muster.

---

[1] Dillon Papers, 'Diary', 20 Dec. 1890. 'I long with an unspeakable longing to get out of politics and have done with the sordid misery of that life, and get to read and think and live at least for a few years before I die, but I fear it is too late now.'

[2] Ibid., W. O'Brien to Dillon, dated 'Saturday'. As O'Brien left on Saturday, December 13 and refers in his letter to having seen 'this morning's *Herald*', presumably his letter was written on the day he sailed.

VIII

THE
BOULOGNE NEGOTIATIONS

~~~~~~~~~~~~~~~~~~~~~~~~~

(1)

BEFORE O'BRIEN and his party had even set foot on French soil a tender came out to their ship bearing Justin McCarthy, Thomas Sexton, T. J. Condon and Fr D. Humphreys (a Tipperary priest closely identified with the evicted tenants), and with them the latest news of a situation which had changed radically while the *Obdam* had been at sea.[1] The Kilkenny election had run its angry course and Parnell's opponents were naturally ready to claim that their victory had been conclusive proof that the country was behind them. Further negotiation with him would be not merely useless but dangerous—dangerous, because it might give the impression that his enemies were divided and that the issue had not yet been settled after all. From the anti-Parnellites, therefore, O'Brien could only expect the impatient demand that he and Dillon should cease to pose as gods from the machine and throw in their lot with the majority. Everybody—except McCarthy and Sexton—as O'Brien afterwards recorded, 'spoke swords and daggers' and the letters awaiting him in France were full of bitterness against Parnell.[2] One of these had been written by Archbishop Croke

---

[1] *United Ireland*, 27 Dec. 1890; W. O'Brien, *Olive branch*, p. 20; McCarthy and Praed, *Our book of memories*, p. 272.

[2] W. O'Brien, *Olive branch*, pp. 20–2 and footnotes.

while the result at Kilkenny was still in the balance and was likely to influence O'Brien strongly, bound as he was to the archbishop by the most affectionate ties. Dr Croke implored him to have no compromise:

> Parnell has hopelessly fallen. The bishops and priests and all good men are determinedly *against* him, and his future leadership, under any conditions, is absolutely impossible so far as they are concerned.
>
> How then can *you* touch him? What good can he do? See how he has acted towards Gladstone and our English allies. Do not recede a bit from the attitude of declared hostility to him. He will be beaten at Kilkenny on Monday. He will, therefore, be prepared for a compromise. If victorious, he would not think of it.
>
> So for God's sake, and country's sake, and conscience's sake, be staunch and steady and no surrender.[1]

The archbishop was right in his forecast that Parnell, if beaten at Kilkenny, would be prepared to negotiate. One of the first people O'Brien met when he landed at Boulogne was the editor of the *Freeman's Journal*, E. J. Byrne, who brought a letter from Parnell himself promising that as soon as the poll was declared he would come to O'Brien in France. This was encouraging, though deceptively so since it was written a week before O'Brien's arrival, and in that week the harsh crescendo of the Kilkenny election had seriously shaken Parnell's readiness to compromise. Harrington wrote to O'Brien, shortly after the latter's arrival, that Kilkenny had 'widened the breach horribly'.[2] And V. B. Dillon wrote gloomily that the manifesto which his cousin John and T. P. O'Connor had issued after O'Brien had left America had nearly made Parnell change his mind about going to France, and that Redmond, Harrington, Kenny and others had had to argue with him to keep him up to the mark.[3] However, even if the election had embittered the quarrel still further, it had also shown the weakness of the

---

[1] Gill Papers, Archbishop Croke to W. O'Brien, 19 Dec. 1890; quoted by O'Brien, *Evening memories*, pp. 478–9. A few days earlier Dr Croke had expressed considerable misgivings about O'Brien's attitude and especially about his leanings towards compromise (Walsh Papers, Archbishop Croke to Archbishop Walsh, 16 Dec. 1890).

[2] Gill Papers, T. Harrington to W. O'Brien, 27 Dec. 1890; W. O'Brien, *Olive branch*, p. 23, *n*. 1.

[3] Gill Papers, V. B. Dillon to W. O'Brien, 28 Dec. 1890; W. O'Brien, *Olive branch*, p. 23, *n*. 1.

Parnellite position and Parnell was not likely to miss the significance of such a warning. Defeated at Kilkenny, he could not afford to let slip the chance of separating Dillon and O'Brien from their colleagues or, failing that, at least of driving a wedge between O'Brien and Dillon. In his own mind he made a sharp discrimination between the two men, as appears from a passage in Harrington's letter to O'Brien already quoted.

When I met him first [wrote Harrington] he was most anxious for the meeting with you. It appears that all through he has expressed to his supporters the utmost faith in your affection for him. I am sorry to learn that he made a wide distinction between Dillon and yourself in this respect. He has told his followers all along that he would [rely?] to the fullest upon your sincerity, but they tell me he never could be induced to make a similar declaration with regard to John.[1]

Ominous though this might be for the future, the fact remained that Parnell was willing to come to France, and O'Brien lost no time in cabling his readiness to open discussions.[2] First, however, he had to find out how far Parnell's opponents would be prepared to go in order to reach a settlement by compromise. This was the subject of his talks with McCarthy, Sexton and Condon the day he arrived. To judge by notes he and Gill made immediately after this conference, the prospects seemed favourable. O'Brien evidently began by saying that the delegates in America were agreed that Parnell's retirement must be the first condition of the negotiations, though they reserved to themselves the right of deciding—in the event of his refusal—whether they would resign or join in the struggle. If Parnell showed a willingness to retire then, said O'Brien, the delegates were in favour of giving every kind of solace to his feelings, consistent with retaining the liberal alliance. To all this McCarthy and Sexton agreed, making it clear nonetheless that voluntary retirement by Parnell was, in their belief, extremely unlikely. Asked by Sexton what sort of satisfaction for Parnell he had in mind, O'Brien recapitulated most, but not all, of the items he had discussed with Dillon, O'Connor and Gill in New York. Thus, he put it to them first that Gladstone should be persuaded to make some acknowledgment that he had been

[1] Gill Papers, T. Harrington to W. O'Brien, 27 Dec. 1890.
[2] *F.J.*, 4 Nov. 1891.

precipitate in publishing his famous letter of November 24 without having consulted the party. This was agreed to 'if Mr G. could be got to consent'. Next, O'Brien proposed that the whole party should reassemble on the understanding that McCarthy was to be re-elected unopposed and that a resolution should be passed acknowledging the informality of his previous election and expressing the gratitude of the party to Parnell. This also was agreed to by McCarthy, Sexton and Condon. Thirdly, O'Brien suggested that Parnell should retain his position as president of the National League. The notes made by O'Brien and Gill describe the reaction to this proposal as follows:

Assented to by all, Mr Sexton adding that he would go further and suggest that a deputation of Mr P.'s prominent supporters in party should accompany him to first meeting of League in Dublin, P. presiding there, Sexton offering to be himself one of the deputation. Mr Sexton also remarked that Irish parliamentary party had no power to depose Mr Parnell from any position except that of chairman of party.

There were two other propositions. One was that Parnell should be retained as one of three treasurers of the party funds, the other two being nominated by the party. This again was agreed to, though McCarthy doubted whether Parnell would accept such an arrangement. The other was that Parnell's followers should have equal representation with his opponents on any committee of the party—and to this also no objection was raised.[1]

Knowing as we do that the delegates in New York had envisaged a far wider field of compromise than this, it is clear that O'Brien at this conference was skirting round some of the more important concessions that the anti-Parnellites might be asked to make. Thus it seems that nothing was said about inducing the two archbishops to retract their denunciations of Parnell, nor about assuring the latter that his influence would always be dominant and his absence probably only temporary. Above all, no mention apparently was made of giving him a special position in any discussions that might be held about the details of a future home rule bill. No doubt O'Brien, just beginning to

[1] Gill Papers, 'Note of interview at Boulogne, Christmas day, 1890, between Messrs Justin McCarthy, M.P., Sexton, M.P., Condon, M.P., on one part, and Messrs William O'Brien, M.P., and Gill, M.P., on other'.

realise the vehemence of the feeling against Parnell, was still only groping his way, and was anxious not to alarm the anti-Parnellites at the very outset. Indeed, even as it was, although their conference reached agreement on the limited agenda O'Brien disclosed, and although both Sexton and McCarthy promised to do all they could to smooth the way, McCarthy remained pessimistic to the end, urging that Parnell would not yield and that anyway the struggle was practically over.[1]

(2)

Nevertheless, the way had been cleared for the long-awaited meeting with Parnell and on December 30 he arrived at Boulogne with a party which included the two Redmonds, Dr Kenny, J. J. Clancy, Henry Campbell, E. J. Byrne and J. M. Tuohy (the two last-named representing the *Freeman's Journal*).[2] The negotiations were conducted in secrecy and at the time only the barest reports of what had happened were allowed to appear in the press. It was, in fact, only after Parnell's death that different versions of this meeting began to appear. First, William O'Brien made a lengthy statement to the press early in November 1891; this was quickly followed by a joint communiqué from John Redmond and Timothy Harrington challenging O'Brien's account, and a little later by a detailed and much documented narrative which Harrington published in the *Freeman's Journal* on 12 November 1891. These disclosures, together with the fusillade of accusations and counter-accusations which they touched off, were available to William O'Brien when, in 1910, he considered the whole episode afresh in the second chapter of his *Olive branch in Ireland*. It is probable also that in writing that book he had access to certain original documents which have only recently come to light as part of the collection of the T. P. Gill Papers, now in the National Library. The other main source for the history of these events is the *Life of Parnell* by R. Barry O'Brien, which was based not only upon

[1] Privately he doubted O'Brien's capacity to be 'as strong with Parnell as he ought to be' (McCarthy and Praed, *Our book of memories*, p. 272, Justin McCarthy to Mrs Praed, 26 Dec. 1890).

[2] W. O'Brien, *Olive branch*, p. 25, gives the date of Parnell's arrival at Boulogne as December 31, but the newspapers place it as December 30 (*F.J.*, 31 Dec. 1890).

the press revelations in 1891 but also upon the personal recollections John Redmond gave him at some date (unspecified) between 1891 and 1898 when the *Life of Parnell* first appeared. During the last few years it has been possible to supplement these sources not only from the Gill Papers, but also from the Gladstone Papers, the Spencer Papers, the Harcourt Papers and the John Dillon Papers; those of Harrington, John Redmond and William O'Brien have also been consulted, but yield little that has not been reproduced elsewhere.[1]

The opening phase of the negotiations was brief, though eventful. Parnell, according to John Redmond's account, was cold and aloof in his manner, while O'Brien was effusive. The latter wished to plunge into business straight away, but Parnell insisted that they should first have lunch. He also insisted that the initial conversation should take place between O'Brien and himself alone.[2] This preliminary encounter was discouraging. Parnell, according to O'Brien's version, which in this particular at least was not contradicted, seemed disposed to launch into a long tirade against the conduct of the majority ever since the outbreak of the crisis. O'Brien refused to listen to this and at one stage left the room.[3] He told John Redmond that though he had proposals to make it was useless to bring them forward while Parnell was in such a mood. During the meal, however, Gill outlined these proposals to Redmond. After lunch

[1] Thus the Harrington Papers contain copies—in two different hands which I have been unable to identify but neither of which is Harrington's—of many of the documents that Harrington published on 12 Nov. 1891. The O'Brien Papers contain little, presumably because O'Brien went straight from the conferences in France to serve the six months' sentence awaiting him in Ireland; the documents, many of them addressed to O'Brien or copies of letters written by him, which one would expect to find in his papers are in fact in those of T. P. Gill, who acted as unofficial secretary during the negotiations.

[2] R. B. O'Brien, *Parnell*, ii. 310–1. O'Brien for his part saw in Parnell 'the pathetic air of a cedar struck by lightning' (*Olive branch*, p. 25).

[3] R. B. O'Brien, *Parnell*, ii. 311; W. O'Brien, *Olive branch*, pp. 25–7, and in *F.J.*, 4 Nov. 1891. Redmond's narrative to Barry O'Brien places this incident after lunch, William O'Brien puts it before, but they agree otherwise in their accounts of the first interview. According to Gill, the interview took place 'before dinner' (Gill Papers, 'Memorandum of Mr John Redmond M.P.'s and Mr T. P. Gill M.P.'s conversations at Boulogne, 30 and 31 Dec. 1890'). This memorandum is in Gill's hand and is on the notepaper of the Hotel du Louvre, Boulogne, where the conference was held.

Redmond passed them on to Parnell, but when Gill appeared he was required to state them himself. He did so and a long conversation followed between himself and Parnell, the upshot of which was that O'Brien was asked to resume his talks with Parnell. He came back accordingly, and took up the threads again, John Redmond and T. P. Gill being present on this occasion. It seems, from a memorandum in Gill's hand, that they discussed most of the topics originally covered by the delegates in New York, including some of those which O'Brien had not mentioned to McCarthy and Sexton.[1]

Unfortunately this memorandum, after indicating the topics which were discussed, breaks off in mid-sentence, thus: 'The conversation proceeded on these lines when Mr Parnell said—.' For what Parnell said we are dependent on William O'Brien's recollections, but it was something so staggering that O'Brien was not likely soon to forget it. It was nothing less than that the only conditions upon which Parnell could accept the terms offered him would be that he, O'Brien, should agree to succeed him as chairman of the re-united parliamentary party, and at the same time should decline the chairmanship of the new *National Press* company which the anti-Parnellites were anxious to persuade him to undertake. O'Brien, not unnaturally suspecting that this was a transparent manoeuvre to alienate him from the majority, or even to separate him from Dillon, tried to laugh the suggestion out of court. But when he saw that Parnell was serious, he countered by proposing that John Dillon was a far more suitable candidate than himself, a proposal—his account implies—from which Parnell recoiled.[2] Eventually, after long discussion, O'Brien agreed to consider Parnell's suggestion, but safeguarded himself by stipulating that before he accepted it he must have time to find what Dillon's reaction would be.[3] And on that note they parted for the night.

The next day Parnell left for England bearing with him a memorandum written for him by T. P. Gill and listing the terms proposed by O'Brien to secure his retirement. This was a document which was later to cause great embarrassment to

[1] Gill Papers, 'Memorandum of . . . conversations at Boulogne, 30 and 31 Dec. 1890'; W. O'Brien, *Olive branch*, p. 27, and *F.J.*, 4 Nov. 1891.

[2] W. O'Brien, *Olive branch*, pp. 27–9; *F.J.*, 4 Nov. 1891.

[3] W. O'Brien, *Olive branch*, p. 29.

O'Brien and Gill, for the latter had no time to make a copy of it and when O'Brien attempted to summarise its contents in his statement to the press of 4 November 1891 he made several serious mistakes which his opponents lost no time in pointing out.[1] In the end it was published by Harrington on 12 November 1891, and as this was the most complete record of the terms which were discussed at Boulogne it is worth quoting at length. The terms were as follows:[2]

1. Meeting of the whole party; acknowledgment of informality of McCarthy's election and re-election of McCarthy as chairman by agreement of whole party.

2. All possible personal satisfaction in shape of public declaration of party expressing gratitude, and enumerating circumstances of misunderstanding tending to account for conflict.

3. All possible efforts to be made to secure from Gladstone acknowledgment of mistake of precipitate publication of his letter and admission that he had not taken sufficient account of national sentiment in Ireland and of Parnell's position.

[1] On the day O'Brien's statement appeared, John Redmond and Harrington drew up a joint declaration in which they asserted that there was no excuse for O'Brien having mis-stated the terms of the memorandum since there was a copy of it in his possession. This was categorically denied by both O'Brien and Gill (*F.J.*, 5 and 6 Nov. 1891). In fact, even before Parnell's death, when he had hinted in his Listowel speech of 13 Sept. 1891 at certain revelations he could make about Boulogne, his opponents had been in a flutter of anxiety when they realised they had no copy of the document (Gill Papers, W. O'Brien to Gill, 19 Sept. 1891, and Gill to W. O'Brien, 21 Sept. 1891; Dillon Papers, W. O'Brien to Dillon, 'Saturday' (26 Sept. 1891): 'I have told him (Gill) not to let P. know we have not a copy, or Heaven knows what he might be tempted to do in his desperation').

[2] *F.J.*, 12 Nov. 1891. Harrington, introducing the memorandum, said that the original was in Gill's handwriting on the notepaper of the Hotel du Louvre. This original seems not to have survived, though a copy of it—identical with the version printed by Harrington—is in the Harrington Papers. This, like the published version, bears no date. Just before Harrington published the memorandum, Gill wrote to O'Brien that if it *was* published it might put him, O'Brien, in an awkward position, and offering to take full responsibility for the wording of it. 'The terms, by the way', he added, 'were in the main identical with those of the document drawn up in New York' (Gill Papers, Gill to W. O'Brien, 10 Nov. 1891). Later, after it had been published, Gill wrote to the press taking responsibility for the phraseology of the memorandum (*F.J.*, 14 Nov. 1891). The fact that he—the author of the original—did not dispute the accuracy of the published document may be considered strong evidence of the latter's authenticity.

4. Possible retraction, in some shape, of bishops' manifesto by Dr Croke or Dr Walsh.

5. Vote of party only to affect chairmanship of party; P. to continue president of the National League; and, if desirable, prominent men of both sections to accompany him to a meeting, under his presidency, of the central branch in Dublin.

6. In case committee appointed by party, Parnell to have nomination of half thereof.

7. Any special recognition of Parnell that he can suggest that would secure his influence in all negotiations touching the home rule bill or other Irish legislation.

8. In case of agreement on these lines, O'Brien to decline chairmanship of new newspaper company, and any rival committee to National League to be discouraged.

It will be seen that, apart from the omission of any reference to the party funds and the introduction of the clause relating to the newspaper company, these proposals were substantially the same as the original ones sketched out in New York by Dillon, O'Brien, T. P. O'Connor and Gill. From Parnell's point of view they afforded a wonderful opportunity of turning disaster into victory. Fresh from defeat at Kilkenny as he was, all that was asked of him was that he should retire from the chairmanship of the parliamentary party, and even this without any hard and fast arrangement that his retirement should be permanent.[1] In return he was to remain at the head of the National League; he was to have a say—which might well be a decisive one—on the details of the home rule bill and on other Irish legislation; he was to receive a resolution of gratitude from the party that was deposing him; and—richest irony of all—a large part of the blame for the crisis was to be laid upon the liberal party, and especially upon Gladstone's letter, without any mention of the divorce court verdict or of his own manifesto. If these terms were actually accepted by the various parties concerned, Parnell would only surrender the appearance of power and would retain the reality. If, on the other hand, as was very much more likely, the liberals indignantly rejected the attempt to make them

[1] O'Brien later insisted that it was to have been permanent; the Parnellites as strongly urged that it was to have been temporary (*F.J.*, 4, 5 and 6 Nov. 1891). The terms of the memorandum quoted above clearly leave the whole issue open—there is nothing to say whether retirement was to be permanent or temporary.

shoulder the blame (or some of it) for what had happened, Parnell would still be in a strong position. For he could then say that his English enemies were so intent upon his destruction that they thrust aside an offer of peace which came, not from him alone, but from some of the most influential members of the party. It was not, perhaps, an argument that would carry much weight in England, but in Ireland, where the struggle was by no means over, much might yet be made of it.

Nor was this all. The fact that O'Brien had been induced to consider taking the chairmanship of the party himself was a further advantage to Parnell, since it was certain to make it more difficult for the former to pose much longer as a mediator. O'Brien, by even contemplating such a step, was in a fair way to find himself at odds with the majority of the party. Still inclined to underestimate the passions let loose in Committee Room Fifteen and in Ireland, he was proposing to wipe out the events of weeks which could never be forgotten by those who had lived through them, and in doing so to set aside the choice of the party in his own favour. Doubtless his motives were entirely unselfish, but he was running a fearful risk by thus swimming against a tide whose strength he had not yet fully realised. For, although Sexton and McCarthy had seemed sympathetic when consulted on Christmas Day, there was still the more extreme wing of the party to reckon with. It was hardly likely that Healy, for example, would have approved for a moment the kind of agreement with which O'Brien was dallying. And even if he had been amenable, it was highly improbable that either of the two archbishops could have been brought to retract anything said by themselves as individuals or by the hierarchy as a body.

So far as O'Brien was concerned, however, the most immediately important factor in the situation was Dillon, always Dillon. On December 31 he cabled to New York the news of Parnell's 'astonishing proposal', that is, his offer to retire if O'Brien would take his place. It was, said O'Brien, a solution personally distasteful to him, but it seemed the only one likely to succeed. He would be guided, however, by Dillon's advice.[1] Dillon was in a quandary. Like O'Brien, indeed even more than

[1] Dillon Papers, cable from W. O'Brien to Dillon, 31 Dec. 1890; W. O'Brien, *Olive branch*, p. 30.

O'Brien, he was ready to suspect a trap. On the other hand if, as O'Brien seemed to think, Parnell really meant what he said, then scarcely any price would be too great to pay for his retirement. His diary accurately reflects his bewilderment:

I never imagined it was possible that I could be put into such a position of perplexity as I am now placed in by cable received from W. O'B. this afternoon. Men say here that Parnell is mad, but it seems to me that his astuteness is absolutely infinite, and in all the reflections on the possible outcome of the situation which have passed thro' my head in the last few days what has now happened never occurred to me. The moment I read the cable I felt that P. had executed a master stroke and all my reflection since has only deepened this conviction—and increased my alarm and uneasiness.[1]

Later that same day there came a second cable saying that McCarthy and Sexton had approved the delegates' original proposals, but that Parnell objected to their being told of the suggestion about the leadership until O'Brien had heard from Dillon.[2] The latter hastened to consult T. P. O'Connor, and together they sent a reply to O'Brien assuring him of their warmest co-operation and that his name would have a splendid effect everywhere, especially in America. They urged him, however, before committing himself to ascertain the feelings of the majority and to be sure that he was not led into an impossible position.[3] Late that night Dillon drafted a further cable saying that he strongly favoured the proposed solution, but feared that O'Brien might be trapped into a position of hostility towards the majority. Above all, he insisted, O'Brien must make sure that McCarthy should not be put in a position where he could say he was badly treated.[4] O'Brien, for his part, much pleased with this evidence of support, notified Parnell next day that he had had a satisfactory message from Dillon,

[1] Dillon Papers, 'Diary', 31 Dec. 1890.

[2] Ibid., cable from W. O'Brien to Dillon, 31 Dec. 1890. The same day John Redmond and Gill cabled urging Dillon to support the proposed solution.

[3] W. O'Brien, *Olive branch*, p. 31; Dillon Papers, draft cable in T. P. O'Connor's hand, 1 Jan. 1891.

[4] Dillon Papers, copy in Dillon's hand of cable from Dillon to Gill, 1 Jan. 1891. Presumably this was sent to Gill. I have not been able to trace the original in the Gill Papers, but some of the documents in that collection have been destroyed by fire and this may have been among them.

but asked, in view of newspaper rumours, that he should be allowed to take McCarthy and Sexton into his confidence.[1] But Parnell, that inscrutable man, having had twenty-four hours in which to reflect, had once more seized the initiative and launched the Boulogne negotiations upon the second phase of their history.

(3)

On New Year's Day 1891 he wrote a long letter to O'Brien from the Westminster Palace hotel, London, in which he set out in detail his views upon their conference at Boulogne. The second paragraph began with the ominous announcement that he had a growing conviction that the proposals laid before him in France, 'however kindly meant towards myself personally', would neither permit O'Brien and the party to stand upon solid ground in the future nor—and here was the sting—allow him to retire 'with any consistency or regard for my responsibility'. He then went on to say that he himself had another proposal 'of a much more simple and workable character' which, if accepted, *would* enable him to retire, and would at the same time ensure as far as possible that the liberal promises of a satis-factory home rule bill would be carried out when the oppor-tunity arose. His plan, he said, resembled the compromise, which had been adopted by the party in Committee Room Fifteen, based upon Clancy's resolution and John Redmond's amendment modifying it. He was referring, of course, to the attempt made by the delegation which had visited Gladstone to obtain from him assurances concerning the land and police questions, and which had retired baffled in view of Gladstone's refusal to hold any negotiations with the Irish party until the issue of the leadership had been settled. Parnell's new proposal attempted to get round this difficulty. Here it is in his own words:

1. That you should suggest to Mr McCarthy to obtain an inter-view with Mr Gladstone at Hawarden and ask from him a memor-andum expressing the intentions of himself and his colleagues upon these views and details, as explained by the delegates in their inter-view with Mr Gladstone on December 5.

2. That Mr McCarthy should transfer this memorandum to your

[1] W. O'Brien, *Olive branch*, p. 31.

custody and that if, after consultation between yourself and myself, it should be found that its terms are satisfactory, I should forthwith announce my retirement from the chairmanship of the party.

3. That the terms of this memorandum should not be disclosed to any other person until after the introduction of the home rule bill and not then unless the bill failed to carry out those terms; but that if the bill were satisfactory I should be permitted to publish the memorandum after the passage of the former into law.

If this were done, Parnell concluded, he would be prepared to agree that the limit of two years as the time within which the police should be disarmed and turned into a civil force under the control of the Irish executive might be extended to five years—though it was vital, he added, that the home rule bill should fix the term precisely and not leave it indefinite.[1]

This new move of Parnell's was extremely subtle and it is hard to avoid the conclusion that he was making it with the primary purpose of putting his opponents in a very awkward position. It could, of course, be interpreted as a sensible and magnanimous offer—he would retire if the party got a good price for him. That was what he had said in Committee Room Fifteen and, as he himself freely admitted, what he was now doing was to revive the proposal made and adopted in Committee Room Fifteen. But with this essential difference—that in the interval McCarthy had been elected as chairman by the majority of the party. Gladstone had said that he would not negotiate until the leadership issue had been settled. With McCarthy duly elected by the majority what excuse could Gladstone have for refusing to negotiate with him? Therefore, let McCarthy go to Hawarden and obtain the same guarantees which Gladstone had refused to the delegation a month earlier. And, since Parnell's proposal was in place of O'Brien's suggestions, the new scheme would have the advantage of doing away with all those apologetic and laudatory resolutions from the Irish party, the Irish bishops and the liberals contemplated in the earlier plan, resolutions which it would probably have been impossible to obtain in any event.

[1] The letter was printed in full by William O'Brien and by Harrington in *F.J.*, 11 and 12 Nov. 1891; their versions are the same save for a few verbal differences. R. B. O'Brien, *Parnell*, ii. 312–3, printed part of the letter, as did W. O'Brien, *Olive branch*, pp. 32–3. There is a copy of the letter in Gill's hand on Hotel du Louvre notepaper in the Gill Papers.

From this standpoint Parnell's plan might seem to offer a possible solution. But it could also be seen in a more sinister light, for on closer inspection it was clear that he was far from abandoning his control over the situation. McCarthy, under this scheme, would be no more than a go-between. Having secured the necessary guarantees, he would hand them over to Parnell and O'Brien and then withdraw discreetly into the background. Nor was Parnell content merely to demonstrate how little importance he attached to McCarthy's chairmanship of the party. He must also retain a veto over the liberal assurances, for that was in effect what was intended by the second of his proposals. And further, he retained for his own future use a very strong card when he laid it down that the liberal assurances might be published if they were not embodied in the next home rule bill, and that even if the bill were satisfactory they might still be made public in his vindication. Thus, in the first eventuality Parnell would be able triumphantly to produce tangible evidence of that liberal untrustworthiness which had been the main theme of his speeches since the beginning of the crisis; and in the second eventuality he would still be able to claim a large share of the credit for whatever might have been achieved.

What Parnell was doing, in short, was to place his opponents firmly on the horns of a most ingeniously contrived dilemma. Either his conditions, involving as they did so many concessions by so many people, would be fulfilled and he would make a graceful exit from the leadership of the party, having demonstrated to the end his self-sacrifice and political acumen—but having done nothing to indicate whether his exit was to be permanent or temporary. Or else, somewhere along the line, the proposals would break down and he would be able to appear in the congenial rôle of a much persecuted patriot whose best efforts for his country were constantly being foiled by the selfishness and petty jealousies of lesser men. When one reflects that McCarthy's consent to his own execution had still to be obtained, that the majority's approval of the whole transaction would be necessary, and that the liberals were certain to take alarm if once they sensed—which they could scarcely help doing, as all eyes were fixed upon these Boulogne negotiations —that McCarthy was not acting upon his own initiative but was simply the agent of Parnell, it is hard to see how anyone can have expected the proposals—in this form at least—to succeed. So far as Parnell was concerned, however, failure would be no great hardship provided it left his freedom of action unimpaired, while, if it proved to be the means of bringing a disillusioned O'Brien into his camp, it might even be an advantage.

O'Brien, for his part, was not unnaturally perplexed by this new development. All his inclinations led him to hope that it was a genuine and unselfish offer, but at the same time he could hardly help realising that it carried with it conditions that were likely to rob it of all value. Also, it did not even make clear whether—if the assurances were given and Parnell retired—McCarthy or O'Brien himself was to be the chairman of the party. His first reaction, therefore, was to cable Harrington that if the new proposal meant that McCarthy was to continue in the chair he, O'Brien, would be prepared to support it. Harrington's answer was that on the contrary the proposal was subject to the chair being taken by O'Brien, and by no-one else.[1] The next day—January 4—O'Brien, in his considered reply to Parnell, wrote that if the latter were to stand by his first determination—that O'Brien should replace McCarthy in the chair—then to send McCarthy to Hawarden would not only be painful for McCarthy, but would raise formidable difficulties in the way of securing the required guarantees from the liberals. When they met again he would offer an alternative solution which might provide a way out of the *impasse*. He added that those who were 'bent on thwarting peace at any price' were building great hopes upon a breakdown of the Boulogne negotiations, but, 'we may still be able to hit upon some agreement that will relieve the country from an appalling prospect, and that neither you nor I will have any reason to regret hereafter'.[2]

The reference to those 'bent on thwarting peace' may well have been provoked by the presence of T. M. Healy who, together with John Barry, was at that moment in Paris attempting to secure O'Brien's aid in the launching of the *National Press* and who sought, at the same time, to make him more appreciative

---

[1] W. O'Brien, *Olive branch*, pp. 33–4; R. B. O'Brien, *Parnell*, ii. 315.

[2] *F.J.*, 11 Nov. 1891; R. B. O'Brien, *Parnell*, ii. 314–5.

of the position of the anti-Parnellites.[1] It does not seem that they were very successful and Healy, writing to his wife on January 5, was pessimistic about the future. O'Brien, he said, had shown no sympathy for the troubles they had gone through, though he did seem to be in agreement with the majority on every point save one. That one point, however, was an important exception, for it concerned Parnell's retirement, which O'Brien wanted to bring about in his own way. Healy admitted that Dillon and O'Brien both wanted Parnell deposed, but said that neither would associate himself with anything that had been done by the majority. There was not, he said, the slightest hope that O'Brien would have anything to do with the new paper. 'On the contrary, having failed to bring about Parnell's retirement, he will go to jail and wash his hands of us. Fight Parnell I don't believe he will, as he thinks the cause is lost if Parnell will not retire and O'Brien will not take part in a struggle against him.'[2] In a second letter, written the same day, Healy threw further light on O'Brien's attitude. He was evidently proving secretive about the latest proposals that were passing between Parnell and himself, and he exasperated Healy by the naïve remark that Parnell would have been easier to deal with if he had not been so heavily beaten at Kilkenny. Well might Healy comment: 'Apparently, everything that we have done has been ill done, and nothing has been done that ought to have been done, and William and Gill are the only men to put matters right. Anything more hopeless it is impossible to conceive.' O'Brien seemed impervious to criticism and when told that his independent action laid him open to a charge of arrogance and indiscipline, he bore this attack, wrote Healy, 'with a gentle egoism beyond reproof'.[3]

Such, then, was O'Brien's mood on the eve of his second interview with Parnell. This took place on January 6 and 7 and they met, as before, in the Hotel du Louvre at Boulogne. According to John Redmond and Harrington, both of whom accompanied

---

[1] Healy was not the only one to bring pressure to bear upon O'Brien. At about the same time he received a letter from his old friend, Archbishop Croke, urging him to end his conference with Parnell (Gill Papers, Archbishop Croke to W. O'Brien, 31 Dec. 1890).

[2] Healy, *Letters and leaders*, i. 347.

[3] Ibid, i. 349.

Parnell on this occasion, the conference first discussed the possible solution which O'Brien had hinted at in his letter to Parnell of January 4. It was simply that if Parnell insisted upon O'Brien becoming chairman, then O'Brien and not McCarthy should go to Hawarden to obtain the liberal assurances; if these were not satisfactory, O'Brien would resign and throw in his lot with Parnell.[1] The latter, by Redmond's account, was highly amused at the vision of O'Brien confronting Gladstone at Hawarden and refused to take it seriously.

The discussion then centred round the proposals that Parnell had put forward in his letter of January 1. O'Brien, finding that Parnell was not prepared to alter these in any way of his own accord, categorically declared that nothing would induce him to take the chair and at the same time ask McCarthy to go to Hawarden 'with a halter round his neck'.[2] Instead, he made three counter-suggestions of his own. The first was that John Dillon should be chairman. The second was that he, O'Brien, should be free to take McCarthy and Sexton into his confidence as to all that had passed already. And the third was that McCarthy should be associated with Parnell and himself in determining the adequacy of the liberal guarantees. It was now Parnell's turn to hesitate. The mention of Dillon's name aroused his strong opposition, and for a time it seemed as if a breakdown could not be avoided. That it was avoided seems to have been due less to O'Brien than to Parnell's own followers, who eventually persuaded him to accept Dillon as the prospective chairman of a reunited party.[3] They also—according to Harrington —prevailed upon him to forgo another condition—which would almost certainly have been fatal—that guarantees should be secured from Harcourt as well as from Gladstone![4] In addition, though Harrington does not mention this in his account, O'Brien secured permission to acquaint Sexton and

[1] *F.J.*, 12 Nov. 1891; R. B. O'Brien, *Parnell*, ii. 315–6. O'Brien does not mention this episode either in his reminiscences or in the account he published in *F.J.*, 4 Nov. 1891. On the other hand, he did not deny the accuracy of Harrington's version of it, and this although the air at the time was thick with challenges and counter-challenges.

[2] *F.J.*, 4 Nov. 1891; O'Brien, *Olive branch*, p. 34.

[3] *F.J.*, 12 Nov. 1891; O'Brien, *Olive branch*, p. 34.

[4] *F.J.*, 12 Nov. 1891; this is supported by O'Brien's letter to Archbishop Croke of 12 Jan. 1891 in *Evening memories*, pp. 479–80.

McCarthy with the nature and progress of the negotiations.[1] The outcome was that Parnell with his own hand drafted a form of agreement which, it was hoped, would provide a solution of all their problems. It ran as follows:

Heads of agreement between Mr Parnell and Mr O'Brien.

1. That Mr O'Brien ask Mr McCarthy to obtain an interview with Mr Gladstone and ask from the latter a memorandum (a) stating whether he and his colleagues intend to deal with the Irish land question themselves by legislation in the imperial parliament, or to regard this as one of the questions the power of dealing with which would be conferred upon the Irish parliament, and if the former course is to be adopted, whether this question is to be dealt with by purchase or upon the lines of the measure annually introduced by the Irish party during this parliament and supported by the liberal party; (b) stating whether Mr Gladstone and his colleagues will agree to insert a provision in the next home rule bill that the control of the imperial authority over the Irish constabulary shall cease within a definite number of years (say five) and that this force, with such modifications in its character and numbers as may be deemed necessary, shall then be transferred to the control of the Irish executive responsible to the Irish parliament; (c) stating whether Mr Gladstone and his colleagues will consent that the solution of these questions dealt with in (a) and (b) upon the lines agreed upon shall be regarded as vital.

2. That Mr McCarthy should transfer this memorandum to the custody of Mr William O'Brien and that if Mr Parnell and Mr O'Brien should find from its terms that the intentions of Mr Gladstone and his colleagues are in accordance with the views expressed in sub-sections (a), (b), and (c) that thereupon:

3. A meeting of the whole party shall be called and a resolution proposed acknowledging the informality of Mr McCarthy's election, and after the passage of this resolution Mr Parnell will retire from the position of chairman, and Mr McCarthy from that of vice-chairman, and Mr Dillon shall be elected chairman.

4. That the terms of the memorandum shall not be disclosed to any persons save the persons named in these heads of agreement until after the introduction of the home rule bill, and not then unless such bill should fail to carry out those terms; but if the bill should be found satisfactory, Mr Parnell should be permitted to publish the memorandum after the passage of the former into law.[2]

[1] O'Brien, *Olive branch*, p. 34.

[2] The heads of agreement were published by O'Brien and Harrington in *F.J.*, 4 and 12 Nov. 1891, respectively, with only a few verbal differences,

In this memorandum Parnell to a great extent succeeded in combining the proposals he had put forward in his letter of January 1 with the demands which the party had agreed to make to Gladstone towards the end of their debates in Committee Room Fifteen, and which Gladstone had then refused to answer.[1] True, he had to accept Dillon instead of O'Brien as prospective chairman, and he had to agree that McCarthy and Sexton should at least be told of what was going on, but his other main propositions were unaffected. McCarthy was to be displaced from the chair, yet he was still to be the intermediary between O'Brien and Gladstone. The onus of judging the adequacy of the liberal promises was to rest solely upon Parnell and O'Brien. And—above all—Parnell was to have the opportunity of vindicating himself either soon, if the liberals played false, or later, if home rule were actually achieved. Of course, the entire agreement was contingent upon securing the assent of the various parties involved. McCarthy, the liberal leaders and John Dillon had all yet to be consulted, and O'Brien at once threw himself with characteristic energy and enthusiasm into the task of reconciling these different and possibly conflicting forces.

(4)

He began with Dillon, since without Dillon nothing at all could be achieved. The latter, who had no inkling of what was in the wind, was astonished to receive, on the evening of January 6, the following cable:

Difficulties about first proposal. Parnell now agrees instead other conditions. You elected chairman if McCarthy first obtains from Gladstone private guarantees constabulary and land satisfactory to Parnell and myself on lines previously defined. We agreeing side with Parnell if guarantees refused. If McCarthy consents this course much preferable. Question arises if McCarthy refuses what should be our action. Myself think resign.[2]

and by O'Brien again in *Olive branch*, pp. 35–6. There is an undated copy in Gill's hand in the Gill Papers, but I have not been able to trace the original.

[1] The assurances detailed in the 'heads of agreement' between Parnell and O'Brien and which McCarthy was to secure from Gladstone, were identical with those demanded by the deputation which the latter received on December 5 (*F.J.*, 6 Dec. 1890).

[2] Dillon Papers, cable from O'Brien to Dillon, received 7.30 p.m., 6 Jan.

It is scarcely surprising that his first reaction should have been a blank refusal. That same night he replied thus:

> Could not think of accepting chairmanship; proposed terms my judgment intolerable; not bona fide. Consider proposal about Gladstone trap. Would never bind myself any course in event of refusal by Gladstone. I sail France Saturday. Insist truce till I arrive.[1]

This was emphatic enough, but that night in his diary he expressed himself even more strongly. Feeling, as he put it, 'very seedy', he was clearly exasperated beyond measure by the way the situation was developing. It was 'bad as bad can be', and the proposal in O'Brien's cable astounded him. 'He seems to have walked into the very trap into which the party walked before, and for doing which we all blasphemed against the party in Chicago. Now the proposal is that I am to get the chairmanship on terms such that I would rather earn an honest living by blacking shoes than accept.' He had, he noted, discussed the matter with T. P. O'Connor who did not feel quite so strongly as he did, and seemed to believe that Gladstone in some way or other might be induced to give the required guarantees. 'I *cannot* think there is the slightest reason to suppose that he would entertain the idea.'[2]

The next day he repeated his warnings to O'Brien. He could not, he said, be a party to demanding pledges from Gladstone and still did not believe that Parnell's offer was bona fide. However, if McCarthy and O'Brien were agreed upon a policy he would not stand in the way, though as he was still in the dark on many essential points he would prefer them to postpone a final decision until he got to France.[3] O'Brien, for his part, bent his efforts to allaying Dillon's anxieties. In one cable that day he announced that Parnell had waived the condition binding their

1891. Five minutes later came another cable from Gill who thought Parnell's offer positively committed him; he added that it was O'Brien who had suggested Dillon as chairman.

[1] Dillon Papers, copy in Dillon's hand of cable to O'Brien, and marked as sent 9.45 p.m., 6 Jan. 1891.

[2] Ibid., 'Diary', 6 Jan. 1891. O'Connor did in fact send a cable supporting the line taken by Dillon (Dillon Papers (copy in O'Connor's hand, headed by Dillon), sent at 10 p.m., 6 Jan. 1891).

[3] Gill Papers, cable from Dillon to O'Brien, 7 Jan. 1891 (much damaged by fire); Dillon Papers, copy in Dillon's hand with note that it was sent at 4.5 p.m., 7 Jan. 1891.

action in case of Gladstone's refusal; he, O'Brien, thought McCarthy ought to be asked to approach Gladstone (and this though only the previous day he had recoiled from obliging McCarthy to go to Hawarden 'with a halter round his neck').[1] In another cable he sent word that the proposals were now in writing. With his usual incorrigible optimism he added: 'If McCarthy shows self-sacrifice believe contains germ satisfactory settlement.'[2] He followed this up next day with further reassurances. Parnell's concession, he believed, was genuine. Gladstone's guarantees would be secret and would remain in O'Brien's custody unless they were violated, or until after a satisfactory home rule bill had become law. He was convinced that Parnell was only concerned to test the sincerity of the liberals, but if he did play false then—so he asserted—Redmond, Harrington, Clancy and Kenny would resign.[3]

Upon Dillon these hopeful cables made little very impression. He answered, indeed, that they put him in a cruel and unfair position. 'Cannot join pressing McCarthy course which am convinced most unwise and event Gladstone refusal would bind us absolutely.' He had never approved of demanding pledges from Gladstone, but if O'Brien on his own responsibility could make an arrangement with McCarthy he would not interfere. However, as he clearly ought to be there, he would announce his departure publicly next day, appealing for a truce until he arrived.[4] His published statement appeared on the morning of his departure—January 10—and its tone was moderate. Difficulties had arisen at Boulogne, he said, and he had been called upon to commit himself definitely upon some of the points in dispute. He had therefore decided to go to France:

No man will desire to see those negotiations broken off so long as there is hope of uniting the party. Everything is to be gained by delay. It is clearly the duty of those parties to the negotiations who really desire to succeed to abstain from public comment until every effort has been used to bring about a settlement. A repetition of the Kilkenny scenes, or the Parnell scenes at Dublin and Cork would

[1] Dillon Papers, cable from O'Brien to Dillon, 7 Jan. 1891 (no time of arrival given).

[2] Ibid., cable from O'Brien to Dillon, received 5.58 p.m., 7 Jan. 1891.

[3] Ibid., cable from O'Brien to Dillon, received 11 a.m., 8 Jan. 1891.

[4] Gill Papers, cable from Dillon to O'Brien, 8 Jan. 1891; Dillon Papers, copy in Dillon's hand, with note that it was sent at 1.20 p.m., 8 Jan. 1891.

ruin the cause for years. In my judgment there is but one hope of saving the movement—that is an agreement uniting the Irish party. I believe it is still possible to re-unite the party, save the general election and secure home rule within three years.[1]

Thus the public man. But in his diary he had already recorded the anxiety with which he contemplated his re-entry into the battle. 'Long cables from O'Brien yesterday and to-day make situation practically hopeless. Parnell seems to have captured him and I fear P. has succeeded in dividing O'Brien from me... How William can have been persuaded to agree to this proposal as to demanding guarantees from Gladstone I cannot begin to understand.'[2]

And in this despondent mood he sailed for France.

---

[1] *Insuppressible*, 12 Jan. 1891.   [2] Dillon Papers, 'Diary', 8 Jan. 1891

IX

THE LIBERAL GUARANTEES

THE FACT THAT Dillon had not closed the door on further negotiations—however sceptical he may have been about their usefulness—allowed O'Brien to continue his efforts to transform his very hypothetical agreement with Parnell into a workable reality. The difficulties surrounding him were immense and he was well aware of them. On the other hand, the consequences of a premature break with Parnell seemed to him so catastrophic that he was determined to persevere. As he wrote to Archbishop Croke at this very time, people in England and Ireland were making a fatal mistake if they imagined that the battle was over because Parnell had been beaten at Kilkenny. On the contrary, it was only beginning and would go on as long as Parnell lived. Further, he pointed out:

. . . he will not only rally the hot-headed youths but hundreds of thousands of the best men in the country, if his offer to give way to Dillon on certain private assurances that all nationalists know to be indispensable should be flung back with insult in his face. . . We have a dozen excellent front-bench men in our party, but there is no other Parnell.[1]

This passage shows very clearly the gulf that lay between

[1] W. O'Brien, *Evening memories*, pp. 479–80, letter to Archbishop Croke, 12 Jan. 1891.

O'Brien and the anti-Parnellites who had been locked in close combat with their adversary for more than a month past. Healy and Davitt, and those who thought with them, were convinced not only that Parnell was far from indispensable, but that a short, sharp fight would finish him. From their point of view he was already a doomed man and no good could come of dealing with him. O'Brien, on the other hand, perhaps still a little influenced by his affection for the leader and by the glamour of his prestige, yet considered him a formidable force and capable of doing great damage to the home rule cause before he could be subdued. Feeling as he did, therefore, he was bound to insist that war to the death should only be resorted to as the last desperate expedient and that every possible effort should be made to enable Parnell to retire on honourable terms.

But the decision as to whether or not these terms should even be offered to Parnell did not rest with Dillon and O'Brien alone. Much depended on the liberal party's attitude and it had yet to be discovered if Gladstone, Harcourt and Morley would agree to consider a proposal which so suspiciously resembled the one they had already rejected out of hand when submitted to them in December. One thing was certain—the developments in the Irish situation since Committee Room Fifteen had subjected the liberal faith in home rule to a very severe shock and had revealed all sorts of stresses and strains which it taxed Gladstone to the uttermost to overcome. At the outset the mood had been one of sympathy for Parnell's opponents, and in the days immediately after the split in the Irish party some liberals were toying with the idea—though John Morley noted that it would need 'the very utmost reserve' to carry it out—of raising money for those who had followed Justin McCarthy in the break with Parnell.[1] Gladstone himself was prepared to contribute £500 to such a fund, though he later cancelled the letter in which he made this offer and nothing more was heard of the project.[2] It was not long, however, before such magnanimous thoughts gave place to anxious calculations about the effect of the Irish quarrel upon English public opinion. A by-election at Bassetlaw

[1] Gladstone Papers (B.M., Add. MS 44,256, f. 87), John Morley to Gladstone, 7 Dec. 1890.
[2] Ibid. (B.M., Add. MS 44,254, f. 58), Gladstone to Arnold Morley, 10 Dec. 1890 (marked 'Cancelled, W.E.G.').

offered a convenient chance of testing this opinion and the result—the unionists retained the seat with an increased majority—confirmed the forebodings of many home rule sympathisers in Britain. It was the first serious electoral set-back the liberals had suffered for a long time and a leading liberal newspaper, the *Daily News*, drew the obvious conclusion, and drew it in no uncertain language:

If the tide of liberal successes were really turned back, so that an event like yesterday's became not as now the exception, but an instance of the rule, the cry for Irish self-government must be made either to the tories or to the moon. . . Unless Mr Parnell can be decisively overthrown, unless his followers resume their old places and the strife is healed, there will be no Irish parliament in this generation.[1]

Even Gladstone, whose faith usually burned so brightly, was disheartened by the Bassetlaw result. John Morley visited him at Hawarden and found him half recovered from a cold, wrapped in a worsted jacket and looking 'with his white, deep-furrowed face like some Ancient of Days'. The by-election, he told Morley, seemed to portend a return to the position of 1886. 'For me that is notice to quit. Another five years' agitation at my age would be impossible—*ludicrous*.' They went on to speak of the situation in Ireland and of the scenes at Kilkenny which Gladstone could only compare with the quarrels among the Jews in Jerusalem while Titus and his legions were marching on the city.[2] From there the talk wandered, as it was so often apt to do, into the by-ways of Homeric study, but there was no disguising the fact that the old man had received a heavy blow—'the heaviest I have ever received', as he described it to Lord Acton a few days later.[3] On the eve of the Kilkenny result, but with the worst of the violence and bitterness already known, Morley summed up for him what he thought the effect of the crisis would be. It was not a cheerful survey. The situation, he wrote, had changed for the worse in several ways, which may be summarised as follows:

1. There was now no responsible or authoritative Irish leader to deal with.

[1] *Daily News*, 17 Dec. 1890.
[2] Morley, *Gladstone*, iii. 452–4; Gardiner, *Life of Harcourt*, ii. 90, John Morley to Harcourt, 18 Dec. 1890.   [3] Ibid., *Gladstone*, iii. 456–7.

2. Irish faction had renewed the old English misgiving as to Irish fitness for self-government.

3. While England would be more averse than before from a wide scheme of home rule, Irish parties would be less able than ever to acquiesce in a lesser scheme (he meant, of course, for fear of leaving themselves open to the charge of undue subservience to the liberals).

4. Anti-Parnellite dependence on the clergy would weaken the liberal case in Britain, to say nothing of Ulster.

5. There would be a 'vague, general, presumptive and indirect discredit' of the home rule cause in the minds of a decisive margin in the British constituencies.[1]

If Morley was pessimistic, Harcourt—with whom he corresponded constantly over Christmas—was not the ideal person to enliven him, for Harcourt had little sympathy to spare for his Irish allies after contemplating the likely effect of the crash upon the prospects of the liberal party, and in his letters undertones of irony were never far away. 'I myself cultivate such stoicism as I can', he wrote at this time. 'Like Grattan we can say, "We sat by its cradle and we follow its hearse". And I at least suffered quite as much from the pangs of its birth as I ever can from the agony of its decease.' His complaint, as he explained to Morley, was that Parnell's appeal to the Irish people 'rests on the denial of *all mutuality*. His demand is that Ireland alone shall prescribe the terms of H.R.' And he continued: '*I have no hesitation in saying that on such conditions I am as much opposed to H.R. as anyone in the unionist camp.*'[2] Morley, however, was unconvinced. He was for fighting 'to save something of what we have gained at such great cost, by convincing the Irish that for once an English party is thoroughly to be relied on'. Replying to this, Harcourt showed a trace of the cloven hoof, of which much more was to be seen in the next few weeks. Parnell's action, he suggested, had checked for the time at least the positive advance of the liberals towards home rule and therefore 'we should operate on the negative and defensive lines as against coercion'. Again Morley strongly disagreed. To announce that home rule was no longer regarded by the liberals as '*actual*' or practical politics would

---

[1] Gladstone Papers (B.M., Add. MS 44,256, ff. 96–8), memorandum by John Morley, 21 Dec. 1890.

[2] Gardiner, *Life of Harcourt*, ii. 91.

fling the nationalists back into Parnell's arms. 'It would be taken to justify Parnell's charge that Mr G. seized the divorce as a pretext for getting rid of the leader.'[1]

None the less, though Morley himself seemed untouched by the prevailing panic, there were signs towards the close of the year, not perhaps that the liberal attachment to home rule was wavering, but that some liberals were thinking of a postponement until times were more propitious. Gladstone himself—so he informed John Morley—was considering how 'to rally ourselves by some affirmative legislation taken up by and on behalf of the party'.[2] What he meant by this is clear from a letter the chief whip, Arnold Morley, wrote him a week later reporting Harcourt's opinion that 'we should do as you suggest—i.e. push forward English and Scottish questions so as to attract and hold any of our friends who may be hesitating'.[3] The particular subjects that Arnold Morley mentioned were 'the drink question', the franchise ('one man, one vote') and something—he did not specify what—for the agricultural worker. Another of Gladstone's confidants, Lord Ripon, agreed that 'one man, one vote' and a reform of registration had possibilities—but subject to two reservations. First, there must be no move in the direction of shelving home rule; that would be inconsistent with everything they had said and done since 1886 'and would be dishonouring to the liberal party'. And secondly, the registration issue 'would not form a basis sufficiently wide or attractive to be made the chief "plank" (forgive the Americanism) of an election platform'. If home rule were dropped, he suggested, a whole series of labour questions would come to the front and would have to be faced.[4] As it turned out, Gladstone's apprehensions seem to have been needless, for a few days later he had a

[1] Gardiner, *Life of Harcourt*, ii. 92. Harcourt, however, was quite unrepentant, as appears from the following, written a few days later. 'What I have to say about home rule may be packed up in a very small parcel as thus: "I believe the present system of government in Ireland to be a bad one. I was very willingly a party to an attempt to create a better. The Irish people and their leaders have proved themselves incapable and unworthy of it. *Voilà tout*"' (Harcourt Papers, Sir W. Harcourt to John Morley, 3 and 4 Jan. 1891).

[2] Morley, *Gladstone*, iii. 457, Gladstone to Morley, 23 Dec. 1890.

[3] Gladstone Papers (B.M., Add. MS 44,254, ff. 67–8), Arnold Morley to Gladstone, 1 Jan. 1891.

[4] Ibid. (B.M., Add. MS 44,287, ff. 81–2), Lord Ripon to Gladstone, 30 Dec. 1890.

reassuring letter from Arnold Morley who said that for every letter he received advocating that English and Scottish measures be placed before home rule he received a hundred asking that their Irish policy should not be affected. 'I should very much regret', he added, 'if it became known that the abandonment of home rule was even being considered.'[1] 'Abandonment' was too strong a word, but the fact remains that there *had* been a recoil, a recoil by which even Gladstone had been affected. It was only a momentary weakening, but it indicated a hesitancy and confusion in the liberal party which did not promise well for the success of O'Brien's mission.

(2)

That mission was already running into difficulties in another direction. It was, of course, essential that Justin McCarthy should not only agree to retire, but should also undertake the humiliating task of obtaining from the liberals the assurances which would be his own order of release. At first all seemed to be going well. On Friday, January 9 McCarthy and Sexton crossed to Boulogne and in the course of a long interview with O'Brien were told of the latest developments in the latter's talks with Parnell.[2] Next day they returned to England and, although no communiqué was issued, O'Brien himself was evidently satisfied, for he cabled at once to Parnell that the indications were favourable and that he presumed Parnell would have no objection to McCarthy having a voice as to the satisfactoriness of the liberal assurances. There would be no obstacle on their side to Parnell making a guarded reference to the Boulogne conference in his forthcoming speech,[3] though, he added, McCarthy had declared that if Parnell made any public statement insisting on his retirement this would prevent him from taking the first step—that is to say, approaching Gladstone.[4]

Parnell, on his arrival in Limerick, had called for three cheers for O'Brien, but this genial gesture made no difference to the

---

[1] Gladstone Papers (B.M., Add. MS 44,254, ff. 71-2), Arnold Morley to Gladstone, 5 Jan. 1891.   [2] *F.J.*, 10 and 12 Jan. 1891.

[3] Parnell was then in Limerick where he spoke on Saturday and Sunday, January 10 and 11.   [4] *F.J.*, 12 Nov. 1891.

firm front he maintained as a negotiator. His Limerick speeches, certainly, were not calculated to smooth the way for O'Brien's approach to the liberals. On Saturday night he told his audience that he claimed for them 'that the decision on all matters relating to your own affairs . . . shall be decided by you, and by you alone'. And on Sunday he went over once more the old story of the Hawarden conversations and showed himself quite unrepentant. Indeed, for good measure he threw in some acid comments on Gladstone's lack of a coherent policy on the Irish land question which, he said, was due to pressure from 'the tail of the liberal party'—as he called the radicals.[1] In this mood his answer to O'Brien's plea to admit McCarthy to their delibera- tions was a foregone conclusion. He was, he replied, at all times willing to consult McCarthy on points of special diffi- culty, but he had to insist that O'Brien adhere to the terms of the agreement reached at Boulogne.[2] This was bad, but worse was to come. It began to seem as if O'Brien, with his habitual over-optimism, had miscalculated McCarthy's reactions also, for on January 12 he received a cable from him explaining that he could not resign without the consent of those who had elected him.[3] To Tim Healy McCarthy wrote the same day assuring him that no definite conclusion had yet been reached at Boulogne. Parnell had accepted Dillon as chairman but the rest of the position was unaltered. 'We simply say that we can do nothing without the knowledge and consent of the party— which we maintain to be *the* party.' As to Parnell's stipulation that the proceedings which had led to his deposition should be regarded as invalid and informal, while O'Brien seemed to have given in to that idea, he and Sexton regarded any discussion about the validity of those proceedings as quite inadmissible; the most they had offered to do was to submit the question of McCarthy's resignation to their own section of the party.[4]

It was ominous, from O'Brien's point of view, that McCarthy should still feel it necessary to preserve a close liaison with Healy, for O'Brien was becoming more and more incensed by the violence of the attacks made upon Parnell by Healy and his following. He had been for a while convinced that the most

[1] *F.J.*, 12 Jan. 1891.　　　　　　　　　　　[2] Ibid., 12 Nov. 1891.
[3] Gill Papers. McCarthy to O'Brien, 12 Jan. 1891.
[4] Healy, *Letters and leaders*, i. 350, McCarthy to Healy, 12 Jan. 1891.

virulent articles in *Insuppressible* were written by him until the
editor told him that they were in fact by Healy's uncle, Donal
Sullivan.[1] Not that this materially affected the issue, for while
Parnell was at Limerick Healy had a field day at Nenagh.
Having on Saturday said that he personally entertained no hope
whatever of a settlement at Boulogne and that Parnell was
playing the game of Committee Room Fifteen over again, on
Sunday he referred in provocative terms to the divorce court
proceedings. Contrasting the recent records of Parnell and
O'Brien he observed that 'when Mr Parnell was on the fire-
escape at Eltham, William O'Brien was on the plank bed at
Tullamore'.[2] At the same time the unfortunate O'Brien was
also under fire from the Parnellite camp for permitting *Insuppressible* to go on appearing under his name. V. B. Dillon wrote
to him that some of the articles were so violent that they might
affect the Boulogne negotiations. He instanced particularly the
issue of January 10 which carried a leader entitled 'Irrevocable
retirement' in which it was said of Parnell that 'when he goes,
he goes for ever'.[3] As another article in the same issue ('Parnell's
surrender') spoke of the former leader having gone to Boulogne
'to entreat the intercession of William O'Brien for terms of
surrender', it scarcely needed a letter from V. B. Dillon to draw
O'Brien's attention to the seriousness of the situation; though,
as the latter pointed out reasonably enough, if he *did* suppress
Insuppressible he would be virtually disarming himself and his
power over Parnell would be gone.[4]

His most urgent task, however, was to bring McCarthy back
into the fold, for if he refused to co-operate the whole scheme
would come to nothing. To achieve this he bombarded Gill,
Sexton and McCarthy himself with letters all written on the
same day and all in much the same vein. The point he tried to
make was that no one would expect McCarthy to resign until
after he had interviewed Gladstone. As he put it to McCarthy:

The only thing settled between us was that you would undertake

[1] Gill Papers, Bodkin to O'Brien, 5 Jan. 1891.
[2] *F.J.*, 12 Jan. 1891; *Insuppressible*, 12 Jan. 1891.
[3] Gill Papers, V. B. Dillon to O'Brien, 11 Jan. 1891; *Insuppressible*, 10 Jan.
1891.
[4] Ibid., O'Brien to V. B. Dillon, 13 Jan. 1891 (copy in the handwriting of Mme Sophie O'Brien).

the first step proposed—viz. seek an interview with Mr Gladstone, and submit our suggestions to him, on condition that Mr Parnell agreed to give you an equal voice as to the satisfactoriness of the assurances of Mr Gladstone, if obtained, and that Mr Parnell in his Limerick speech should avoid any allusion to your resignation of the chairmanship.[1]

When he wrote this letter—which McCarthy accepted as satisfactory[2]—O'Brien presumably had not received Parnell's cable from Limerick refusing to include McCarthy in their examination of the liberal assurances,[3] but next day, better informed, he renewed his demand.[4] Parnell's reply, when at last it arrived, was even more crushing than before. He was anxious to meet O'Brien on this question, he said, but he was unable to see how 'I can in any way admit that Mr McCarthy is a free agent or can be an independent judge, knowing as I do how completely he has delivered himself over to Mr Gladstone and how willing he is to accept as satisfactory any statement or assurance of the former'.[5] And from this position it was impossible to move him.

(3)

While O'Brien was gyrating among these Irish cross-currents, the first tentative move was being made to establish contact with the liberals. On January 12 T. P. Gill both wrote to and visited John Morley and found him—so he told O'Brien—'with us wholly' and ready to go to Hawarden later that week. However, said Gill, Morley appeared to have grave doubts about Harcourt and 'went so far as to say that the present aspect of things in the liberal party looked remarkably like a vindication of P.'s apprehensions'.[6] In his own letter to Morley, with which

[1] Gill Papers, O'Brien to McCarthy, 12 Jan. 1891; this, like the letters of the same date to Gill and Sexton, is a copy made by Mme O'Brien.

[2] Ibid., cable from McCarthy to O'Brien, 13 Jan. 1891.

[3] Parnell's cable from Limerick was not dated, but could only have been sent on January 10 or 11. He arrived back in Dublin in the early morning of January 12 (*F.J.*, 13 Jan. 1891).

[4] *F.J.*, 12 Nov. 1891.

[5] Gill Papers, Parnell to O'Brien, 16 Jan. 1891. This is the original; also in the Gill Papers there is a copy in Gill's hand.

[6] Ibid., Gill to O'Brien, 12 Jan. 1891.

he enclosed copies of a letter from Parnell to O'Brien (presumably the letter of January 1)[1] and of the heads of agreement drawn up at Boulogne, Gill outlined the strategy by which it was hoped to obtain Gladstone's co-operation. Officially, he said, Gladstone was only to know that McCarthy, whom he recognised as leader of the Irish party, had come to ask him, in that capacity, for certain confidential assurances. Unofficially, he was to be enlightened on every point on which they could inform him. 'It is simply a terrific emergency . . . and it becomes a question at the very utmost of *straining a point* to avert what would be certain ruin and anarchy for Ireland in our time.'[2] In the interview he had with Morley—according to the account the latter sent Gladstone—Gill covered much the same ground as in his letter, but added the more precise information that O'Brien had persuaded Parnell to retire in favour of Dillon and that McCarthy, 'tho' sore at Parnell's insults', was also ready to withdraw.[3] Further, reported Morley, McCarthy would ask Gladstone for a memorandum on land and police. After describing the circumstances under which Parnell might be free to publish this otherwise secret memorandum, Morley commented: 'A desperately childish sort of device if ever one was. . . Among other impossibilities is the condition that your memo is to bind your colleagues (whoever they might be).'[4] Next day he forwarded the proposals to Gladstone, but with the air of one taking no responsibility for them. 'I think I was bound to submit them to you', he wrote, 'painful in some ways as they are and childish in others.'[5]

Clearly, Morley in private was by no means so favourably disposed as Gill represented him to be. In public on the other hand, he did what he could to help. The day after seeing Gill he made at Newcastle a very important speech, and one which probably did more than anything else to convince the anti-Parnellites that they could still depend on the liberals. For the

[1] See pp 204-5 above.

[2] Gill Papers, Gill to Morley, 12 Jan. 1891 (copy in Gill's hand).

[3] In saying this Gill was evidently unaware of McCarthy's reservations on the subject, conveyed—as we have seen—on that same day to both O'Brien and Healy.

[4] Gladstone Papers (B.M., Add. MS 44,256, ff. 115-6), John Morley to Gladstone, 12 Jan. 1891.

[5] Ibid., f. 117, John Morley to Gladstone, 13 Jan. 1891.

most part he ignored the provocations of Parnell's Limerick speeches, but he did take him up sharply on his claim that it was for the Irish people alone to decide all matters relating to their own affairs. To this Morley replied: 'I don't believe that any rational Irishman makes that demand. I don't believe that any rational Irishman expects that Englishmen and Scotchmen are not to have a voice in this great transaction. And I am very certain of this—that no rational Englishman will assent to any such claim whether made by Mr Parnell or anybody else.' On the vexed questions of the land and the police he asserted that there had been no going back by the liberals from their proposals of 1886. If, he said, a community was not fit to have control of its own civil police, then it was not fit to have home rule at all. The only reservation was that while the civil police force was being created, the existing armed and semi-military police (the Royal Irish Constabulary) would have to be maintained, partly because the imperial government had to honour its commitments to that force, and partly to bridge over the transitional period, in order to maintain law and order until the civil police had come into being. As to the land question, Morley declared that he stood where he had stood in 1886. While he thought it would be best if the land question could be solved at Westminster concurrently with the establishment of home rule, if British opinion determined that this should *not* be done, then of course it would have to be dealt with by the Irish parliament. All this —though not very specific—was balm to the negotiators at Boulogne, since it was at least on the lines of the assurances they sought. For the general public, however, which could only guess at what was going on behind the scenes, the most heartening part of the speech was its peroration:

It is for Irishmen to choose. If they are true to themselves we will never betray them. . . Let us watch, let us extenuate, let us hope. When the obscuring smoke has rolled away, let Irishmen know that they will see the beacon of friendship and sympathy still burning clear on the English shore.[1]

Meanwhile Gladstone had been digesting the Irish proposals and now sent his comments to Morley. They were, briefly, that the liberals could only deal with the *de facto* leader of the Irish

[1] *F.J.*, 14 Jan. 1891; *Pall Mall Gazette*, 14 Jan. 1891.

party and that the Irish must make up their minds who that was to be; that 'a document binding colleagues presents great difficulties'; and that no assurances could be given on the land question until the measure then before parliament had received its final shape.[1] On January 16 Morley had another interview with Gill and told him of Gladstone's comments. Reporting their conversation to Hawarden, Morley wrote that Gill had pointed out that when McCarthy came with his demands Gladstone 'would not be in any official sense aware that he was about to abdicate' and that what they did about the leadership was their own business. 'Technically', noted Morley, 'this is true', and he added a remark of his own which indicates that he was beginning to consider that the difficulties of giving assurances were out-weighed by the evil consequences of not giving them. 'If no assurances can be given', he wrote, 'and the Boulogne device falls through, then I anticipate that Dillon and O'Brien will throw all up; will go to prison and will come out to find the whole movement in pretty complete collapse, or else Parnell practically master of a demoralised party.'[2]

But there was Harcourt as well as Gladstone to contend with. That same day the newspapers carried a letter from him which was obviously provoked by Parnell's Limerick speeches. The burden of it was that if the Irish people and party continued to maintain towards the liberal party the same friendly co-operation, mutual good-will and honourable confidence as before, all might yet be well. However, he said, if Parnell succeeded in inflaming Irish sentiment, in rejecting constitutional action and in poisoning the Irish mind against Gladstone and his colleagues —if 'separation and hostility to Great Britain, and not an honourable and cordial alliance is aimed at . . . then I have no hesitation in saying that home rule has no chance and ought to have no chance'. All therefore depended on what decision the Irish people made. He, Harcourt, had little doubt of the outcome, but he added: 'The sooner that decision is made apparent the sooner it will be possible to pronounce on the future of home rule.'[3]

This letter with its undertone of menace—so different from

---

[1] Gardiner, *Life of Harcourt*, ii. 96, John Morley to Harcourt, 16 Jan. 1891.
[2] Gladstone Papers (B.M., Add. MS 44,256, ff. 120–1), John Morley to Gladstone, 16 Jan. 1891.   [3] *F.J.*, 16 Jan. 1891.

Morley's language of sympathy and faith—indicates how uncompromising was Harcourt's mood even before he learnt of the Boulogne negotiations. When on January 16 John Morley told him of them and of Gladstone's reaction to them, his indignation knew no bounds and he erupted at once in vehement letters to Hawarden and London. To Gladstone he wrote that the whole scheme was 'worthy of the Beggar's Opera'. 'I can scarcely bear to think or speak with patience of their daring to suppose that we should be parties to such an infamous intrigue.' And to Morley he expressed his alarm and disappointment that even the suggestion of such a proposal 'should not have been at once extinguished by a peremptory negative such as you would present to a gentleman who asked you to be his partner on the understanding that he marked the cards'. And he added indignantly: 'I for one will be no party to buying off this Gaul of Eltham with pledges.'[1]

This was no idle ranting. On the contrary, it underlined a deep division between Harcourt and his colleagues which, for a few days, threatened to paralyse their action. It is clear from the agitated letters which passed to and fro that not only John Morley, but Arnold Morley and Earl Granville were all convinced that Harcourt was only too ready for an excuse to shelve home rule.[2] Even Gladstone was moved to observe that while he admired 'the great talent' of Harcourt's published letter, he believed that it would supply Parnell 'with the exact material he wants' and that it would suggest to the voters in the pending West Hartlepool by-election that if there was so much uncertainty as to what Ireland would say and do, it was no time to commit themselves to supporting the liberal candidate.[3] To Harcourt himself he wrote in a tone of mild and muffled

[1] Gardiner, *Life of Harcourt*, ii. 96–7. In another letter at this time Harcourt stressed particularly that there should be not even a shadow of dealing with Parnell. 'If he is to be the Lord Bute of the Irish party, we are just as far as ever from a solution' (Harcourt Papers, Sir W. Harcourt to John Morley, 17 Jan. 1891).

[2] Gladstone Papers (B.M., Add. MS 44,254, ff. 75–6), Arnold Morley to Gladstone, 17 Jan. 1891; (B.M., Add. MS 44,180, ff. 200–3), Earl Granville to Gladstone, 20 Jan. 1891; Spencer Papers, John Morley to Earl Spencer, 19 Jan. 1891.

[3] Granville Papers (P.R.O. 30.29, box 29A), Gladstone to Earl Granville, 19 Jan. 1891.

reproof. There was, he said, scarcely a single proposition of Harcourt's letters (to himself and to the press) which he would question. 'Yet, in my inner consciousness, I do not seem mentally to come to close quarters with the question in exactly the same *attitude* as you.' Like Harcourt, he shrank from the notion of secret agreements; also, he viewed the leadership and home rule as perfectly distinct questions; he 'distrusted entirely the O'Brien proceedings'; and he could not conceive how there could be confidential conversations on Irish land until they knew how the government's present purchase bill would alter the situation. On the other hand, he said, if home rule was to be killed, he was most anxious to have nothing to do with the killing of it. 'I look at Ireland through the majority of the constitutional representatives of the country favourable to home rule. They have deposed Parnell. I will not, and I think ought not to, suppose it possible that the country will disown its parliamentary party . . . I think Healy and his friends have the strongest claims, political and moral, on both our consideration and our support.'[1]

At this stage, indeed, it seemed as if Gladstone would have a rift between his two lieutenants on his hands in addition to his other troubles, for John Morley took Harcourt's protests in very bad part and refused to meet him to discuss the matter. And, even though Harcourt handsomely withdrew his most wounding remarks, Morley's resentment was not easily assuaged. It was not only a personal grievance—though it *was* that—but a fundamental difference of policy that divided them. As he bluntly put it: 'Is our attitude on Irish affairs to be that indicated in my Newcastle speech, or that of your letter to Mr Gladstone and me?'[2] Fortunately, just when the relations between the two men seemed to have reached breaking-point, the liberal victory at the West Hartlepool by-election restored their sense of proportion. In view of the ominous result at Bassetlaw the previous month the West Hartlepool verdict had been awaited with great anxiety. In 1886 the seat had been won by a liberal unionist with a majority of over a thousand. Now, in 1891, after a tense struggle, it was captured by the

[1] Harcourt Papers, Gladstone to Sir W. Harcourt, 19 Jan. 1891, quoted in Gardiner, *Life of Harcourt*, ii. 97–8.
[2] Ibid., ii. 99, Morley to Harcourt, 21 Jan. 1890.

liberal candidate—C. Furniss—by 298 votes. In spite of the
fact that it was an industrial constituency where labour issues
might have been expected to be dominant, the victorious liberal
was convinced both that the election had been won primarily
on home rule, and that if he had not endorsed Gladstone's
repudiation of Parnell, he would not have stood a chance.[1] This
success gave a much-needed stimulus to the home rule cause in
England, and in Harcourt's phrase 'spread a holy calm' among
the liberal leaders.[2] Not that Harcourt himself relaxed his
suspicions of Parnell who, he told Gladstone, had only proposed
his retirement 'in order to get us into a mess. . . I don't believe
he has or ever had the smallest intention to retire upon any
terms'.[3] On the other hand, he could not but be aware of the
formidable body of opinion among his colleagues in favour of
taking up the negotiations. And since they all seemed to agree
that the negotiations were not to be secret, the worst of his
objections was removed and he put no further barrier in the
way.[4]

(4)

While the liberals were grappling with their own internal
difficulties, John Dillon arrived in France, being met at Le
Havre on January 18 by O'Brien and Gill.[5] O'Brien found him,
rather surprisingly, imbued with 'the best possible spirit'[6] and
although he was probably over-optimistic as usual, Dillon himself later noted down a variety of factors which had brought
him to believe that the negotiations did in reality offer the best
hope for the future. Here they are in his own words:

[1] Interview reported in *Review of Reviews* (Feb. 1891), iii. 142. The poll was
declared on January 21 (*Daily News*, 22 Jan. 1891).

[2] Gardiner, *Life of Harcourt*, ii. 99.

[3] Gladstone Papers (B.M., Add. MS 44,202, ff. 56–7), Harcourt to Gladstone, 20 Jan. 1891.

[4] Arnold Morley, Earl Spencer and Lord Herschell, as well as John
Morley, all seem to have favoured negotiating (Gladstone Papers (B.M.,
Add. MS 44,254, ff. 75–7), Arnold Morley to Gladstone, 17 Jan. 1891).
Granville tended more to agree with Harcourt, but even so wished he would
'not say or do more in public or private till after consultation with you and
his colleagues' (Gladstone Papers (B.M., Add. MS 44,180, ff. 200–3), Earl
Granville to Gladstone, 20 Jan. 1891).

[5] *F.J.*, 19 Jan. 1891.

[6] Cable to Parnell, 21 Jan. 1891, in *F.J.*, 12 Nov. 1891.

1. I found that both McCarthy and Sexton had practically agreed to seek the guarantees without any pressure from me.

2. Morley's attitude—as to which I knew nothing whatever up to that, I found that he thought the guarantees ought to be given and promised his active co-operation.

3. Morley's Newcastle speech.

4. The information communicated to me by W. O'B. confirmed me in the conviction that there was absolutely no other way by which it would be possible to save the movement except by a treaty with Parnell.

5. The outrageous attitude assumed by Healy's faction, by John Deasy etc., and by the bishops. And the scandalous attempts made by Healy and others to misrepresent W. O'B. and to thwart his attempt to make peace.[1]

6. I was to some extent influenced by O'B.'s strong conviction that Parnell was really anxious for peace on the terms he offered and was determined to act with good faith. And still more by the evidence I got then and afterwards that John Redmond and some other of Parnell's men were sincerely and earnestly desirous of peace.[2]

Not long after his arrival he had a letter from McCarthy which promised well. According to this, Gladstone was full of vigour and good-will and the attitude of other leading liberals was favourable. McCarthy, it seemed, did not believe the cause had suffered any loss in England or Scotland from what had happened and thought the chances of success at the general election were as good as ever. 'Of course you understand that all this means—if Parnell shall no longer be leader.' Then came the news for which Dillon had been waiting. McCarthy wrote that he was ready to re-open negotiations with Gladstone, though he pointed out that the latter might behave as he had done previously and refuse to discuss the question of assurances until the leadership crisis had been resolved. True, McCarthy would be going to him as leader and presumably he would be ready to negotiate with him:

[1] At the Leinster Hall, Dublin, on January 23, Healy launched a severe attack on the negotiations which, he said, should never have been undertaken. The tone of his speech is sufficiently indicated by the remark that 'Mr Parnell was hanged at Kilkenny, but cut down again at Boulogne' (*Insuppressible*, 24 Jan. 1891).

[2] Dillon Papers, 'Diary', an undated note in Dillon's hand at the back of the diary.

But we shall have to tell him that the pledges now sought are a condition of Parnell's retirement, and are to be submitted to Parnell himself. Is it not at least possible that he may declare this to be the old question over again and decline to go into it. . .? It seems to me that there might be a way of getting over this by settling once for all the question of leadership *before* going into the negotiations and thus approaching Gladstone through a leader whose leadership should be fixed and certain as recognised and accepted by the whole party.[1]

The point was certainly an important one, and was, indeed, the main difficulty in the way of the negotiations being pushed through to a conclusion, but there were two favourable omens which suggested that even this difficulty might not be insuperable. One was that McCarthy had apparently dropped his claim to be a judge of the adequacy of the liberal guarantees, for he made no mention of the matter throughout this letter; if this was so, then it was the best possible evidence of McCarthy's readiness to find a peaceful end to the crisis at all costs.[2] The other was his insistence upon the friendliness of the liberals; and if this were true, then they might not be disposed to take up again the unyielding attitude they had done in December. Certainly, when Dillon heard from Gladstone two days later, the tone of his letter was warm and friendly. He promised every support in his power to the Irish parliamentary party—amongst whom, he said, he did not include Parnell's followers—but he emphasised the fact that 'the British liberal party, loyal as before to home rule, refuses to follow Mr Parnell'.[3]

During the next few days there was much coming and going by both liberals and nationalists as a result of which a pattern for a possible settlement began gradually to emerge. On the liberal side, it is clear that the fundamental problem to be solved —as McCarthy had anticipated—was how to help Dillon and O'Brien without at the same time appearing to truckle to Parnell. It was evident that McCarthy himself was anxious to resign the leadership—'as it prevents him earning his bread by

[1] Dillon Papers, McCarthy to Dillon, 19 Jan. 1891.
[2] W. O'Brien, *Olive branch*, pp. 34–5, later claimed that McCarthy's right to share in the task of judging the liberal assurances had been conceded. There is no evidence that this was actually so and neither in that book, nor in the statement he published on 4 Nov. 1891, does he give any indication that McCarthy was present at the final conference with Parnell.
[3] Dillon Papers, Gladstone to Dillon, 21 Jan. 1891.

writing'[1]—but what was the best way of getting him to do it? Gladstone, from the safe remoteness of Hawarden, showed signs of not wishing to be involved directly himself. Writing to Granville, he suggested that he, Harcourt and the two Morleys should confer together, and then proceeded to give him his views:

> I feel persuaded we shall be of one mind. My leanings are:
> 1. No *secret* agreement.
> 2. No mixture of leadership with conditions of home rule.
> 3. No dealings with Parnell.
> 4. Free and confidential communication with the actual leader, as previously with Parnell.

Dillon, he added, 'does not seem to be a bit stiffer in the back than O'Brien. I should like to hear something of Healy who is of stiffer material'.[2]

This was so very negative and general that it is not surprising that when the group did meet in London—even though Harcourt was 'as mild as a lamb'—they did not come to any final decision.[3] John Morley, upon whom fell the main burden of these negotiations on the English side, saw McCarthy and Gill at least twice each within two days and on January 22 gloomily reported his findings to Gladstone. From McCarthy, whom he found quite willing to retire in any way that would make things easy for Dillon, he learnt that Sexton must not be understood to promise to support Dillon as chairman. On the other side, when he suggested to Gill that McCarthy should abdicate, Dillon be elected, and *then* either approach Gladstone for private assurances or be content with a public letter, Gill told him that this would not satisfy Parnell. Thus balked and harassed by both parties, it was little wonder that Morley was despondent. As he saw it, O'Brien and Dillon provided the only effective counterweight to Parnell. And if the negotiations were broken off and they went to jail their adversary would have un-limited chances of mischief for the next six months. 'It is well

---

[1] Gladstone Papers (B.M., Add. MS 44,180, ff. 204–5), Earl Granville to Gladstone, 21 Jan. 1891.

[2] Granville Papers (P.R.O. 30.29, box 29A), Gladstone to Earl Granville, 21 Jan. 1891.

[3] Lord E. Fitzmaurice, *Life of the second earl Granville*, p. 499, Earl Granville to Gladstone, 22 Jan. 1891.

enough', he wrote, 'for Healy to flourish his tomahawk, but he has no weight in Ireland; he is a mere *gamin*. If the Boulogne attempt fails, as I feel that it *must*, and as Parnell means it to fail, I see nothing before Ireland but the worst.' And he ended by saying he would simply tell Gill that a secret agreement was impossible, and that the details of a home rule bill could not be discussed in connection with McCarthy's deposition from the chairmanship.[1]

For several days longer the issue remained in suspense, though, as most of the discussions appear to have been carried on by word of mouth, little has been recorded of their course. It seems clear from John Morley's letter to Gladstone just quoted that Gladstone himself was aware that Parnell was being consulted by the negotiators in France about the guarantees, and the other leading liberals must have shared this knowledge, since they had all either been told about or had seen copies of Parnell's heads of agreement with O'Brien.[2] Once they had decided against making any secret agreement, they were faced with the further decision as to whether or not they would go on insisting that the leadership question must be finally settled *before* they gave their public assurances. If they did so, they faced the total collapse of the negotiations; but if they did not so insist, then they were in effect withdrawing under Parnell's pressure from the position they had taken up the previous December. It was a very unpleasant dilemma, and had it not been for John Morley it might well have been solved merely by repeating the earlier refusal to negotiate while the leadership question was still in dispute. Morley, however, was becoming more and more convinced that Dillon and O'Brien held the key to the situation and that to boggle about giving assurances—even though Parnell was lurking in the background—would make their position impossible. 'We know nothing as to future manoeuvres', he wrote to Earl Spencer. 'But what is certain is that if Mr G. does not give assurances as to land and police, we shall lose Dillon and O'Brien. The assurances constitute the only

[1] Gladstone Papers (B.M., Add. MS 44,256, ff. 127–30), John Morley to Gladstone, 22 Jan. 1891. Next day he wrote in the same sense to John Dillon (Dillon Papers, John Morley to Dillon, 23 Jan. 1891).

[2] Ibid. (B.M., Add. MS 44,256, f. 117), John Morley to Gladstone, 13 Jan. 1891; Spencer Papers, John Morley to Spencer, 19 Jan. 1891; Gardiner, *Life of Harcourt*, ii. 95–6.

instrument by which they baffle Parnell. I don't believe that P. means to withdraw, but the battle against him will be hopeless unless we have Dillon and O'Brien with us.'[1]

The day after writing this letter Morley again saw the indefatigable Gill and was able to tell him that half-a-dozen of the old cabinet were to meet and that he was 'very sanguine' that assurances would be given, though he was uncertain whether they would be in the form of a private letter to McCarthy or of a published statement. Gill, while pressing him to adopt the former method, admitted that he had been to see Parnell to find out whether he would accept, if need be, a public letter by Gladstone 'entirely independent of the Boulogne negotiation' in place of a private communication to McCarthy. He reported that Parnell had agreed and that he had found him in a reasonable frame of mind.[2]

At length, after a meeting of the liberal leaders in Gladstone's room on January 28, the terms of the guarantees were agreed upon.[3] They were then handed over to the Irish intermediaries and by them duly transmitted to O'Brien in France.[4] The original of this document has not come to light, but the essential portions were published nearly a fortnight later and appear in the minutes of the Irish parliamentary party in the form of a newspaper cutting. The text, which is reproduced below, shows that there was nothing revolutionary about the long-awaited assurances and that, on the contrary, they followed very closely what Morley had laid down in his Newcastle speech. Gladstone, indeed, later maintained that on the subject of the police 'I said what Mr Morley had said' and that on the question of the land 'I am not aware that anything was named which had been withheld in 1886'.[5] The details, then, were as follows:

[1] Spencer Papers, John Morley to Earl Spencer, 27 Jan. 1891.

[2] Gill Papers, note in Gill's hand of interview with John Morley at the latter's house on 28 Jan. 1891; the document has been damaged by fire and some words are missing.

[3] Harcourt Papers, memorandum by John Morley dated 1891 and written on Harcourt's notepaper; Gardiner, *Life of Harcourt*, ii. 99. Those present in Gladstone's room were Gladstone himself, Spencer, Ripon, Harcourt and John Morley.

[4] Dillon Papers, 'Diary', 30 Jan. 1891.

[5] Letter from Gladstone to the editor of *The Star* in *Pall Mall Gazette*, 9 Nov. 1891.

Land

It would obviously be inconsistent with the concession of home rule to Ireland that the power to deal with the laws relating to land in Ireland should be permanently confined to the imperial parliament to the exclusion of the Irish legislature.

The land question must, therefore, either be settled by the imperial parliament simultaneously with the establishment of home rule, or within a limited period thereafter to be specified in the home rule bill; or the power to deal with it must be committed to the Irish legislature.

Police

Mr Gladstone expressly said in introducing the home rule bill in 1886 that he and his colleagues had no desire to exempt the police of Ireland in its final form from the ultimate control of the Irish legislative body.

The complete organisation of the civil force by the Irish government to take the place of the present armed and semi-military police ought not to require more than a moderate amount of time—say, five years or less.

During that interval the present armed police under the control of the Lord-Lieutenant would undergo a rapid reduction or transformation (subject, of course, to a strict observance of all engagements made by the imperial government with the Royal Irish Constabulary), and would, on the completion of the arrangement for a civil force, finally disappear.[1]

When, some days later, Sexton was reporting to the Irish party on the last phase of the negotiations, he explained that when the terms were given to them they were told that they embodied the provisions on the two topics of land and police 'which Mr Gladstone and his colleagues would regard it as their duty to insert in the home rule bill, and treat as essential provisions'.[2] O'Brien, having received the assurances on January 30, talked them over with Dillon and found them on the whole satisfactory.[3] He was now free to move and that same day he cabled to Parnell that he had received 'materials for a final decision' and that it was important that he should come and see them at once.[4] As O'Brien had already a week earlier withdrawn his name from *Insuppressible* he could certainly not be accused of any lack of good-will or readiness to bring the negotiations to a

[1] Dillon Papers, 'Minutes of the Irish parliamentary party', 12 Feb. 1891.
[2] Ibid., 12 Feb. 1891. [3] Ibid., 'Diary', 30 Jan. 1891.
[4] *F.J.*, 12 Nov. 1891; R. B. O'Brien, *Parnell*, ii. 318.

successful end.[1] There was nothing more he could do, and all
depended now upon Parnell. He was due to speak on Sunday,
February 1 at Ennis and from there travelled without a break to
Calais where he was to meet O'Brien.[2] He spent two nights upon
the journey, arriving at Calais almost worn-out and in a state of
high indignation at newspaper rumours that everything had
been decided already behind his back.[3] However, O'Brien
smoothed him down and they set to work to consider the liberal
assurances.

(5)

The accounts of what then took place are confused and difficult to disentangle. O'Brien himself is responsible for much of
the confusion, because at different times he gave very different
versions. In November 1891 he contented himself with explaining simply that when Parnell read the liberal proposals he made
certain amendments in them and that after he, O'Brien, had
accepted these amendments, Parnell departed for London.[4] In
the general election of 1895, however, he went out of his way to
repel a suggestion made by Redmond that Dillon (at that time
still O'Brien's closest political associate) was to blame for the
failure of the negotiations. 'So far from the breakdown of the
arrangement at Boulogne being due in any way to John Dillon,
he played a more unselfish part and faced more cruel mis-repre-
sentation and injustice than probably any man ever faced before.'[5]
Fifteen years later, now identifying Dillon with everything that
thwarted his grandiose schemes for solving the Irish question by
'conciliation and consent', he gave in his memoirs a quite

[1] W. O'Brien, *Olive branch*, pp. 38–9; *Insuppressible*, 24 Jan. 1891. This was
the last issue of the paper. If it had not collapsed, the editor probably would
have done so from sheer physical exhaustion, as he had been working eighteen hours a day since it started (Gill Papers, Bodkin to Gill, 17 Jan. 1891 (he
has '1890' but this was obviously a slip); Bodkin, *Recollections of an Irish
judge*, pp. 175–7).

[2] His mood at Ennis was uncompromising and he assured his hearers that
he would tolerate no home rule bill which gave England a veto over Irish
legislation (*F.J.*, 2 Feb. 1891).

[3] *Daily News*, 3 Feb. 1891; W. O'Brien, *Olive branch*, p. 45.

[4] *F.J.*, 4 Nov. 1891.

[5] Ibid., 24 July 1895; see also W. O'Brien, 'Was Mr Parnell badly
treated?' in *Contemporary Review*, lxx (Nov. 1896), 683.

different account. He passed lightly over his own interview with
Parnell, mentioning the latter's amendments very briefly, and
devoted most of his space to the interview which took place between Parnell and Dillon the next morning. The two men, he
said, were amicably discussing Dillon's future tactics as chairman
of the party and naturally came to the topic of the Paris fund.
Parnell suggested that the fund should be lodged in his name and
Dillon's. Dillon—according to O'Brien—retorted that this would
mean that the first time he was in need to pay the parliamentary
salaries Parnell would be in a position to cut off his supplies and
render his position hopeless. The effect of this remark upon Parnell
was electric. He rose to his feet 'white with passion' and told Dillon
that this was not the language he had a right to expect
from him. The moment passed, and apparent calm descended
again, but in O'Brien's view—that is to say, the O'Brien of
1910—the incident was the rock upon which all their hopes
foundered.[1]

It is only fair to point out that we do not have to rely solely
upon O'Brien to know that the interview was an unhappy one.
Within a week of its taking place John Redmond wrote to him
that he was afraid 'John's interview with P. at Calais had a *very
bad effect*', and about the same time Harrington also wrote: 'I
think John said something to him about the funds in Paris
which wounded him terribly. . . .'[2] According to Harrington's
own published account (for which he did not give his sources,
but which seems not to have been contradicted, though closely
scrutinised by hostile eyes) Dillon had asked that Parnell should
release and place at his disposal as much of the Paris fund as
would sustain the parliamentary party for three years. Harrington added: 'I have it both from Mr Parnell and from Mr Dillon
that the latter gentleman declined to take the chair if this was
not done.'[3] T. M. Healy, also, though not of course directly
concerned, thought the clash of personalities was the significant
issue. The real reason for the breakdown, he wrote to Archbishop Walsh a few days later, was that 'P. won't have Dillon
for leader. He "blasted" Dillon to Gill coming over on the boat
and said, "I never could get on with that man. You know
O'Brien was the man I wanted." ' Healy added, and if he was

[1] W. O'Brien, *Olive branch*, pp. 46–8.
[2] Ibid., pp. 44–5; *F.J.*, 4 Nov. 1891.   [3] *F.J.*, 12 Nov. 1891.

right it is an interesting indication of how far the anti-Parnell-ites were prepared to go, that they were ready even at that late date to accept O'Brien as chairman, but that they were unable to get in touch with Parnell at the critical moment.[1] It is clearly impossible to elicit the true facts of the case where the evidence is so conflicting, and where, although three men were involved, only one broke silence. That the Parnell-Dillon interview was a complicating factor may be admitted, but the events of the next few days were to show that it was far from being the funda-mental cause of the break-down of the negotiations.

On the contrary, so far from washing his hands of the whole business, Parnell gave every indication that he was prepared to take the liberal assurances seriously, and even his arch-enemy, Healy, was for a moment under the impression that he was yielding.[2] When Parnell got back to London he wrote to Gill that, on looking over the section of the memorandum relating to the land question, he had failed to notice that there was no provision for the retention of the full number of the Irish mem-bers in the event of the imperial parliament taking the proposed 'limited period' for dealing with the land problem after the establishment of home rule. 'It will', he said, 'be absolutely necessary to insert a provision in the memorandum for such retention during the limited period, as it would never do to reduce the number of members during the interval in which both the constabulary and the land question would be under imperial control.'[3] Next day Gill met him and noted down, not merely the suggestion about retaining the Irish members, but also a further demand that when the Royal Irish Constabulary was abolished this was 'to be brought about *legislatively by an essential provision of the home rule bill.* . . .' What Parnell feared, evidently, was that if this were left to the executive action of the lord-lieutenant, it might happen that after the liberals had passed home rule, a subsequent unionist lord-lieutenant might either refuse to disband the R.I.C. or might even raise such a

[1] Walsh Papers, T. M. Healy to Archbishop Walsh, 10 Feb. 1891.

[2] Ibid., T. M. Healy to Archbishop Walsh, 4 Feb. 1891.

[3] Gill Papers, Parnell to Gill, 3 Feb. 1891. This letter was handed to Gill by Joseph Nolan (a Parnellite M.P.) on his arrival at Victoria Station from Calais on the night of February 3. (Note in Gill's hand at the top of the letter.) Also in the Gill Papers is a copy in Gill's hand of 'amendments sug-gested at Calais, Feb. 3, by Mr Parnell to memo. of liberal assurances'.

force anew if he chose.[1] While one may feel that this was an extremely remote contingency, the fact that Parnell was prepared to consider and provide against it does not suggest that he had already written off the negotiations as hopeless.

Nevertheless the breaking-point was near, for in quite another direction Gill's interview with him turned out to be of decisive importance. We have only Parnell's version of what Gill said (Gill himself only made a note of Parnell's amendments), but it seems that he was incautious and conveyed to Parnell that the liberal leaders had laid it down, as a condition of continuing the negotiations, that their assurances were not to be submitted to him, but to O'Brien alone, and that the latter would be required to bind himself to accept them before they could be published.[2] This, at any rate, was the burden of a letter Parnell wrote to Gill on February 5. These 'new proposals and demands' of the liberals would, he said, materially increase the difficulties of a settlement. They put him in 'a humiliating and disgraceful position' and neither his own self-respect nor that of the Irish people would allow him to occupy it for a single moment.

This was bad enough—but worse was to follow. He went on to say that within the last twenty-four hours 'information of a most startling character' had reached him from a reliable source, though what source he did not specify. He recalled that when he had met Gladstone at Hawarden the future position of the Irish members at Westminster was still uncertain. At that time it seemed likely that some would be retained as a symbol of imperial unity, but not a large number, so as not to give grounds for imperial intervention in Irish affairs. The information which had now reached him was that the full number *would* be retained permanently—a prospect he described as

---

[1] Gill Papers, a copy in Gill's hand of a memorandum which he made of a conversation with Parnell after receiving Parnell's letter of 3 Feb. 1891. These amendments of Parnell's were reproduced by O'Brien and Harrington in almost identical terms (*F.J.*, 4 and 12 Nov. 1891).

[2] This was an accurate enough statement of the liberal position, since, as we have seen, they had always insisted that they were not dealing with Parnell. But for the peace-makers in France, who, whatever the liberals might say, did have to deal with him, Gill's tactlessness was a heavy blow. If the negotiations were to have any hope of succeeding it was essential that Parnell should be given no ground whatever to claim that he was being slighted or by-passed.

'ominous and most alarming'.[1] Even apart from this, however, if the 'degrading condition' he had referred to at the outset—that is, his exclusion from pronouncing upon the liberal assurances—was insisted upon, he could not be a party to further negotiations.[2]

It was probable enough that Gill had been unguarded in his language. O'Brien had evidently feared that this might happen and had earlier impressed upon him that at all costs he must not drop any hint to Parnell which would allow the latter to say that the liberal offer was made upon the condition of throwing him over.[3] This, however, had not prevented Gill, as he admitted to Morley, from telling Parnell on a previous occasion that 'Mr G. seemed determined that any action he might take could not be said to arise out of a bargain over the Irish leadership'.[4] If Gill had talked as freely as this once, he might have done so again and thus opened the way for a misunderstanding which—given the cumulative strain of the long-drawn-out negotiations—was quite likely to occur anyway. However, he seems to have been genuinely astonished to receive Parnell's letter and wrote at once that it was of vital importance he should see Parnell, the first part of whose letter was founded on a misunderstanding which he could remove.[5] To this Parnell merely replied that he would be very glad if it turned out as Gill said—would he kindly write and explain the misunderstanding?[6] Thereupon Gill wrote again by return, saying he knew nothing whatever about these proposals or new conditions and that in any event he had no authority to speak for anyone save O'Brien.[7] Parnell, however, brushed him on one side and devoted himself to acquainting O'Brien with the new situation.

In France the first rumblings of disaster fell upon incredulous

[1] It is perhaps significant that Morley the previous week had said to Gill on this topic: 'Unfortunately I am afraid they are going to be kept on altogether, more's the pity' (Gill Papers, Gill's memorandum of his conversation with Morley, 28 Jan. 1891).

[2] *F.J.*, 4 and 12 Nov. 1891; R. B. O'Brien, *Parnell*, ii. 319–22.

[3] Gill Papers, O'Brien to Gill, 27 Jan. (in error dated February) 1891.

[4] Ibid., Gill's memorandum of his conversation with Morley, 28 Jan. 1891. [5] *F.J.*, 12 Nov. 1891; copy in Harrington Papers.

[6] Gill Papers, Parnell to Gill, 6 Feb. 1891; *F.J.*, 12 Nov. 1891; R. B. O'Brien, *Parnell*, ii. 322.

[7] *F.J.*, 12 Nov. 1891; copy (Gill to Parnell, 7 Feb. 1891) in Harrington Papers.

ears. Indeed, the news O'Brien had received from the Parnellite
camp had so far been extremely hopeful. From J. J. Clancy he
had two letters in rapid succession, urging him not to lose heart,
insisting that Parnell was sincere and that a little more concession would satisfy him.[1] On February 5 John Redmond also
wrote 'as one who is quite as anxious for the settlement as you
are yourself'. He suggested that the assurance as to the police
could be strengthened so as to satisfy Parnell and that as regards
the land question there was not much difference between the
proviso in the memorandum and what Parnell asked. 'Of
course I quite understand a feeling of impatience on the part of
G. and his friends and God knows *you* have special reasons for
impatience, but so much is at stake and we have approached so
near an agreement that it would be horrible if a breakdown
came now.' He added, however, and it was an ominous addition
in view of what was to come, that while he, Clancy and Harrington were using all their influence in the right direction,
'there are other influences among his friends besides ours'.[2] Yet
another of Parnell's followers, V. B. Dillon, wrote even more
strongly. Redmond and Harrington, he said, were leaving for
London 'and go, I assure you, not to allow as far as they can any
alteration from the original proposals as agreed to by you and
John to be made'. He did not, he added, think that Parnell
intended to make any, but if he did 'he won't have these men
or his other best friends with him'.[3]

It is not surprising, in view of these letters, that Dillon and
O'Brien were on the whole optimistic. It was true, as Dillon
recorded in his diary, that letters and telegrams from Gill were
unfavourable, but he wrote: 'There is now, however, so trifling
a difference between what P. demands and what the liberal

[1] Gill Papers, J. J. Clancy to O'Brien, 4 and 5 Feb. 1891.

[2] *F.J.*, 4 Nov. 1891; W. O'Brien, *Olive branch*, p. 49. The original of this
letter is in the Gill Papers. It was written from Dublin on black-bordered
notepaper (Redmond's mother had just died there) and has been much
damaged by fire.

[3] Gill Papers, V. B. Dillon to O'Brien, 6 Feb. 1891 (also damaged by fire);
F.J., 4 Nov. 1891; W. O'Brien, *Olive branch*, p. 50. This reaction had been
anticipated in the anti-Parnellite camp, for already on January 31 Healy
was writing to Archbishop Walsh: 'If he shows bad faith I understand his
followers, or some of them, will come over to us under a Dillon leadership,
and of course if they or any responsible section of them quit him, and Dillon
and O'Brien issue a strong manifesto, he is dished' (Walsh Papers).

leaders offer that it is almost inconceivable that a break-off can occur.'[1] But the next day brought bad news, for Gill cabled that the liberals had refused to alter a comma of their assurances and that Parnell was showing an intractable spirit.[2] That night the now somewhat discredited envoy arrived in person, bringing with him Parnell's letter of February 5, which seemed to Dillon 'a most treacherous document'. Parnell's alleged information that it was proposed to retain the Irish members after home rule, and the conclusion he drew from it that this would give a pretext for English intervention in Irish affairs, suggested at once to Dillon that 'he now proceeds to raise the veto question . . . which is a question that could only be raised at this juncture with the intention of doing mischief'.[3] From what Gill told them it certainly seemed as if Parnell's mood had changed sharply for the worse. His principal supporters had been called to a meeting in London on the night of Saturday, February 7 (Harrington and Redmond had been summoned from Dublin, but Redmond, said Gill, had not come over) which had apparently been stormy, as they had all come downstairs looking disconcerted and had told Gill that Parnell was very much out of temper. It is clear from Dillon's diary that he and O'Brien were both convinced that after the letter of February 5 the negotiations were doomed; this description of Parnell's attitude towards his own followers can only have strengthened their conviction.[4]

Accordingly, O'Brien wrote next day to Redmond that it was no use prolonging the agony. 'The story of the "new conditions" is of course absolute rubbish—not a shadow of foundation for it.' Parnell, he observed, was by his action making Healy 'the happiest man in London' and was himself 'now entering a conflict which at the very brightest can only end in making the country a hell-fire of discord and defamation'. He did not, however, entirely close the door and ended by saying that if Parnell accepted the assurances without more ado all would still go splendidly, 'but I fear me all is over and my last word is said'.[5] To Parnell himself he wrote that, while the story that had

[1] Dillon Papers, 'Diary', 6 Feb. 1891.   [2] Ibid., 7 Feb. 1891.
[3] Ibid., 9 Feb. 1891.   [4] Ibid., 9 Feb. 1891.
[5] Redmond Papers, W. O'Brien to John Redmond, 'Sunday night' (8 Feb. 1891).

reached him was purely imaginary and nothing had occurred to alter the terms on which they had met at Calais, the terms of his letter to Gill made it apparently idle to proceed further with their negotiations.[1] He followed this with another letter the next day in the same vein, but deploring the consequences if the negotiations were broken off.[2]

Parnell, however, was immovable. Writing to O'Brien on February 10 he declared that neither his letters nor Gill's had thrown any light on the 'misunderstanding' which the latter had undertaken to dispel. He then repeated for O'Brien's benefit the circumstances under which the 'misunderstanding' with Gill had arisen. 'I assumed', he said, 'that you would receive a memorandum on which you would be required to form and announce your judgment apart from me.' And he finished on an even more ominous note by referring to the recently published pastoral letters by several of the Irish bishops.[3] 'They create great doubts in my mind as to whether the peace we are struggling for is at all possible, and as to whether we are not compelled to face even greater and larger issues than those yet raised in this struggle.' This letter had a curious history. It was not published until after Parnell's death and when it appeared O'Brien immediately denied that he had ever received it.[4] A few days later Gill explained to Redmond that Parnell *had* written it, but after he, Gill, had seen him on February 10 he 'had resolved to drop the letter he had written breaking off the negotiations [sic] on the misunderstanding'.[5] This apparently was because Gill at last had been able to convince him that the misunderstanding really *was* a misunderstanding.[6] But this made no difference to the final outcome, for at this interview Gill had also to tell him that the liberals refused to make any changes in their offer.

[1] *F.J.*, 12 Nov. 1891; Gill Papers, copy in Gill's hand on Hotel du Louvre notepaper, 8 Feb. 1891.

[2] Ibid., 12 Nov. 1891; Harrington Papers, copy of O'Brien to Parnell, 9 Feb. 1891.

[3] Ibid., 9 Feb. 1891. The bishops of Elphin and Galway, and the archbishop of Armagh (Cardinal Logue) were particularly strong in their hostile references to Parnell and Parnellism.

[4] Ibid., 12 and 14 Nov. 1891; R. B. O'Brien, *Parnell*, ii. 324–6, published the letter, but gave no indication that it had not been sent.

[5] Redmond Papers, Gill to Redmond, 27 Nov. 1891.

[6] *F.J.*, 14 Nov. 1891, letter from T. P. Gill, 13 Nov. 1891.

Thereupon Parnell cabled at once to Boulogne as follows: 'On learning amendments will not be accepted, I must adhere to my position at Calais. Misunderstanding with Gill cleared up. Writing fully.'[1]

Clearly, even though Parnell did not send the letter of February 10, it represented his mood accurately enough and all that Gill's interview had done had been to make him change his ground. His resolve to break off the negotiations was in no way affected. O'Brien, on his side, had no doubts that the cable—which he received late on the night of February 10—marked the end of all their efforts, and with Dillon he sat until midnight talking over the situation with very little hope for the future.[2] The next day came two letters from Parnell which put the issue beyond all possible doubt. One, which was private, was full of affectionate regard for O'Brien and for 'the kindness and gentleness of spirit' he had shown throughout their conferences. The other —which was for publication and had actually been drafted by Gill during his interview with Parnell the previous day—simply explained that the last information Gill had conveyed to him (that is the liberal refusal to amend the assurances) being 'of a final character' there was nothing to be done but to bring the episode to a close.[3] Thereupon Dillon and O'Brien, having issued dignified but singularly uninformative statements to the press, crossed to Folkestone on February 12, where they were at once arrested and taken to Scotland Yard as the first stage of their journey to an Irish jail.[4]

(6)

Thus vanished the last chance Parnell was to have of obtain-

---

[1] Gill Papers, cable to O'Brien, 10 Feb. 1891, unsigned but later published by O'Brien as coming from Parnell (*F.J.*, 4 Nov. 1891). In the Harrington Papers there is a copy of a letter from Redmond to Parnell, 9 Feb. 1891 (I have not been able to trace the original), in which Redmond suggested that the refusal of the liberals to accept any amendments put Parnell in the position to break off on that ground 'which I'm sure you see would be an infinitely safer ground than the "new conditions" which O'Brien never heard of and did not agree to'.   [2] Dillon Papers, 'Diary', 10 Feb. 1891.

[3] Gill Papers, Parnell to O'Brien, 11 Feb. 1891 (in a copyist's hand, but signed by Parnell); Redmond Papers, Gill to Redmond, 27 Nov. 1891; *F.J.*, 4 and 12 Nov. 1891; W. O'Brien, *Olive branch*, p. 53.

[4] Dillon Papers, 'Diary', 12 Feb. 1891; *F.J.*, 12 and 13 Feb. 1891.

ing terms from the majority section of the Irish party. Thence-forward it was certain that the struggle in Ireland would go on unchecked, for with Dillon and O'Brien out of the way there was nothing to prevent a head-on clash between Parnell and the most extreme and resolute of his opponents. Since the terms were so favourable, and the consequences of his repudiation of them so serious, it may well be asked why he broke off the negotiations when he did. As he never explained his action publicly, other than in the letters already quoted, we cannot know the inner workings of his mind and all explanations of his decision must be highly speculative. It was, however, widely suspected at the time, as we have seen, that he never intended to withdraw and that the negotiations were undertaken and kept in being as part of his grand strategy. His close follower and biographer, Barry O'Brien, has suggested that his aim was partly to divide his various Irish opponents and partly to drive a wedge between them and the liberal party.[1] In the first of these objectives—if he was indeed striving consciously for either of them—he undoubtedly had some success. Both Dillon and O'Brien risked their popularity and prestige by conceding as much as they did, and they were regarded with much suspicion by the Healyite section of the party.[2] On the other hand, a clash between what might be called the extreme anti-Parnellite wing (Healy's group) and the moderate centre, which looked to Dillon and O'Brien for leadership, would probably have come anyway, since there were certain to be many who would sooner or later recoil from a repetition *ad nauseam* of the scenes at Kilkenny. And, although the negotiators were to be off the stage for the next six months, it is significant that their final words before going to prison were directed towards this body of moderate opinion, when they denounced the methods used against Parnell and asserted that peace might have been achieved but for the irreconcilables on both sides.[3]

If, however, it was also Parnell's intention to sever the alliance between his Irish enemies and the liberals, he was doomed to disappointment. If the liberals had refused to make any offer to

[1] R. B. O'Brien, *Parnell*, ii. 326–8.
[2] Of the two, O'Brien came worse out of the affair in Healy's eyes (Healy, *Letters and leaders*, i. 335, letter to his brother, 23 Feb. 1891).
[3] *F.J.*, 12 Feb. 1891.

the anti-Parnellites, then there might indeed have been a chance of breaking up the coalition. But once they had overcome their qualms about giving assurances, and once O'Brien had accepted these as broadly satisfactory, it was hopeless to expect any rift between them to develop. And, though Parnell did induce O'Brien to forward his amendments to the liberal leaders, the effect of this manoeuvre was less to embroil the anti-Parnellites with their English allies than to cause both of them to regard the author of the amendments with even greater suspicion than before.

If Barry O'Brien was right and these really were Parnell's aims, it is hard to resist the conclusion that he never intended the negotiations to succeed. Before accepting this conclusion, however, two things are worth recalling. One is that many of those who were closest to him—for example, John Redmond, J. J. Clancy and Valentine Dillon—were, as we have seen, convinced that he was genuinely anxious for a settlement.[1] And this view seems to have been shared by William O'Brien, by T. P. Gill and even for a time by John Dillon.[2] The two last-named in later years considered that Parnell had been several times on the verge of a compromise, but that Mrs O'Shea had stiffened him and sent him back as obdurate as ever.[3] There is no proof that this was so—though it may have been—but the fact that Dillon and Gill (especially the latter, who was in such close touch with Parnell) thought it a factor in the ultimate break-down at least indicates that they believed Parnell himself meant business.

The second point that needs to be stressed is that the terms offered were extremely favourable—so favourable, indeed, that he would have been foolish not to consider them seriously. All that was asked of him was that he should resign the chairman-

[1] See p. 241 above.

[2] Dillon Papers, 'Diary'. On 6 Feb. 1891 Dillon still thought a settlement likely, but four days later he wrote: 'I never could bring myself to look with hope or satisfaction on the proposed arrangement. It might have come off alright, but I could not see how it could.'

[3] W. S. Blunt, *My diaries*, i. 218–9, conversation with T. P. Gill, 7 Mar. 1896; ii. 381, conversation with Dillon, 10 Mar. 1912. This may have been what Redmond meant when he wrote to O'Brien (see p. 241 above) that there were other influences on Parnell's side besides those of his friends who were working for peace.

ship of the parliamentary party—he was, presumably, to be left in control of the National League, despite the obvious dangers which this entailed. And not only had Parnell's opponents acquiesced in what might well have turned out to be a disastrous division of powers, but they had failed to make it clear whether Parnell's retirement from the chairmanship was to be permanent or temporary. O'Brien later asserted vehemently that it was to have been permanent.[1] Parnell's followers just as vehemently declared that the only reason they had been prepared to accept the arrangement was because it was to have been 'a sham retirement . . . for the purpose of placating Mr O'Brien's English friends'.[2] John Dillon, for his part, long afterwards told Wilfred Blunt that he had repeatedly promised Parnell that he would resign the chairmanship back to him after six months—'indeed, I would only act as vice-chairman for him during his retirement'.[3] True, this was more than twenty years after the event, but it had been a critical event in Dillon's life and one which he was likely to have remembered very vividly. These differences of opinion are impossible to reconcile, but the significant fact surely is that the Parnellites believed that the retirement was only to be temporary, for such a belief can only have served to make the proposed settlement even more desirable in their eyes.

If, then, the terms were so generous and if, as so many people were convinced, Parnell was prepared to take them seriously, why did he break off the negotiations when he did? Certainly, if his primary aim was, as Barry O'Brien suggested, to sow discord among his enemies, he was more likely to achieve it by drawing out the discussions as long as possible than by taking the initiative in bringing them to a close. And in fact, if that *was* his policy, then his cutting the link with Dillon and O'Brien while the hostile alliance remained intact was virtually an acknowledgment of failure. If, on the other hand, his intention was to secure a genuine peace his action, though it may have been ill-judged, was at least consistent. Given that guarantees had at last been extracted from the liberals, and given that he

[1] *F.J.*, 4 Nov. 1891; W. O'Brien, *Olive branch*, p. 30, *n*. 1.
[2] Ibid., 5 Nov. 1891, statements by John Redmond, T. Harrington and J. J. Clancy and letter from Dr J. E. Kenny.
[3] W. S. Blunt, *My diaries*, ii. 381, entry under 10 Mar. 1912.

had asserted his right to examine them, it would have been perfectly natural for him to feel that he was entitled to suggest amendments which would make the assurances even more satisfactory.

Unfortunately this line of thought, which no doubt seemed logical enough to him, was precisely the one best calculated to set the taut nerves of the liberal leaders jangling with alarm. The frame of mind in which they received the amendments may be judged from a letter John Morley sent Spencer while the issue was still in the balance. Referring to Dillon and O'Brien, he wrote: 'They (no doubt at the instigation of Parnell who was over there on Sunday) pressed for small changes. Mr G.—most wisely—stuck to it that we would not alter a comma.' And further down he added that Gladstone had been inclined to dissuade McCarthy from resigning, but that he, Morley, had pointed out to him that it was not their business to offer advice on the leadership issue.[1] Parnell's conduct and speeches during the previous three months had evidently brought the liberals to such a pitch of exasperation that they were ready to start at shadows and smell conspiracy in what were, after all, quite straightforward proposals. But, although the provocation was admittedly great, it can scarcely justify the unyielding attitude they took up. It was a sad commentary on their loss of balance that they should have refused even to consider what they themselves admitted to be only small changes in their guarantees; while Gladstone's hankering to interfere in the question of the leadership, despite his earlier recognition that this was for the Irish party to decide, was a startling indication of how much his own individual judgment had been affected by the crisis. No doubt the explanation for their harshness lies in their intense distrust of Parnell, and in their determination to use every weapon they could to defeat him. This, however, does not absolve them from their failure to count the cost of their intransigence. By agreeing to make changes, or at least to give them proper consideration, they would have put themselves in a strong position, for they would have left Parnell with the alternative of either accepting their terms and retiring, or of rejecting them on grounds he would have found it very difficult to justify. As it was, their blank refusal to 'alter a comma' made it certain that the

[1] Spencer Papers, Morley to Earl Spencer, 8 Feb. 1891.

struggle would go on and that in future there would be further bitter variations by the Parnellites on the familiar theme of liberal dictatorship.

Parnell himself was in no better condition than his opponents to take a detached view of the situation. As we know, his health had not been good for some time, and the incessant travelling and speaking in the exceptionally severe weather of that winter must have taken a heavy toll of his strength. But psychologically, as well as physically, he had been under intense strain. With his private life exposed to every kind of insult, and his political career in jeopardy, it is not surprising that his pride was deeply wounded and that this was reflected in his behaviour. It was only to be expected that he should appear hesitant, irritable and supersensitive to anything that might seem to threaten his honour or self-respect. Certainly, his interview with Dillon, his 'misunderstanding' with Gill, his angry conference with his own followers, his resentment at newspaper paragraphs and at the bishops' pastoral letters, all suggest that he was near the limit of his patience. For a man in this condition, the abrupt rejection of his amendments by the liberals must have seemed like a blow in the face, leaving him little option but to discontinue the negotiations.

Whether or not this is the correct explanation of his attitude we shall probably never know for certain. There is little evidence that he said very much on the subject even to his own followers, and what he did say—so far as we can judge—tended to be inconsistent. Thus, on one occasion he admitted to Barry O'Brien that some good might come out of the negotiations, but another time, when the latter told him that people were saying he was talking peace but meant war, he replied smiling: 'Oh, indeed, do they? Well you know, if you want peace you must be ready for war. We must show these people we are not afraid to fight.'[1] Perhaps this very inconsistency expressed his own innermost uncertainty about the final outcome. And in the last analysis the truth may simply be that he was pulled different ways by conflicting currents—that in one mood he may sincerely have wanted a settlement, that in another he may have found the prospect of retirement (even temporary retirement) intolerable, and that in yet another he may have been unable

[1] R. B. O'Brien, *Parnell*, ii. 328–9.

to resist the temptation to foment trouble among his enemies. But whatever his aims may have been, the consequences of the break-down are clear. So long as the negotiations continued, his fate still hung in the balance. The moment they had ended the way was clear for the fight to go on again—and this time to the death.

X

IN DECLINE

‹‹‹‹‹‹‹‹‹‹‹‹‹‹‹‹‹‹‹‹‹‹‹‹‹‹‹‹‹

(1)

ALTHOUGH IT MAY have seemed in retrospect that the negotiations in France were, as Morley called them, 'idle from the start' they were not—from the viewpoint of Parnell's opponents—entirely fruitless.[1] The liberal assurances were not withdrawn because Parnell had rejected them, and this at least was an advance on the blank negative which was all the delegates from Committee Room Fifteen had received from Gladstone two months earlier. Further, the fact that they were published to the world meant that the liberal party had been committed in advance on the two important topics of the land and the police in a manner it would be impossible to repudiate.[2] And apart from this, the meetings between McCarthy and Parnell had resulted in the liberation of £8,000 from the Paris fund mainly, if not entirely, for the support of the evicted tenants. It is true that this was the subject of angry exchanges as to who had taken the initiative and how much was really allotted to the evicted tenants and how much otherwise, but it seems beyond doubt that not less than £5,000 was released for the benefit of these unfortunate people, and this too was a positive gain.[3] Finally, if the break-down of the negotiations

[1] Morley, *Recollections*, i. 263.

[2] Dillon Papers, 'Minutes of the Irish parliamentary party', 12 Feb. 1891; *F.J.*, 13 Feb. 1891.

[3] Parnell's speech at Waterford, *F.J.*, 26 Jan. 1891; Dillon Papers,

meant that Dillon and O'Brien had been detached from Parnell, then the anxieties and delays of the past weeks would, for that alone, have been worth while. The obliging officials at Scotland Yard allowed them to hold virtually open house for their friends, and during the night they were there they had many visitors. Among these was John Morley, who found them still inclined to regard Parnell as a formidable force, and who therefore impressed on them that his Ennis speech repudiating a veto power in the imperial parliament had been 'absolutely fatal' to any scheme of home rule associated with him.[1] Justin McCarthy, who also saw them, was persuaded that both men would never accept Parnell's leadership again.[2] Others, notably T. M. Healy and T. J. Condon, reporting that night to the party, confirmed that Dillon certainly had declared he would not serve under Parnell again, but apparently they said nothing about O'Brien.[3] Many people at the time seem to have believed that when the two went into jail Dillon was an anti-Parnellite and O'Brien a Parnellite, though how far this was correct only the sequel would show.[4]

Parnell himself was still full of fight and either did not realise, or would not allow himself to realise, the weakness of his position. True, the church was against him, but he had expected that and, as Kilkenny had indicated, he might choose to conjure up the spirit of fenianism as a counter-weight. True also, the

'Minutes of the Irish parliamentary party', 13 Feb. 1891. In the Gill Papers, there is a copy in Gill's hand of a letter from him to Parnell, 16 Jan. 1891, acknowledging receipt of Parnell's order to Munroe & Co. to pay £8,000 to William O'Brien, £5,000 for relief of the evicted tenants and £3,000 to meet a draft by the National League, 'the understanding being that the £5,000 is to be replaced to the credit of the general account at Paris, if you should desire it, on the arrival of funds from America'. With the letter is a copy (also made by Gill) of Parnell's order to the bankers. Later, Gill wrote a public letter explaining that the whole £8,000 had been used for the evicted tenants (*F.J.*, 18 Feb. 1891).

[1] Morley, *Recollections*, i. 264. At Ennis Parnell had told his audience that their attitude had shown the world that Ireland 'stands fast to her claim to be sovereign within her own kingdom and country, that she refuses to admit any English veto. . . .' (*F.J.*, 2 Feb. 1891).

[2] McCarthy and Praed, *Our book of memories*, p. 280, letter to Mrs Praed, 13 Feb. 1891.

[3] Dillon Papers, 'Minutes of the Irish parliamentary party', 12 Feb. 1891.

[4] R. B. O'Brien, *Parnell*, ii. 327.

majority of the party was against him, but he could—and did—claim that the balance would be redressed at the next general election. Holding this view, he could afford to make light of the verdict of a single constituency and explain it away, as his followers were prone to do, as the outcome of clerical dictation. Besides, Dublin was enthusiastically on his side; other towns, notably Waterford and Kilkenny, could be reckoned to be so, and in Cork he had had a rousing reception. Above all, of course, he still had the invaluable support of the *Freeman's Journal*.

All these factors have to be taken into account when considering his conduct in the months after the breakdown of the negotiations. Without them his career would be difficult to explain in rational terms. His policy—such as it was—was very simple. He would go to Ireland as often as he could, and wherever he could, and preach the doctrine of independent opposition as he had already many times defined it. Week-end after week-end, with very few intermissions, he would make the laborious journey from Brighton to Dublin and thence to all parts of the country—one week Roscommon, another Galway, then Cork, Drogheda, Ballina, Clonmel, Newbridge, Mullingar—and so on for month after month. Considering that his health had been poor all that winter, and that the winter was so harsh, the mere physical strain of these expeditions, which often necessitated three or more speeches, was overwhelming. Even his enemies noticed the change in him as spring merged into summer. Healy, seeing him at close quarters in the house of commons, wrote of him that while sometimes like cast-iron, at others he was 'awfully haggard'; and at the end of June, during the Carlow by-election, as so white that he felt sorry for him.[1] Justin McCarthy, who met him quite often on financial business connected with the evicted tenants, also described him as 'pale and haggard' and remonstrated with him for over-doing it. To which Parnell only replied that he liked it and that it was doing him a lot of good.[2]

But these Irish adventures were not conducted in a vacuum. There was always the opposition to contend with, and that opposition—as we shall see presently—grew steadily more intense and powerful. And as it did so the old vicious circle of Kilkenny repeated itself, only on a larger scale. The more

[1] Healy, *Letters and leaders*, ii. 361, 362.   [2] R. B. O'Brien, *Parnell*, ii. 345.

Parnell was attacked, the more violently he—and his most devoted followers—reacted. He himself was all too easily drawn on from the at least defensible position of independent opposition to other, extremer statements which did him nothing but harm. He was always liable to lash out at the liberal party, and at Gladstone in particular, and this could only result in alienating many honest men who had been convinced over a long period of years—during which Parnell had done nothing to disillusion them—that it was to Gladstone and no-one else they must look for home rule. Thus, it was not enough for him to attack the guarantees that the liberal party had given,[1] but he must also accuse Gladstone of trying to usurp the powers of the sovereign in saying that the liberals would never give home rule to Ireland if he, Parnell, was to be the first Irish prime minister.[2] Even a meeting designed to promote the cause of amnesty for dynamiters undergoing long terms of imprisonment was turned into an attack on Gladstone for not releasing some of these prisoners in 1886.[3] And from that it was but a step to proclaiming that Gladstone had tried every other policy first before he tried conciliation. What, for example, were moderate nationalists to make of the following, delivered at Wicklow on 31 May 1891?

He [Gladstone] taught the tories how to pass a crimes act, he suppressed public meetings in Ireland . . . he prohibited organisation, the forces under his control shot down the people and bayoneted women and children. All these things were tried by Mr Gladstone and the liberal party before they adopted the policy of conciliation and concession to the Irish national demands . . .[4]

Even if the fact of Gladstonian coercion be admitted, the whole tone of such a speech, ignoring the circumstances under which coercion was used, and making it appear that conciliation was only tried as a substitute when force failed, was a gross misrepresentation of a statesman who, more than any other, had

[1] Speeches at Roscommon and Strokestown, *F.J.*, 23 and 24 Feb. 1891.
[2] Speech at Drogheda, *F.J.*, 23 Mar. 1891. Gladstone at Hastings on March 17 had said that after the divorce disclosures the liberal party had had to decide whether (under a home rule settlement) it should place the constitutional leadership of Ireland in Parnell's hands (*F.J.*, 18 Mar. 1891).
[3] Speech in Phoenix Park, Dublin (*F.J.*, 6 Apr. 1891).
[4] *F.J.*, 1 June 1891.

shown in his Irish policy breadth of vision and generosity of
spirit. Yet even this was no more reckless than the assertion
Parnell made at Bermondsey a couple of weeks later: 'Supposing Mr Gladstone comes into power at the next general
election he will not give Ireland her legitimate freedom. Supposing this dispute had never arisen Mr Gladstone, upon coming
into power, would not have given Ireland her legitimate freedom.'[1]

It was fatally easy to pass from the thesis of independent
opposition, or from abuse of his former allies and followers, to
even more uncompromising speeches in which Parnell seemed
to hint—as he already had in Kilkenny—at the inadequacy of
constitutional action. For example, on one occasion he began a
speech in Navan by telling his audience that though they were
'men of royal Meath', someone in the distant future 'may have
the privilege of addressing you as men of republican Meath'.[2]
At another meeting he reverted to a favourite theme—declaring
that he would not repeat Grattan's mistake in disbanding the
Volunteers. 'We will refuse to surrender one particle of power,
one single soldier, one single weapon, until such a measure of
legislative independence has been granted to Ireland as will
enable her to take care of her own future. . . .'[3] And again, on
St Patrick's Day at Cork he claimed that he had never magnified
the efficiency of parliamentary action. 'I only have seen the
weakness of the position of any Irish parliamentary party.'[4]
This, it seems, was not merely for public consumption, but
expressed a deeply considered opinion. That night, in conversation with his host, the Cork solicitor M. J. Horgan, he said that
he foresaw the failure of Gladstone's Irish policy, and that in
that event the only course for the Irish members would be to
return home and organise what would in effect be a policy of
civil disobedience. Military opposition to England, it seems—
despite his predilection for martial metaphors—he considered
impracticable and hopeless.[5]

Such themes formed the staple of his Irish speeches during
these months, but it is only fair to say that they were not the

[1] *F.J.*, 18 June 1891.
[2] Ibid., 2 Mar. 1891; at the end of this speech he referred to Gladstone as
a 'grand old spider'.
[3] Speech to a gathering of Gaelic clubs in Dublin (*F.J.*, 25 Feb. 1891).
[4] *F.J.*, 18 Mar. 1891.   [5] J. J. Horgan, *Parnell to Pearse*, p. 48.

only ones. He was not entirely obsessed with attacking the liberals and on several occasions spoke more constructively. Unfortunately, the two causes with which he concerned himself most only brought him into further disrepute—in one case undeservedly, in the other perhaps less so. The first was the support he gave to Balfour's land bill, which was passed into law during the session of 1891. This bill, though naturally, being a unionist measure, it treated the landlords tenderly, was a mile-stone in the history of Irish land legislation for two reasons. One was because it took the principle of land purchase further than had yet been attempted, and did so by providing the unprecedentedly large sum of £33,000,000 in the form of credits to enable tenants to become the owners of the holdings they occupied. The other was that, in setting up the Congested Districts Board, it indicated that the unionist government was prepared to make a determined effort to remedy the endemic poverty and distress of the over-crowded districts in the west of Ireland.[1] This measure was by no means a final solution, but it had in it the possibility of real betterment for many Irish tenants, and accordingly Parnell threw himself behind it, rejecting scornfully the notion, as he put it 'that if you were any better off you would become less determined nationalists, and less anxious to obtain home rule'.[2] On the contrary, as he told an audience at Ballina, he would welcome from any English government or minister any action that would be some reparation for the wealth taken from the west in times past.[3] 'My views', he said on another occasion, 'are to accept anything good that we can get for Ireland from any English party, but at the same time not to surrender our independence to any English party.'[4] Since the unionist intention, of which the bill of 1891 was a striking example, was obviously to weaken the demand for self-government by remedying material grievances, Parnell's policy of accepting whatever any English party chose to give clearly involved a certain amount of risk, and could only

[1] For the significance of the act of 1891 see J. E. Pomfret, *The struggle for land in Ireland*, pp. 263-9.

[2] Speech at Irishtown, county Mayo (*F.J.*, 20 Apr. 1891).

[3] *F.J.*, 21 Apr. 1891.

[4] Speech at Carlow *F.J.*, 4 July 1891). Other speeches in which he developed his views on the land bill are reported in *F.J.*, 29 and 30 June, 2 and 3 July, 1891.

be carried out with the utmost watchfulness to see that the removal of some of the most fruitful sources of discontent did not rob the home rule movement of its momentum. But provided this caution was observed—and Parnell's speeches showed that he was alive to the danger—to welcome a measure which promised so much advantage for Ireland was a constructive and intelligible viewpoint, and did not deserve Healy's sarcastic remarks that Parnell had become 'a tory and an orange agent',[1] or that he was 'blowing the bellows for Balfour'.[2] The anti-Parnellites were quite justified in trying to improve the bill as it passed through parliament, or even in attacking Parnell for accepting some of its provisions too uncritically, but they were scarcely in a position to condemn him as whole-heartedly as they did, in view of the very real benefits it conferred on the country.

The other case, however, was different. It became clear during that spring and summer that Parnell intended to make a strong bid for working-class support in both England and Ireland. He opened this phase of his campaign with a speech at Clerkenwell in which he made a rather obvious attempt to drive a wedge between the liberals and labour, saying that he was now freer to express his sympathy with the English working-man since he had no longer to think about the leaders of the liberal party, and suggesting a number of labour reforms which parliament should carry through.[3] Ten days later he spoke in Dublin to a conference of Irish labour unions and, after repeating his Clerkenwell declaration that he was at last able to express his views more openly on labour questions, he even went so far as to assert that in the past, out of deference to the liberals, he had in Mid-Lanark thrown the weight of the Irish vote against Keir Hardie, despite the protests of R. B. Cunninghame Graham, 'a very dear friend of mine'.[4] His main purpose, however, was to

[1] Speech at Newry (*National Press*, 9 March. 1891).

[2] Speech during the Carlow election (*National Press*, 30 June 1891).

[3] *F.J.*, 5 Mar. 1891. Among other things he advocated shorter hours for miners and others; the setting up of boards of conciliation; and some degree of intervention in the affairs of the big monopolies, e.g. the railway companies.

[4] For the Mid-Lanark by-election of 1888 see T. W. Moody, 'Michael Davitt and the British labour movement, 1882–1906', in *Transactions of the Royal Historical Society*, fifth series (1953), iii. 65. Keir Hardie's own

develop a programme for Irish labour and he proceeded to declare his agreement with most of the objectives laid down by the conference. He was, he said, for manhood suffrage (one man, one vote); he was for the eight-hour day, though he thought it would need to be adopted internationally before it was practicable; he was for social legislation which, he hoped, would do more for the workers' conditions than strikes or combinations; he was, he further declared, for the nationalisation of the land— not (with a slap at Davitt) that he believed in the crude theories hitherto put forward, but rather that there should be heavier taxation of land so that taxes could be taken off food and other commodities; finally, he was for taxing unoccupied land, ground rents and unoccupied houses in towns, for the promotion of Irish industries, for extension of the factory acts and the employers' liability acts, for building labourers' cottages and for increased provision of labourers' allotments.[1]

Considering how little many of these subjects had occupied his mind in the past—except for the development of Irish industry, which was really a part of the home rule programme—it is hard to avoid the suspicion that this new-found faith was a somewhat sudden conversion, or rather a death-bed repentance. Davitt, who more than any other Irish nationalist could claim to speak for labour, made great play with this revelation of Parnell as a recruit to the workers' cause, remarking that Parnell's speech would have had an electrifying effect if made six months earlier, and that anyway the entire programme had been borrowed from his own *Labour World*.[2] Parnell, however, went on his way unregarding, and two months later at Inchicore (Dub-

admiration for Parnell was unaffected by the circumstances of the split. After Parnell's death he wrote of him as 'the one man in politics for whom I was ever able to feel a genuine respect' (*Labour Leader*, 17 Nov. 1894, quoted in E. Hughes ed., *Keir Hardie's speeches and writings, 1888–1915*, p. 38).

[1] *F.J.*, 16 Mar. 1891.

[2] Speech at Newry (*National Press*, 16 Mar. 1891). At that very time the two men were at loggerheads over one of those exasperating side-issues which did so much to embitter the politics of the day. Davitt claimed that when in 1890 he had tried to launch a labour movement in Cork (the Irish Democratic Labour Federation) Parnell had sought to prevent—or at least to discourage—him. Parnell, on the other hand, denied that he had asked Davitt to withdraw from the movement, though he admitted questioning him about its possible effects on nationalist unity; being, as he said, reassured by Davitt on this point, he had not pressed the matter further (*F.J.*, 11 and 16

lin) he was to be found advocating further limitation of the hours of work in mines and other dangerous and unhealthy trades, though he took care—as before—to add that he thought these regulations would only be effective if internationally applied. 'The future', he proclaimed, 'is undoubtedly with the working-classes.'[1] These efforts to develop a programme of advanced social legislation may have been sincerely meant—we cannot after all tell what was in his innermost mind. But his long indifference to such problems, combined with the fact that he was himself not only a land-owner but an employer of labour on a considerable scale in his Wicklow mines and quarries, inevitably left these speeches open to the inference that they were in fact nothing but the crudest of appeals for the support of Irish working-men.

Perhaps it is unfair to analyse too closely his speeches at this time. They were the desperate utterances of a man fighting for his political existence. For Parnell it was above all essential to put his case to as many people as often as he could. And while the basic themes were repeated over and over again, it was obvious policy to vary his approach according to the kind of audience he was addressing. But running through these speeches there was an unmistakable note of urgency, as if he realised that time was now against him. In the early stages of the struggle, before anyone knew what the reaction in Ireland was going to be, his best course had been to adopt delaying tactics, partly perhaps in the hope that the initial scandal of the divorce court might die down, partly to allow time for the differences which undoubtedly existed among his opponents to come out into the open. It was only after the Kilkenny election had shown the strength of the feeling against him that the time-factor began to operate the other way, though the full significance of this was hidden until the Boulogne negotiations had broken down. So long as they lasted Parnell might still have been justified in playing for time, but once they collapsed and it became plain that—in the immediate future at least—he had nothing to hope for from Dillon and O'Brien, then it became urgent for him to use his still very considerable personal prestige

Mar. 1891; *National Press*, 16 Mar. 1891; F. Sheehy Skeffington, *Michael Davitt: revolutionary leader and labour agitator*, pp. 177–9).

[1] *F.J.*, 8 June 1891.

on as wide a front as possible, to prepare the way for what
he hoped would be a crushing victory at the general election—
and the general election might come at any moment. Further,
it was vitally important for him to seize the chance which his
possession of the national newspaper and the national organisation gave him, for, until his opponents could improvise
counter-weights to these powerful forces, he had here an
advantage which might prove decisive.

(2)

Unfortunately for him, the speed with which these opponents
regrouped robbed him of his advantage all too soon. The
Boulogne negotiations finally broke down on February 12; in
little more than three weeks a rival to the *Freeman's Journal*—the
National Press—was launched. The first issue appeared on
March 7, and from then until his death it was Parnell's implacable enemy. From the beginning it was dominated by the
Healyite section of the party and Healy himself wrote many of
its leading articles. Without Healy, indeed, it is hard to see how
it could have been produced as speedily as it was. Neglecting
his law practice, he gave almost his whole time to the preparation of the paper. When it first appeared its standard of printing
left something to be desired, but this was soon changed and
within a few weeks it stood out as a formidable competitor to the
Freeman's Journal. On the morning of its first day Healy wrote
to his brother that they had sold 62,000 copies and could have
sold 100,000 if their printers had not been exhausted.[1] Within
a few days there was an inevitable falling-off of circulation, but
even so, Healy estimated it at 34,000.[2] It was, however, an
expensive venture, for not only did it cost £37,000 to launch,[3]
but one of its directors, T. A. Dickson, admitted to John Morley
not long after Parnell's death that it was then losing £400 a
week.[4] Its chief weakness seems to have been that it was never
able to compete with the *Freeman's Journal* for advertisements,

[1] Healy, *Letters and leaders*, ii. 358, letter to Maurice Healy, 7 Mar. 1891.
[2] Ibid., ii. 358, letter to Maurice Healy, 11 Mar. 1891.
[3] Healy's estimate, ibid., ii. 358.
[4] Gladstone Papers (B.M., Add. MS 44,256, ff. 175–6), John Morley to
Gladstone, 18 Nov. 1891. Dickson also told him that Healy was 'practically
in editorial control'.

and in the end it was obliged to amalgamate with that paper, though not before it had done the work for which it had originally been designed.[1]

Almost simultaneously with the founding of the *National Press*, the anti-Parnellites created the Irish National Federation, which was their counter to the Irish National League. It resembled the League in its structure, and branches of the latter, if they wished to join the Federation, had only to change the name of their organisation. Like the League, the Federation was firmly under the control of the parliamentary party. It did not receive its final constitution until November 1892, but in the interval it was governed by an executive committee which consisted entirely of the leading members of the party, with the solitary addition of Michael Davitt. The main business of this executive committee at the outset was to assist by every means in its power the formation of local branches of the Federation in every constituency, so that wherever Parnellism showed its head there should be a body of organised opinion ready to combat it.[2]

It is probably true to say that it was several months before the Federation swung fully into action. Certainly, the next head-on collision between Parnell and his opponents occurred before the new organisation could possibly have taken root in the country. In the middle of March the death of P. Macdonald created a vacancy in North Sligo. He had not been a prominent member of the party, and his obituarist in the *National Press* could find nothing better to say of him than that while he had been 'a strong advocate of the interests of the licensed trade', and had guarded those interests zealously, he had done it so quietly that 'they were for the most part unaware how much they were indebted to his unostentatious exertions'.[3] Nothing in his political life was so important as his leaving of it, for, inevitably, there would be a tense and ruthless struggle to fill his place and the verdict of North Sligo would be just as eagerly awaited as that of North Kilkenny had been.

The early stages of the contest were, however, overshadowed

[1] Healy, *Letters and leaders*, ii. 372–86.
[2] Dillon Papers, 'Minutes of the Irish National Federation'; *National Press*, 11 Mar. 1891; *F.J.*, 11 Mar. 1891; F. S. L. Lyons, *The Irish parliamentary party, 1890–1910*, pp. 185–92.
[3] *National Press*, 13 Mar. 1891.

by an incident which could have developed into something of major importance and which, though it failed to do this, certainly added to the bitterness with which the fight was carried on. Speaking at Cork on St Patrick's Day, Parnell had offered to resign his seat if his fellow-member for the city, Tim Healy's brother Maurice, would do the same.[1] Healy at once replied that though there was no obligation on him to notice the challenge—after all, it was not his leadership that was being questioned—he would resign concurrently with Parnell so that both writs for the by-elections might be issued at the same time.[2] For a day or so there was great speculation as to whether or not Parnell would follow up his offer, but when his answer appeared it struck a curiously evasive note. Maurice Healy's letter, he said, had been written in a tone of 'studied insult' and several of his statements had been 'of an untruthful character'. This made it impossible for him to have any dealings with Healy or his friends and impossible to hope that he would keep any promises or agreements 'any longer than he might find it expedient'. However, Parnell concluded, he had sent his application for the Chiltern Hundreds to Colonel J. P. Nolan, the chief whip of his party, with instructions to forward it to the chancellor of the exchequer 'as soon as Mr Maurice Healy has submitted himself to the judgment of, and gone to, his constituents'.[3] This, as Healy was quick to point out, was very different from the simultaneous resignation he had envisaged, since it suggested that he, Healy, should resign 'trusting to your honour to do the same'. 'A trick of this kind', he wrote tartly, 'imposes upon nobody, and simply covers you with contempt.' Skilfully, he tossed the ball back to Parnell, announcing that he was sending *his* application for the Chiltern Hundreds to the anti-Parnellite whip, who would hand it to the chancellor of the exchequer when Colonel Nolan assured him that he would hand Parnell's concurrently.[4] There were some more angry exchanges, but the fact remained that Parnell did not take the challenge any further. The truth was that each side trusted the other so little that neither would move first, though on balance Healy seemed to have had the better of the argument. There was no compelling reason why he should resign at all, let alone first;

[1] *F.J.*, 18 Mar. 1891.
[2] Ibid., 19 Mar. 1891.
[3] Ibid., 23 Mar. 1891.
[4] Ibid., 24 Mar. 1891.

on the other hand, if Parnell were serious about resigning, there was nothing to prevent him from accepting Healy's offer of simultaneous resignation, since, if the whips agreed to act in unison, there could be no possible opportunity for trickery.

With the scene set in this fashion, the atmosphere of the North Sligo election was likely to be turbulent. The Parnellites complained furiously of clerical influence, while the anti-Parnellites denounced the stone-throwing of the Parnellite mobs.[1] Since no petition was lodged to unseat the victor, the accusations and counter-accusations that were bandied to and fro were never sifted judicially, but there can be little doubt that tempers ran high and that speakers on both sides were sometimes subjected to more than a merely verbal barrage from unruly audiences.[2] So far as clerical influence was concerned—though opinion differed widely on what constituted 'influence'—it would have been surprising if the weight of the church had not been thrown firmly behind the anti-Parnellite candidate, a Sligo merchant and alderman named Bernard Collery. At the convention which selected him many priests and two bishops were present, and clergy certainly attended anti-Parnellite meetings.[3] On the polling-day itself, however, they did not—as the *National Press* took care to point out—accompany their flocks to the voting-booths.[4] While this was admitted by the Parnellites, the latter maintained that despite this the clergy made 'extraordinary efforts' on Collery's behalf, though—with a natural desire to make the best of both worlds—this did not prevent them from claiming a few priests as supporters of Parnell.[5] What worried them particularly was that the illiterates were apparently very numerous and that these, having to declare their choice, were thus denied the privilege of a secret ballot. 'It is a remarkable fact', commented the *Freeman's Journal* acidly (but perhaps too sweepingly), 'that all the illiterates voted for alderman Collery.'[6]

---

[1] *F.J.*, 3 Apr. 1891; *National Press*, 30 Mar. 1891.

[2] At an anti-Parnellite meeting in Tireragh stones were thrown at Davitt and one of his party, John Pinkerton M.P., received a severe blow on the head (*National Press*, 30 Mar. 1891). On the other hand, at Grange the Parnellites had been roughly handled by their opponents a few days earlier (*F.J.*, 21 Mar. 1891).

[3] *Sligo Champion*, 21 Mar. 1891; *National Press*, 23 Mar. 1891.

[4] *National Press*, 3 and 4 Apr. 1891.

[5] *F.J.*, 1 and 4 Apr. 1891.   [6] Ibid., 3 Apr. 1891.

Parnell's candidate was the Dublin solicitor, V. B. Dillon, who, as we have seen, was a channel of communication between the Parnellites and his cousin John Dillon. He was a very active supporter of Parnell's, but his name cannot have meant very much to the electors, who were at least familiar with his opponent. In point of fact Parnell concerned himself little with the merits and de-merits of the rival candidates, and devoted much of his time to assuring his hearers that the interests of the congested districts had always been near his heart,[1] and to telling them that the small tenants' needs could be satisfied if the government stopped—or reduced—police recruiting for the next six years. This, he calculated, would result in a saving of £500,000 a year which, if properly applied, would allow 250,000 small tenants to live rent free for ever. As for the larger tenants, their rents would have to be reduced by 30 per cent.[2] But, though some of the more simple of his hearers may have been swayed by these allurements, the outer world was more interested in what he had to say of the political situation in general. And what he had to say held out little prospect of peace or unity in the future. He urged the electors not to allow their representatives to take their orders from Gladstone or the National Liberal club. 'It was not on that principle that we founded our party and that we made it respected by both the great English parties.'[3] A day or two later he turned savagely on his former followers as 'latter-day nationalists', 'men who rush in now when they think there is an opportunity of gathering up some of the swag, bearing off the spoils, and cheating the Irish nation of her level right and of her nationhood'. During the same speech, after saying that he would gladly give way to a leader whenever such appeared, he declared that not one of 'the seceders' was fit for the post:

Can you make any one of them a leader? Who would unite with him any section of the country or any section of his colleagues? Can you select the foul-mouthed Tim Healy? Can you trust in uncertain and wobbling Tom Sexton? And can you follow hysterical Davitt who never belongs to any one party for twenty-four hours together? You cannot.[4]

[1] *F.J.*, 25 Mar. 1891. [2] Ibid., 26 and 27 Mar., 1891.
[3] Ibid., 26 Mar. 1891. [4] Ibid., 30 Mar. 1891.

It was clear that adversity had done nothing to chasten Parnell. Language such as this put any kind of reconciliation beyond the pale. It may have impressed some of the electors, but it did not affect the result. When the poll was declared on April 3 Collery had a majority of 768 votes—3,261 against 2,493.[1] For most voters, it seemed, Parnell's broadsides were of less importance than Davitt's assertion that he, Davitt, and his colleagues stood for Ireland and not for the dictatorship of any one man, and Sexton's warning that with Parnell they could not win the general election and could not preserve the essential liberal alliance.[2]

The margin of victory was not large, but it was the fact of victory which was important. A few days before the verdict William O'Brien had smuggled out of prison a letter to T. P. Gill in which he summed up the position very acutely. 'Any bad beating for P. in Sligo', he said, 'will make the others so cockahoop that there will be no standing them.' On the other hand, he added, if Parnell won 'he would be quite entitled to say the country was with him, and I for one should not say him nay'.[3] In the event, the anti-Parnellites were naturally jubilant, but mixed with their jubilation was a bitter, irreconcilable note which was ominous for the future. The *Sligo Champion*, though its language was extreme, caught the mood of the moment when it called Parnell 'a fallen idol, a burst balloon, a cheat, a fraud, a wreck. He would be pitied if he were not insolent'.[4] It was war to the knife and both sides knew it. The Parnellites, on their side, showed no sign of weakening, and with dogged optimism the *Freeman's Journal* proclaimed that another such victory 'and the seceders shall be undone'.[5] Thus, although in retrospect the North Sligo election may be seen to have tilted the balance of power markedly—perhaps even decisively—against Parnell, in its immediate effects it seemed only to have intensified the struggle without offering any prospect of ending it.

[1] *F.J.*, 4 Apr. 1891.

[2] *National Press*, 30 Mar. and 2 April 1891. The main burden of opposing Parnell in this campaign fell upon Davitt and Sexton. T. M. Healy was out of action, having been assaulted and injured on a visit to Cork (*National Press* and *F.J.*, 30 Mar. 1891).

[3] Gill Papers, O'Brien to Gill, 'Wednesday'; the post-mark on the envelope was 19 Mar. 1891 (which was a Thursday).

[4] *Sligo Champion*, 4 Apr. 1891.   [5] *F.J.*, 4 Apr. 1891.

But, while electoral battles such as these, with their angry scenes, their personal dramas and their publicity, were the obvious land-marks in the disintegration of the parliamentary party, it was also being subjected to a different kind of strain which, in the long run, probably did quite as much to damage the relations between the rival sections. One of the most unhappy features of the quarrel was that from the moment the Boulogne negotiations broke down until Parnell's death (and, indeed, beyond it) the opposing parties were locked in one controversy after another which solved nothing, but which—especially since they were carried on in the press and on the platform—resulted in ill-tempered and unforgivable things being said, leading sometimes to estrangements that lasted for many years. Almost any topic could provoke such angry exchanges, but the most important of them centred round two of the fundamentals of the human condition—religion and money. And—given the original occasion of the crisis and the church's reaction to it—it was not hard to see which of these two would loom larger in the eyes of contemporaries.

For Parnellites who were also Roman Catholics the dilemma was a cruel one and it is not surprising that they sought to evade it by seeking to delineate different spheres of conduct—that of faith and morals on the one side, and that of politics on the other—and by insisting that the two could and should be separate. Not long after the Boulogne failure had ended the partial truce, John Redmond—who by no stretch of the imagination could be regarded as one of the more hysterical Parnellites—developed this concept in a significant speech in Dublin.

God forbid (he said) I should deny to the prelates of my church the most plenary powers in matters of faith and morals. In such matters they shall command my obedience and my devotion. God forbid also that I should echo the false and hollow cry of no priests in politics. Priests and bishops cannot by reason of their sacred office lose their civil rights or evade their duties as patriotic Irishmen, but for my part I say the two things must be kept apart. Gentlemen, I have received during the course of this struggle letters from many catholic priests . . . and some of these gentlemen have said to me that whatever my individual political opinion might have been at the commencement, that the moment the bishops spoke it was my duty as a catholic to obey. Now, gentlemen, I protest with all the vehemence in my power against any such doctrine as that. I claim the right to exercise absolute freedom of action. I am entitled, when the bishops, in a political question, advocate a course which my intelligence and my conscience tell me is a wrong one, to perfect freedom to dissent from them, and to recall how, time and time again in the history of our country, the prelates took action which has since been proved to be short-sighted and unpatriotic.

It had been suggested, he continued, that those who supported Parnell were condoning sin. But, he said, when the Leinster Hall meeting was held no word was then spoken to suggest that they were condoning sin. And he went on:

If it was not condoning sin before Mr Gladstone's letter, how was it after? The question of Mr Parnell's leadership was a purely political question and for my part I don't hesitate to say that if in this purely political question the bishops and priests of Ireland are able to make their power paramount and to overbear the will of the country, they will thereby have created the most formidable obstacle to the granting of home rule by the English people that the wit of man could devise.[1]

Redmond's arguments, though they might be—and were— disputed, were at least on a rational plane. It was, however, fatally easy for the Parnellites, harassed as they were, to step down from this level and yield to the temptation to embarrass the hierarchy in whatever way they could. In March, for example, Timothy Harrington, by a calculated indiscretion, published a letter Cardinal Logue had written to Parnell in 1890 expressing the dissatisfaction of the bishops with some aspects of the Plan of Campaign and at the lack of supervision over *United Ireland*.[2] A month later he was again in controversy, when he asserted that in 1890 the selection of E. F. V. Knox as parliamentary candidate for West Cavan had been objected to by the local bishop on the grounds that Knox was a protestant,

[1] *F.J.*, 25 Feb. 1891. A leading article, praising this speech, observed: 'Irish history has, unfortunately, presented too many examples of how wrong Irish bishops can go in matters political.'

[2] Ibid., 11 and 12 Mar. 1891; Healy, *Letters and leaders*, i. 353–4. Earlier Harrington had sent a copy of this letter to Dillon, while the latter was still in America (Dillon Papers, Harrington to Dillon, 3 Jan. 1891 and enclosure).

and that after the latter had been elected, the bishops had debated—though not adopted—a resolution protesting against the number of protestants whom Parnell was bringing into the party.[1] This was at once vigorously denied by the bishop of Kilmore, Dr E. M'Gennis, who explained that his ground for complaining of Knox's selection had not been personal to Knox, nor that Knox was a protestant, but that he had felt that a properly constituted convention for West Cavan should have been held.[2]

Incidents like these were not, perhaps, very important in themselves, but they were exactly the sort of thing that was likely to happen once the habit of common action in the national movement had been lost. And the movement would not long retain the broad basis which had been its strength if irritations of this kind were allowed to multiply. We can see now that the problem was all but insoluble—that at any time it was certain to be difficult to define the limits of the part played by the church in politics, but that in the present instance, when the crisis had been touched off by apparently incontrovertible evidence of moral offence, the bishops would have been open to severe criticism if they had not spoken. And, even if it had been proved in court that O'Shea had been a conniving husband, this would have made no essential difference to the over-riding fact that a sin had been committed. From the church's point of view, what transformed Parnell's sin from a personal matter between him and his conscience to a national concern, was the fact that he was a public figure and not merely a private individual. This was brought out very clearly by Archbishop Croke in a reply to questions put to him by the editor of the *National Press*. Dr Croke explained that what he had to say applied to the *leadership* and to nothing else. Parnell's offence need not prevent him from being elected for any constituency, or indeed

[1] *F.J.*, 9 Apr. 1891.

[2] Ibid., 10 Apr. 1891. Other exchanges followed, but took the subject no further (April 11, 14 and 16). Earlier, Archbishop Walsh had warned Dillon and O'Brien to treat as absolutely groundless any rumours about the bishops having protested to Parnell about the election of protestant members. The bishops had considered a complaint that the original programme for selecting members as defined in 1885 had been departed from, but even this had been dropped nem. con. on Walsh's suggestion (Dillon Papers, Archbishop Walsh to Dillon, 26 Jan. 1891).

from exercising any influence he might have in helping the home rule cause 'almost as effectively as if he were leader'. But not *as* leader—that was the crux. And, in case this seemed to his readers too subtle a distinction, he took care to define his position very carefully:

You ask me is he fit, or unfit, to be the leader of the Irish nation? I answer, with the bishops, *decidedly unfit*. You further enquire—is he unfit *because* he has confessedly committed a grievous offence against the moral law? I answer—not precisely for that, but because, having committed it, and having never expressed his repentance for it but, on the contrary, as far as possible minimised it, he *should* not be set up, as on a pinnacle by a Christian people, to be respected, consulted and dealt with as a leader must be, and *could* not be so placed without manifest disregard of every moral sentiment, without sensibly lessening the social and mundane sanction that does so much for its support, and without leading young persons especially to think that, as Luther profanely put it, they may 'sin boldly' and be none the worse for it, here or hereafter. In other words you cannot support Mr Parnell's leadership without giving public scandal, condoning his offence, at least to some extent, and thus disturbing the landmarks of social morality.

Thus, in the archbishop's view, it was Parnell's obduracy and his prominence that together made him unacceptable. But there was a further point to be considered. Redmond—and Dr Croke also singled out Leamy and Clancy—had declared their willingness to follow their bishops in faith and morals, while claiming that Parnell's leadership fell outside that category. But, said the archbishop in effect, who is to decide into what category any issue will fall? Surely, catholics are bound to admit that it is the church which decides, and that the church will speak through its bishops. He continued:

And now, pray, where would be the practical advantage of having the prelates of the church endowed with a plenary jurisdiction as regards faith and morals, and the further privilege of deciding authoritatively on both, if individual members of the fold can at pleasure, or according to their caprices, render that jurisdiction nugatory by stating that they cannot accept the ruling of the bishops in a particular case, inasmuch as it involved only secular issues.[1]

The archbishop here put his finger on the weakest link in the

[1] *National Press*, 9 Mar. 1891.

Parnellite argument. Once they had admitted the authority of the bishops in matters of faith and morals, they put themselves in an impossible position. For who except the bishops—speaking for the church—could define what constituted faith and morals? It could not but seem illogical, therefore, at one and the same time to admit the bishops' authority and to deny their power of definition. It was all very well to insist that politics was a thing apart but in politics—which, after all, was only another aspect of men's relations with one another—there was virtually no situation into which faith or morals might not be said to enter. If the Parnellite claim to exempt politics from the sphere of faith and morals was accepted, this would open the way to a host of independent judgments on a host of different subjects— which, from the church's point of view, was akin to anarchy. In a sense, this whole dispute was an Irish variation on a theme which was common enough in late nineteenth-century Europe —the reaction of modern man against the claims of the church. It was a reaction which took various forms, though sooner or later it usually expressed itself in anti-clericalism of one form or another. It would be idle to deny that in the Parnell crisis in Ireland the elements of anti-clericalism—though not of anti-catholicism—were present. That they did not develop was partly because the Parnellites were in such a decisive minority, and partly because those who looked to Gladstone for home rule had, in Parnell's behaviour to him, a perfectly intelligible political argument, without concerning themselves exclusively with the moral issue.

(4)

The disputes which racked the once-united party over money, though they did not go so deep as those about the rôle of the church in politics, were no less bitter. One of the most irritating, and most tragic in its implications, was a quarrel about the best way of releasing the Paris funds for the benefit of the evicted tenants. Parnell wanted the money to be handled simply by McCarthy and himself, and he wanted also to make sure that other evicted tenants besides those who suffered under the Plan of Campaign should have a share in what was going. McCarthy's colleagues, however, were anxious at all costs to avoid exposing their good-natured and easy-going leader to the wiles of Parnell, and, after consultation with them, he made various suggestions designed to associate others with Parnell and himself in the administration of the fund. To every such suggestion Parnell simply replied that he could not share his responsibility with anyone save McCarthy, and a nagging controversy was carried on between them from February to May without any result except a worsening of tempers all round. Each side naturally was anxious to gain the credit for relieving the evicted tenants, but neither trusted the other enough to come to a working arrangement for disposing of the funds. And in fact, although the money was there, and the tenants were in dire need, the matter was still unsettled when Dillon and O'Brien came out of prison at the end of July.[1]

But worse—much worse—than this was still to come. Towards the end of May, Archbishop Croke went on a visitation through his archdiocese and took the occasion to make a number of hostile speeches against Parnell. In one of them—at Kilteely —he asked how it was that Parnell was able to go once a week by special train through Ireland 'to knock the bottom out of the priests'. It was a pity, he said, that there was no proper audit of public funds—and he instanced the 'Parnell tribute', the Defence Fund organised for the purposes of the special commission, the £10,000 given by Cecil Rhodes (of which he had heard that £5,000 was still unaccounted for), and a cheque of £1,000 from John Morrogh M.P., which was also unaccounted for. And how much was there really in the Paris fund? 'I do not', he said, 'for a moment wish to insinuate that there was any embezzlement going on or any misapplication of the funds, but I simply express my opinion that a public audit of all national financial transactions is absolutely necessary.'[2]

The archbishop might shroud his observations in cautious and diplomatic language, but his words were a challenge, a direct reflection upon Parnell's honour which the latter dare not

[1] The earlier correspondence on the subject is in *F.J.*, 7 Mar. 1891; the later exchanges are in *F.J.*, 14, 16, 17, 22, 23, 24, 27, 28 Apr. and 5, 6, 8 and 12 May, 1891. In the National Library, Dublin, there are copies in Parnell's hand of his letters to McCarthy of 18, 20 and 28 Feb. and 6 Mar., 1891 (N.L.I., MS 5934).

[2] *National Press*, 30 May 1891.

ignore. The very next day at Wicklow he dealt with Dr Croke's charges in detail. The 'Parnell tribute' was for his own personal and private benefit and he did not have to account for it.[1] The balance of the Defence Fund he held in his own hands and would use for public purposes in his own good time. As for the second £5,000 from Cecil Rhodes, part of that he had given to William O'Brien for Plan of Campaign tenants and the rest was still in his possession.[2] As for the £1,000 given by John Morrogh, that cheque—he said—had been given several months before Morrogh had become a member of the party, but he did not explain what had happened to it. The Paris fund, according to Parnell, had grown from £25–26,000 in 1882 when he took it over from Patrick Egan, to £43–44,000—its present figure. He pointed out that withdrawals from it were controlled by joint treasurers and that when bonds were from time to time sold, the proceeds went either to the National League, or to the National League of Great Britain, or to the parlimentary party. So far as the two former were concerned, there was an annual inspection by an accountant; as for the party, its books were in the possession of the treasurer, J. F. X. O'Brien, and no doubt he would publish an audit.[3]

To this detailed reply there came the bombshell—no other word will do—of the article in the *National Press* entitled 'Stop, Thief', which may claim to be the hardest blow delivered in the entire history of the split. That the article—though, of course, anonymous—was written by T. M. Healy appears to be beyond question, and indeed he later accepted responsibility for every word on the subject that appeared in the press.[4] Starting from a remark made by Dr Croke in his Kilteely speech that two or

[1] For the 'Parnell tribute' see R. B. O'Brien, *Parnell*, ii. 22–8. It was a national collection made on his behalf in 1883 and amounted to £37,000.

[2] The circumstances of Rhodes's gift of £10,000 are described in R. B. O'Brien, *Parnell*, ii. 184–9.

[3] *F.J.*, 1 June 1891.

[4] *National Press*, 11 June 1891. His authorship of the article is accepted by his daughter, Mrs M. Sullivan (*No man's man*, pp. 197–8). Earlier, he had been anxious that Parnell should be 'probed' about the balance of the Defence Fund. He wrote to his brother at the height of the Kilkenny election that the expenses of the special commission had been £31,000 and that the balance (which he reckoned at £10,000) was—together with £5,000 of Rhodes's money—being used against them in the election (Healy, *Letters and leaders*, i. 343–4, letter to Maurice Healy, 15 Dec. 1890).

three years earlier he had tried in vain to discuss with Parnell
the question of auditing funds, the article stated:

The silence of Mr Parnell now is the best explanation of his refusal
to face, even in five minutes' friendly conversation, a powerful and
determined nationalist. Why? Because for years *he has been stealing
the money entrusted to his charge*.[1]

It went on to question Parnell's account of what had happened
to the money from Cecil Rhodes, pointing out that at Clonmel
in April Parnell had said he had handed William O'Brien a
cheque for £5,000 in a lump sum, which had been given to him
by Rhodes to spend as he thought best.[2] But at Wicklow Parnell
had stated that *some* money was given to O'Brien and that he
had kept the balance. What balance? Of the original £10,000,
£5,000 was entered in the books of the parliamentary party and
there was no dispute about that.[3] Therefore, the argument
concerned the other £5,000 of which Parnell had given inconsistent accounts. Finally, the article ended by asserting that
Parnell had passed the money from Morrogh into his own
private account and in effect put it in his pocket.

The next day the attack was resumed with an article which
began by saying that the *National Press* had been awaiting a
writ from Parnell but had not received one. 'We called Mr
Parnell a thief. We repeat that epithet.' The concluding passage
ran as follows:

This charge, if he fails to face it, has come to stay. It will haunt Mr
Parnell on platform and in parliament, at bed and board, for the
remainder of his career. We will force him to face it, or amidst the
contempt of his own supporters, 'lash the rascal naked through the
world'.[4]

Nothing can give a better idea of the pitch of ferocity that the

---

[1] *National Press*, 1 June 1891. Parnell's explanation of this at Wicklow had
been that he had believed the archbishop wanted to see him about the Plan
of Campaign and that, as he disapproved of that venture, he had made no
effort to meet Dr Croke (*F.J.*, 1 June 1891).

[2] *F.J.*, 27 Apr. 1891.

[3] I have examined the books of the parliamentary party and have only
been able to trace one payment of £5,000 which may have been an instalment of Rhodes's contribution. See also C. Cruise O'Brien, *Parnell and his
party*, p. 266, n 4.

[4] *National Press*, 2 June 1891.

struggle had now reached than the tone of these two articles. Over many months the constant bickering, the endless controversy, the strain of two bitterly fought elections, had combined to break down all barriers of restraint. The man who had led a united party for ten years, who had received the most extreme devotion from his fellow-countrymen, was now in plain terms called a thief. All that had been said by Archbishop Croke, and he stressed this himself a day or so later, was that the public had a right to know how money was spent that had been intended for the national cause.[1] He was not suggesting that Parnell had pocketed the money; but this was what the *National Press* was doing.[2] And so, on the basis of the archbishop's remarks, and of Healy's own suspicions as to how Parnell was finding the money to carry on the struggle, this structure of accusation was raised. It might have been true that Parnell had not publicly accounted for money he had received, and this might have been reprehensible of him. Healy's suspicions might have been well-founded, and Parnell might have been found to have used the money for carrying on the war against his opponents. But even if that had been what he was doing, there was a case which could be argued for and against. For, it could be said that in his own view he was still the leader of the party and that the money was being legitimately spent if it helped to crush a revolt and to restore unity to the movement. Against, it could be maintained that when the money was given to Parnell, it was given to him as the leader of a national movement, and that to use it for sectional purposes was to misuse it, that it would have been better to keep it apart, used by neither side, or best of all to have used it for the evicted tenants. But to throw out the epithet 'thief' without further argument or discussion, was to strip the quarrel of the last vestiges of restraint.

Of course, as a purely tactical move, it was ingenious enough. The charge was dramatic, sensational, direct—it was certain to catch the public eye. And it placed Parnell at once on the defensive. If he did *not* bring a libel action, this would leave him open

[1] *National Press*, 3 June 1891.

[2] Ibid., 5 June 1891. 'His Grace nowhere suggested that Mr. Parnell pocketed the money. We did. His Grace did not say he was in possession of knowledge as to the disposition of the moneys. We are. He never suggested that Mr Parnell was a thief. We say so.'

to the suspicion that he dare not bring it because the comment was fair comment and not libel. On the other hand, if he did bring an action then his financial resources and the inner workings of his movement would be exposed to searching and hostile scrutiny by counsel, a process which might or might not substantiate the charges against him, but which would certainly provide his opponents with much useful information about the strength and weakness of his position. And, although he might get a verdict against the *National Press*, and even obtain heavy damages, the cost might well prove too dear.

Whether this was his reasoning, or whether—as would have been psychologically typical—he merely disdained to notice the accusation, the fact remains that he took no action against the *National Press*, and contented himself with a brief promise in a speech at Inchicore a few days later that he would prepare a balance-sheet to explain the disputed items and would submit this balance-sheet to O'Brien when he came out of jail. The latter could then make what public report he thought proper.[1] This offer was contemptuously received by the *National Press*, which commented that 'stupider balance-sheets than Mr Fox[2] can prepare have passed alerter arithmeticians than Mr O'Brien before now . . .' Making further capital the writer seized the chance of suggesting that the offer was really made with the object of driving a wedge between Dillon and O'Brien and that, in any event: 'The position of nominee-auditor for an accused thief is not one to be coveted, and after the experience of Mr Parnell in Boulogne, it is hardly likely to be accepted'.[3] No such balance-sheet seems to have been presented to O'Brien. At any rate, no record of it has survived in O'Brien's papers, and even the *National Press* seems subsequently to have avoided the topic, though on one occasion in August it announced ironically that in a speech he was about to make at Kells 'Mr Parnell will explain his reasons for now refusing to submit the proposed balance-sheet to Mr O'Brien'.[4] Parnell, of course, did nothing of the sort, and as Dillon intervened privately to prevent any

---

[1] *F.J.*, 8 June 1891.
[2] Mr. Fox, as was shown at the divorce trial, was one of the aliases adopted by Parnell in his efforts to avoid publicity.
[3] *National Press*, 8 June 1891.
[4] Ibid., 13 Aug. 1891.

further references to the matter, it was allowed to drop.[1] The truth probably was that by then the struggle with Parnell had passed into a new phase and neither side was much interested in taking the issue further.

(5)

Meanwhile, the month which had produced the most virulent attack Parnell had yet had to face, also brought him intense personal happiness. Very early on the morning of June 25 he drove Katharine O'Shea to the registry office at Steyning (in Sussex) where they were married, with two of her maids as witnesses. That day they spent quietly by the sea at Shoreham.[2] It was the only honeymoon they were to know, for their peace was soon shattered. Two days earlier the first move had been made in the third and last battle Parnell was to fight in the constituencies, when his opponents selected a local merchant named John Hammond to fill the vacancy at Carlow caused by the death of the O'Gorman Mahon, the old man who, if Mrs O'Shea's account is to be trusted, had been among the first to arouse her interest in Parnell.[3] And, on the day before Parnell's wedding, a Parnellite convention had already met in Carlow and chosen as their candidate Andrew Kettle, who had been a Land Leaguer in days gone by, and who had been an important link between that organisation and the constitutional movement.[4] A by-election was too important an opportunity for Parnell to test opinion in the way that mattered most for him to be able to spare much time away from Ireland. He was married on Thursday and by Sunday he was in Carlow. And from then until the declaration of the poll he flung himself into the contest with the same fierce abandon he had shown at Kilkenny and Sligo.

[1] Dillon Papers, M. Bodkin to Dillon, 19 and 21 Aug. 1891.

[2] *F.J.*, 26 June 1891; O'Shea, ii. 250–8.

[3] *National Press*, 24 June 1891; O'Shea, i. 132–4. The O'Gorman Mahon died on 16 June 1891 at the age of 89. He had been ill at the time of Committee Room Fifteen, but had declared against Parnell.

[4] *F.J.*, 25 June 1891. Years later Kettle recalled that Dr Kenny had approached him in despair of finding any Parnellite candidate and that he, Kettle, had agreed to stand provided his election expenses were paid for him. (A. J. Kettle, *Material for victory*, ed. L. J. Kettle; these memoirs were published in 1958, but appear to have been written about 1910.)

After a fairly quiet opening the election developed into a very rowdy affair. There was some stone-throwing, and the Parnellite candidate's name unfortunately suggested to the wilder element an easy way of drowning his speeches, which were on occasion accompanied by much banging of tin cans.[1] On the other hand, Parnell himself admitted that—in contrast to Kilkenny and Sligo—he had no difficulty in penetrating to every part of the constituency and speaking and canvassing freely.[2] It was noticeable also that the Parnellites complained less than before about clerical interference—though they *did* complain of it[3]—and that they even succeeded in finding a parish priest, the Very Reverend B. O'Neill of Bagenalstown, to sign Kettle's nomination paper.[4] The arguments used by both sides ranged over all too familiar ground and need not long detain us. Parnell devoted much effort to explaining his attitude towards the land bill (which by then had reached the house of lords) and to declaring that his view had always been that if the tenant farmer were made the owner of his holding 'he was thereby a stronger soldier and more fit to fight in the ranks of Irishmen'.[5] For the rest, he repeated yet again his attacks upon Gladstone and his warnings against departing from the principle of independent opposition.[6] His late followers also came in for their share of abuse—some of them being described as having 'no more brains than would sit cross-legged on the point of a pin'[7]—and Healy in particular was the target for some of his most bitter speeches.[8] This was natural enough, for Healy, who dominated the campaign on the anti-Parnellite side, was certainly the man to give as good as he got. Not, indeed, that even

[1] *F.J.*, 2 and 6 July 1891. It was reported that on Sunday, July 5, Dr Hackett's glasses were broken by a stone and one eye hurt. This was the same man who had attended Parnell when his eye had been injured in the Kilkenny election.

[2] Ibid., 4 July 1891. He had, however, been shouted down at Rathvilly (*F.J.*, 2 July 1891).

[3] Ibid., 8 July 1891.   [4] Ibid., 30 June 1891.

[5] Ibid., 29 June 1891. See also *F.J.*, 30 June, 3 and 4 July, 1891 for other speeches by Parnell on the same subject.

[6] Ibid., 29 and 30 June and 1 July, 1891.   [7] Ibid., 6 July 1891.

[8] 'This man has thriven at all stages of his career by slanders and by lies. He has left every party that he ever belonged to and he has always bitten every hand that cherished him' (*F.J.*, 1 July 1891). See also *F.J.*, 3 and 4 July 1891.

he could disguise the staleness of the arguments. There was nothing for him to do but to hurl the familiar abuse at Parnell, to justify the action of the majority in Committeee Room Fifteen, to caution the farmers against land purchase in the tory manner, and to impress upon the electors that there was no means of winning the struggle for home rule 'except by becoming friends of the English democracy, of the English working-classes'.[1]

The result was announced on July 8, and it was a crushing defeat for Parnell's candidate. Hammond had received 3,755 votes, Kettle 1,539—giving an anti-Parnellite majority of 2,216.[2] This margin, so much greater than those at the other two by-elections, could leave little doubt as to what would happen when the general election came. Parnell was being repudiated by the electors and nothing could conceal the fact. He himself presented, as always, an iron front to disaster. In his speech after the poll was declared he proclaimed his intention to contest every by-election and the general election, and if beaten then, still to fight on. That he meant what he said was indicated by the fact that, within little more than a fortnight of the Carlow result, he had summoned a much-publicised convention of the National League to encourage his followers and to give them an idea of his future policy. His supporters did their best to magnify the importance of the occasion and the *Freeman's Journal* estimated that it was attended by some 2,500 delegates.[3] It was not, however, a very convincing demonstration, for, as the *National Press* was quick to point out, the convention was not really representative of the country as a whole. Of the 1,648 delegates who were actually named in the official report of the proceedings, four counties—Dublin, Meath, Wicklow and Kildare—accounted for more than fifty per cent. Dublin city and county together supplied over one-third of the total whereas Ulster, at the other extreme, had only 52 delegates.[4]

The clouds were now gathering fast. On the day of Parnell's wedding the archbishops and bishops held their first full meeting since the crisis had begun. A week later their unanimous

[1] *National Press*, 24, 29, 30 June, and 1 July, 1891.
[2] *F.J.*, 9 July 1891.   [3] Ibid., 24 July 1891.
[4] *National Press*, 25 July 1891.

resolution condemning him was given to the press. It fully
endorsed the declaration made by the standing committee the
previous December and brought it up to date:

... since the issuing of that declaration, Mr Parnell's publication,
and that of his recognised agents and organs in the press, especially
their open hostility to ecclesiastical authority, has supplied new and
convincing proof that he is wholly unworthy of the confidence of
catholics; and we, therefore, feel bound on this occasion to call on
our people to repudiate his leadership.[1]

This, of course, was not novel. But it had not been said before
with such masssive unanimity, and its impact upon public
opinion was sure to be heavy. In one quarter, especially, it had
a very powerful effect and directly contributed to the drawing
away from Parnell of one of his most valuable allies—the
Freeman's Journal. The paper was run by a company and its
board of directors had, as we have seen, followed Parnell
unswervingly from the very beginning of the crisis. Large blocks
of shares, however, were owned by the widow of the late manag-
ing director and one time M.P., and by her son, Edmund
Dwyer Gray, who only came of age during 1891. He had been
absent in Australia when the split in the party first began and
on his return had acquiesced for a time in the course followed
by his directors. In May 1891, however, there were rumours
that he was thinking of changing sides and towards the end of
April he had actually had interviews with McCarthy and
Sexton. McCarthy was much taken with him and saw him as a
kind of latter-day *Vivian Grey* and a future prime minister of an
Irish cabinet.[2] For the time being, however, he refused to commit himself and in May he was observed at the house of commons in company with Parnell.[3] It may be that he was persuaded by Parnell, or that he was nettled by the sneers in which
the *National Press* indulged at his expense,[4] or even—as he

---

[1] *National Press*, 2 July 1891. The bishop of Limerick's signature was missing from this resolution, but he later published a letter (dated July 15) in
which he 'heartily concurred' in the action taken by the hierarchy and
denied firmly that he was a Parnellite (*National Press*, 16 July 1891).

[2] McCarthy and Praed, *Our book of memories*, p. 290; *F.J.*, 15 and 16 May,
1 Aug. and 22 Sept., 1891.   [3] *National Press*, 13 May 1891.

[4] Ibid., 14, 15, 16 and 26 May 1891. See also Gray's interview in
F.J., 15 May 1891.

apparently wrote to John Morley—that he was waiting until Dillon and O'Brien were free.[1] Whatever the reason, he had made no move in May, and in July his paper was still behind Parnell. But with the resolution of the hierarchy made public and the growing evidence of Parnell's desperate plight before his eyes, it was a question how much longer he would be content to remain passive.

As July drew near its close Parnell seemed a doomed man—the church against him, the *Freeman's Journal* wavering, the tide in the constituencies flowing strongly in his opponents' favour. The only factor that was still to a certain extent unknown was the attitude Dillon and O'Brien would take when they emerged from jail at the end of the month. When they had gone into prison Dillon, as we have seen, had been classed as an anti-Parnellite, O'Brien as still inclined to be Parnellite in his sympathies. But who could tell how the events of the intervening months might have affected them? Perhaps they had been so disgusted by the methods used against Parnell that they would refuse to join in hounding him down. Perhaps, on the other hand, Parnell's own conduct, combined with the defeats he had suffered, would decide them to have done with him as quickly as possible. Or perhaps they would say 'a plague o' both your houses' and either withdraw altogether from politics or attempt to form a centre party purged of extremists of all kinds. Their influence was still great and they had the advantage of not having been involved in the sordid quarrels of the past six months. Their decision was sure to have an important effect on the future course of the struggle and both sides awaited it anxiously. Until the prison-gates opened, therefore, an uneasy calm descended on the scene.

---

[1] On which Morley commented: 'This I cannot believe. What possible good can come to Dillon and his aims from giving Parnell the *Freeman's* support for three months longer?' (Gladstone Papers (B.M., Add. MS 44,256, ff. 141–2), John Morley to Gladstone, 23 May 1891).

XI

THE LAST PHASE

~~~~~~

(1)

THE CONDITIONS under which Dillon and O'Brien were confined in Galway jail, though irksome, were an improvement upon those which O'Brien at least had had to undergo in Tullamore a few years earlier. The prisoners had each a reasonably comfortable cell, could get up and go to bed when they wished, and were not limited in their exercise by the ordinary regulations. Their diet—an important point especially for Dillon, who had been suffering severely from dyspepsia while in America—was supervised by the prison doctor. They were not allowed to meet each other, but they did do so once shortly before they left, and they were not allowed newspapers, though there are indications that they contrived to see one now and again. They could, however, have what books they liked from the library of the neighbouring Queen's College. Dillon was reported to be spending most of his time reading Schlegel and Heine, while O'Brien was at work upon a novel dealing with his beloved Clew Bay in the time of Grace O'Malley—gratifying news to a public still old-fashioned enough to value some evidence of intellectuality in its heroes.[1] It does not seem that the precautions taken by the authorities against the prisoners communicating with each other or with the outside world were very

[1] *National Press*, 17 May 1891. The novel was eventually published under the title *A queen of men*.

stringent, and they were apparently able to keep themselves abreast of the political situation.[1]

The main source for the development of their ideas during this period is the correspondence carried on between them while they were in prison. This had of necessity to be surreptitious and the letters have not all survived. Those that have survived are with one exception undated save for the day of the week, and even that exception is wrongly dated. Since they had to be smuggled from one prisoner to another, probably with the aid of a friendly warder, the letters were scribbled hastily on small scraps of paper and enclosed in tiny envelopes.[2] Unfortunately, the gaps left in the correspondence are considerable and it throws only a fitful light upon many subjects it would have been interesting to know more about. O'Brien's letters seem to have suffered more than Dillon's, for the collection in the Dillon Papers is disappointingly small. Dillon's letters, on the other hand, which are in the O'Brien Papers, though also far from complete, are longer and more coherent. However, despite their short-comings, these snatches of conversation on paper, heard as it were from behind locked doors, reveal much of what was passing in their minds.

One thing, at any rate, is quite clear. Nowhere in these letters is to be found any suggestion that either of them regarded Parnell's continued leadership as in the slightest degree possible. What they *were* anxious to achieve, above all, was some kind of settlement which, on the basis of his retirement, would allow the two wings of the party to reunite. Their exchanges, therefore, were almost entirely taken up with discussing how best this should be done, and it is interesting to see how they reflected the very different temperaments of the two men. O'Brien was the more prolific in ideas, but most of his proposals were hopelessly unrealistic. Dillon, by contrast, was—as always—the penetrating critic, judging the proposals by their relation to the actual circumstances, so far as these could be known, and eventually

[1] Letters could pass in and out of the prison, though doubtless with difficulty; e.g. Gill Papers, Archbishop Croke to O'Brien, 22 Mar. 1891, and O'Brien to Gill, 'Thursday' (the contents place it as some time in July, i.e. after the Carlow by-election).

[2] It is, of course, not possible to say with certainty that where two or three scraps of paper are now found in the same envelope they are all part of the same letter; again, there are some fragments which have no envelope.

carrying O'Brien with him in agreement on a moderate, practical programme.

At one stage it appears that O'Brien envisaged a meeting of the whole party (Parnellite as well as anti-Parnellite) where Parnell would make a statement reserving his right to criticise the home rule bill when produced, but promising not to cripple the party's unity by going on with the fight and thus playing into the hands of the tories at the election. If he agreed to this— O'Brien suggested—then it should be settled that none of the sitting members of the party should be disturbed at the general election, save by a two-thirds majority vote of the party against them. Any casual vacancies before the general election should be filled by combined conventions of branches of the Irish National League and the Irish National Federation; those two bodies should be amalgamated anyway under a new name. Finally, to protect the party against misconduct in the next parliament, there should be a definite rule that a man should vacate his seat if called on to do so by a two-thirds majority vote of the party.[1] Admittedly, O'Brien did not really expect Parnell to agree to such an arrangement, but he was concerned less with him than with his more reputable followers:

> If (he wrote) he rejected such a proposal as that, nothing could be clearer than that he was bent upon a policy of wicked destruction, and the men who had stuck to him most faithfully on the personal issue would be completely justified in separating from him on the question whether home rule was to be made impossible.

Further, even if no Parnellites came over, O'Brien reckoned that the effect on the country of such an offer would be overpowering, especially if McCarthy's section agreed to elect Dillon as chairman 'on a policy of rigid abstention from personal blackguardism'. Without some such proposal, O'Brien added, it was difficult to see how the *Freeman's Journal* could be detached from Parnell's side. And he ended by suggesting that if Dillon thought well of these proposals, they should be conveyed to Redmond, Kenny, Clancy and P. O'Brien as their last word before re-entering the fight.[2]

[1] O'Brien presumably considered that the parliamentary pledge (see p. 15 above) which had been designed for just this purpose had hitherto proved inadequate.

[2] Dillon Papers, O'Brien to Dillon, letter dated 'Saturday'.

Dillon's reactions can be gathered from a letter which, on internal evidence, seems to have been written while the Carlow election was in progress—that is, in the last week of June or the early days of July. From this it appears that he was broadly in favour of an approach to the Parnellites, subject to two conditions. First, they should not enter into any formal negotiation with Parnell himself, but deal with Redmond, 'H.' (Harrington?), and others who were on the spot and could be brought to reply quickly one way or the other. Secondly, whatever offer they made to the Parnellites should be definite and they should insist on an equally definite answer within a very few days. But what if the Parnellites refused this offer? To judge from Dillon's letter, he and O'Brien had already considered this possibility earlier in their correspondence, and also at a conversation they had recently managed to have, but had reached no conclusion. O'Brien's view evidently had been that unless some Parnellites were detached, the future would be hopeless. Dillon disagreed. It might, he said, be six months or a year before they could say the position *was* 'utterly hopeless'. Reverting to a suggestion he had already made—perhaps at the conversation with O'Brien just mentioned—he urged again that on their release they should join the Irish National Federation. He now gave more fully his reasons for taking this step. They must, he declared, do one of two things. Either they retire from politics altogether, or they join Parnell's opponents. If they joined the Federation, it would give them a chance of defining their position and of using their influence so that the fight would be carried on on different lines from those pursued by Healy and the *National Press*. There followed a passage so interesting in its bearing both upon the immediate situation and upon Dillon's own attitude that I reproduce it at length:

But I confess that I have always felt that in public life if one agrees with the principle of a party and objects to its methods, the proper course is to join the party and try to alter it from within. And in the present situation in Ireland these views appear to hold with the greatest possible force. Suppose we don't join the Federation? . . . I believe we should be driven into a very ugly corner very quickly and that the results would be to greatly increase Healy's power with the priests and with the party. On the other hand, if we join the Federation that is no reason why we should allow Healy to dictate our action. We should in my judgment be in a much better position to dissociate ourselves from him and to set to work at once amongst the members of the party, to ascertain what amount of support we could secure for a decent policy. I believe that it would be utterly impossible to give a chance to a policy of moderation unless we frankly and promptly joined the anti-Parnell party.

You seemed the other evening to be under a very false impression as to my estimate of Healy's power. I consider Healy a most formidable element in the situation. And by a little mis-management he might easily be made so influential as to render it perfectly hopeless to rescue the [country?] from the extreme faction. But consider how it has been that Healy acquired the influence he now has. I believe it has been largely due: (1) to the outrageous language used by Parnell and some of his men towards the majority of the party . . . and (2) to the foolish, most unwise attacks made by Harrington and Joe Kenny on the priests and bishops, which have thrown them more into Healy's hands than would otherwise have been the case. If we were to stand aloof from the Federation, and adopt an attitude of 'outside', hostile criticism of Healy and his set, I am convinced the result would be to make Healy even more formidable than he now is. And it is just because I think Healy and the spirit which he is gathering round him so dangerous that I consider it essential, if we are to remain in public life at all, that we should without delay get into the party and try it out with H. and his gang.[1]

The Carlow election came and went, but it brought no weakening either by Parnell or by his supporters. It began to look as if Dillon was right and as if the two prisoners might reconcile themselves to joining the Federation and doing battle on two fronts, against Parnellites without and Healyites within. O'Brien, however, was not yet willing to abandon all attempts at peace-making. Writing to Dillon after the Carlow result had been declared, but before the Parnellites convention had met in Dublin, he was still optimistic about the possible outcome of an approach to the more moderate of Parnell's followers.

Carlow (he wrote), upon the whole, was a tremendous advantage. It takes away the last hope of P.'s securing a majority by fair means

[1] W. O'Brien Papers, Dillon to O'Brien, dated 'Sunday'. The writ for the Carlow election was issued on Monday, June 22, and the result was known on Wednesday, July 8. Probably, therefore, this letter was written on either Sunday, June 28, or Sunday, July 5. Earlier in the letter Dillon had said that he hoped that if the Parnellites were badly beaten at Carlow, some of Parnell's men might refuse to go further with him.

and brings his moderate supporters nakedly face to face with the question—are they going to help him to defy the country and wreck everything in mere vengeance?

Might it not therefore be reasonable to hope that some Parnellites would now at last break away from their leader? O'Brien certainly thought so and pinned his hopes on John Redmond. If Redmond—he said—would write to Parnell advising the postponememt of his projected convention until Dillon and O'Brien were released, and declining to participate if Parnell insisted on going ahead with it, he would have a splendid opportunity for a break—'but I am afraid he is not resolute enough'.[1] However, even if Redmond could not be brought to this pitch, O'Brien still felt that some olive branch ought to be held out to him and others like him, before Dillon and himself threw in their lot with the anti-Parnellites. O'Brien's idea apparently was that McCarthy and *his* moderates should be asked to agree to an offer being made to the *Parnellite* moderates. If this arrangement were accepted by McCarthy's group, but refused by the Parnellites, then Dillon and O'Brien should side with the former. If, however, Healy and his following insisted on a policy of no quarter, then O'Brien would be for washing his hands of the whole business. But the solution he obviously preferred was a settlement by consent between the less extreme men on both sides. And he added, a trifle ingenuously, 'if we could once sever the decent element from P.'s following I don't know that P.'s hostility might not be even useful in keeping our ranks united and the liberals up to the mark'.[2]

Upon Dillon, however, the Carlow election had made a different impression. An approach to the Parnellites, he considered, would now be fraught with great danger, not least because it would give Healy the opportunity 'to write a series of offensive articles specially intended to make it impossible for

[1] In fact, though twenty-three Parnellite M.P.s were at the convention, John Redmond was not among them. His telegram of apology merely stated that he was detained at Wexford on a murder trial and regretted he could not be present—but did not include the good wishes customary on these occasions (*F.J.*, 24 July 1891).

[2] Dillon Papers, O'Brien to Dillon, dated 'Thursday' and written either on Thursday, 9 July (the day the Carlow result was published) or Thursday, 16 July 1891. About the same time—possibly even the same day—he wrote to Gill in similar terms (Gill Papers, O'Brien to Gill, 'Thursday').

us to make any move in the direction of peace'. With this observation he began a reply to O'Brien which is the longest of these letters to have survived and which seems to have been decisive in shaping their course. The burden of it was that until they had definitely joined the majority they would be in no position to do anything towards securing a peaceful settlement. In other words, he reversed what he took to be O'Brien's order of procedure and proposed instead that they should first take sides and then, by the light of experience, find out whether they could go on with the struggle or not. If the Parnellites, on their side, still showed themselves irreconcilable things might turn out in one of two ways:

1. If Parnell were to succeed in consolidating and holding together a considerable party, and carrying on an aggressive fight—it is quite possible that in spite of all we could do the majority of the party would gradually become a Healy-bishops' party, and if I found that their forces were too strong for us, I should then with a good conscience retire and have done with Irish politics.

2. On the other hand—and I confess I am very sanguine since recent events that this would be the course—by joining the party frankly and immediately, we might find that our influence in the party even at the outset would be too strong for Healy. And in any case, if while announcing our determination to fight Parnell, and to insist on giving the liberals a fair trial, we set up a standard of moderation and openly announced that our influence would be used in favour of a policy of conciliation and of holding out the hand to every man who wished to come back to the party, I believe there would rapidly rally to our support an immense amount of public sympathy all over the country. And I confess I have strong hopes that Parnell's party would begin to crumble away. And if a movement of that kind set in, it would be extremely rapid.

You see, my point is that being *inside the party* we could effectively and safely advocate a policy of reconciliation—whereas if we attempted to do so from outside, or to make terms for our support, we should put Healy in an immensely strong position to attack us. Once committed to the party, we have as good a right to lay our views before the country as he or anyone else, and he would then be obliged to declare himself. If he declared himself in favour of a policy of 'No Terms', as I hear he has headed an article in the *Press* yesterday,[1] I would take up the challenge immediately and I am confident

[1] Dillon was mistaken about the date here. His own letter is dated 'Monday' and the *National Press* was not published on Sundays. The article

we could beat him with slaughter. A fight of that nature might be the very occasion for getting over a lot of P.'s men.

Dillon then went on to consider what should be their procedure on release. He suggested that, if questioned by reporters, they should say that they had no intention of opening further negotiations, but that they would always be glad to do anything in their power to bring about peace. As soon as possible they should see Redmond and make their proposals—to him alone at first. But it would be no good making any communication to the other side, that is the anti-Parnellites, about the proposals 'unless and until we are in a position to say that—if agreed to— a considerable body of P.'s men will join the party'. To a suggestion from O'Brien that he, Dillon, should take the chair of the party, Dillon returned a vehement refusal:

. . . it is utterly out of the question to make my being elected chairman a condition of our joining the McCarthy party. I have thought over that point carefully and *nothing* would induce me to consent to such a proposal. I believe it would be exceedingly bad policy. It would be taking up a position utterly indefensible before the country and which might lead to a hideous disaster, to say nothing of the intolerable position in which I should be personally put . . .

. . . To sum up then—my proposal is: immediately after we have seen Redmond, if a number of the Parnellites don't accept our proposals, that we should frankly and without conditions of any kind throw ourselves in with the McCarthy party. Then define our position and endeavour to rally a party on the platform of fighting Parnell, giving Gladstone a fair chance, and a friendly welcome to all who will join from the other side. If H. objects, fight him inside the party. If we are beaten, leave public life. If we win, I believe we should succeed in disintegrating Parnell's following and that all would go right.[1]

This powerful and persuasive letter seems to have ended the matter, for a few days later O'Brien replied accepting Dillon's arguments and agreeing that they ought to join the majority, 'always provided it is clearly understood that if the "*vae victis*" policy triumphs, that is, if any of P.'s men are willing to come

—which was actually entitled 'No Conditions'—appeared in the *National Press*, 14 July 1891. This suggests that Dillon's letter may have been written on the following Monday, i.e. 20 July 1891.

[1] W. O'Brien Papers, Dillon to O'Brien, 'Monday', probably 20 July 1891 (see previous footnote).

over and are repulsed and insulted, we shall clear out'.[1]

From these exchanges, two things emerge. The first is that O'Brien was not exaggerating when he wrote, twenty years later, that although he and Dillon had differed somewhat about what they should do when they came out of prison, he had subordinated his own judgment to that of his colleague.[2] The other is that quite evidently the two men were already in imagination planning and fighting the battles that would have to be won *after* Parnell had been beaten. In other words, the course of events in the six months since they had entered Galway jail had already shown plainly the elements of discord amongst Parnell's opponents, which were to fill the history of the next ten years. A split between Healy on the one hand, and Dillon and O'Brien on the other, might well have come in any event; they were men of very different temperaments and there were many things on which they did not see eye to eye. But the dominant rôle Healy had played in the fight against Parnell, the power he had gained and the way he had used that power, above all his control of the *National Press*—these things made him a formidable rival to men such as Dillon and O'Brien who, in view of their own previous records, might be pardoned for thinking that it was they who should rule the party from behind Justin McCarthy's unstable throne. We shall, therefore, only grasp the true inwardness of what was to follow if we realise that below the surface a complicated war of manoeuvre was being waged. Both sections of the anti-Parnellites were agreed that Parnell himself must go, but beyond that everything was, as Dillon himself said in one of his prison letters to O'Brien, 'a shifting sand'.[3]

[1] Dillon Papers, O'Brien to Dillon, 'Thursday'. The letter contains a reference to William Redmond arriving from America 'just now'. He landed on Sunday, July 19 (*F.J.*, 20 July 1891), so it seems likely that O'Brien's letter was written on July 23, as that was the only Thursday after Redmond's return from America that Dillon and O'Brien spent in jail.

[2] O'Brien, *Olive branch*, pp. 54–5. O'Brien says that, apart from the Carlow election, Dillon was influenced partly by a sense of their responsibility towards the evicted tenants and partly by the news which had reached O'Brien that E. D. Gray was only awaiting their release to swing the *Freeman's Journal* on to the anti-Parnellite side.

[3] O'Brien Papers, Dillon to O'Brien, the letter quoted on pp. 284–5 above.

(2)

We have seen what Dillon and O'Brien thought of the situation. For Healy's attitude we have to depend mainly upon the files of the *National Press*, since his memoirs unfortunately throw little light upon these critical months of his career. It is, however, impossible to believe that so astute a politician should not have realised how the land lay, and there are in fact indications that he was well aware of what was going on. On July 9, for example, a friend told him that he had just met Harrington and had found him 'crushed' and depressed. Harrington had apparently said that Healy was the only obstacle to peace and that if Dillon were recognised as leader, perhaps *he* would be able to restrain him. Healy's only comment on this at the time was that it showed 'a wholesome frame of mind',[1] but the incident reappeared a few days later as the basis of the article 'No Conditions' which, as we have seen, attracted Dillon's attention in Galway jail. The article began by saying that there were rumours from London that some Parnellites were anxious to make terms and that Harrington had mentioned Healy as the main difficulty in their way, but it then went on to declare that those Parnellites whose conduct, language and sentiments had not made it impossible to receive them could come back into the fold. It ended, however, on a sufficiently uncompromising note:

With Parnell and Parnellism there can be no second parleying; with ribald railers there can be no truce; better fight till the pledge-breakers are annihilated than expose the vast issues that are involved to the dangers of treachery, deceit and, mayhap, of absolute disaster, by yielding to a timid apprehension of the harm they can yet inflict.[2]

This article may be regarded as a fair indication of Healy's mood immediately after the Carlow by-election and—if the *National Press* may be taken to represent his views—there was no sign whatever in the weeks following that he was in the slightest degree disposed to become any more conciliatory.[3] The very

---

[1] Healy, *Letters and leaders*, ii. 363, letter to Maurice Healy, 9 July 1891.
[2] *National Press*, 14 July 1891.
[3] See, for example, the article on the 'red herring' of Parnell's convention which, it was said, was designed to distract attention from the real issue. 'But the country is now in full cry on Mr Fox's track and resolved to hunt

fact that in the *National Press* he possessed such a powerful weapon was itself a further barrier in the way of peace, because the more closely he identified himself with it, the harder it would be for him to relinquish it, as he surely must, if the *Freeman's Journal* ever deserted Parnell. In this connection he let fall a revealing remark in a letter to his father, when he said: 'The *National Press* is doing well. I am afraid the *Freeman* will come round—we are cutting in on it so.'[1] In view of the fact that the *National Press* had been started only because the *Freeman* had refused to 'come round', this comment suggests that the newspaper war was tending to become for him an end in itself, and not merely a means to a greater end. His relations with the *Freeman's Journal* could thus never have been friendly. They were further bedevilled by the fact that at this very time he had taken a libel action against the rival paper for various state-ments it had published about his alleged conduct during the Maryborough trials of 1889. Proceedings had been begun in April, but the trial only came on early in July, when the jury found that there had been libel, but disagreed about the extent of the damages. It was not until 1892 that Healy got his damages (£700), but the fact that the case came when it did certainly made it no easier for E. D. Gray to come over to the anti-Parnellite camp.[2]

As the date for the release of the two prisoners approached, both sides gave ample proof that they regarded the event as being of great—possibly decisive—importance. The *Freeman's Journal*, as was to be expected, looked to them as a moderating influence, hoping they would use all their efforts to bring about a reunion of the party; though—as if to demonstrate that it was after all still Parnellite—it also printed one of Harrington's more outspoken speeches in which he commented scathingly on what he called the attempt 'to prostitute religion at the feet of Mr Gladstone in Ireland'.[3] Next day, the leading article

him from public life, and it is merely puerile to attempt to draw a red herring across the trail. What the country wants is not a new national policy, but only to get rid of the degraded and treacherous leader who strove to ruin the old' (*National Press*, 24 July 1891).

[1] Healy, *Letters and leaders*, ii. 361, letter to his father, undated—but attri-buted by him to June 1891.

[2] *F.J.*, 27 Apr. and 8 and 9 July 1891; Healy, *Letters and leaders*, ii. 360–3, 373–5.   [3] *F.J.*, 29 July 1891.

studiously avoided referring to Dillon and O'Brien as partisans
of either side, and spoke of them as being anxious 'to bring the
existing divisions to a close honourable to all concerned and
beneficial to the country'.[1] The writers of the *Freeman's Journal*
were no doubt hampered by the knowledge that the ground was
shifting under their feet, but the *National Press* felt no such
inhibitions. On July 27 a leader declared flatly: 'Parnellism must
not merely be defeated. It must be annihilated.'[2] On July 30—
the day of the release—after an innocuous first leader entitled
'Welcome' which was a simple tribute to the past services of
Dillon and O'Brien, there followed another article—'A per-
fidious appeal'—which was in a very different vein. Starting
with the assertion that the 'Parnellite mutiny' had been completely quelled, it went on to recall the early declarations Dillon
and O'Brien had both made against Parnell while they were
still in America. Then followed a savage attack on E. D. Gray,
asking if he was at the bottom of 'this whining appeal' to the
two prisoners to mediate when they came out, and recalling, in
most insulting terms, his vacillations during the past few months.
It ended thus:

> The appeal to Mr Dillon and Mr O'Brien to resume dilatory
> 'negotiations' can have no tangible object that we can find other than
> the treacherous one of giving a plausible show of truth to the persis-
> tent Parnellite calumny that in spite of all their outspoken protesta-
> tions they are still half-Parnellite in their hearts, and so weakening or
> destroying their influence for good in the country.[3]

Thus, with perverse brilliance, in one short column the article
had contrived to remind readers of Dillon's and O'Brien's determined opposition to Parnell at the outset of the crisis, to make it
more difficult than ever for the *Freeman's Journal* to change sides,
and to warn the two prisoners that they would be well advised
not to become involved in any further negotiations.

A considerable crowd had collected outside the jail to welcome them when they emerged, among them O'Brien's wife
Sophie, Maud Gonne, and various representatives of the evicted
tenants, including Patrick McDermott, who headed a delegation from the notorious Clanricarde estate at Woodford, and
was on familiar ground, since he had himself, it was said, been

[1] *F.J.*, 30 July 1891.   [2] *National Press*, 27 July 1891.   [3] Ibid., 30 July 1891.

an inmate of the prison no less than seventeen times. The two men drove off at once to breakfast with the bishop of Galway.[1] Afterwards they went to the Temperance Hall where, having received the inevitable addresses, they made their long-awaited declarations. Dillon spoke first and lost no time in assuring his audience that the reasons he had had for signing the original manifesto against Parnell in America had only been strengthened in the interval. He could not accept Parnell's leadership in what he called 'the new policy' he was proposing to the country—the very reverse of the policy the party had advocated under Parnell's own leadership since 1886. It was, he insisted, necessary to give the liberals a fair chance of passing a home rule bill—they could still be fought if and when their bill proved to be unsatisfactory. From this he passed on to condemn the violent language used by both sides, but blamed Parnell for beginning it with the opening sentences of his manifesto. It was rather surprising, knowing as we do what he expected from John Redmond, that of recent speeches he singled out especially one made by the latter's brother, Willie, at the Parnellite convention.[2] Then, after a pledge of support for the evicted tenants there came—whether his hearers realised it or not—the most important sentence of Dillon's entire speech. 'I say deliberately that my voice shall always be given in favour of welcoming any rational, patriotic and reasonable offer which comes from any quarter—I care not where—and which points towards a reunion of the national ranks in this country and the banishment of the demon of discord from the people of Ireland.'[3]

[1] As they stepped into the bishop's carriage, says O'Brien (*Olive branch*, p. 58), an old Parnellite called out, 'We're sorry to see ye in bad company, but God bless ye, anyhow'. While the novelist in O'Brien may have been uppermost in recounting this incident, it symbolises aptly enough the mingled regret and respect with which the Parnellites saw them passing into the ranks of their enemies.

[2] William Redmond had said that he was glad a split had occurred and that the grain had been sifted from the chaff. Thenceforth when he went to a meeting he need not fear to find 'any weak-kneed, miserable, surrendering wretches who gave up their independence when the first Englishman asked them' (*F.J.*, 24 July 1891).

[3] *National Press*, 31 July 1891; *F.J.*, 31 July 1891. The latter has a slightly different wording for the sentence quoted above, but the sense is the same in both versions.

O'Brien's speech, which followed, covered very much the same ground, and stressed the fact that they were completely at one. A little later they went on to the Railway Hotel where they received more addresses, including one from the local Parnell leadership committee; in receiving this, however, they made it clear that their break with Parnell was absolute. From Galway they travelled to Dublin, and after that paid a flying visit to London to confer with Justin McCarthy.[1] They then returned to Ireland—Dillon to Dublin and O'Brien to Old Head Lodge near Louisburgh—to await reactions before making their next move.

These reactions soon came thick and fast. One of the first was from E. D. Gray. On the very day when the *Freeman's Journal* published its account of the release of the two prisoners, it also carried a letter and a long statement from Gray about his position and future course. He announced—what indeed most people knew already—that he had for some time past held views similar to those expressed by Dillon and O'Brien. Their example he was now prepared to follow and to declare himself opposed to Parnell. Apart, however, from the political aspect of the matter he had also been influenced by Parnell's marriage which, he said, had 'rendered it impossible that he should ever be recognised by the catholic hierarchy as the leader of the catholic people of Ireland'.[2] While it was true that Gray could not change the policy of the paper overnight, in fact, not until the shareholders met a few weeks later, his announcement did at least indicate that the Parnellites in a very short time would find themselves in the same position as their enemies had been in at the beginning of the crisis—without a national newspaper to report their meetings and to keep their policies before the public. So far from having been intimidated by the *National Press*, it is clear that Gray was prepared to be as bold in his attitude as Dillon and O'Brien had ever dared to hope.[3]

---

[1] *National Press*, 5 Aug. 1891; McCarthy and Praed, *Our book of memories*, p. 298.

[2] *F.J.*, 31 July 1891. A few days later there appeared a letter from Archbishop Walsh pointing out that both catholic and anglican teaching agreed that marriage with a divorced woman was no real marriage. Parnell's offence was thus deepened rather than mitigated (*National Press*, 6 Aug. 1891).

[3] Gray was also influenced—so he said—by the three by-elections and by

Gray's attitude had been one of the imponderables which Dillon and O'Brien had turned over so often in their minds while still in Galway jail. More predictable were the responses of the extremists on both wings. The *National Press* on one side and Dr Joe Kenny on the other showed all too clearly the obstacles in the path of a policy of conciliation. The former had professed to find their Galway speeches encouraging, both for the reunion of the party and the succour of the evicted tenants. But the benign spirit of the article which expressed these hopes was belied by one sharp paragraph warning them of the uselessness of negotiating with Parnellism. 'It is hardly needed that they should crush it by argument or eloquence. The fierce battle was fought, and the victory won, while prison walls shut them out from the strife.'[1] Dr Kenny, on the other side, breathed defiance against all anti-Parnellites, Gray and Dillon and O'Brien included. Dillon, he suggested, instead of singling out William Redmond for attack would have been better advised to turn his attention to admonishing clerical intolerance.[2]

These skirmishings on either flank, however, could be ignored. The central problem was—how would Parnell himself react to the Galway speeches and would those speeches open the way for a rupture between him and his more moderate followers? On Sunday, August 2, he was in Thurles and both there and on

the curious affair of Henry Campbell. Campbell—Parnell's secretary—had taken a libel action against the *Cork Herald* which had imputed to him the hiring of certain houses for the immoral purposes of Parnell. The allegation was based on certain letters produced in the divorce court and purporting to have been signed by him. Campbell in his action against the *Cork Herald* swore that he had not signed them and that his name had been used without his consent. The jury found for him and awarded him £250 damages. Next day there appeared a letter from Parnell to Campbell's solicitor explaining that he had had Campbell's authority to use his name in a 'negotiation' at Eastbourne, but could not recall whether or not he had told him that the business in question was the renting of a house—if he had used his own name he would have had to pay a higher price. More was made of the affair than it deserved, but it lent itself to the designs of those who wanted to give a sinister twist to what in reality was only an attempt by Parnell to secure privacy for Mrs O'Shea and himself, before their relationship became public property. The trial is reported in detail in *National Press*, 22 to 26 and 29 June 1891.

[1] *National Press*, 31 July 1891. [2] *F.J.*, 1 Aug. 1891.

his return to Dublin that night he referred several times to Dillon and O'Brien. It was noticeable that whereas he spoke with great affection of O'Brien, most of his remarks were directed towards Dillon, accusing him of indiscipline over the land act of 1881 and the Plan of Campaign and suggesting that while Dillon had spoken much about unity at Galway, he had ignored the idea of independence. 'I ask Mr Dillon', he said, 'not to throw away his sword, not to disband his army, not to give up any force or strength which he now possesses, until we have tested the promises of these English liberals by their performances.'[1] Since at Thurles he also made one of his periodic references to the possible limitations of constitutional action, it was quite evident that he had no intention of trying to bid for the support of either O'Brien or Dillon, despite the immense prestige and influence they could bring to bear.

This, however, was only what they had expected. From their point of view, the more irreconcilable Parnell appeared, and the more violent his speeches, the better chance they might have in their main objective of drawing his more moderate followers away from him. Precisely what steps they took to achieve this objective we do not know, since of necessity they would have had to be taken in the strictest secrecy. It is clear from their exchanges in Galway that they hoped to interview John Redmond and to make him the pivot of the whole effort to break up the Parnellite party. But whether they actually succeeded in seeing him or not remains a mystery. If a meeting did take place, and if any record of it was made, such a record does not seem to have survived among the papers of Dillon, O'Brien or Redmond, and there is no mention of a conference in the various memoirs and biographies dealing with the period.[2] For obvious reasons, the contemporary press makes no reference to

[1] *F.J.*, 3 Aug. 1891. This speech called forth a detailed refutation from Dillon the next day (*F.J.*, 4 Aug. 1891).

[2] That a meeting was at least intended seems clear from a note from William O'Brien to Redmond, which has been preserved in the Redmond Papers. It says simply: 'We are both ever so sorry to have missed you to-day. Could you drop in for a while any time during the evening—say at nine?' It was written from Dillon's house in North Great George's Street and dated 'Friday evening'. The date, '1 August 1891', has been scribbled on the envelope; this may be the date the letter was received—the previous day, July 31, was a Friday.

it either. This silence, of course, does not prove that no meeting took place. It may have done, but it equally well may not—it is impossible to say which.[1]

However, it is worth pointing out that at such a conference Dillon and O'Brien would almost certainly have found the obstacles to success greater than they had anticipated when planning their action in Galway jail. They never set down in writing—or if they did, it is no longer extant—just why they expected so much from Redmond. They knew, of course, that at Boulogne he had been a good influence for peace, while remaining perfectly loyal to Parnell. They were probably aware also that since Boulogne the tone of his speeches had been on the whole restrained, and it can scarcely have escaped them that during July he had been conspicuously inactive in politics. Possibly they may also have had other sources of information unknown to us. But, whatever the reasons for their belief, they *did* believe that Redmond was their best hope. Yet, in adopting this notion and basing their plans upon it, they were making a grave miscalculation. They forgot—or failed to realise—that anxious as Redmond doubtless was for the unity of the party to be restored, even this mattered less to him than loyalty to his leader. It has to be remembered that Parnell had a very warm affection for Redmond and that the latter was devoted to him. Was it therefore likely that he would agree to abandon Parnell under any circumstances? True, he might have disapproved of Parnell's methods and his absence from the convention might even have been an outward sign of this disapproval. But disapproval did not mean desertion—and desertion was what O'Brien and Dillon would have had to propose to him, however tactfully the appeal might be phrased. The most that one can conceive Redmond being prepared to consider would have been some kind of conference reproducing the later stages of the Boulogne negotiations and resulting, possibly, in a temporary retirement by Parnell. But this would have been no use to Dillon and O'Brien. They were finished with Parnell and were only concerned to heal the breach in the party as quickly as

[1] If a meeting did take place, that may explain an otherwise cryptic reference in Arthur Griffith's paper years later to the effect that Redmond had attempted to betray Parnell on the eve of his death (*United Irishman*, 1 June 1901).

possible. Redmond was *not* finished with Parnell, and it was a serious error on the part of the two intending mediators to suppose that he might be.

Whatever happened behind the scenes—if anything did—it seems clear that when Dillon and O'Brien made their next important public appearance, no arrangement with the Parnellites had yet been reached. They had elected to speak on August 9 at Mallow—O'Brien's home-town—and the meeting had all the signs of a major occasion. There was a very large crowd and it was said to have been the biggest anti-Parnellite demonstration that had yet been held. Both the principals spoke twice and Dillon's first speech especially was dignified, moderate and persuasive. He had, he said, been bound to Parnell by close ties in the past, but he could not follow him at the sacrifice of the home rule cause and of the evicted tenants. However, he then went out of his way to say that he felt no hostility towards the true and convinced Parnellites, adding that if any such were to abandon their opposition and join the majority even at this late date he would hold out the hand of friendship to them. O'Brien similarly pleaded for an end to 'this hateful war between Irishmen' and urged that they should re-establish a solid and united party which would either be able to co-operate in the passing of a satisfactory home rule bill, or else be 'as free as air to hunt down, to pursue and to destroy any liberal party or any liberal minister that could be guilty of the baseness or of the infamy of attempting to betray their pledges to us'.[1] These two speeches, with their emphasis on friendly reunion, suggested that Dillon and O'Brien had not yet given up all hope of winning over the moderate Parnellites but, on the contrary, were anxious to advertise that their offer was still open. It was never again to be repeated on such favourable terms, for only three days later Dillon took the decisive step of presiding at a meeting of the Irish National Federation in Dublin, and so identified himself beyond all question with the anti-Parnellite section.

In the speech which he made on this occasion Dillon took the opportunity of giving his hearers—who included a watchful Tim Healy—an extended account of his actions and reactions since the beginning of the crisis. It was delicate ground and he probably succeeded only in irritating both Parnellites and anti-

[1] *F.J.*, 10 Aug. 1891; *National Press*, 10 Aug. 1891.

Parnellites. Thus, on the one hand he stigmatised the Leinster Hall meeting as 'a most dreadful political mistake' and, on the other, condemned Parnell for not being more accessible to the liberal leaders and for turning the loyalty of his own followers against themselves and leading them into a 'rat-trap'. Perhaps unwisely, he did not rest content with this and went on to suggest that Parnell, who now accused his opponents of undue subservience to the liberals, had himself been guilty of the same fault on two earlier occasions—at the time of the Kilmainham 'treaty', and when he offered his resignation to Gladstone after the Phoenix Park murders. It is interesting to see how under provocation Dillon, against all his inclinations, was being swept into the prevailing fashion of turning the past history of the movement inside out to find ammunition with which to assail the other side. Admittedly, Parnell had set him the example by impugning his own behaviour in 1881, but what Dillon had not yet had a chance to realise was that the more the main quarrel was confused by the intrusion of side-issues of this kind (which were really over and done with) the better it suited Parnell. The more Dillon became involved in controversy with him, the less the likelihood of his winning over those moderate (if increasingly hypothetical) Parnellites of whom he had had such great hopes.[1] So that, although his speech to the Federation contained yet another appeal to the moderates, the effect of that appeal was certain to be neutralised by the censures upon Parnell which accompanied it. The situation, of course, was extremely difficult and Dillon was hardly to be blamed for taking some time to get his bearings after a six months' absence, during which most of the familiar landmarks had disappeared. He cannot have been very comfortable at that meeting anyway, and his discomfort was not likely to have been diminished when

[1] The most fruitful source of controversy, however, was not the past, but the present—the plight of the evicted tenants. At Mallow—and again to the Federation—Dillon had suggested that a committee be formed of two Parnellites and say, O'Brien and himself, that money be released from the Paris fund and placed at the disposal of this committee for the relief of *all* evicted tenants (i.e. League as well as Plan of Campaign tenants), and that a fresh appeal for subscriptions should be made to the country. The only effect was to initiate a lengthy and acrimonious dispute which continued more or less in public until Parnell's death. In fact the correspondence was published on the day of his death (*F.J.*, 6 Oct. 1891).

Healy, seizing his chance with both hands, poured cold water on the idea of reconciliation. Parodying Emerson's remark about the slavery dispute in America, that it had become 'a question for the gun', he suggested that, so far as Parnell's immediate followers were concerned, it was 'a question for the sweeping-brush'. True, he claimed that he would be the first to welcome erring Parnellites back into their ranks—but only if it could be done with safety to the cause. In this matter, he added, it was necessary to act with 'political prudence'—they should not allow their hearts to get the better of their heads. Those who heard this speech, and those Parnellites who read it, might perhaps have been forgiven if they considered the qualifications more significant than the welcome.[1]

(3)

Dillon's decision to take the chair at this meeting of the Federation may fairly be regarded as the last turning-point in the long and bitter road that led from Committee Room Fifteen to the final eclipse of Parnell. While he and O'Brien were safe in Galway jail, it was easy to think of them as indeed they thought of themselves—as above the battle, uncommitted, free either to throw their great influence into one scale or the other, or to mediate between the two extremes. In fact, however, when they came face to face with the realities of the situation, they found that they had very little room in which to manoeuvre. Given their own unshakable conviction that any reconciliation must be on the basis of Parnell's retirement, and given the equally unshakable devotion of Parnell's followers to him, there was no hope of arbitration and the two men, if they wished to stay in politics, had no alternative but to join the anti-Parnellites. But—and here was the irony of the whole situation—although they went into the majority party reluctantly and hating its methods, once they *had* done so, they became the target for some of the most angry Parnellite attacks. Thus, when Redmond eventually broke silence, he reproached them with having let slip a golden opportunity, 'and he was bound to say that they had let slip with it their own power or influence with either one or the other in this controversy'. Their weakness, he implied,

[1] *F.J.*, 13 Aug. 1891; *National Press*, 13 Aug. 1891.

was that while they detested the methods used against Parnell they had not the courage to denounce them. 'Allied to the party led by Mr Healy', he added, 'their power for good was absolutely nil.'[1]

Redmond no doubt was angry and disappointed, and due allowance must be made for the fact, but it was palpably unfair for him to say they had not denounced the methods used against Parnell, when in fact they had done so at Galway and at Mallow. It was unfair also to condemn them for coming down on the anti-Parnellite side, without taking into account the reasons for their action. It was unfair, but it was only human; and that Dillon and O'Brien of all people should have been attacked by John Redmond, from whom they had expected so much, was after all only a measure of the general disintegration which the long months of quarrelling and recrimination had produced.

But, while Redmond's strictures might be excused as a natural reaction to an intolerable situation, Dillon was not prepared to treat others with the same forbearance. Towards the end of August, John Devoy wrote to him, criticising his Mallow speech as showing that 'nothing less than Parnell's scalp' would satisfy him, and enclosing certain proposals for ending the struggle. Briefly, these were that both sections should agree to a joint session of the whole parliamentary party and that at this meeting Parnell and McCarthy should resign from the leadership of their respective sections; that Parnell should be re-elected by the whole party and then resign, his resignation being accepted with a resolution from the party acknowledging his past services and asking him to remain a member; and that John Dillon should be elected chairman. Devoy further suggested that Parnell should then be requested by the party to go on a fund-raising tour of the U.S.A., Canada and Australia, and that the party should pledge itself to accept no home rule bill that did not include an executive responsible to the Irish parliament, and confer the right to appoint the judiciary and the magistracy, as well as the control over police, land and public works; no member of the party, Devoy also proposed, was to take office

---

[1] *F.J.*, 15 Sept. 1891. This provoked a reply from O'Brien, regretting that 'after a long period of deliberation' Redmond should have chosen to speak in such fashion (*F.J.*, 21 Sept. 1891).

under any British ministry, until the home rule bill had become law. Dillon's reply to this was simply that something very similar had been offered to Parnell at Boulogne. His rejection of terms then, and his subsequent declarations that he would only accept reunion on the basis of his continued leadership, had made it impossible for O'Brien and himself to make any fresh proposals on their release from Galway. They had, how-ever, announced that they would do their utmost to restore peace. 'Our advances', Dillon said, 'were rejected with con-tempt. . . .' Parnell proving obdurate, they were bound to fight him. 'Against such a programme as this we have no choice. We must fight against it or give up all claim to the name of the Irish nationalist party. It is with the Irish party a struggle for existence. For parley with such a policy would be the basest cowardice.'[1]

Always it came back to Parnell. So long as he lived, the war would go on. And, as summer turned to autumn, his furious energy seemed to show no sign of ebbing. Despite the symptoms of defeat which steadily accumulated, he still continued his expeditions to Ireland and his preparations for the general election which many people thought to be imminent. Towards the end of that summer, when he was talking with Barry O'Brien at Euston station before leaving on the boat train, he asked him what he thought the result of the general election would be. O'Brien, who knew how he valued a straight answer, told him he might come back to Westminster with five followers, but that he would not be surprised if he came back alone. To which Parnell merely replied that if he did come back alone, at least he would represent a party whose independence had not been sapped.[2] Not even annihilation at the polls, it seemed, would crush his indomitable spirit. No disappointments seemed to have any effect upon him. The by-elections were brushed on one side and he continued to speak wherever he could find an audience.[3] Even the defection of the *Freeman's Journal* failed to shake him. It was expected that this would take place when the

[1] W. O'Brien and D. Ryan (ed.), *Devoy's post-bag*, ii. 319–28. A copy of Devoy's proposals to Dillon and a draft of Dillon's reply are in the Dillon Papers.　　　　　　　　　　　　　　[2] R. B. O'Brien, *Parnell*, ii. 347.

[3] Kells, August 16; Dublin, August 28 and 30; Westport, September 6; Listowel, September 13; Cabinteely, September 20; Creggs, September 27.

shareholders held their meeting at the end of August. But Harrington, on the ground that insufficient notice had been given and that the proceedings were therefore invalid, managed to postpone the inevitable and it was not until September 21 that the paper finally abandoned Parnell.[1] He, however, had by that time set on foot plans for a new paper, to be called the *Irish Daily Independent*.[2] These had not got very far before his death, but the fact that he meditated such a venture at all is yet another proof of his extraordinary tenacity.

But the strain was telling. Those who were near him noticed curious indications of tension—for instance, his reluctance to be left alone for any long period. Patrick O'Brien, one of those moderates whom Dillon and O'Brien had hoped to win over, saw a good deal of him in these last months and later recalled, as an example of this, how on one occasion Parnell had insisted on going to the theatre with him (something he had not done for many years), and how afterwards he had kept O'Brien walking to and fro between Morrison's Hotel and the National Club until the small hours of the morning.[3] It was not all gloom of course. He had found happiness in his marriage and that happiness often reflected itself in his manner. Pierce Mahony, who entertained him in Kerry shortly before his death, found him pleasant and friendly and noted that 'he used to talk more during the split than ever before'.[4] His sister Emily—Mrs Dickinson—thought him 'in capital spirits' at his Cabinteely meeting only three weeks before he died, and she, too, noticed his unusual talkativeness.[5]

Had his health been able to withstand the endless demands he was making upon it, his occasional fits of depression and loneliness might not have been so alarming. But his strength was failing, and the long journeys across Ireland week-end after week-end required more and more of an effort. It was about this time that he wrote to his mother that he was 'weary of these troubles, weary unto death';[6] and Michael Macdonagh, when he saw him at Listowel, was struck by how pale he seemed in

---

[1] *F.J.*, 29 Aug. and 22 Sept. 1891.

[2] R. B. O'Brien, *Parnell*, ii. 340, 349, 350; O'Shea, ii. 261. In the Parnell Letters in the National Library there is an envelope containing documents relating to the new paper (N.L.I., MS 8314).

[3] R. B. O'Brien, *Parnell*, ii. 341-4.   [4] *Ibid.*, ii. 344-5.   [5] *Ibid.*, ii. 348.

[6] *Ibid.*, ii. 348; O'Shea, ii. 176.

the September sunlight, addressing a devoted, but not very large, crowd in the market-square. His speech, however, was as full of fire as ever, and showed no sign of weakening:

If I were dead and gone to-morrow [he said], the men who are fighting against English influence in Irish public life would fight on still. They would still be independent nationalists. They would still believe in the future of Ireland as a nation. And they would still protest that it was not by taking orders from an English minister that Ireland's future could be saved, protected or secured.[1]

These were brave words, but when the speech was done and the meeting over Macdonagh saw him in a different aspect—sitting hunched at a table behind the jug of flowers one of his admirers had set there, his overcoat collar turned up, his silk-hat low over his eyes, his face care-worn and remote as he lost himself in thought, oblivious of his surroundings.[2]

The Listowel meeting was on September 13, and on September 20 he spoke at Cabinteely. On Saturday, September 26, he was back in Dublin again, en route for Creggs in county Galway. He was far from well on his arrival and sent for Dr Kenny.[3] Kenny urged him not to go, but he had never been one to pay much attention to advice and it was a part of his rigid personal code to spare himself nothing in the fight he had set himself. He had promised he would speak and he would keep his promise. There was no more to be said. He travelled in company with the *Freeman's Journal* reporters and talked optimistically of his new paper, but he admitted that he felt very ill, and indeed he carried his arm in a sling—the rheumatism which had attacked him off and on during the past year was becoming more severe. As it happened, the day of the meeting—Sunday, September 27 —was wet. Parnell, however, rejected the umbrella which was offered him and spoke bareheaded; to make matters worse, the small bag in which his wife had packed a change of clothing for him was mislaid, and for several hours after the meeting he was obliged to sit in damp clothes. His speech began so haltingly

---

[1] *F.J.*, 14 Sept. 1891. To William O'Brien this speech showed "that he is almost desperate and as incoherent as in the wildest of his Kilkenny speeches . . . and that he is falling back more and more on the hill-side boys' (Dillon Papers, O'Brien to Dillon, 15 Sept. 1891).

[2] M. Macdonagh, *The home rule movement*, pp. 238-9.

[3] R. B. O'Brien, *Parnell*, ii. 349; O'Shea, ii. 176.

that it was possible to take it down in longhand. Parnell excused himself on the ground that his doctor had forbidden him to come. 'However', he said, 'I do not think that any very material harm will come to me from this meeting. If I was to allow the suggestion of such a thought we should have our enemies throwing up their hats and announcing I was buried before I was dead.' In one respect he was more cautious in this speech than he had been in some of his other utterances, for he proclaimed that he had never pledged himself to extreme courses, for the man who did so without powder and shot was, he insisted, only attempting to delude the Irish people. But towards his Irish opponents he was as unbending as ever. No matter what subject he touched—the Boulogne negotiations, the Plan of Campaign, the Kilmainham 'treaty'—he seemed intent only upon discrediting his enemies. There was no hint of reconciliation in anything he said, and it was only fitting that the final words he spoke at this, the last public meeting he was ever to address in Ireland, should have been an exhortation to his followers to fight on:

We shall continue this fight. We fight not for faction but for freedom. If there ever was a fight which men would have desired to avoid, it would have been the fight which my friends throughout Ireland are now waging and waging so bravely. I honour them for their courage and I will not leave them until they get a better leader. I regret that you should have to submit to this persecution. I know that you look to Ireland's future as a nation if we can gain it. We may not be able to gain it, but if not it will be left for those who come after us to win; but we will do our best.[1]

On the journey back to Dublin he was restless and in much pain. Arrived in the city, he went to Dr Kenny's house and stayed there for several days attending to business connected with the launching of his new paper. All that time he was far from well and was suffering acutely from his rheumatic left arm, but on Wednesday night, brushing aside as usual the protests of Dr Kenny, he sailed for England. He would come back, he said, 'on Saturday week'.[2] On reaching London he took the grave

[1] *F.J.*, 28 Sept. 1891; R. B. O'Brien, *Parnell*, ii. 349–50; O'Shea, ii. 266; Macdonagh, *The home rule movement*, pp. 239–40.
[2] *F.J.*, 2 Oct. 1891; R. B. O'Brien, *Parnell*, ii. 351; Macdonagh, *The home rule movement*, p. 240, has 'Sunday week'.

risk—for a man in his condition—of having a Turkish bath
before catching the train to Brighton. There, his wife was
waiting for him, and though he attempted to pass it off she could
see that he was very ill. So much so that she spoke again about
fetching his specialist (Sir Henry Thompson) from London; she
had apparently threatened to do this before he left for Ireland,
but he had refused to allow her. That evening, though he ate
well, he needed a blazing fire, despite the warm weather. On
his way to bed, Katharine had to help him up the stairs. He
never came down them again alive.

During the night he was restless and spoke of writing to
Thompson. In the morning he seemed a little better, but nevertheless it seems that on that day—Saturday, October 3—he did
write to the specialist describing his condition.[1] Although he
stayed in bed, he grew worse on Sunday and this time Mrs Parnell was not to be denied. She sent for the local doctor, who did
what he could for him. But Parnell did not improve and that
night he got no sleep. His old superstitions and fears about himself (one of them, according to his wife's account, was that he
would die if he did not sleep on two consecutive nights) rose to
the surface of his mind, and towards morning he became very
feverish.[2] During Monday he was in great pain and appears to
have been delirious. Again that night he did not sleep and during Tuesday he lay most of the time without movement. Late
that evening he opened his eyes and spoke his last words: 'Kiss
me, sweet wifie, and I will try to sleep a little.' Almost at
once he lost consciousness and died shortly before midnight.[3]

[1] R. B. O'Brien, *Parnell*, ii. 351; O'Shea, ii. 271, letter from Sir Henry
Thompson to Mrs Parnell, 7 Oct. 1891.

[2] It is curious that at each of his last three meetings in Ireland he gave
examples of his superstition. At Listowel he was disturbed at the prospect of
thirteen sitting down to dinner; at Cabinteely he was upset by the breaking
of glass; and at Creggs he refused to pass a reporter on the hotel staircase
(R. B. O'Brien, *Parnell*, ii. 344, 349, 350).

[3] This account of his last days is based upon his wife's recollections
(O'Shea, ii. 266–76). While this is in several ways (see ch. 11 above) an
untrustworthy book, written in her old age, this part of it at least rings true.
It is not likely that she would forget the least detail of the poignant climax to
the supreme event of her life, and she could have no reason for distorting her
picture of it. It is, of course, the only first-hand account we have of the close
of Parnell's life. I have accepted her version of his last words rather than the
one which appeared in the press a few days later—'Let my love be given to

The doctor who attended him, Dr Jowers junior, later stated that death was due to rheumatic fever, though he added that Parnell in any event had a weak heart.[1] It was, however, the opinion of Sir Henry Thompson that the illness need not in itself have been fatal, had he not so overtaxed his strength in the last months of his life. As it was, Thompson doubted that anything could have saved him even by the time he had reached London on his way home. As he put it: 'He wanted no medicine to combat the attack. He wanted physical force, increased vitality to keep the attack at bay.'[2] At the time of death the body temperature was so high that it was not possible to make a death-mask, and the body itself had to be placed in a lead coffin without delay. It was not true, however—as was rumoured—that no-one was allowed to see the dead Parnell. On the contrary, apart from his widow, he was seen certainly by Dr J. G. Fitzgerald and by Henry Harrison. The latter, like most people, had only learnt of Parnell's death from the evening papers of October 7 and he, with other Parnellites and with the dead man's sister, had gone at once to Brighton. It was, apparently, due to their efforts that Mrs Parnell overcame her natural reluctance to consent to a public funeral in Ireland.[3] She did overcome it, however, and on Saturday, October 10, the *cortège* set out from Brighton. On Sunday morning it arrived at Kingstown and thence, through the stricken city, Parnell's body was carried to Glasnevin, where his grave lies close by O'Connell's monument.

my colleagues and to the Irish people' (*F.J.*, 9 Oct. 1891). The latter has the air of being manufactured for the occasion and does not sound at all characteristic of Parnell.

[1] *F.J.*, 9 Oct. 1891.
[2] O'Shea, ii. 272–4, Sir Henry Thompson to Mrs Parnell, 10 Oct. 1891.
[3] H. Harrison, *Parnell vindicated*, pp. 92–9.

CONCLUSION

~~~~~~

WHEN THE CURTAIN was rung down at Brighton, moderate
men might have been excused for thinking that the tragedy had
been played out and that peace and reconciliation would
follow. Such hopes, if they were ever widely held, were soon
shattered. Parnell was not even in his grave before his enemies
and his friends were at each others' throats again. On the eve
of the funeral the *Irish Catholic*, in a leading article which John
Dillon subsequently described as 'un-Catholic, un-Christian . . .
a disgrace to Irish journalism',[1] not only attacked the memory
of the dead leader with extreme brutality, but also took a very
menacing tone against his surviving followers.[2] For the other
side, on the same day, Edmund Leamy in *United Ireland* retorted
passionately that Parnell had been 'sacrificed by Irishmen on
the altar of English liberalism. . . . Murdered he has been as
certainly as if the gang of conspirators had surrounded him and
hacked him to pieces'.[3] Anger such as this would not pass in a
night. On the contrary, as men laboured through the political
wasteland of the 'nineties, the bitterness and sense of disenchant-
ment seemed to grow greater rather than less.

[1] *F.J.*, 19 Oct. 1891, speech at Dungarvan on Saturday, 17 Oct. 1891.
[2] *Irish Catholic*, 10 Oct. 1891. This article is missing from the copy in the
National Library, Dublin. Part of it was reprinted in the issue of October 17.
The general tone is sufficiently indicated by the following: 'The evil that
men do lives after them, and the weeds which grow upon the grave of a dead
cause are often rank and noxious. We have no fear that those which spring
from the tomb of Parnellism will be able to thwart the course of Ireland into
freedom. Her feet are strong enough to tread down the miserable tangles of
an unholy and unblessed growth.'
[3] *United Ireland*, 10 Oct. 1891; M. Leamy, *Parnell's faithful few*, pp. 102–3.

Time, however, dealt more kindly with Parnell than with his opponents. The idea of the lonely, heroic figure, deserted by his party, fighting to the end against overwhelming odds, had a nobility which made an irresistible appeal to those—such as John O'Leary, for example—who saw the issue primarily in terms of the ancient struggle against England; to others, like Yeats, whose pity and indignation were stirred by the spectacle of greatness overthrown by mediocrity; and to such as Joyce, for whom the fall of Parnell symbolised the triumph of all that was disgusting and degrading in Irish life. There had, of course, already been a Parnell legend while Parnell himself was still alive, but from the day he died it was assured of immortality. And as he receded further into the past, and the sharp outlines of memory were blurred, the real man became merged in the legend, and the legend in its turn exerted a powerful influence upon a fresh generation, which knew little of the rights or wrongs of the split, but was ready to interpret it in the light of its own hopes and aspirations.

But the historian who wishes to pierce beyond the legend has to take account not only of the man's nobility but also of his weakness. For it is, after all, impossible to deny that Parnell was to a great extent responsible for his own ruin, and that he took the first steps towards disaster very far back in his career—from the moment he allowed himself to drift into an impossible situation with Katharine O'Shea. That he loved her with the whole force of his nature, and that she soon became indispensable to him, no-one can doubt. But this does not excuse his fatal acquiescence in her desire to have both him and her fortune too. For her sake, as we have seen, he agreed to keep their affair secret until her aunt's death brought her the wealth she coveted. We know from what she herself told Henry Harrison that Parnell detested this concealment and wished to make her his wife openly and as soon as possible. Unhappily, he failed to do so until—politically, at any rate—the damage had been done. By keeping up the deception for so long he not only involved himself in a series of humiliating shifts, which must have been almost intolerable to a man of his pride, but also left himself vulnerable to attack in a way no responsible leader— especially with the example of Sir Charles Dilke before him— should ever have done. No doubt, even if the relationship had been made public in 1881 or 1882 there would still have been criticism and there might still have been pressure on him to retire. But if he *had* retired then, the retirement might possibly only have been temporary (this, after all, was what was suggested first when the crash eventually came) and would surely have been less damaging both for him and for his party than what actually happened in 1890. Certainly, it could have been no worse.

This initial mistake meant that he fought his last fight under a heavy disadvantage. He showed, indeed, all his old resource, but at the same time his efforts to distract attention from the divorce led him into serious errors of judgment. One was his refusal to consider resigning at any time between the verdict and the moment when the publication of Gladstone's letter so greatly increased the difficulty of doing so. Another was the manifesto, which did him immense harm. A third was his decision to break off the Boulogne negotiations despite the very favourable terms offered to him. It must be admitted, however, that in making these errors he was in a sense the victim of his own most outstanding qualities. The very things that had served him so well in the past now led him over the precipice. His indifference to English hostility, his aloofness from his own followers, his tenacity, above all his invincible pride—these conspired to make him quite immovable and deaf to every kind of appeal. And, revolting as were some of the methods used against him, it is scarcely surprising that his opponents took the view that nothing short of total war was likely to have much effect upon him.

This is not to say, however, that his enemies do not bear a share—and a very large share—of the responsibility for the course the struggle ultimately took. In such a complex and long-drawn-out crisis it was almost impossible to avoid making mistakes and nearly everyone made them sooner or later. Gladstone, for example, always apt to fumble when delicate handling of individuals was needed, showed himself at his worst when he decided so impetuously to publish his letter to John Morley before the Irish party had had a chance to consider its implications. Gladstone again, with his liberal colleagues, took up a narrow and grudging attitude about the guarantees they were asked to give during the negotiations in France, refusing to 'alter a comma' when faced with amendments which they themselves admitted to be of minor importance—this at a time when the negotiations offered the only hope, albeit a faint one, of a peaceful solution. And apart from the liberal leaders, liberal public opinion as expressed in the newspapers, on the platform and from a multitude of pulpits, showed itself extraordinarily insensitive to Irish national pride, and made it very difficult for those of his countrymen who opposed Parnell to do so without seeming to have yielded to the dictation of their English allies.

No doubt it was galling to be exposed to such a charge and no doubt the Parnellites frequently misrepresented the motives of their adversaries. This, however, scarcely justifies the latter—or at least the more extreme of them—in adopting such a forbidding attitude towards the efforts made by Dillon and O'Brien to reach a settlement at Boulogne and Calais, especially when those efforts were being sympathetically received by some of the leading men on the other side. Still less does it excuse the campaign of vilification which anti-Parnellite speakers and newspapers carried on so unceasingly. It is true that where passions ran so high rough words would probably have been inevitable anyway, and Parnell and his followers were certainly not backward in name-calling. But it is hard to believe that it was necessary in attacking them to descend to the level of the 'Stop, thief' article, or of the coarse insults which were heaped on Mrs O'Shea's name on every possible occasion. Few things, probably, have done more to discredit the opposition to Parnell in the eyes of posterity than this endless, monotonous vituperation.

Contemporaries, naturally, were obsessed by these absorbing personal issues but now, after more than sixty years, it should be possible to attempt a more dispassionate estimate of the effects —apart from the enmities it created between individuals— which the split had upon the home rule movement. These seem to have been three-fold. In the first place, the parliamentary party was deeply and permanently changed by its ordeal. Secondly, the relations between the church and a section of the laity were subjected to a severe, perhaps unprecedented, strain. And finally, the whole future of Anglo-Irish relations was influenced by the way in which the crisis emphasised, indeed perpetuated, the dependence of the Irish nationalists at Westminster upon the all-important liberal alliance.

The nature of the change in the parliamentary party is easily stated. The split was in essence the overthrow of the dominance of one man; more accurately, perhaps, it was the replacement of a dictatorship by an oligarchy. Parnell may have been a very inadequate dictator by modern standards. He was not omnipotent and he was certainly very far from ubiquitous—but he did have a very real ascendancy over his party. For Irishmen, who had often in the past shown a tendency to exalt, or even idolise, their leaders, the picture they had gradually built up of 'the chief' had a romantic fascination. But a *führer-prinzip* of this kind held grave dangers for a parliamentary party. Such a party, if it was to have any meaning at all, must base itself upon the broad, democratic process of majority rule. This was recognised in theory by the custom of electing the chairman afresh at the beginning of each parliamentary session but, since Parnell was of course chosen time after time, it is not surprising that the theory became a little rusty over the years. Yet, in logic, what a vote could do, a vote could undo. The party which at one meeting had voted Parnell into the chair, was quite within its rights when subsequently it attempted to vote him out of it. And, although the minority were entitled to criticise the motives from which they felt the majority were acting, this did not allow them to frustrate the will of the latter indefinitely. For, while it is technically true that no vote was actually taken in Committee Room Fifteen on the precise issue of Parnell's leadership (though the vote on Colonel Nolan's amendment was an accurate enough indication of how the party was likely to divide), no-one who is familiar with the debates can doubt that the absence of such a vote was not because the majority lacked the intention, but because they were denied the opportunity.

Thus, although the immediate consequence of the withdrawal of the forty-five from Committee Room Fifteen was the disruption of the party, its ultimate significance was its vindication of majority rule. And this had a permanent influence both upon those who went with McCarthy and those who stayed with Parnell, for in the nine years that the split lasted after Parnell's death each section was careful to avoid placing any individual in a position of arbitrary power; there were chairmen, but there were no leaders. On the anti-Parnellite side, McCarthy, if he could be said to have led his party at all, did so like the duke of Plaza Toro—from behind. Dillon, who succeeded him, tried harder to make his authority real, but he nearly broke his heart in the attempt, and in fact retired baffled a year before the party came together again. And although John Redmond stood out more conspicuously among the Parnellites—it was, after all, easier to do so in a group which most of the time numbered less than a dozen—when the time came to pick a leader for the reunited party he was so far from being regarded as pre-eminent that it was an open question until almost the last minute whether the choice would fall on him or on his colleague, Timothy Harrington.

After the reunion in 1900, it is true, Redmond's obvious parliamentary skill and immense personal integrity gradually gained him great authority. But the party he had to govern was not the party of Parnell's prime and, though he did his best to restore the discipline of other days, there were recurrent symptoms of disunity which he was never quite able to master. In other respects also, he was much less powerful than Parnell had been. At one time, for example, the party was little better than the client of the national organisation which had taken the place of the old National League and National Federation. This was the United Irish League, which had been founded by William O'Brien in 1898 when the prestige of the parliamentarians had been at its lowest ebb. For a few years after unity had been restored, the United Irish League held the whip hand in Irish politics, and although eventually the party reasserted itself, it was never able to control the new organisation as effectively as it had controlled either of the old ones.

It was the same with the constituencies. During the split the county conventions, which were responsible for selecting nationalist candidates to contest the various parliamentary divisions, succeeded to a considerable extent in shaking themselves free of party control—either Parnellite or anti-Parnellite—and even after 1900 this habit of independence persisted. The consequence was that many of the members elected after that date were men who either lived in or had close connections with their constituencies and were primarily representatives of, and spokesman for, local interests.[1] Whether this was desirable or not—and something could be said on both sides of the question—it was a clear illustration of the way in which the party, having involuntarily relaxed its hold over the county conventions, found itself much more at the mercy of local peculiarities than it had been in the 'eighties.

It would, however, be wrong to make too much of this, or to deny that under Redmond's guidance the party regained much of its influence in the country. Indeed, it is probably fair to say that it was not until the crisis of the third home rule bill that its power began to be seriously undermined. But, while it recovered its efficiency, it failed to recover what had been one of its greatest assets—its appeal to the popular imagination. Where Parnell had been the poetry of nationalism, Redmond was the very embodiment of its prose. And by 1912 it was beginning to become clear that the young men of the country were not prepared to exist indefinitely on a régime of prose alone.

The changes in the government and power of the party probably escaped the attention of most people except those directly affected. This, however, could not be said of the second major consequence of the split, which involved both party and country. That was the clash it precipitated between the church and the Parnellites. In a sense this clash resembled the conflicts between church and state which were frequent all over western Europe in the later nineteenth century. True, there could obviously be no separate Irish 'state' so long as Ireland remained under the union, but it could reasonably be argued that the parliamentary party, from which presumably the government would be chosen if home rule ever became a reality, represented the civil power as it were in embryo; and that as such its relations with the church were of the same order of importance as the relations between church and state elsewhere.

For most of the Parnellite period, and especially from 1882 on, this relationship between the church and the Irish party had been in general an amicable one. There had, of course, been

[1] These points are developed in detail in F. S. L. Lyons, *The Irish parliamentary party, 1890–1910*, ch. III and V. 'Local' members had in fact made a considerable showing as early as 1885, though it seems that either Parnell or his principal lieutenants could dispose of seats very much as they pleased between 1886 and 1890. See C. Cruise O'Brien, *Parnell and his party, 1880–90*, ch. IV and VIII.

awkward moments—during the Plan of Campaign, for example —but there had been little trace of that extreme hostility with which clergy and laymen so often confronted each other on the continent. Indeed, given the genuine devotion of the Irish people to their religion, and the scarcity and feebleness of rival attractions, the kind of collision which had occurred in other countries might have been avoided altogether. But the split ensured that it was not avoided and soon the angry protests against the intervention of the church in politics, so familiar elsewhere, began to be heard in Ireland also.

It was, however, unfortunate for both sides that the debate had to be carried on in such a context. Unfortunate for the church because, while the hierarchy as a whole was circumspect and dignified in its behaviour, the violent anti-Parnellism of individual priests placed a very damaging weapon in the hands of those who were only too ready to repeat the old gibe that home rule meant Rome rule. Unfortunate, also, for the Parnellites, whose attempt to draw a line between morals and politics and to confine the church to the former, might have been more convincing if the particular case they were trying to argue had not seemed to contradict their thesis so obviously. They asserted, of course, that the divorce case should have no bearing on the question of the leadership. Nowadays many people—though not, perhaps, in Ireland—would probably accept their argument. But—and this is the essential point—at that time public opinion, protestant as well as catholic, English as well as Irish, took it for granted that the moral and political issues were inextricably bound up together, and that precisely because Parnell was a proven and unrepentant adulterer he was unfit to remain at his post. Where English non-conformists had already rushed in, it was unthinkable that Irish catholics should forbear to follow.

Furthermore, apart altogether from the divorce, the Parnellite appeal to fenian sentiment was a challenge which the church dared not ignore. Even if the extent of fenian influence was not so great as some imagined, fenianism did exist and it had not abjured the use of force to achieve its aim of total separation from England. From this it followed that those who worked with the fenians might ultimately, under certain conditions, find themselves involved in acts of violence; and acts of violence, it could be argued, raised moral issues upon which the church was bound to express an opinion. In 1890–1 this might have appeared a remote enough possibility, but the bare fact that the possibility existed would, from the church's point of view, have tended to make the Parnellite distinction between morals and politics more unreal than ever. Parnell himself denied that he contemplated any appeal to force and, despite the wildness of some of his speeches, there seems no good reason to believe that he was ready to abandon constitutional methods, acutely aware though he was of their limitations. On the other hand, the enthusiasm with which the fenians rallied to him certainly suggested that if he wanted to make common cause with them, he could easily do so. We can scarcely be surprised, therefore, that the clergy, with the evidence of this enthusiasm before them, should have spoken out as vehemently as they did against the threat of what they could only have regarded as a pernicious alliance.

The result was easy to foresee. As the struggle intensified, each side became more deeply committed. Among the Parnellites the *Freeman's Journal* (until it changed sides), and a few individual members of parliament, threw all restraints aside and carried on a bitter vendetta against those who—since they did not cease to be catholics—were still their spiritual leaders. The spiritual leaders, for their part, were driven to press their claims further and further until, as we have seen, Archbishop Croke ended by asserting the over-riding right of the church to decide in the last resort what were and what were not 'secular issues.'[1] Such a claim might at any other time have provoked a sharp—and healthy—reaction, leading perhaps to a clarification of the relations between church and laity. But in the shadow of the split the challenge could not be taken up except by those who, in the nature of the case, were in the worst possible position to do so.

It was an added misfortune for Parnell and his followers that, leaving the moral issue on one side, their enemies had an intelligible political reason for opposing them. Men who were genuinely convinced both that the liberal alliance was vital for the winning of home rule and that the alliance could only be saved by sacrificing Parnell, had no option but to take sides

[1] See p. 269 above.

against him, however much they disliked the savagery with which he was being attacked in the name of morality. It was, indeed, the fundamental weakness of Parnell's position that, by combining in his own person the offence to religion and the threat to the liberal connection, he united against him in England and Ireland an assortment of allies whom scarcely any other set of circumstances would have brought into action together.

It remains only to mention the third important consequence of the split—its effect upon the position of the Irish party at Westminster. The anti-Parnellite majority asserted over and over again that their supreme political justification for deserting their leader was the necessity for keeping the liberal alliance intact. The inescapable corollary of this was that, since the alliance had only been saved by jettisoning Parnell, thenceforward the party must stand or fall with the liberals. Irish parliamentarians, indeed, never ceased to proclaim the doctrine of independent opposition. But that doctrine, capable only of a very limited application since 1886, had become more than ever impracticable after 1890. The party was in the position of a gambler obliged to stake everything on a single throw, but denied a choice of hazards. For, given the inexorable hostility of the unionists to home rule, there was little the nationalists could do but cling desperately to their liberal allies.

So long as the liberals remained faithful all might yet be well. But would they remain faithful? It is clear from what we have seen of their various reactions before, during and after the split, that among the leaders of the party there was considerable confusion and disagreement as to what home rule really entailed. Gladstone, by the force of his immense prestige, was able to overcome these differences and to rally both his colleagues and liberal opinion as a whole to such good effect that within two years of Parnell's death he had actually managed to carry a home rule bill through the house of commons. And even the fact that this was promptly killed by the house of lords does not take away either from the greatness of his individual achievement or from its value to the Irish parliamentary party. That party, split into two—virtually into three—sections was in a bad enough way by 1893. The near prospect of a home rule bill was almost the only thing that kept it alive, and if Gladstone had not produced one it is hard to see how the party could have survived as a political force.

But the failure of 1893, however magnificent, was still a failure. The liberals could scarcely be expected to go on ignoring the claims of their English, Scottish and Welsh supporters in pursuit of a policy which had brought them so much hardship and so little tangible success. It was not surprising, therefore, that when Lord Rosebery succeeded Gladstone as prime minister in 1894 he lost no time in placing home rule publicly and firmly on the shelf. And indeed, given his small majority in the house of commons and the implacable hostility of the house of lords, it was only common-sense for him to do so.

In 1906, however, when after ten years in opposition the liberals came back to power with an immense majority, there seemed—to Irish eyes at least—no further excuse for delay. Yet, though Campbell-Bannerman and Asquith were prolific of promises, they were slow to take effective action. Neither of them, it was all too clear, had inherited Gladstone's zeal for the cause, but even if they had been temperamentally inclined that way (which they were not) Gladstone's zeal was a luxury they were hardly able to afford. The liberal majority of 1906 was not a majority for home rule alone. On the contrary, to many British electors it represented primarily a means of achieving a variety of long-deferred social reforms. Those reforms, and the running fight with the house of lords which accompanied them, occupied the main energies of the government until 1911 and, although the victory over the upper house which was won in that year was as vital to Redmond as to Asquith, there was no disguising the fact that the delays and disappointments of those years had placed a heavy strain upon the liberal-nationalist alliance, and had considerably embarrassed the parliamentary party in its attempts to justify itself before the bar of Irish public opinion.

The result was that although a home rule bill was introduced in 1912, and although Redmond contrived to keep the Irish demand in the forefront of politics for three successive years, the long, hard journey had taken its toll. More and more, as the crisis neared its peak, he and his party, with every energy centred on the house of commons, found themselves out of touch with the new forces that were gathering in Ireland. By

1914 they were dangerously isolated and faced catastrophe if, at the last moment, anything should baulk them of victory. Yet the difficulties in their way were almost overwhelming. Apart from the fact that Redmond's hold over nationalist Ireland was becoming increasingly precarious, the liberal ministry—on which, in the last resort everything depended—was beset by a variety of problems which only seemed to grow graver and more insoluble as time went on. With the shadow of war in Europe, industrial unrest and the suffragette agitation at home, the menace of an armed rising in Ulster and the mounting tide of party passion in England, the outlook could hardly have been bleaker or the prospects for home rule more unpromising. True, the two elections of 1910 had allowed Redmond to hold the balance of power between liberals and conservatives, but, though he exploited this advantage with great skill, his freedom of action was circumscribed by the fact that, while he could destroy the government, in doing so he would destroy with it the last remaining hope of gaining home rule by constitutional means. To the very end, therefore, the Irish party was chained, Prometheus-like, to the rock of the liberal alliance.

For a brief moment, when the third home rule bill, albeit with serious qualifications, reached the statute-book despite the outbreak of the war, it did perhaps seem as if that alliance had after all been justified by results. We know now that this was an illusion, that the legislation of 1914 solved nothing, and that the issue was ultimately to be decided outside the house of commons. The era of constitutional agitation was ending, the key to the future lay elsewhere. And when in 1916 an older, deeper tradition in Irish history emerged once more into the open, the days of the parliamentary party were numbered. Within three years of the Rising it had ceased to exist.

Appendix I

THE PARNELL MANIFESTO

~~~~~~

TO THE PEOPLE OF IRELAND[1]

THE INTEGRITY and independence of a section of the Irish
parliamentary party having been apparently sapped and
destroyed[2] by the wirepullers of the English liberal party, it has
become necessary for me, as the leader of the Irish nation, to
take counsel with you, and, having given you the knowledge
which is in my possession, to ask your judgment upon a matter
which now solely devolves upon you to decide.

The letter of Mr Gladstone to Mr Morley, written for the
purpose of influencing the decision of the Irish party in the
choice of their leader, and claiming for the liberal party and
their leaders the right of veto upon that choice, is the immediate
cause of this address to you, to remind you and your parliamentary representatives that Ireland considers the independence of her party as her only safeguard within the constitution,
and above and beyond all other considerations whatever. The
threat in that letter, repeated so insolently on many English
platforms and in numerous British newspapers, that unless
Ireland concedes this right of veto to England she will indefinitely postpone her chances of obtaining home rule, compels
me, while not for one moment admitting the slightest probability

---

[1] The text reproduced here is that published in *F.J.*, 29 Nov. 1890.

[2] Some versions omitted the word 'apparently', but Parnell on December
3 confirmed that it should have been included (*F.J.*, 4 Dec. 1890).

of such loss, to put before you information which until now, so far as my colleagues are concerned, has been solely in my possession, and which will enable you to understand the measure of the loss with which you are threatened unless you consent to throw me to the English wolves now howling for my destruction.

In December of last year, in response to a repeated and long-standing request, I visited Mr Gladstone at Hawarden, and received the details of the intended proposals of himself and his colleagues of the late liberal cabinet with regard to home rule, in the event of the next general election favouring the liberal party.

It is unnecessary for me to do more at present than to direct your attention to certain points of these details, which will be generally recognised as embracing elements vital for your information and the formation of your judgment. These vital points of difficulty may be suitably arranged and considered under the following heads:

(1) The retention of the Irish members in the imperial parliament.

(2) The settlement of the land or agrarian difficulty in Ireland.

(3) The control of the Irish constabulary.

(4) The appointment of judiciary (including judges of the supreme court, county court judges, and resident magistrates).

Upon the subject of the retention of the Irish members in the imperial parliament Mr Gladstone told me that the opinion, and the unanimous opinion, of his colleagues and himself, recently arrived at after most mature consideration of alternative proposals, was that, in order to conciliate English public opinion, it would be necessary to reduce the Irish representation from 103 to 32.

Upon the settlement of the land it was held that this was one of the questions which must be regarded as questions reserved from the control of the Irish legislature, but, at the same time, Mr Gladstone intimated that, while he would renew his attempt to settle the matter by imperial legislation on the lines of the land purchase bill of 1886, he would not undertake to put any pressure upon his own side or insist upon their adopting his views—in other and shorter words, that the Irish legislature was not to be given the power of solving the agrarian difficulty, and that the imperial parliament would not.

With regard to the control of the Irish constabulary, it was stated by Mr Gladstone that, having regard to the necessity for conciliating English public opinion, he and his colleagues felt that it would be necessary to leave this force and the appointment of its officers under the control of the imperial authority for an indefinite period, while the funds for its maintenance, payment, and equipment would be compulsorily provided out of Irish resources.

The period of ten or twelve years was suggested as the limit of time during which the appointment of judges, resident magistrates, etc., should be retained in the hands of the imperial authority.

I have now given a short account of what I gathered of Mr Gladstone's views and those of his colleagues during two hours' conversation at Hawarden—a conversation which, I am bound to admit, was mainly monopolised by Mr Gladstone—and pass to my own expressions of opinion upon these communications, which represent my views then and now.

And, first, with regard to the retention of the Irish members, the position I have always adopted, and then represented, is that, with the concession of full powers to the Irish legislature equivalent to those enjoyed by a state of the American union, the number and position of the members so retained would become a question of imperial concern, and not of pressing or immediate importance for the interests of Ireland. But that with the important and all-engrossing subjects of agrarian reform, constabulary control, and judiciary appointments left either under imperial control or totally unprovided for, it would be the height of madness for any Irish leader to imitate Grattan's example and consent to disband the army which had cleared the way to victory.

I further undertook to use every legitimate influence to reconcile Irish public opinion to a gradual coming into force of the new privileges, and to the postponements necessary for English opinion with regard to constabulary control and judicial appointments; but I strongly dissented from the proposed reduction of members during the interval of probation and I pointed to the absence of any suitable prospect of land settlement by either parliament as constituting an overwhelming drag upon the prospects of permanent peace and prosperity in Ireland.

At the conclusion of the interview I was informed that Mr Gladstone and all his colleagues were entirely agreed that, pending the general election, silence should be absolutely preserved with regard to any points of difference on the question of the retention of the Irish members.

I have dwelt at some length upon these subjects, but not, I think, disproportionately to their importance. Let me say, in addition, that, if and when full powers are conceded to Ireland over her own domestic affairs, the integrity, number, and independence of the Irish party will be a matter of no importance; but until this ideal is reached it is your duty and mine to hold fast every safeguard.

I need not say that the questions—the vital and important questions—of the retention of the Irish members, on the one hand, and the indefinite delay of full powers to the Irish legislature on the other, gave me great concern. The absence of any provision for the settlement of the agrarian question, of any policy on the part of the liberal leaders, filled me with concern and apprehension. On the introduction of the land purchase bill by the government at the commencement of last session, Mr Morley communicated with me as to the course to be adopted. Having regard to the avowed absence of any policy on the part of the liberal leaders and party with regard to the matter of the land, I strongly advised Mr Morley against any direct challenge of the principle of state-aided land purchase, and, finding that the fears and alarms of the English taxpayer to state aid by the hypothecation of grants for local purposes in Ireland as a counter-guarantee had been assuaged, that a hopeless struggle should not be maintained, and that we should direct our sole efforts on the second reading of the bill to the assertion of the principle of local control. In this I am bound to say Mr Morley entirely agreed with me, but he was at the same time much hampered—and expressed his sense of his position—in that direction by the attitude of the extreme section of his party, led by Mr Labouchere. And on a subsequent interview he impressed me with the necessity of meeting the second reading of the bill with a direct negative, and asked me to undertake the motion. I agreed to this, but only on the condition that I was not to attack the principle of the measure, but to confine myself to a criticism of its details. I think this was false strategy, but it was strategy adopted out of regard to English prejudices and radical peculiarities. I did the best that was possible under the circumstances, and the several days' debate on the second reading contrasts favourably with Mr Labouchere's recent and abortive attempt to interpose a direct negative to the first reading of a similar bill yesterday.

Time went on. The government allowed their attention to be distracted from the question of land purchase by the bill for compensating English publicans, and the agrarian difficulty in Ireland was again relegated to the future of another session. Just before the commencement of this session I was again favoured with another interview with Mr Morley. I impressed upon him the policy of the oblique method of procedure in reference to land purchase, and the necessity and importance of providing for the question of local control and of a limitation in the application of the funds. He agreed with me, and I offered to move, on the first reading of the bill, an amendment in favour of this local control, advising that, if this were rejected, it might be left to the radicals on the second reading to oppose the principle of the measure. This appeared to be a proper course, and I left Mr Morley under the impression that this would fall to my duty.

But in addition he made me a remarkable proposal, referring to the probable approaching victory of the liberal party at the polls. He suggested some considerations as to the future of the Irish party. He asked me whether I would be willing to assume the office of chief secretary to the lord-lieutenant of Ireland, or to allow another member of my party to take the position. He also put before me the desirability of filling one of the law offices of the crown in Ireland by a legal member of my party. I told him, amazed as I was at the proposal, that I could not agree to forfeit in any way the independence of the party or any of its members; that the Irish people had trusted me in this movement because they believed that the declaration I had made to them at Cork in 1880 was a true one and represented my convictions, and that I would on no account depart from it. I can only speak of what I know. I considered then that, after the declarations we have repeatedly made, the proposal of Mr Morley, that we should allow ourselves to be absorbed into English politics, was one based upon an entire misconception of our position with regard to the Irish constituencies and of the pledges which we had given.

In conclusion, he directed my attention to the Plan of Campaign estates. He said that it would be impossible for the liberal party when they attained power to do anything for these evicted tenants by direct action; that it would be also impossible for the Irish parliament, under the powers conferred, to do anything for them, and, flinging up his hands with a gesture of despair, he exclaimed: 'Having been to Tipperary, I do not know what to propose in regard to the matter.' I told him that this question was a limited one, and that I did not see that he need allow himself to be hampered by its future consideration; that, being limited, funds would be available from America and elsewhere for the support of those tenants as long as might be necessary; that, of course, I understood it was a difficulty, but that it was a limited one, and should not be allowed to interfere with the general interests of the country.

I allude to this matter only because within the last few days a strong argument in many minds for my expulsion has been that, unless the liberals come into power at the next general election, the Plan of Campaign tenants will suffer. As I have shown, the liberals propose to do nothing for the Plan of Campaign tenants by direct action when they do come into power, but I am entitled to ask that the existence of these tenants, whom I have supported in every way in the past, and whom I shall continue to support in the future, shall not constitute a reason for my expulsion from Irish politics. I have repeatedly pledged myself to stand by these evicted tenants and that they shall not be allowed to suffer and I believe that the Irish people throughout the world will support me in this policy.

Sixteen years ago I conceived the idea of an Irish parliamentary party independent of all English parties. Ten years ago I was elected the leader of an independent Irish parliamentary party. During these ten years that party has remained independent, and because of its independence it has forced upon the English people the necessity of granting home rule to Ireland. I believe that party will obtain home rule only provided it remains independent of any English party. I do not believe that any action of the Irish people in supporting me will endanger the home rule cause, or postpone the establishment of an Irish parliament; but even if the danger with which we are threatened by the liberal party of to-day were to be realised, I believe that the Irish people throughout the world would agree with me that a postponement would be preferable to a compromise of our national rights by the acceptance of a measure which would not realise the aspirations of our race.

Appendix II

A NOTE ON PARTY FINANCES

ONE OF THE most immediate consequences of the split in the Irish parliamentary party was of course that each section found itself very short of funds. This situation, indeed, was to persist until the party was reunited in 1900, but it was especially acute in 1890–1, partly because both Parnellites and anti-Parnellites had hurriedly to improvise ways and means of raising money and partly because, having raised it, they had to spend so much of it on fighting each other. It is unfortunately impossible to speak with equal confidence about the financial resources of the two sides. The anti-Parnellite position is well-documented, since the treasurer's books have survived and are now in the National Library in Dublin. No Parnellite books, however, have so far come to light and no authoritative and detailed statement of their resources or expenditure was made public from the time of the split until the time of Parnell's death. Thus, while we can be precise about the anti-Parnellite funds even to the smallest item, it is only possible to make the vaguest guesses about those of their opponents.

So far as the anti-Parnellites, then, are concerned the following table of receipts and expenditure, based upon a balance-sheet in the ledger of the Irish parliamentary fund, may be taken as giving an accurate picture of the state of affairs during the vital year December 1890 to December 1891.[1]

[1] J. F. X. O'Brien Papers (N.L.I., MS 9231), 'Ledger of the Irish Parliamentary Fund, 7 Dec. 1890–4 Apr. 1896', p. 169.

RECEIPTS	£	s.	d.	EXPENDITURE	£	s.	d.
Irish Parliamentary				Expenses of A.			
Fund, old a/c	76	1	5	O'Connor, M.P.			
Irish Parliamentary				and J. F. X.			
Fund, new a/c	841	1	0	O'Brien, M.P., on			
John Dillon special				mission to Paris	41	8	4
(evicted tenants)				General expenses	234	16	4
a/c	1,000	0	0	*Insuppressible*	200	0	0
Irish National				Election expenses	975	13	5
League of Great				Irish National			
Britain	350	0	0	Federation	400	0	0
Irish National				Australian mission			
Federation	3,500	0	0	of J. R. Cox, M.P.	50	0	0
National Fund	1,250	0	0	Meetings in England	35	1	4
Loan from John				Meetings in Ireland	66	15	7
Barry, M.P.	1,550	0	0	Liberal meetings in			
General Election				England, special a/c	44	13	10
Fund	420	11	4	Members' salaries	6,900	0	0
				Cash in hand	1	0	0
				Credit balance in			
				bank 31 December			
				1891	38	4	11
TOTAL	£8,987	13	9	TOTAL	£8,987	13	9

The items on the expenditure side of this table are largely self-explanatory. The only two which call for special mention are the sum of £975 13s. 5d. paid out in election expenses and the £6,900 spent on members' salaries. The former was almost entirely devoted to the Kilkenny election. The latter represented the payments made to twenty-eight members of parliament during the period 8 Dec. 1890–31 Dec. 1890. The average payment was £200 per head, though one member received £500, three £400, four £300 and three £250. The total of £6,900 expended in this way also included one payment of £300 on account for 1892.[1]

The receipts were drawn from such a variety of sources as to suggest—what, indeed, was only the truth—that the anti-Parnellites were ready to exploit almost any source that would bring them revenue. The old parliamentary fund—£76 1s. 5d. —was what stood to the party's credit in the bank when the split occurred. The new parliamentary fund was made up

[1] J. F. X. O'Brien Papers (N.L.I., MS 9231), 'Ledger of the Irish Parliamentary Fund', p. 80.

partly of money subscribed by the members themselves, partly of contributions from their well-wishers. The sum of £1,000 from John Dillon's special account was a partial repayment of money formerly advanced by the party to aid the evicted tenants.[1] The contribution from the Irish National League of Great Britain represented part of the proceeds from the sale of premises in Smith street, London.[2] Nothing was specified about the £3,500 derived from the Irish National Federation, but almost certainly this consisted of subscriptions and collections from local branches of the organisation in Ireland. The general election fund was collected mainly in London, Manchester, Liverpool and other towns in Great Britain under the auspices of the Irish National League of Great Britain.[3] As the name implies, it was ear-marked for a special purpose, but anyway was so small that it scarcely affected the general situation. The loan from John Barry, of course, though extremely useful at the time, was a liability which sooner or later would have to be paid back.[4] The remaining item of importance—the national fund —represented an attempt by the party to whip up enthusiasm in the country and to persuade their supporters to contribute afresh, no matter what their other commitments might be. It was launched in September 1891 after the committee of the party had held several meetings in Dublin to discuss the position.[5] Its nucleus appears to have been a sum of £99 11s. 9d. left over from the Irish Tenants' Defence Fund,[6] and by the end

---

[1] J. F. X. O'Brien Papers (N.L.I., MS 9231), 'Ledger of the Irish Parliamentary Fund', p. 70.   [2] Ibid., p. 80.   [3] Ibid., p. 18.

[4] It is just possible that this 'loan' may not have been made by Barry himself, but may have been instead a concealed contribution from English sympathisers. In November 1891 Henry Labouchere wrote to Harcourt recalling that after the Kilkenny election the anti-Parnellites had needed money badly to pay both the election expenses and the salaries of some of their members. Labouchere said that funds had been found 'without it being possible to say that they came from the liberal party'. They were, he added, given to John Barry (whom he wrongly described as the treasurer) and apart from him the only person to know of the transaction was said to have been Healy (Harcourt Papers, Labouchere to Sir W. Harcourt, 6 Nov. 1891). Labouchere is not the most reliable of witnesses and I know of no other evidence to support his statement. On the other hand, we have seen above that there was a strong disposition amongst some English liberals to help the anti-Parnellites financially, so Labouchere's account is not inherently improbable.   [5] F.J., 25 Sept. 1891.   [6] F.J., 16 Nov. 1891.

of the year £5,259 13s. 3d. had been acknowledged.[1] The proportion of this claimed by the party for its own use (£1,250) was, therefore, just under twenty-five per cent.

Two final comments suggest themselves. One is that the receipts during this vital year were almost entirely from English or Irish sources. American contributions appear to have been negligible and such American money as did cross the Atlantic seems to have been devoted mainly to relieving the needs of the evicted tenants. For all practical purposes the anti-Parnellites could not—at least for parliamentary purposes—look to the United States for aid.[2] And the other comment is that even despite the strenuous efforts that had been made the majority section were only able to close the year 1891 with a credit in the bank of £38 4s. 11d. And if we subtract from their receipts the general election fund of £420 11s. 4d. which was in effect mortgaged, and the loan of £1,550 from John Barry, it is plain that even this credit balance was an illusion and that in reality they ended with a deficit of nearly £2,000.

When we turn to the financial position of Parnell and his group all is vagueness and uncertainty. There is in fact only one solid piece of evidence to guide us. This is that in March 1891 his followers launched the Parnell Leadership Fund and that the last acknowledgment of contributions published in the *Freeman's Journal* before it changed sides (three weeks before Parnell's death) gave the total collected up to that time as £4,697 17s. 4d.[3] There is no subsequent information—even in *United Ireland* which after the defection of the *Freeman's Journal* was the main Parnellite newspaper—during the rest of 1891 about this fund. Probably it lapsed with Parnell's death; if so, it can scarcely have reached the £5,000 mark.

It is hardly likely that Parnell could have fought three by-elections, held innumerable meetings in Ireland and paid the parliamentary salaries of a number of his supporters on this money alone. To some extent he may have supplemented it from his own private resources. These, however, were not large, for even the Parnell tribute of his earlier years seems to have been almost altogether used in paying previous debts and in

---

[1] *F.J.*, 31 Dec. 1891.

[2] F. S. L. Lyons, *The Irish parliamentary party, 1890–1910*, p. 202.

[3] *F.J.*, 7 Mar. and 18 Sept. 1891.

developing his quarries and mines in county Wicklow.[1] These continued to absorb considerable quantities of capital up to the time of his death, but the fact that—according to his brother, who inherited Avondale from him—Parnell died £50,000 in debt, suggests that towards the end of his life his political activities may have added considerably to the burden of expense he was already carrying.[2] There is, however, no way of proving whether, or to what extent, he did commit his private fortune to the struggle, though it would have been very much in character for him to have pledged it to the hilt.

As we have seen, his opponents had very definite ideas about where he got the money for his campaign, asserting that he used for his own purposes what had been intended for the benefit of the home rule movement as a whole—instancing, especially, the balance of the defence fund, £5,000 from Cecil Rhodes and £1,000 from John Morrogh.[3] Parnell of course insisted that the money was entrusted to him to spend as he saw fit, but since no detailed account was apparently ever given of what happened to it, there is no means of knowing whether or not he did use it as a campaign fund, or whether it was still intact at his death.

Apart from these sums, and apart from his own private resources, there seems to have been only one further source of supply open to him. This was the Irish National League, which continued to collect subscriptions from its members during the crisis. The League seems to have put out no general statement of its finances during 1891 so it is impossible to tell what its total revenue was, though the treasurer's fortnightly reports published in the press indicate that a contribution of even three figures was something of a rarity. For example, from the beginning of June to the end of September only one of the subscription lists was over £100[4] and the total collected in those four months was £610 4s. 7d.[5] Evidently salvation was not to be looked for in that quarter. Nor was it to be sought in the United States, for such American contributions as were made—and they were neither large nor numerous—appear to have been included either in the Parnell Leadership Fund or in the periodic

---

[1] J. H. Parnell, *Charles Stewart Parnell: a political memoir*, p. 286.
[2] Ibid., p. 288.   [3] See pp. 271–3 above.   [4] *F.J.*, 17 June 1891.
[5] *F.J.*, 3 and 17 June, 1, 15 and 29 July, 12 and 26 Aug., 9 and 23 Sept., 1891.

reports by the treasurer of the Irish National League. It is true that a Parnellite mission spent some months in America in 1891, but its appeal for funds was primarily on behalf of the evicted tenants rather than for the purposes of Parnell and his parliamentary followers. And even this appeal was described by the delegates on their return home as only 'fairly successful'.[1]

The truth is that at every turn we are met by a scarcity of reliable evidence. The meagre evidence we have, indeed, suggests that the financial problems of the Parnellites must have been at least as severe as those of their opponents, but more than that it is impossible to say. It seems, in short, as if the mystery which surrounded Parnell's revenues in the last year of his life must remain a mystery still.

BIBLIOGRAPHY

~~~~~~~~~~~~~~~~~~~~~~~~~~~~~~~~~~~~~~~

A useful guide to the printed sources for Irish history in the period covered by this book is to be found in the *Bibliography of Irish history, 1870–1911*, compiled by Mr James Carty, M.A., and published in 1940 for the Department of Education by the Stationery Office, Dublin. Reviews and short notices of works dealing with the events of 1890–1, and published since 1938, appear in the relevant numbers of *Irish Historical Studies* (Dublin, 1938–).

Of the manuscript sources listed below, only one—the Gladstone Papers—has been classified in a printed catalogue. Some, though not all, of the other collections are known to scholars, but, as most of the items used here have not appeared anywhere before, they are recorded in detail under their appropriate heads.

Except where otherwise stated, all books listed in this bibliography were published in London.

A. SOURCES
I. COLLECTIONS OF PRIVATE PAPERS.
In England

(1) *The Dilke Papers*

These are in the British Museum and, at the time of writing, are being bound. While this book was in the press I was allowed to see them but, owing to pressure of time, I confined my researches to those parts of Sir Charles Dilke's diaries and memoirs which threw some light on the Parnell-O'Shea affair and which had, in part, been previously consulted by Henry Harrison.

The relevant diary entries (1882 and 1887) are to be found in B.M., Add. MSS 43,924 and 43,927 respectively.

The relevant memoir material (for the same dates) is in B.M., Add. MSS 43,936 and 43,941 respectively.

(2) *The Gladstone Papers*

For a full description of this collection see *Catalogue of additions to the manuscripts in the British Museum: the Gladstone Papers* (1953).

Correspondence with Lord Acton, 1888–97 (B.M., Add. MS 44,094).

Correspondence with the second Earl Granville, 1887–91 (B.M. Add. MS 44,180).

Correspondence with Sir William Harcourt, 1890–2 (B.M., Add. MS 44,202).

Correspondence with Cardinal Manning, 1872–91 (B.M., Add. MS 44,250).

Correspondence with Arnold Morley, 1890–5 (B.M., Add. MS 44,254).

Correspondence with John Morley, 1889–25 Sept. 1892 (B.M., Add. MS 44,256).

Correspondence with the first Marquess of Ripon, 1883–97 (B.M., Add. MS 44,287).

Correspondence with the fifth Earl Spencer, 1889–97 (B.M., Add. MS 44,314).

General correspondence 20 Sept.–Dec. 1890 (B.M., Add. MS 44,511).

Memoranda, mainly relating to the Irish question, 1887–91 (B.M., Add. MS 44,773).

(3) *The Granville Papers*

As the second Earl Granville died in March 1891 his papers do not contain very much material on the event of 1890–1. Some individual items, however, were valuable and are listed below. The collection is now housed in the Public Record Office, London and is under the index number 30.29.

Sir William Harcourt to Earl Granville, 27 Oct. 1889 (box 29A).

Earl Spencer to Earl Granville, 29 Dec. 1889 (box 22A).

Sir William Harcourt to Earl Granville, 29 Nov. 1890 (box 29A).

Gladstone to Earl Granville, 21 Jan. 1891 (box 29A).

(4) *The Harcourt Papers*

The papers of Sir William Harcourt are preserved at Stanton Harcourt and I am grateful to Viscount Harcourt for his kindness in allowing me to see them there and also for his permission to quote from them. They were, of course, extensively used by A. G. Gardiner in his biography of Sir William Harcourt and I have only listed here those items which he either did not use, or from which I have made different quotations.

Sir William Harcourt to John Morley, 27 Oct. 1889.

Sir William Harcourt to Gladstone, 4 Dec. 1890 (copy in Harcourt's hand).

Notes dictated by Sir William to Louis (Lulu) Harcourt on the Parnell crisis, undated but apparently made in December 1890.

Sir William Harcourt to John Morley, 3 and 4 Jan. 1891.

Sir William Harcourt to John Morley, 17 Jan. 1891.

W. E. Gladstone to Sir William Harcourt, 19 Jan. 1891.

H. Labouchere to Sir William Harcourt, 6 Nov. 1891.

Memorandum written at Malwood by John Morley on the subject of liberal-nationalist dealings at the time of the Boulogne negotiations, 1891 (no more precise date given).

Memorandum by Sir William Harcourt on the Irish party, 1891. It is in his son's hand, but with pencilled corrections in his own writing, and, although it has no precise date, appears to date from November or December 1891, after William O'Brien and others had made their various 'revelations' about the Boulogne negotiations.

(5) *The Spencer Papers*

These papers, which are admirably arranged and in excellent condition, are now at Althorp. I am much indebted to Earl Spencer for permission to quote from them. The items of importance for the period of the Parnell split are as follows:

Earl Granville to Earl Spencer, 22 Oct. 1889.

Sir William Harcourt to Earl Spencer, 25 Oct. 1889.

John Morley to Earl Spencer, 17 Nov. 1890.

Sir William Harcourt to Earl Spencer, 29 Nov. 1890.

John Morley to Earl Spencer, 1 Dec. 1890.

Sir William Harcourt to Earl Spencer, 1 Dec. 1890.

Earl Granville to Earl Spencer, 20 Dec. 1890.

John Morley to Earl Spencer, 19 Jan. 1891.

John Morley to Earl Spencer, 27 Jan. 1891.

John Morley to Earl Spencer, 8 Feb. 1891.

In Ireland

(6) *The Dillon Papers*

These papers are at present housed in Dublin in temporary quarters. I am most grateful to Professor Myles Dillon for his courtesy and kindness in making them available to me. They constitute one of the main Irish manuscript sources for the history of the Parnell split. The relevant items used in this book are given below; except where otherwise stated, the documents listed are letters received by Dillon from various correspondents.

The minutes of the Irish parliamentary party, 1890–1.

The diary of John Dillon, 1890–1.

Cable from T. P. Gill to John Dillon, 26 Nov. 1890.

'Memorandum for Paris negotiations', 11 Dec. 1890.

V. B. Dillon to John Dillon, 13 Dec. 1890.

J. E. Kenny to John Dillon, 13 Dec. 1890.

William O'Brien to John Dillon, probably 13 Dec. 1890.

Mrs Kate Rea to John Dillon, 15 Dec. 1890.

Two cables from William O'Brien to John Dillon, 31 Dec. 1890.

Draft cable from John Dillon and T. P. O'Connor to William O'Brien, 1 Jan. 1891.

Copy of cable from John Dillon to T. P. Gill, 1 Jan. 1891.

T. C. Harrington to John Dillon, 3 Jan. 1891.

Cable from William O'Brien to John Dillon, 6 Jan. 1891.

Cable from T. P. Gill to John Dillon, 6 Jan. 1891.

Copy of cable from John Dillon to William O'Brien, 6 Jan. 1891.

Copy of cable from T. P. O'Connor to William O'Brien, 6 Jan. 1891.

Copy of cable from John Dillon to William O'Brien, 7 Jan. 1891.

Two cables from William O'Brien to John Dillon, 7 Jan. 1891.

Cable from William O'Brien to John Dillon, 8 Jan. 1891.

Copy of cable from John Dillon to William O'Brien, 8 Jan. 1891.

Justin McCarthy to John Dillon, 19 Jan. 1891.

Gladstone to John Dillon, 21 Jan. 1891.

John Morley to John Dillon, 23 Jan. 1891.

Archbishop W. J. Walsh to John Dillon, 26 Jan. 1891.

Three letters from William O'Brien to John Dillon in Galway jail; they are undated, but two certainly were written in July 1891.

M. McD. Bodkin to John Dillon, 19 and 21 Aug. 1891.

John Devoy to John Dillon, 27 and 30 Aug. 1891, and draft reply by John Dillon.

William O'Brien to John Dillon, 15 and 26 Sept. 1891.

Memorandum by Michael Davitt on Paris fund, 23 Oct. 1894.

(7) *The Gill Papers*

The papers of T. P. Gill are of exceptional importance in the history of the Parnell crisis, partly because Gill acted as an intermediary between the various persons involved in, or interested in, the Boulogne negotiations and partly because many of the letters addressed to William O'Brien came into Gill's possession when O'Brien left France in February 1891 to serve his sentence in Ireland. Unfortunately, just before the papers were acquired by the National Library of Ireland (where they now are) they were damaged by fire and many of the documents are in very poor condition. Enough have survived, however, to make this collection a very important source for the events of 1890–1. The documents listed are letters, unless otherwise specified. The items used in this book are:

Parnell to Gill (in a secretary's hand, but signed by Parnell), 31 Dec. 1889.

Cable from J. E. Kenny and J. J. Clancy to Gill, 26 Nov. 1890.

Cables from William O'Brien to Gill, and from John Dillon and T. C. Harrington to William O'Brien, 26 Nov. 1890.

Cable from T. M. Healy and T. Sexton to T. P. O'Connor, 27 Nov. 1890.

Cable from Parnell to John Dillon and William O'Brien, 28 Nov. 1890.

Copy of cable from John Dillon, William O'Brien, T. P. O'Connor, T. D. Sullivan, T. P. Gill to Parnell, 28 Nov. 1890.

Cable from John Redmond to Gill, 29 Nov. 1890.

Cable from McCarthy to John Dillon and William O'Brien, 6 Dec. 1890.

Cable from Parnell to William O'Brien, 8 Dec. 1890.

Cable from J. E. Kenny to William O'Brien, 8 Dec. 1890.

Cables from M. McD. Bodkin to William O'Brien, 10 and 11 Dec. 1890.

'Memorandum for Paris negotiations', 11 Dec. 1890. This is a copy, but made at the same time as the original which is in the Dillon Papers.

John Dillon to William O'Brien, 13 and 18 Dec. 1890.

T. P. O'Connor to William O'Brien, 19 Dec. 1890.

Archbishop T. W. Croke to William O'Brien, 19 Dec. 1890.

'Note of interview at Boulogne, Christmas Day 1890, between Messrs Justin McCarthy, M.P., Sexton, M.P., Condon, M.P., on one part, and Messrs William O'Brien, M.P., and Gill, M.P., on other' (in Gill's hand).

T. C. Harrington to William O'Brien, 27 Dec. 1890.

V. B. Dillon to William O'Brien, 28 Dec. 1890.

'Memorandum of Mr John Redmond, M.P.'s and Mr T. P. Gill, M.P.'s conversations at Boulogne, 30 and 31 Dec. 1890 (in Gill's hand).

Archbishop T. W. Croke to William O'Brien, 31 Dec. 1890.

M. McD. Bodkin to William O'Brien, 5 Jan. 1891.

Two cables from John Dillon to William O'Brien, 7 and 8 Jan. 1891.

V. B. Dillon to William O'Brien, 11 Jan. 1891.

T. P. Gill to William O'Brien, 12 Jan. 1891.

William O'Brien to McCarthy, 12 Jan. 1891.

McCarthy to William O'Brien, 12 Jan. 1891.

Copy (in Gill's hand) of letter from him to John Morley, 12 Jan. 1891.

Cable from McCarthy to William O'Brien, 13 Jan. 1891.

William O'Brien to V. B. Dillon, 13 Jan. 1891.

Parnell to William O'Brien, 16 Jan. 1891.

M. McD. Bodkin to William O'Brien, 17 Jan. 1891.

William O'Brien to Gill, 27 Jan. 1891.

Note (in Gill's hand) of his interview with John Morley, 28 Jan. 1891.

Parnell to Gill, 3 Feb. 1891.

Copy (in Gill's hand) of memorandum made by T. P. Gill of conversation with Parnell after receiving Parnell's letter of 3 Feb. 1891 (undated, but probably 4 Feb. 1891).

J. J. Clancy to William O'Brien, 4 and 5 Feb. 1891.

John Redmond to William O'Brien, 5 Feb. 1891.

V. B. Dillon to William O'Brien, 6 Feb. 1891.

Copy (in Gill's hand) of letter from William O'Brien to Parnell, 8 Feb. 1891.

Cable from Parnell to William O'Brien, 10 Feb. 1891.

Parnell to William O'Brien, 11 Feb. 1891 (in a secretary's hand, but signed by Parnell).

William O'Brien to Gill, probably 19 Mar. 1891.

Archbishop T. W. Croke to William O'Brien, 22 Mar. 1891.

William O'Brien to Gill, 'Thursday' (probably July 1891).

William O'Brien to Gill, 19 Sept. 1891.

Gill to William O'Brien, 21 Sept. and 10 Nov. 1891.

(8) *The Harrington Papers*

These papers are also in the National Library of Ireland and, at the time of writing, are being classified. There is not a great deal that is relevant to the subject of this book, but what there is is listed below:
The diary of T. C. Harrington, Nov.–Dec. 1890 (N.L.I., MS 2195).
A group of documents consisting of copies of letters, cables and memoranda connected with the Boulogne negotiations. They are in two different hands which I have not been able to identify, but neither of which is Harrington's. Almost all of these—including the more important ones—were published by Harrington in *F.J.*, 12 Nov. 1891. The only exception is the copy of a letter from John

Redmond to Parnell, 9 Feb. 1891, referred to on p. 244, footnote 1 above.

Copies of affidavits of J. F. X. O'Brien and Justin McCarthy, 27 and 28 Apr. 1891 (N.L.I., MS 8930).

(9) *J. F. X. O'Brien Papers*

This collection, also in the National Library of Ireland, consists of letters, letter-books, ledgers, cash-books, pass-books and other documents accumulated by J. F. X. O'Brien during his tenure of office as treasurer of the Irish parliamentary party. Only those books have been used here which throw light upon the financial position of Parnell's opponents in the years 1890–1. They are:

Cash-book of the Irish Parliamentary Fund, 7 Dec. 1890–6 Apr. 1896 (N.L.I., MS 9230).

Ledger of the Irish Parliamentary Fund, 7 Dec. 1890–6 Apr. 1896 (N.L.I., MS 9231).

(10) *William O'Brien Papers*

This collection too is in the National Library of Ireland but, although it is a valuable source for the general history of the party, it has little to offer on the events of the split. The reason is—as already stated elsewhere—that O'Brien went straight from France to prison in Ireland and his papers passed into the possession of T. P. Gill. The only item of importance, therefore, is the small group of letters O'Brien received from Dillon while they were both in Galway jail (N.L.I., MS 8555).

(11) *Parnell Correspondence*

There are no 'Parnell Papers' properly so called, but from time to time letters written by him or to him are acquired by the National Library. There are two groups relating to the period with which this book is concerned:

Drafts or rough copies in Parnell's hand of letters to Justin McCarthy in connection with the release of the Paris fund for the benefit of the evicted tenants (N.L.I., MS 5934). They are dated 18, 20 and 28 Feb. and 6 Mar., 1891 and were all subsequently published in the press (*F.J.*, 7 Mar. 1891).

A bundle of letters (Aug.–Sept. 1891) promising support for Parnell's projected newspaper to fill the void left when the *Freeman's Journal* went over to his opponents (N.L.I., MS 8314).

(12) *John Redmond Papers*

This large collection has been received too recently by the National Library to have been catalogued at the time of writing, though work on it is proceeding steadily. So far as can be judged, however, it reveals disappointingly little about the split, perhaps because the leading Parnellites saw each other so frequently that little correspondence was necessary. However that may be, only two items have been used in this book:

Letter from William O'Brien to John Redmond, 8 Feb. 1891.

Letter from T. P. Gill to John Redmond, 27 Nov. 1891.

(13) *W. J. Walsh Papers*

The papers of Archbishop Walsh are in the archives of Archbishop's House, Drumcondra, Dublin, and I am deeply indebted to the present archbishop, the Most Reverend Dr J. C. McQuaid, for permission to quote from them. The collection formed the basis of Monsignor P. J. Walsh's biography of Archbishop Walsh, but I have been able to use a number of items not previously published. They are as follows:

Dr J. Gillooly, bishop of Elphin, to Archbishop Walsh, 19 and 28 Nov. 1890.

Dr B. Woodlock, bishop of Ardagh, to Archbishop Walsh, 25, 26 and 27 Nov. 1890.

Dr J. Donnelly, bishop of Clogher, to Archbishop Walsh, 28 Nov. 1890.

W. M. Murphy to Archbishop Walsh, ten telegrams between 1 and 6 Dec. 1890.

W. M. Murphy to Archbishop Walsh, 6 Dec. 1890.

Archbishop T. W. Croke to Archbishop Walsh, 16 Dec. 1890.

T. M. Healy to Archbishop Walsh, 31 Jan., 4 and 10 Feb. 1891.

(14) *Miscellaneous*

Two items of interest in private ownership have come to my notice:

A letter from Archbishop W. J. Walsh to W. M. Murphy, 26 Dec. 1890. I am grateful to Miss Eva Murphy for allowing me to make use of this letter.

A group of telegrams in support of Parnell sent to him in Cork from various parts of the country, 11 Dec. 1890. These were in the possession of the late Dr M. O'Hea.

II. NEWSPAPERS

Cork Examiner.
Daily News.
Evening Telegraph.
Freeman's Journal.
Insuppressible.
Irish Catholic.

Kilkenny Journal.
Labour World.
Nation.
National Press.
Pall Mall Gazette.
Pall Mall Gazette 'Extra' : 'The Story of the Parnell Crisis'.
Sligo Champion.
'Suppressed' United Ireland.
The Times.
The Times: 'The Parnellite Split'.
United Ireland.

III. CONTEMPORARY WORKS OF REFERENCE

Dod's parliamentary companion, 1832—work still in progress.
Thom's Irish almanac and official directory, Dublin, 1844—work still in
    progress.
Thom's Irish who's who, Dublin, 1923.
Who was who (1897–1916), 1920. *Who was who (1916–1928),* 1929.

IV. MEMOIRS, DIARIES, LETTERS AND SPEECHES

Blunt, W. S., *The land war in Ireland,* 1912.
Blunt, W. S., *My diaries,* 2 vols. (2nd ed.), 1921.
Bodkin, M. McD., *Recollections of an Irish judge,* 1914.
Chamberlain, Joseph, *A political memoir, 1880–92,* ed. C. H. D.
    Howard, 1953.
Clarke, Sir Edward, *The story of my life,* 1918.
Davitt, Michael, *The fall of feudalism in Ireland,* London and New
    York, 1904.
Devoy's post-bag, vol. ii, ed. W. O'Brien and D. Ryan, Dublin, 1953.
Esher, Reginald, Viscount, *Journals and letters,* vol. i, ed. Maurice V.
    Brett, 1934.
Gladstone, Herbert, Viscount, *After thirty years* (1st ed.), 1928.
Gladstone, Mary, *Letters and diaries,* ed. L. Masterman, 1930.
Hardie, J. Keir, *Speeches and writings, 1888–1915,* ed. E. Hughes,
    Glasgow (3rd ed.), 1928.
Healy, T. M., 'The rise and fall of Mr Parnell', in *The New Review,*
    iv, 194–203 (Mar. 1891).
Healy, T. M., *Letters and leaders of my day,* 2 vols, 1928.
Horgan, J. J., *Parnell to Pearse,* Dublin, 1948.
Kettle, A. J., *Material for victory,* ed. L. J. Kettle, Dublin, 1958.
Leamy, Margaret, *Parnell's faithful few,* New York, 1936.
Lucy, Sir Henry, *Diary of the Salisbury parliament, 1886–92,* 1892.
McCarthy, Justin, 'The deposition of Mr Parnell', in *North American
    Review,* clii, 234–44, New York (Feb. 1891).

McCarthy, Justin, *Reminiscences*, vol. ii, 1899.
McCarthy, Justin, *The story of an Irishman*, 1904.
McCarthy, Justin, and Praed, Mrs Campbell, *Our book of memories*, 1912.
Morley, John, Viscount, *Recollections*, vol. i, 1917.
O'Brien, William, 'Was Mr Parnell badly treated?' in *Contemporary Review*, lxx, 678–94 (Nov. 1896).
O'Brien, William, *Recollections*, 1905.
O'Brien, William, *Evening memories*, 1907.
O'Brien, William, *An olive branch in Ireland*, 1910.
O'Connor, T. P., *The Parnell movement* (1st ed.), 1886.
O'Connor, T. P., *Memoirs of an old parliamentarian*, 2 vols., 1929.
O'Donnell, F. H., *History of the Irish parliamentary party*, 2 vols., 1910.
Oxford and Asquith, Earl of, *Fifty years of parliament*, vol. i, 1926.
Redmond, J. E., *Historical and political addresses, 1883–97*, 1898.
Rendel, Lord S., *Personal papers*, ed. F. E. Hamer, 1931.
Ryan, M. F., *Fenian memories*, Dublin, 1945.
Sullivan, Donal, *The story of room fifteen*, Dublin, 1891.
Sullivan, T. D., *Recollections of troubled times in Irish politics*, Dublin, 1905.
Tynan, Katharine, *Twenty-five years: reminiscences*, 1913.
West, Sir A., *Private diaries*, ed. H. G. Hutchinson, 1922.
Yeats, W. B., *Autobiographies*, 1955.

V. PARLIAMENTARY DEBATES AND PAPERS

Annual register, 1889–91.
Hansard, parliamentary debates, 3rd series, vols 313, 328, 349–56.
Return of the number of agrarian offences in each county in Ireland in each month of the year 1880, H.C. 1881, lxxvii.
Special commission act, 1888; reprint of the shorthand notes of the speeches, proceedings and evidence taken before the commissioners appointed under the above-named act, 12 vols, 1890.
Report of the evicted tenants' commission [c. 6935], H.C. 1893, xxxi.

B. SECONDARY WORKS

I. BIOGRAPHIES OF PARNELL

Included in this section are not only those biographies which deal with the whole of Parnell's life, but also a number which throw light merely upon certain aspects of it. Sketches of his career which appeared in newspapers or periodicals are not included, though a few of the books listed above are based on that or similar material.

Johnston, R., *Parnell and the Parnells*, 1888.

Short and necessarily incomplete, but contains a useful account of Parnell's early career.

O'Connor, T. P., *Charles Stewart Parnell: a memory*, 1891.

Bears the marks of having been written in a hurry to take advantage of a favourable market, but has some shrewd and informative comments.

O'Brien, R. Barry, *Life of Charles Stewart Parnell*, 2 vols (2nd ed.), 1899.
Barry O'Brien comes as near as possible to being Parnell's Boswell, though—since it was produced so soon after Parnell's death—his book suffers from the fact that he had to be careful to avoid offending the susceptibilities of many who appeared in it and who were still very much alive when it was published. The treatment of the O'Shea affair, for example, is so cautious as to be almost valueless and in some other instances—such as the Boulogne negotiations—it is scarcely more satisfactory. But as a record of Parnell's personality the book is unsurpassed. It is particularly valuable for the period of the split, since Barry O'Brien saw a great deal of Parnell at that time; allowance has to be made, of course, for the author's strong Parnellite bias.

Dickenson, Emily Monroe, *A patriot's mistake*, Dublin, 1905.
The authoress was one of Parnell's sisters and saw a certain amount of him in the months before he died. Her book, however, was written in her old age and is very untrustworthy, especially about Parnell's early life.

O'Shea, Katharine, *Charles Stewart Parnell: his love-story and political life*, 2 vols (1st ed.), 1914.
Not a biography in any real sense, but of the greatest interest and importance in the history of Parnell's relations with Mrs O'Shea herself and with her husband. It contains a number of valuable letters and is, in addition, virtually the only first-hand source for Parnell's last days. It was, however, written in old age and under influences hostile to Parnell. For evaluations of its worth see chap. II above and Henry Harrison, *Parnell vindicated*.

Parnell, John Howard, *Charles Stewart Parnell*, 1916.
Like Mrs Dickenson's book this was written in old age and is suspect on that account. It has many inaccuracies, but the picture it gives of Parnell is recognisably a likeness, even if not a good one.

O'Hara, M., *Chief and tribune: Parnell and Davitt*, Dublin, 1919.
Of some interest in that it emphasises the importance of the relations between Parnell and Davitt, but very far from being the last word on the subject.

Ervine, St John, *Parnell*, 1925.
This is an exceedingly misleading biography and has been exhaustively criticised by Henry Harrison in his *Parnell vindicated* listed below. It must in fairness be added, however, that a great deal more is known now about Parnell's life than when Ervine wrote his book.

O'Brien, William, *The Parnell of real life*, 1926.
Some of the chapters in this book are reprints of earlier pieces by O'Brien, but it is a convenient and interesting summing-up of the impressions of one who knew Parnell well.

Robbins, Sir A., *Parnell: the last five years*, 1926.
Useful as the comment of an experienced liberal-unionist journalist on the period of Parnell's greatest triumphs and disasters.
Harrison, Henry, *Parnell vindicated: the lifting of the veil*, 1931.
This important work is chiefly valuable for the light it throws on the Parnell–O'Shea triangle. It also deals with some other aspects of Parnell's career and has useful criticisms of the earlier literature on the subject. For a discussion of the validity of some of Harrison's own theories, see chap. II above.
Haslip, Joan, *Parnell: a biography*, 1936.
A useful popular study of Parnell based on some, though not very extensive, original research.
Ó Broin, León, *Parnell: Ceathaisnéis*, Dublin, 1937.
A full-length biography which has the unusual distinction of having been written in Irish.
Sherlock, Thomas, *Life of Charles Stewart Parnell*, Dublin, 1945 (first published as newspaper articles in 1882).
Of some value for Parnell's early years, but of little importance otherwise.

II. OTHER BIOGRAPHIES

Askwith, Lord G. R. A., *Lord James of Hereford*, 1930.
Barton, D. P., *T. M. Healy*, Dublin, 1933.
Dictionary of national biography, and supplements, 1908–40.
Dugdale, Blanche E. C., *Life of Arthur James Balfour*, vol. i, 1936.
Fitzmaurice, Lord E., *Life of the second earl Granville* (1st ed.), 1905.
Fyfe, H., *T. P. O'Connor*, 1934.
Gardiner, A. G., *Life of Sir William Harcourt*, 2 vols, 1923.
Garvin, J. L., *Life of Joseph Chamberlain*, vol. ii, 1932.
Gwynn, D. R., *Life of John Redmond*, 1932.
Gwynn, S., and Tuckwell, G., *Life of Sir Charles Dilke*, vol. i, 1917.
Jenkins, Roy, *Sir Charles Dilke*, 1958.
Leslie, Sir Shane, *Henry Edward Manning: his life and labours*, 1921.
Macdonagh, Michael, *Life of William O'Brien*, 1928.
Mills, J. Saxon, *Life of Sir E. T. Cook*, 1921.
Morgan, J. H., *John, Viscount Morley*, 1924.
Morley, John, *Life of Gladstone*, vol. iii (1st ed.), 1903.
O'Brien, R. Barry, *Life of Lord Russell of Killowen*, 1901.
O'Flaherty, Liam, *The life of Tim Healy*, 1927.
Skeffington, F. Sheehy, *Michael Davitt: revolutionary leader and labour agitator*, 1908.
Sullivan, M., *No man's man*, Dublin, 1943. A study of T. M. Healy by his daughter.
Thorold, A. L., *Life of Henry Labouchere*, 1913.
Walsh, P. J., *William J. Walsh, archbishop of Dublin*, 1928.
Whyte, F., *Life of W. T. Stead*, vol. ii, 1925.

III. SPECIAL STUDIES

Hammond, J. L., *Gladstone and the Irish nation*, 1938.

Harrison, Henry, *Parnell, Joseph Chamberlain and Mr Garvin*, 1938.

Harrison, Henry, 'Parnell's vindication', in *I.H.S.*, v. 231–43 (Mar. 1947).

Harrison, Henry, *Parnell, Joseph Chamberlain and The Times*, Belfast and Dublin, 1953.

Howard, C. H. D., ed. 'Documents relating to the Irish "central board" scheme, 1884–5', in *I.H.S.*, viii. 237–63 (Mar. 1953).

Howard, C. H. D., 'Joseph Chamberlain, Parnell and the Irish "central board" scheme, 1884–5', in *I.H.S.*, viii. 324–61 (Sept. 1953).

Lyons, F. S. L., *The Irish parliamentary party, 1890–1910*, 1951.

Macdonagh, Michael, *The home rule movement*, Dublin, 1920.

Moody, T. W., 'The new departure in Irish politics, 1878–9', in H. A. Cronne, T. W. Moody and D. B. Quinn (ed.), *Essays in British and Irish history in honour of James Eadie Todd*, 1949.

Moody, T. W., ed. 'Parnell and the Galway election of 1886', in *I.H.S.*, ix. 319–38 (Mar. 1955).

Moody, T. W. ,'Michael Davitt and the British labour movement, 1882–1906', in *Transactions of the Royal Historical Society*, fifth series, iii. 53–76 (1953).

O'Brien, C. Cruise, 'The machinery of the Irish parliamentary party, 1880–85', in *I.H.S.*, v. 55–85 (Mar. 1946).

O'Brien, C. Cruise, *Parnell and his party, 1880–90*, 1957.

Palmer, N. D., *The Irish land league crisis*, New Haven and London, 1940.

Pomfret, J. E., *The struggle for land in Ireland*, Princeton, 1930.

Scott, J. W. Robertson, *The life and death of a newspaper*, 1952.

Strauss, E., *Irish nationalism and British democracy*, 1951.

INDEX

also America, Irish delegates in, O'Brien, William, Parnell, Charles Stewart

Dillon, John Blake, 23

Dillon, Valentine B., corresponds with John Dillon, 188–9; and with William O'Brien, 194, 222, 241, 246; Parnellite candidate at North Sligo, 264–5

Donnelly, Dr J., bishop of Clogher, 77 *n* 3

Drogheda, 253, 254 *n* 2

Dublin, Parnell and Devoy meet in, 7; Parnell arrested in, 11; *The Nation* published in, 26; meeting of Irish National League in, 72; support for Parnell in, 72, 73–4, 76, 85, 112, 125–6, 128, 131, 135 *n* 1, 155, 159, 253; E. J. Kennedy, lord mayor of, 73; proposed meeting of party in, 122, 125, 146; rival committees in, 154–5; struggle for possession of *United Ireland* offices in, 155–7, 160–1, 181, 213; T. M. Healy assaulted in, 155; Parnell's Rotunda speech in, 159–60; Parnell's return to from Kilkenny, 177; proposed meeting of Irish National League in, 196; Parnell's later visits to, 253, 255, 257–8, 258–9, 275, 296, 302 *n* 3; Parnellite convention in, 278; Dillon and O'Brien in, 294; Irish National Federation meeting in, 298–300; Parnell's last appearance in, 304, 305; Parnell's funeral in 307; anti-Parnellite committee in, 329

Eastbourne, Parnell and Mrs O'Shea at, 52, 294 *n* 3

Eccles, by-election, 82

Edinburgh, 22

Egan, Patrick, 6 *n* 1, 11 *n* 5, 272

Eighty club, Parnell's speech at, 18, 22

Eltham, Mrs O'Shea's house (Wonersh Lodge) at, 37, 57, 222, 227; Parnell at, 40, 42, 45, 46, 47, 49, 50–1, 52; Captain O'Shea at, 37, 44, 45–6

England, public opinion concerning Parnell leadership in, 80–1, 83–4, 85–6, 87, 90, 91 *n* 4, 216–17, 311, 315; *see also* Gladstone, Harcourt, Liberal party, Morley

Ennis, Parnell's speech at in 1880, 10; and in 1891, 236 and *n* 2, 252

Esmonde, Sir Thomas, *M.P.*, 121 *n* 2, 149 *n* 1

Evicted tenants, and Plan of Campaign, 18–19; problem of providing for, 73, 75, 95, 124, 134 *n* 1, 154, 182, 187, 293, 298; financial accounts of, 151, 328–9, 330, 332; represented at first Boulogne conference, 193; grant from Paris fund for, 251, 270–1; Dillon-Parnell correspondence concerning, 299 *n* 1

Fenianism, and Isaac Butt, 2–3; Parnell's early dealings with, 3–7, 9; Davitt and, 6–7; Dillon suspected of sympathy with, 23; O'Brien attracted by, 25; Parnellite appeal to at Kilkenny, 168–70, 176, 252, 315–16; Dillon's later attitude towards, 189

Finucane, J., *M.P.*, 121 *n* 2, 149 *n* 1

Fitzgerald, Dr J. G., *M.P.*, and Parnell manifesto, 99; in Committee Room Fifteen, 121 *n* 2, 140, 149 *n* 1; and death of Parnell, 307

Flynn, J. C., *M.P.*, 121 *n* 2, 149 *n* 1

Foley, P. J., *M.P.*, 121 *n* 2, 149 *n* 1

Folkestone, 244

Forster, W. E., *M.P.*, chief secretary for Ireland, 13 *n* 1

Fowler, H. H., *M.P.* (later Viscount Wolverhampton), 191

'Fox, Mr', alias of Parnell, 275, 290 *n* 3

Fox, J. F., *M.P.*, 121 *n* 2, 149 *n* 1

Freeman's Journal, early attitude of, to Parnell, 9; William O'Brien on staff of, 25; Parnell gives interview to, 39–40; on divorce case, 39–40, 72; on leadership issue, 90; supports Parnell, 95–6, 109, 118, 253, 316; reports Committee Room Fifteen debates, 119–21; advocates Boulogne conference, 158; policy of Dillon and O'Brien towards, 187; E. J. Byrne, editor of, 194, 197; rivalry of *National Press* with, 260–1, 291–2, 294; and North Sligo by-election, 263, 265; and Parnellite convention, 278; wavers in support of Parnell, 279–80, 283, 289 *n* 2, 294–5; T. M. Healy's libel action against, 291; and release of Dillon and O'Brien, 291–2; abandons Parnell, 294, 302–3, 316, 330

Furniss, C., *M.P.*, 229

Galway, Plan of Campaign in, 18; by-election (1886) in, 27–8, 30, 49, 166; bishop of, 243 *n* 3, 293 *n* 1; Dillon and O'Brien in jail in, 244, 252, 265, 271, 281–92, 297, 300; Queen's College, 281; speeches of Dillon and O'Brien at, 293–4, 295–6, 301; Parnell leadership committee in, 294; *see also* Creggs

General election, (1880) 8–9, 35; (1885) 15, 16; (1886) 17; anticipated, 82, 86–7, 92, 95, 99–100, 101 *n* 2, 102, 112, 123, 182, 191, 219, 253, 265, 302; fund, 328–30

Gilhooly, J., *M.P.*, 121 *n* 2

Gill, T. P., *M.P.*, reassured by Parnell about divorce case, 40; on Parnell's case against O'Shea, 40 *n* 2; early support of Parnell, 74–5; and Parnell manifesto 113–15; and draft proposals for Parnell-O'Brien conference, 183–7, 195–7, 201; leaves America for France, 187; at Christmas Day conference in Boulogne, 197–8; memorandum by, on Parnell-O'Brien conference, 199–201 and *n* 1, 2; and proposed chairmanship of Dillon, 211 *n* 2; correspondence with W. O'Brien, 222, 265; negotiations with John Morley, 223–4, 226, 232–4, 240; and later negotiations in France, 229, 237, 238, 241–2, 249; and 'misunderstanding' with Parnell, 230–43; on political influence of Mrs O'Shea, 246; and evicted tenants' funds, 251 *n* 3; *see also* America, Irish delegates in

Gilooly, Dr J., bishop of Elphin, 77, 243 *n* 3

Gladstone, Mrs Catherine, 87

Gladstone, Herbert (later Viscount), 65

Gladstone, Mary, 22–3

Gladstone, William Ewart, *M.P.*, and earlier history of Irish land question, 9–10, 11, 221, 321; and the 'Kilmainham treaty', 12–13; and Parnell's offer of resignation, 14, 84 and *n* 3, 299; and special commission, 22 *n* 1; oratory of, 29; on Parnell, 31; and Parnell's relations with Mrs O'Shea, 40–1, 64–5; Cardinal Manning and, 80; attitude of to

Parnell's leadership, 80–90, 127, 136, 142–5, 146, 179, 186, 219, 230, 232, 248, 264, 270; his letter to Harcourt (23 Nov. 1890), 84–5; his letter to John Morley (24 Nov. 1890), 87–8, 91–4, 97, 102, 105, 113, 116, 127, 129, 135, 144, 184, 189, 195–6, 129–30, 130 *n* 3; 200–1, 267, 310, 320; McCarthy's interviews with, 98–9, 129–30, 130 *n* 3; Parnell's hostility towards, 98, 99, 105, 157–8, 175, 193, 221, 253–5, 277; Parnell's visit to at Hawarden, 99–100, 103–5, 107, 125, 128–9, 143, 239, 320–3; views of on Irish representation at Westminster, 106, 107, 321, 322; on Parnell manifesto, 110–11, 113, 124, 130, 135, 154; and home rule bill (1886), 126; and proposed liberal guarantees, 129–31, 135–45, 179, 186, 204–7, 210–14, 223–4, 251; papers of, 198, 334; proposed visit of McCarthy to, 204–7, 209, 210, 213, 220, 223–4, 230–1; and liberal dissensions, 108, 216, 227–9; and anti-Parnellite funds, 216; and Bassetlaw by-election, 217; and alternatives to home rule, 219–20; and Boulogne proposals, 225–6, 232–5; his letter to John Dillon, 231; and Parnell's amendments, 240, 241, 248, 310–11; speech of, at Hastings, 254 *n* 2; T. C. Harrington on, 291; and home rule bill (1893), 317–18; *see also* Harcourt, Liberal party, Morley

Glasnevin, Parnell's grave at, 307

Gonne, Maud, 292

Gower, George Leveson, 64

Graham, R. B. Cunninghame, 257

Granville, second earl, and Parnell crisis, 64, 65, 85; on Hawarden conference, 106, 108; and liberal guarantees, 141 *n* 1; on Parnell's sanity, 175 *n* 1; on Harcourt, 227; on Boulogne negotiations, 229 *n* 4

Grattan, Henry, Parnell's analogy with, 100, 164–5, 255; parliament of 177; quoted by Harcourt, 218

Gray, E. Dwyer, and *Freeman's Journal* policy, 279–80, 289 *n* 2, 291, 294–5

Grieves, Tracy, Parnell's interview with, 157–8, 181

STUDIES IN IRISH HISTORY, FIRST SERIES
published by Messrs Faber & Faber